977.7
Sch99p Schwieder
Patterns & perspectives
in Iowa history
80778

DATE DUE

JU 2 1987			
Fe 2 89			
NOV 02 1995			
APR 09 01			

Learning Resources Center
Marshalltown Community College
Marshalltown, Iowa 50158

Patterns and Perspectives in Iowa History

Patterns and Perspectives
in
Iowa History

Edited by Dorothy Schwieder

The Iowa State University Press / Ames / 1973

TO ELMER *who understands*

DOROTHY A. SCHWIEDER holds the B.A. degree from Dakota Wesleyan University and the M.S. degree from Iowa State University. She taught history at Dakota Wesleyan University and she presently teaches Iowa history at Iowa State University. On the WOI weekly radio program, "Iowa Heritage," Mrs. Schwieder discusses important personalities and events that have shaped Iowa's past. Articles by Mrs. Schwieder have appeared in *The Iowan, Annals of Iowa,* and *Montana, The Magazine of Western History.* She is on the Board of Curators of the State Historical Society of Iowa.

© 1973 The Iowa State University Press
Ames, Iowa 50010. All rights reserved

Composed and printed by
The Iowa State University Press

First edition, 1973

Library of Congress Cataloging in Publication Data

Schwieder, Dorothy, 1933–   comp.
    Patterns and perspectives in Iowa history.

    Includes bibliographical references.
    CONTENTS: McAvoy, T. T. What is the Midwestern mind?—Hagen, W. The Sacs and Foxes of the Mississippi Valley.—Swierenga, R. P. A Dutch immigrant's view of frontier Iowa. [etc.]
    1. Iowa—History—Addresses, essays, lectures.
I. Title.
F621.5.S38   977.7   73-928
ISBN 0-8138-1215-1

CONTENTS

Preface   vii

THOMAS T. MCAVOY
What is the Midwestern Mind?   3

WILLIAM T. HAGAN
The Sacs and Foxes of the Mississippi Valley   25

ROBERT P. SWIERENGA
A Dutch Immigrant's View of Frontier Iowa   41

ALLAN G. BOGUE
The People Come   81

MILDRED THRONE
"Book Farming" in Iowa, 1840–1870   105

GEORGE A. BOECK
A Decade of Transportation Fever in Burlington, Iowa, 1845–1855   133

ROBERT EDSON LEE
Politics and Society in Sioux City, 1859   159

DAVID S. SPARKS
The Decline of the Democratic Party in Iowa, 1850–1860   175

MYRTLE BEINHAUER
Development of the Grange in Iowa, 1868–1930   207

MARTHA BROWNING SMITH
The Story of Icaria   231

CORA FREAR HAWKINS
A Doctor's Wife in the Nineties   263

LOUISE NOUN
1872–1920—Carrie Chapman Catt 283

VERNON CARSTENSEN
The University as Head of the Iowa School System 323

THEODORE SALOUTOS AND JOHN D. HICKS
The Farm Strike 359

EDWARD L. AND FREDERICK H. SCHAPSMEIER
A Prophet in Politics: The Public Career of Henry A. Wallace 379

CHARLES W. WIGGINS
The Post World War II Legislative Reapportionment Battle in Iowa Politics 403

DOROTHY SCHWIEDER
Agrarian Stability in Utopian Societies: A Comparison of Economic Practices of Old Order Amish and Hutterites 431

PETER SCHRAG
What Happened to Main Street? 455

PREFACE

STATE AND LOCAL HISTORY is an often neglected area of study. Dominating the field of American history are such issues as the causes of the American Revolution, the nature of Jacksonian democracy, and the impact of the New Deal—to mention only a few. These traditional themes center on the broad and total aspects of the American nation and certainly are essential to a proper understanding of the nation's past. With this approach, however, one is rarely permitted to become acquainted with ordinary Americans upon whose shoulders rested much of the day to day responsibility for living and working. To be sure the political and economic elites are given recognition, but typically these individuals are discussed from the viewpoint of their contributions to the major themes. The study of state and local history allows a closer look at what one historian has called the "Anonymous Americans."[1] These less articulate, less successful, but nevertheless important Americans are often most visible on the state and local level.

Occasionally students will ask if it is not possible to study persons and families rather than to deal primarily with general events? This is a pertinent question since American history in the classroom is frequently presented in general, sweeping terms. Many college students find that their only exposure to the discipline is through an American history survey course. Because of the vast amount of material to be covered within a short period of time, students fail to deal with individuals other than major personalities, or to gain a sense of the so-called "common American." Further, emphasis is often on political events.

In the study of state history the scope of the field is narrowed and students have an opportunity to look more closely

---

1. Tamara Hareven, ed., *Anonymous Americans* (Englewood Cliffs, N.J.: Prentice-Hall, 1971).

at all aspects of a particular situation. It becomes easier, for example, to deal with specific case studies of either individuals or events and it becomes possible to study the history of a specific locality (a township, for example) or a local political happening. Within these frameworks students can gain multi-dimensional views as they examine the many facets of an event and see also its relationship to the broader setting of regional or national history.

In an attempt to help students look closer at Americans of the past, most of the eighteen essays in this book deal with the broad range of human experiences shared by Iowans during their everyday living throughout the nineteenth and early twentieth centuries. The emphasis is not upon political activities nor upon the development of institutions, but upon commonly shared human experiences. Of necessity some material is included on general developments in agriculture and education, but the major emphasis lies in the direction of social history. As students read the selections it is hoped they will develop a sense and feeling for these Americans of the past, understanding their achievements, their frustrations, and their heartaches, as well as their persona. It is, in other words, "people history." Moreover, some of the color, excitement, and fervor of events should be visible through the readings so students can develop some knowledge of what it might have been like to live in Iowa during the nineteenth or early twentieth centuries.

The lack of usable classroom materials in Iowa history significantly influenced the selection of essays. Within the past fifteen years historical research and publication in state and local history has been limited and few monographs have been published. This has greatly reduced the selections available so that finding appropriate material is a serious problem for instructors. In light of these current limitations and because no adequate college level text exists, these essays are intended to accomplish a dual purpose. The first is to indicate—through the broad range of topics selected—the major issues and developments that would be covered in a text. The second and more important purpose, however, is to provide essays that will give students a more intense view of the subject matter. Accompanied by appropriate lectures, this anthology may then serve either for basic or supplemental reading in an Iowa history course.

Preface

One impression that should be guarded against, however; state history cannot be studied of and by itself. As Philip Jordan wrote in his excellent study, *The Nature and Practice of State and Local History*, "the smallest unit is always part of something larger," and "the part cannot be understood without a knowledge of the whole."[2] To study state history one must recognize significant antecedents. Most events in Iowa (as in any state) were greatly influenced by earlier physical, social, economic, and political developments. To recognize these prior influences and in turn perceive their effect on Iowa's formation and growth is to gain a fuller knowledge and understanding of the subject. Thus in all local and state history there is the relationship to the regional and national scene. In any given locality at any given time, the historical process begins with an individual or individuals. The patterns and trends that later emerge on the national level are discernible at least in part because of the prior individualized, localized studies.

I am grateful to the publishers and authors of these essays for permission to reprint them. I would particularly like to thank Dr. Walter Rundell, Jr., formerly chairman of the History Department at Iowa State University and now chairman of the History Department at the University of Maryland, for his continual support and encouragement of my work in this area. Not only was he helpful in the compilation of this book, but his support led to my initial participation as an instructor and researcher in the field of Iowa history.

DOROTHY SCHWIEDER

Iowa State University
May 1972

---

2. Philip Jordan, *The Nature and Practice of State and Local History*, Publication No. 14 (Washington, D.C.: Service Center for Teachers of History, 1958), pp. 7–8.

Patterns and Perspectives in Iowa History

What is the Midwestern Mind?
THOMAS T. MCAVOY, C.S.C.

BECAUSE of its location and physical characteristics, Iowa is part of both the Prairie region and the larger area known as the Middle West. As such, Iowans supposedly share conservative political attitudes as well as social and religious values with other inhabitants of the central region of the United States. Certainly comparisons can be made with the neighboring state of Illinois in regard to farming practices and the background of the early settlers; in many ways these similarities still persist. But to what extent can Iowa be considered a part of the much broader area of the Midwest? Embracing twelve states in the central portion of the United States, the Middle West includes such divergent areas as the flat, dry Dakota plains, and the rolling, fertile prairies of Iowa and Illinois. Do Iowa farmers, representing the corn-hog complex, share many similarities with the wheat farmers of the Plains? This article by Thomas McAvoy explores the idea of the midwestern mind. Believing that there is a commonality of background, personal characteristics, and interests among midwesterners, McAvoy singles out some of the major influences that have produced this particular population. Refuting charges that midwesterners lack culture and distinctive qualities, he cites their growing influence throughout the entire country although admitting to the presence of a certain self-centeredness. The author raises many important considerations about the concepts of the Midwest and its people. To what extent can legitimate generalizations be made about Iowans in relationship to other midwesterners?

From Thomas T. McAvoy, C.S.C., editor,
The Midwest/Myth or Reality?
(Notre Dame: University of Notre Dame Press; © 1961
by The University of Notre Dame Press),
pp. 53–72.

Thomas T. McAvoy, C.S.C.

What is the Midwestern Mind?

PROFESSOR RAY BILLINGTON in a recent essay sadly concluded that the Middle West of today bears "little resemblance to the Garden of the World pictured by propagandists a generation before."[1] Other writers complain that the Midwesterners seem to be out of touch with the rest of America and are not doing their share in bearing the burdens of the modern world crisis.[2] Most of these latter critics either live outside the Midwest or, if they are here as teachers or by business commitments, long to go elsewhere. The major error in these opinions is the failure to recognize the midwestern mind. This mind is the mind of those who recognize the Midwest as their home and intend to make it the best home they know how.

There has been too much of Frederick Jackson Turner in evaluations of the Midwest. Turner, his followers, and most regional litterateurs and historians have placed too much value on the environment—the irrational element—in the region. It is of the essence of the Midwest as a region that it lacks most of the characteristics usually ascribed to European or Asian regionalism. One could almost say that the chief characteristic of the Midwest is that it is lacking in unusual physical characteristics—that most of its landscapes are lacking in mountains and valleys, swift streams and rough waste lands. And this is very important in evaluating the midwestern mind.

What is the midwestern mind? It is the mind of those—the great majority at least—living between the Alleghenies and the Rockies and Canada and the South, who accept the region and intend to stay there. By this definition I exclude that pessimistic view of the Midwest drawn up chiefly by the literary critics who went east to New York or west to Hollywood to reap the benefit of their midwestern origins and who were probably repelled by the very sameness that is the essence of the Midwest.

To pursue the negative side of this problem a bit farther, one must remember that nearly all the historical writing about the Midwest has had as its basic concept a region formed by a frontier—whether that frontier was that of the hunter and trapper, of the cattleman, or of the small farmer. A book has recently been published also on the urban frontier of the Midwest. In the early concept of the Midwest there was, at most, a small community. The inhabitants of this region were the victims of a Federal land policy that cut up all land into squares of 640 acres. They came here first along the mountain passes, the rivers, the Great Lakes, the canals, and then the railroads. As they conquered the prairies they occasionally built market centers, then manufacturing centers, and now combinations of both about which even the farmers are slowly gathering. This is not an erroneous view of the Midwest of the nineteenth century except for one thing—that these plains and rivers, canals, roads and railroads were in the hands of a lower middle-class people who were consciously creating a place to live, making fortunes, and creating homes for their children. Where are these pioneers whom we admire so deeply? Back in the nineteenth century.

What of the living Americans of the Midwest today? They do not live in the past. They are living for themselves. They possess the creations of the nineteenth century but they are molding them anew to create the world in which they themselves want to live.

The frontier thesis after all is a bit of American romanticism. The romanticism of Western Europe which thus found its way over the Atlantic to America was a kind of ancestor worship of the countryside. In the Midwest romanticism, the pioneer farmer was confined to his countryside and forced to find his joys in the simple pleasures of the frontier barn dance, and sewing bees, or in the transitional small towns of the late nineteenth and early twentieth centuries. There has been some of this regional literature that has this spirit of romantic nationalism. But the midwestern farmer was not dominated by any valley of the Wabash, the Fox River Valley, or any lake regions. He had few hills in which a mythical spirit could hide. Such romanticism belongs to Europe of the late eighteenth and early nineteenth centuries, not to twentieth-century Midwest United States.

A second image of the Midwest which has created some of our most delightful literature deals with the other chief constituent of the Midwest, the immigrant. The strong peasant type who found simple freedom and joy or sadness in the wide expanses of the prairie or re-established with differences on the plains the old-world community, or clustered in the filth and poverty of the tenement or shanty regions of the towns or cities, these too have been pictured as part of the Midwest and rightly so, but of an earlier Midwest (or so we hope). These very real people—they are generally also of the lower middle class—have been pictured not as living but as fighting against a harsh sentimental nature or a material-minded people in a world to which they have been drawn by their desire for freedom. Some of these portraitures are of the early twentieth century and some of the darker accounts are well known in Europe and through the writings of the American critics. But here again it is time to stop thinking of these people as foreigners, as migrants from Europe, from the South or the Southwest, as urbanized farmers, and start thinking of them as the Midwest as it is. Most of these people are here to stay and want to create here their future home.

In central Indiana, the Tennesseean who used to come in the summertime has remained to become a resident. In some midwestern manufacturing centers the boy with the Polish or Italian or Greek or Slovak name does not know Polish or Italian or Greek or Slovak. He might not even know the correct pronunciation of his name and cares less about the fatherland of his grandparents. Some of these may think that progress requires change, even moving into a new area, but for the most part the limit of the new horizons is simply suburbia—some region where they can own an attractive home, raise a healthy family, and send their children to good schools. They are like the other migrants and non-migrants, just interested in living. They too have become part of the Midwest.

There is a third element besides the frontierman and the immigrant in this midwestern mind which is probably more important than either of the other two but which has not had its share of literature, except in such tales as the *Hoosier Schoolmaster*, in the accounts of the circuit-riding minister, or in those dull accounts of midwestern politicians ground out in doctoral dissertations. The upholder of the frontier thesis would say that this group is the last wave of the frontier. Others have called them the transplanted Yankees, although a very high percentage also come from the South. They are not very romantic, yet they are really the ones who took over the midwestern land from the Indians and proceeded to create a place to live. They are properly the westerners of the decades before, during, and immediately after the Civil War. One can hardly think of a town in the North Central States in which they were not seen surveying townships, raising grain and animals, building roads, courthouses, small white churches and schools, and making money on one side of the counter or the other. One thing about these men, women, and children is that no one has tried to make them heroic. Some do try to give this Midwesterner Paul-Bunyan-size shoes and make his barrel chest the shrine of manly virtue and heroic honesty, but that is usually on Sunday morning. Most of the week this Midwesterner had always been very practical both in what he did and what he said. Of course in their old age, some of these have retired to Los Angeles and some have gone back East for urban pleasures in their prosperity, but the greater part of this backbone of the Midwestern civilization has always been with us and remains amidst the new homes and electronic instruments of living today.

I have always been impressed by stories of frontier travelers who found that the usual greeting in the fields or at the door of the pioneer log cabin was simply, "What's new?" It expresses the open-minded toleration of the Midwest. One could draw a line about two-thirds from the bottom boundary of the Midwest. Beneath that line the dominant first settler would be from the South, above from the North. There were some differences between the two in their traditional political and their traditional religious practices, but they generally agreed on the chief forms of government, on the need of schools, on the practicality of sharp business, and on a common belief that every man had to look out for himself. They had a limited appreciation of fine arts because they did not have the leisure essential for artistic expression, yet, their literature was enriched by the King James version of the Scriptures, and the ubiquitous small newspaper. In mid-nineteenth century this type was numerically dominant in the Midwest. At the turn of the century they were financially and culturally dominant. By mid-twentieth century they are still dominant but in the current generation it is getting harder and harder to tell them from the great-grandchildren of the immigrants.

Who created this midwestern mind? Probably the early Protestant minister and his associates, especially those who created the innumerable liberal art colleges which polka-dotted the midwestern map: Western Reserve and Miami, Oberlin and Otterbein, Wabash and Knox, Carroll and Coe, and the hundred others. Of course, most of these ministers and teachers were trained in the older liberal arts colleges of the East and came West with many doctors and lawyers from the older colleges. No one has yet measured how much the educational systems of the Midwest were manned and formed by the products of the Eastern schools and seminaries. Then, there was that remarkable midwestern local press which has passed almost without a trace. Not all these midwestern editors were William Allen Whites but his pattern is not much different from those who spoke the mind of the Midwest and directed its politics until at least the end of World War I and the Depression. What did they teach and what did they say? Probably, besides the inevitable local politics, that this is the garden spot of the world where good men prospered and that they intended to keep it that way.

What happened to the Midwest in recent years fills some of the best pages of the annual *Statistical Abstract*.[3] This is not the place to say how many swine and cattle and chickens and turkeys and ducks are raised, nor how much wheat, oats and corn is raised—not to mention the quantities stored along the railroad tracks. Neither is it very important to say how great is the concentration of manufacturing ability in this region or the millions of people who live and work here. But it is rather essential to remember that the Midwest is a permanent part of the country and that most of the millions living here intend to stay and are very busy making the Midwest into the kind of world they want to give to their children.

This midwestern mind has been on the defensive since World War II and the main charges of the press of the other sections of the country seem valid. They claim that the Midwest is isolationist, that it lacks any distinctive qualities, and that it has low cultural ideals. The first of these charges seems the most disheartening. Graham Hutton in *Midwest at Noon* was certain that when the young men who had served abroad in Europe and Asia returned to their old homes they would do away with this isolationism. This has not happened, chiefly because the Midwestern youth after his term of service has rushed into the self-centered life of the midwestern United States and has been too busy with his own tasks to think about the world he saw in his travels with the Army or Navy. Some of these returned service men, of course, have brought back foreign brides and some became interested in commerce with the countries to which they had been sent. But for the most part these youths do not recall that Europeans, or Asians were particularly interested in the Midwest, except perhaps to see what they could get from the people of the Midwest. They know that Europe and Asia are living for themselves and since this is what most of these youngsters are forced to do here after an enforced absence, they must be excused if they are just as self-centered as other people.

The Midwesterner is not opposed to Europeans or Asians. The attempt to read Irish feelings against England or German feelings against England does not explain the same deep opposition to other peoples of Americans of English origins who share the same feelings. Midwesterners gladly help the suffering and deprived peoples of other countries. They are deeply moved at the thought that those countries should fall under the rule of totalitarian governments by foreign conquest, although not so deeply moved at the prospect of their falling by their own carelessness. But at the present time for them, the living, the all-important problem of the Midwest is the Midwest, the land in which they live, earn their livelihood, and plan their future. They are chiefly concerned with the prosperity, the business, the labor relations and the suitability of their own community. Paris and London or Rome or Tokyo are fine places to go for a vacation when money can be had, but the important things for most of the Midwest millions are the hundreds of thousands of new homes, the thousands of new automobiles, radios, television sets, the new household appliances, the new roads, the new or better living conditions of the Midwest. They do not believe that this is the whole of living, they just feel that the better they do their job and the better they make the world in which they and their children live, the better will be the whole of the world.

It is not true that an unscrupulous demogogue can arouse this midwestern mind by claiming that Khrushchev and Mikoyan threaten its peaceful existence. To attribute any anti-foreign notions to the midwestern mind is not correct. Queen Elizabeth II was nowhere more royally greeted than in the heart of the Midwest, nor did Khrushchev find a more friendly reception than in Iowa. There is no narrowness of viewpoint or unfriendliness in the midwestern mind. A basic interest in his own welfare does exist here, but the Midwesterner intends his prosperity for all, for the country, and for Europe and Asia too. He has a conviction based on generations of experience that the prosperity of all will come only through his own prosperity. This conviction that the world's prosperity depends on midwestern prosperity is fundamentally the mind that ruled the Midwest in the nineteenth and early twentieth centuries, and the immigrants adopted it just as completely as the grandchildren of the original transplanted Yankee.

The second charge against the midwestern mind is that it is not distinctive. The Midwest has no Blue Ridge Mountains or Rocky Mountains, no Golden California or Florida coasts. The literary glorifications of life on the prairie or in the plains cities serve rather to emphasize the lack of unique physical and natural phenomena about which a great folk literature would have arisen in other regions of the world. There are indeed other fertile valleys besides the Mississippi and the Missouri, such as the Wabash and the Ohio, but there is little of the picturesque about them. One can survey the patchwork of farmlands and woodlands from the air, and from the thruway the observer can be thrilled by the fertility of the countryside, but he sees little in the countryside that would cause the traveler to make a stop. Even the pattern of the midwestern city is never wholly constant. The midwestern countryside, like its inhabitants, is middle-class—neither naturally beautiful nor technically stupendous.

But this is the mid-twentieth century. Modern man is no longer dominated by the physical element, as he had been in ages past, as he is no longer dependent on natural beauty for his pleasure. The descendant of the peasant whose life was dominated by the physical contours of his old region has become the liberated, widely traveled, and mobile midwestern citizen whose pleasures are more of the mind, whether by book, by radio or television, by movie, or on occasion by a short trip of a few hundred miles. The poignancy of the pioneer of the plains was a sad pleasure of the pioneer Midwest and is often still the plight of the unsuccessful farmer, but it is not the mind of most of the millions of Midwest America, whether in the large expanse of the whole region or in the smaller communities. The sameness of the Midwest arises chiefly from the wide expanse from mountain range to mountain range. The very sameness of men in this wide expanse arises not, however, from the sameness of the land but the sameness of man and is overcome only by concentration on the dignity and higher destiny of man.

This then brings us to the third criticism of the midwestern mind: that it is not cultured enough. This is a criticism that was probably true of the dominant group that has created the present prosperous Midwest. They were chiefly lower middle class, sternly religious, hard working with little time for artistic expression. Most of the artistry came with the pioneer from Europe or was bought carelessly by the new rich until the present prosperity and the new leisure began to create the new Midwest—the permanent home of its people. Let us look more closely. It must be granted at the start that the Midwest does not have, nor will ever have, the Ivy League Universities; it cannot rewrite the American literary products of the Transcendental Era, or of the other romanticists who created the great American literature of the nineteenth century. The Midwest did contribute much in the realistic rebellion of the late nineteenth and early twentieth century, but most of the prose and poetry, philosophy, pragmatic and realistic, and the art of America has been produced east of the Ohio Valley. But not all of it, for it can be seen that many of the great American artists and thinkers were originally from the Midwest. Much of the literature of rebellion, of local color has been produced among the saddened immigrants and their children or the heroic victims of the midwestern farms, even though the days of that literature seem past with the atmosphere that created them. The cultural advances of the Midwest today and of the future depend and will depend upon the ability of the people of the Midwest to make the things of the mind and of the soul more important than the vast material riches and advances of the modern way. We have said that the midwestern mind is the mind of those who intend to make the Midwest their home. These are hard at work creating a Midwest not only of material prosperity, but artistically and culturally superior.

    The outstanding quality of those who are creating the new Midwest is a kind of self-centeredness. This lack of world-wide ambitions has been mistaken for isolationism by those who do not understand the positive elements of much midwestern thinking. Midwestern people are not turning away from other people so much as they are creating here a twentieth-century living.

The heart of this cultural process creating the new Midwest is its system of education. The classical liberal arts colleges which for years dictated the ideals of the old Midwest continue with renewed zeal to speak to a liberal mind of the youth of the region. This youth no longer studies the classics but is literate in new concepts. This new college knowledge has replaced speculative thought with elaborations of the behavioral sciences, and the modern physical and biological sciences. They also show a consciousness of other worlds and other cultures. But the task of directing the cultural development of the Midwest is too great for the small colleges. The local press is just a commercial enterprise with little persuasive power. The new dominant force in the Midwest today is found in its huge universities, mostly but not entirely financed by State funds, and responsible to the political forces of state governments. A few private and religious universities are also important, but the young men and women who fill the positions of leadership in the schools, the governments, and businesses of the region are more and more the products of these state universities. The private universities in the Midwest, even those with large endowments, must lag behind because they cannot draw upon these state funds. Unfortunately, this dominance of non-sectarian education threatens the new midwestern mind with a kind of secularism from the absence of a balancing religious doctrine. However, the churches of the Midwest are very active and draw an increased membership. The Puritanism of early midwestern culture still dominates the press and the public utterances of governmental officers but there is some danger in this cultural imbalance.

European critics of American life have been repelled by the mass education of the Midwest and their criticism has been strengthened by leaders in the Ivy League universities of other regions, but this criticism is premature, and arises from the phenomena of so many lower class people claiming higher education. In the very nature of the circumstances, this higher education tends often to be of a lower caliber or of superficial kind. When one considers the millions of youths living in the region now called the Midwest, the old notion of a small elite group going to a few universities has proved impossible. Some youths will undoubtedly continue to go away from the region for higher studies, and some will go to foreign universities, but the cultural impact of the midwestern mind is being formed in the midwestern colleges and universities and, of course, the lower educational institutions of the region. This public education is quite different from that of the past, chiefly because modern science has changed the living conditions of so many, and because democracy has modified the notion of popular rights. But just as all flowerings of culture have taken time, the perfection of a higher culture among this midwestern people will be a product of time.

While the early nuclear studies at the University of Chicago may not be typical, it is worth recalling that these midwestern universities have been very active in scientific research in this atomic age, and that the thousands of their graduates already active in business and in law and in education are but symptomatic of the new midwestern mind. It is perhaps too soon to say what will be the ultimate ideals of the multitudinous midwestern mind. It is not interested in the reading of foreign languages, even the languages of the grandparents. But by translation it has learned to reach the culture of Greece and Rome, of Europe and of Asia. It is a bit skeptical of the eternal values of a Greek poem or an English ode, but gradually the elements of great literature and philosophy are being transformed into their own ideas. Their appreciation of the great history of mankind and the history of the American people is molding for them a cultural tradition which will best train the midwestern youth to seek the nobility of a Greek ideal in the actual reality of the American commonwealth. The new midwestern citizen must combine prosperity, liberty, and the spiritual ideals with the material wealth of this machine age. Technologically there are enough resources for millions in this region to live in peace and comfort—if there is combined with this a sense of the dignity and spiritual character of man. The sameness and the wide expanse of the midwestern scene creates the hope of attaining these cultural ideals. The tolerance of the Midwest makes room for the church and for the cultural institutions which are to create the higher ideals of midwestern life.

The midwestern mind is no longer that of the frontiersman who gave up comfort and culture to conquer the fields and streams, nor is it the mind of the raw immigrant who had not yet learned to live in the freedom of mid-America, either on the countryside or in the slums. Nor is it yet that of the hardworking pioneer farmer and businessman whose practical ideals laid the foundation for the present prosperity. The leisure and the prosperity of the new day has made possible a new Midwest. The present midwestern mind has formed itself while creating wealth in this fertile and productive region. It has a new concept of human progress, accepting a basic sameness but dedicated to a newer progress, richer living, happier homes amid the possession of the land. It is symbolized by a new architecture, new artistry, new concepts of living, and a new faith in the spiritual dignity of man. If there is some fear of the terrible engines of destruction that have been created by the use of nuclear energy, there is also a faith in human goodness that will prevent their use for war and a very human confidence that the new power will just increase the new physical liberty and prosperity of middle-class America.

Of the criticisms of the midwestern mind, the problem of isolationism is perhaps the easiest to meet, although culturally it is still a bad frame of mind, even when explained as self-centeredness rather than isolationism. With few exceptions, however, there is no midwestern nationalism of the type which would attempt to make the region into a mythical heaven, superior to other regions. The Midwesterner admits that he likes to go to other regions to feast his eyes on the mountains and canyons, and beautifully formed valleys. He has deep sympathy for the down-trodden peasant of Asia, Africa, and some parts of Europe. But he has recovered from the missionary zeal to carry democratic ideals to all these poor people which was characteristic of the Midwestern Progressive at the turn of the century.

On the question of sameness, there is no final answer in a world that has so many things produced on the assembly line. One can have his own color on his Ford or Lark or Cadillac, or on his telephone, but no one would ever think of asking for a different kind of instrument. The same cereals, fruit juices, bread, and packaged meats and vegetables do not seem to have taken very much joy out of living, so long as one gets occasional vacations or respites to create something different for a change.

Even the same schools are not so bad as long as the promotion is by merit and the contents of the course returns to basic education. The same newspapers, nation-wide radio programs, and television shows are usually quite a bit better than local products or none. What is important about the sameness of midwestern living is the fact that it is shared by so many who would be deprived without this leveling, and that it does not seem to have eliminated the personal and the individual for those who can spend more money.

To estimate the cultural and spiritual position of the new Midwest is difficult, just as cultural history is always the last written. It is hard to weigh or measure spiritual goods, and at times the attempt to analyze them seems to destroy their delicate fineness. One has but to travel about the rural regions of the Midwest to note the change from the old architecture of the nineteenth-century Midwest. Some of those large stone courthouses still overshadow the surrounding village in the manner that Tulsa's skyscraper towers over the plains. The newer buildings are smaller, more functional but attractive. Some of these rural shopping centers by their use of glass and electric lights almost create a fairyland. Probably the most attractive buildings of the modern Midwest are the new churches and the new college and university buildings. They, of course, do not have the massiveness of Chicago's skyscrapers, but they combine function with ideas. The universities are no longer building imitations of Oxford or Cambridge, or early Yale, but twentieth-century halls of learning and student quarters.

These universities are more and more the structural supports of the cultural and social life. The faculties of these institutions, of course, are not able to maintain leadership without help because the Midwest has not yet broken away from the American notion that educators need not be paid well. But the successful people are usually graduates of these universities and colleges and have learned to support musical organizations as well as sport centers, to insist on libraries and museums, and to see that the newer civic buildings embody better architectural ideals than those of the city council.

The religion of the Midwest is very difficult to describe. Certainly the moral tone derived from the early Yankees and Southerners has not been entirely dissipated. But there is no moral power like a local New England or Southern theocracy of the nineteenth century to force moral uprightness. Honesty in government and honesty in business is very much the rule in most midwestern communities and departures from that honesty receive quick retribution in elections or in business. Public vice is opposed and even public gambling is not tolerated in many communities. The reaction to the Prohibition laws has broken much opposition to the public sale of intoxicants, but the restrictions on Sunday liquor sales in some other circumstances persist.

The administration of government and police protections in such cities as Chicago, Detroit, and St. Louis is only slightly different from similiar problems and failures in other larger cities of the nation. The only difference seems to be in a greater mobility and in newer types of citizens in the midwestern metropolises.

At the heart of the various regions of the new Midwest are the larger cities with tall buildings, financial centers, urban universities, and social exchanges. These large urban centers of the Midwest, especially Chicago, Detroit, and St. Louis, are mightily affected by two main movements. The immigrants and urbanized farmers of a generation ago have for the most part prospered and feel the need of the benefits of modern city life, which they can best attain only in the suburbs. There they are re-establishing their churches and their schools and even the local politics which had been dominated by the machine in the less attractive districts of the cities. In their places, where the cities have not yet replaced the tenements with modern buildings, have come the newer city residents from the poorer farm regions of the South, the Southwest, and from Spanish America. Religion and government alike face a difficult task in trying to regain the minds and the hearts of these new poor.

Religious membership is higher insofar as the Midwest has participated in the general American trend, but in the Midwest, outside of a few smaller communities there is no moral force demanding membership in a religious organization. Catholicism seems to have prospered in the Midwest, almost justifying the fear of Samuel F. B. Morse of a hundred years ago. The Catholic parochial school prospers best in the Midwest with many large high schools and the few Catholic colleges seem to be successful, with the women's colleges achieving a higher, if more delicate, kind of success. But culturally the Catholics, being for the most part only one or two generations in the English atmosphere of Midwest America, have not been so vocal or so influential in public life as their numbers would suggest. The Midwest remains dominantly Protestant. Most prominent persons in civic life belong with their families to the Protestant Episcopal, Presbyterian, Methodist, Baptist, Lutheran, United Brethren, or Christian churches. There are thriving Gospel and Pentecostal congregations, many of whose membership have recently arrived from the South or Southwestern parts of the country. The dreary meeting houses of another day are being replaced by attractive church buildings and social centers designed by the best architects.

The literature of the Midwest has been handicapped by the lack of prosperous publishing houses in the region and this has forced so many midwestern writers to go on bended knee to eastern firms to attain publication. This dominance of the eastern publishers remains in the realm of fiction, although the opening of newer markets for books in the Midwest will undoubtedly change the quality of the books accepted. Most significant in recent years has been the prosperity and multiplication of university presses with their philosophical, historical and sociological books. The importance of this one item is almost immeasureable, both in strengthening the cultural life of the Midwest and in defending the better ideals of midwestern life.

The instruments of learning and art in the Midwest in recent years has gone far beyond the public libraries which served so well an earlier generation and which are in a grander way continuing intellectual forces of the present day. New buildings for civic and business purposes have begun to display the conceptions of American architects and engineers. The list of public art galleries of the Midwest includes such important collections as the Art Institute of Chicago and the collections at the University of Chicago and Northwestern University, and the galleries of Elgin, Rockford, Springfield in Illinois; those of Fort Wayne, Indianapolis, South Bend in Indiana; Davenport, Des Moines, Fort Dodge in Iowa; Wichita in Kansas; Kansas City in Missouri; those of Detroit, Grand Rapids and Lansing in Michigan; of Minneapolis, St. Paul and Rochester in Minnesota; and many others in Ohio, such as those in Cleveland, Cincinnati, and Toledo; and Milwaukee in Wisconsin. The number of symphony and concert orchestras, beginning with those more noted organizations of Chicago, Minneapolis, Detroit, Cleveland, and Indianapolis, give some measure of the growing interest in the finer musical arts possible in the larger centers of population. Music Departments of the State Universities are contributing much here, not only in faculty and student interest in music, but also in creating centers of the performing arts in their localities.

I have said that the midwestern mind is the mind of those who intend to stay in the Midwest and make it their home. But that is not to say that these same people do not want to retain the strength of character of the pioneer, or the spiritual courage of the incoming immigrant, or the matter-of-fact hard working spirit of the transplanted Yankee of other days. But the mind is something spiritual that cannot be tied down to the limits of a place or a region. The mind is part of the soul and its chief yearnings are for the things of the spirit. The twentieth-century Midwesterner wants to enjoy the riches of his homeland but he is also aware that the crowning jewels among these riches are spiritual.

[1] Ray Allen Billington, "The Garden of the World: Fact and Fiction," *The Heritage of the Middle West*, ed. by John J. Murray (Norman, 1958).
[2] John Bartlow Martin, "The Changing Midwest," *The Saturday Evening Post*, January 11, 18, 25 and February 1, 1958.
[3] *Statistical Abstract of the United States, 1959* (Washington, 1959).
[4] Cf. *American Art Directory, 1958*, Vol. 40. Published by the American Federation of Arts, ed. by Dorothy B. Gilbert (New York, 1958).
[5] Cf. "International Directory of Orchestras and Managements" *Musical America, February*, 1958, pp. 292-300.
[6] Robert C. March "Music in the Midwest," *High Fidelity*, X (February, 1960), 42-44, 106-7.

The Sacs and Foxes of the Mississippi Valley
WILLIAM HAGAN

OF THE MANY Indian tribes that once resided in the upper Mississippi River region, two of the most powerful were the Sac and Fox. Originally located around the Great Lakes the two tribes were forced out of that area by the French. Forming a close confederation they moved southward, living for a time in Wisconsin, then Illinois, and later Iowa. The Sac and Fox—both members of the Algonquin Family—remained closely allied throughout their years in Illinois and Iowa, but never merged so as to lose their tribal identity.

Before the 1830s most of the Sac and Fox lived along the eastern bank of the Mississippi River, but in 1832 the last resisting members were forced across the river into Iowa. Then began a series of land treaties with the federal government which terminated only after all Sac and Fox land had been ceded to the government and the two tribes had been relocated in Kansas. In the mid-1850s, about ten years after their removal from Iowa, several Fox Indians returned to Iowa; they purchased eighty acres of land and reclaimed their original name of Mesquakie. This marked the beginning of the Tama Indian Settlement and today the Mesquakie own more than 3,000 acres of land along the Iowa River in Tama County. Each August hundreds of Iowans attend the Tama Pow Wow where the Mesquakie perform tribal dances and exhibit their art and craft work.

In the first chapter of his book, *The Sac and Fox Indians,* William Hagan relates a brief history of the Sac and Fox as well as their early tribal activities in the vicinity of Iowa. His detailed descriptions help us to visualize how the early Sac and Fox looked and acted in their tribal life.

From *The Sac and Fox Indians,* by William T. Hagan.
Copyright 1958 by The University of Oklahoma Press,
pp. 3–15.

1. The Sacs and Foxes of the Mississippi Valley

IN THE spring of 1800, as Sacs and Foxes on the upper Mississippi deliberated in council, William Henry Harrison, delegate from Northwest Territory, rose in Congress Hall to introduce a bill. The young legislator proposed that Congress divide Northwest Territory into two political units, and a few weeks later President John Adams signed the bill creating Indiana Territory. To serve as governor, Adams chose well-qualified Delegate Harrison. The stalwart twenty-seven-year-old Harrison had served his apprenticeship in the regular army under that taskmaster Anthony Wayne. After resigning his army commission, Harrison became secretary of Northwest Territory in July, 1798. From this office the voters of the territory had sent him to Congress.

From his new capital at Post Vincennes, Harrison surveyed a domain which extended from the Ohio River on the south to the Canadian border, and from what is now the western boundary of the state of Ohio to the Mississippi. Inhabiting this vast region was a scanty population of about 5,500 whites, most of them of mixed French and Indian blood. Using canoes, keels, mackinaws, and flatboats to navigate the rivers of the area, on land the infrequent traveler followed the paths trodden by the buffalo and Indians.

Although they were not included in the census returns of 1800, the population of Indiana Territory included many thousands of Indians. In the summer of 1795, Harrison had been present when Wayne negotiated the Treaty of Greenville with tribes from this area, and as aide to the General he assumed the duty of seeing the provisions of the treaty carried into effect. This training stood Harrison in good stead as governor, for the activities of the traders, the naturally belligerent proclivities of the Indians, and the encroachment of white settlers upon Indian lands brought inevitable clashes between the two contending civilizations under his jurisdiction.

Not so closely in contact with the advancing line of settlement as many of the other Indian nations in the territory of Indiana, the Sac and Fox tribes afforded Harrison many unhappy moments. Residing in several villages scattered along the banks of the Mississippi from around the mouth of the Des Moines River to the French settlement at Prairie du Chien, these Indians, on the grounds that they had never entered into treaty relations with the United States, refused to negotiate with the governor of Indiana Territory.[1] True, they had not signed the Treaty of Greenville, but at Fort Harmar in January, 1789, two Sacs signed the treaty which Governor Arthur St. Clair of Northwest Territory concluded with representatives of several tribes. Article XIV of that treaty specifically mentioned the Sacs as being received into the "friendship and protection" of the United States on an equal basis with the other tribes.[2]

The role of the Sacs and Foxes in the Old Northwest made some settlement with them a necessity. Brave and warlike, they

[1] Harrison to the Secretary of War, July 15, 1801, in *Messages and Papers of William Henry Harrison* (ed. by Logan Esarey), I, 25-31.
[2] The text of any treaty cited in this study may be found in Charles J. Kappler (ed.), *Indian Affairs: Laws and Treaties*.

had dispossessed the Illinois Indians who formerly inhabited their area. Originally, their home had been to the north—the Sacs in the upper Michigan peninsula and the Foxes on the south shore of Lake Superior. Midway in the seventeenth century, Iroquois and French pressure drove the Sacs south to the area around Green Bay. Previously, the Chippewas had eased the Foxes out of their lands on the shore of Lake Superior, and the latter had gradually moved south until they occupied land around Lake Winnebago and along the Fox River.

In the early eighteenth century an attack by the French drove the Sacs and Foxes into the close confederation which marked their relationship until the middle of the next century. When the French sought to punish the Foxes for interfering with their traders, the Foxes sought refuge in the midst of the Sacs. The latter, though friendly to the French, refused to surrender the culprits, and the French vented their wrath upon both tribes. This attack forced the now allied tribes to migrate again, and they jointly attacked the Illinois Indians, whose land they coveted.

By the time Governor Harrison entered upon his duties at Post Vincennes, the Sacs were living in one large village and several small ones on the Mississippi, between the mouth of the Des Moines and the mouth of the Rock. The Foxes were scattered in several villages, from the mouth of Rock River north along the banks of the Mississippi to Prairie du Chien. The largest Sac village, Saukenuk, was the wonder of all who visited it. Occupied by the majority of the Sac nation, in 1817 it contained probably one hundred lodges, and its chiefs could muster one thousand warriors. The location, on a point of land between Rock River and the Mississippi, was an enviable one. The rushing waters at the rapids of the Rock and of the Mississippi teemed with fish. Extensive stands of bluegrass around the village furnished ample pasturage for the horses. On the fertile prairie which ran parallel to the Mississippi, the women of Saukenuk and an adjoining Fox village tilled several hundred acres of corn.

Besides raising enough corn to allow for a surplus to be sold to the traders, the women cultivated pumpkins, beans, and squash. From the bluff which rose out of the prairie bordering the Mississippi gushed several springs of clear, sparkling water. Rock Island and the surrounding country provided in abundance berries, apples, plums, and nuts to enhance the diet of the Sacs and Foxes. In exile, Black Hawk remembered, "We always had plenty—our children never cried with hunger, nor our people were never in want."

One or more families lived in each of Saukenuk's hundred lodges. Occupied only in the summer, the lodges were not constructed for warmth. Forty to sixty feet long and about twenty feet wide, they were simply furnished frames of upright posts covered with white elm bark. Running the length of each side of the lodge was a long bench covered with bark, upon which the women spread blankets and skins. The Indians left the area between the benches open for fires and food preparation. There was no opening for a chimney, and the smoke escaped either through the roof or out the doors. Sometimes fences, consisting of poles over which melon vines trailed, enclosed individual lodges. The entire village gave an impression of neatness and good order unusual among Indian habitations.

The Sacs and Foxes, particularly the Sacs, reflected this pride in appearance. Both nations were of Algonquian stock and had the culture of the eastern Woodland Indians modified by practices adopted from Plains tribes. Although they were so closely allied as to be treated as one nation, they retained definite tribal characteristics. Noted for their fighting ability and the relative efficiency of their political administration, the Sacs were respected throughout the upper Mississippi valley. Well developed physically and tastefully attired in breechclout and beaded moccasins, his scalp lock treated with vermillion and yellow, his face streaked with red, blue, and yellow, a string of wampum or bear's claws around his neck with ear bobs to match, the young Sac brave was an imposing sight.

His counterpart among the Foxes was equally impressive in appearance, although the Foxes did not enjoy the prestige accorded the Sacs. Their smaller number, perhaps 1,600 compared to 4,800 for the Sacs in 1804, was not the only explanation. While the Sacs were noted for their political organization, the Foxes were relatively deficient in this respect. Moreover, among an improvident people the Foxes were noted for improvidence and for their addiction to the white man's firewater. In the confederation the Foxes followed the lead of the Sacs.[3]

At best, government among the Sacs and Foxes was a slack harness for a primitive people. In each tribe, authority for enforcing the simple rules of its society nominally resided in the civil chiefs and a council composed of the chiefs and adult males. The posts of civil chief, of which there were several, one being accorded first rank, were hereditary. Despite the respect accorded the office in matters of social and ceremonial significance, the actual political control exercised by the chief depended largely upon his own personality. If he were wise in council and brave in the incessant warfare, the civil chief might exert considerable authority. If he displayed no such qualities, he found himself with little voice in tribal affairs. But even the influential chief found it expedient to bow to the wishes of the tribal council, which, in the final analysis, wielded what authority there was among the Sacs and Foxes.[4]

In addition to civil chiefs, the tribes distinguished outstanding braves, who were themselves the elite of the warriors, by granting them the title of war chief. They retained the title

---

[3] Thomas Forsyth to Thomas L. McKenney, August 28, 1824; Forsyth to Lewis Cass, May 12, 1822; both in Indian Office Files. Photostatic copies are in the possession of the State Historical Society of Wisconsin (hereafter, the term "Photostat WHS" will be used).

[4] Thomas Forsyth to William Clark, January 5, 1827, in Draper MSS. (State Historical Society of Wisconsin), 9T2-3.

only so long as they maintained their reputation for valor and resourcefulness. Actual leadership of a war party rested with any individual who could attract sufficient followers for such an expedition. A record of successful campaigning was a valuable asset in recruiting men for a war party against the current enemy, but dreams and visions likewise played an important role.

Ma-ka-tai-me-she-kia-kiak, or Black Sparrow Hawk, a Sac brave and war chief of about thirty summers when Harrison became governor of Indiana Territory, was typical of his class. The descendant of a chief, he was of medium but strong build. His sharp, dark hazel eyes, unshielded by eyebrows, peered over a Roman nose. His generous mouth overhung a slightly receding, sharp chin. Only a scalp lock adorned his otherwise shaven head. Not unpleasant, his features, with his light yellow complexion, had a slight Chinese cast.

Several children graced the lodge of Black Hawk, as he was commonly known, and Asshewequa, or Singing Bird, his attractive and devoted wife. Although polygamy was common among the Sacs and Foxes, Black Hawk remained faithful to Singing Bird. More typical of his tribe was the Sac's love of war. At the age of fifteen he had wounded an enemy and won the right to paint, wear feathers, and be called a brave. In the succeeding years Black Hawk led or was a member of many war parties which left Saukenuk in search of enemy scalps.

Whenever he wished to lead a war party, Black Hawk followed the customs of the tribe and prayed and fasted in order to communicate with the Great Spirit and receive some omen to rally others to his side. Since so much emphasis in the Sac and Fox society was placed upon skill and valor in combat, the young Indians were ever ready for war. If Black Hawk, or some other ambitious brave, could announce that the Great Spirit had informed him of the location of a band of unsuspecting Sioux, Osages, or Menominees and had assured him success, he had no difficulty recruiting his force. Individually, those who wished to join him would visit Black Hawk in a lodge which he had erected apart from the others and agree to place themselves under his leadership for the projected expedition. This was all that was necessary to loose a war party whose deeds might provoke retaliation and a general conflagration. Older and wiser heads might attempt to dissuade Black Hawk, but they were not often successful.

Like many primitive peoples the tribesmen displayed considerably more order in their social organization. Each family among the Sacs and Foxes belonged to one of the dozen or more great gens, or groups. Membership in the gens, which bore such names as Bear, Buffalo, Sturgeon, and Thunder, was hereditary. Important for the transmission of property, which had to be hereditary within gens, the groupings also had religious significance, and most of the ceremonials employed the concept.

Nonreligious in content but equally important in the social organization of the Sacs and Foxes was a division of the male population of each tribe into two orders. Like all other parents, Black Hawk and Singing Bird daubed with black or white paint the face of each of their sons at birth, thus enrolling him in one or the other of the orders. Distinguished by their face paint, the youths teamed with others of their order in the tribal games and vied in feats of daring and stratagem in war.[5]

The close social organization of the Sacs and Foxes helped the tribes maintain their unity despite a weak political structure and a migratory mode of life which led Black Hawk and his fellows to occupy their villages only between hunting trips. Normally, in the spring following their winter hunt, the Sacs returned to Saukenuk to plant their crops and deal with the traders. On arrival at the village, Black Hawk would repair his lodge and open the cache which he had left the previous fall.

[5] Sol Tax, "The Social Organization of the Fox Indians," Fred Eggan (ed.), *Social Anthropology of North American Tribes*, 243–44; Major Morrill Marston to Rev. Jedediah Morse, November, 1820, in Draper MSS., 1T58; Forsyth comments on this in Draper MSS., 9T6.

For days he and his family gorged themselves on the bark-packaged contents. The dried corn, squashes, beans, and crab apples, present so sparingly in their diet during the difficult winter months, had been carefully concealed in their hole by a covering of sod which blended with the rest of the prairie.

Having satisfied their immediate cravings, the Indians then turned to other occupations. Black Hawk and the other warriors traded, negotiated with their agent, and relaxed in long convivial sessions marked by smoking, boasting, and drinking liquor donated by the traders.

While Black Hawk and the other men were thus pleasantly engaged, Singing Bird took her hoe and joined the women and children in the fields. Planting in the same hills year after year made it unnecessary to clear new ground—by far the most difficult task of the farmer on virgin land. Three or four cultivations with a hoe sufficed, and after repairing the flimsy fences of poles, Singing Bird could join Black Hawk in the ceremonial feasts and dances which regularly occurred after the planting.

Following the feasting and dancing, the tribe once again dispersed. Black Hawk and the hunters departed for the boundless prairies west of Council Bluffs to stalk the elk and buffalo and the occasional party of Osages or other hostile bands also following the grazing herds. Singing Bird and the children fished and gathered bark for bags and flag reeds, from which the women wove the mats used in making their winter lodges. Or they might go up the Mississippi to the lead region to mine and smelt ore. The Foxes, who occupied the sites of some of the richest lead veins on the Mississippi, were particularly active in the production of the metal. Their annual output of three thousand to four thousand pounds of smelted metal went to the traders.

After a month or six weeks of these activities the hunters, lead miners, fishermen, and reed and bark gatherers reassembled at the village to share their various products and indulge in a riot of feasts, dances, and games. With plenty of food available for all, feast followed feast. As the fresh corn and other garden products became available, the Indians gorged themselves. Dysentery frequently resulted, and every year saw several deaths attributable to this ailment.

In addition to feasting, the Indians raced horses and played ball. With hundreds of excited warriors participating, the ball games on the open prairie were particularly spectacular. The ancestors of modern lacrosse, the games were played on a field perhaps two or three hundred yards long. In crucial games between bands or villages, warriors armed with rackets and fortified by fasting and ceremonials could turn the vigorous sport into a modified form of mayhem. Spectators and participants alike gambled heavily, wagering guns, horses, blankets, and other property on the outcome of the games and races. Infrequently, intertribal games and races provided occasions for great celebration.

Ball games and horse racing came to an end when the crops were in. A tribal council then convened to allot hunting areas for the coming winter and to fix a date for the Indians to leave the village. Caches dug, and corn, beans, and other garden products dried and buried for use the following spring, Black Hawk and his family were ready to depart.

Early in September the crier circulated through the village announcing the date of departure. In the last hours the Indians busily loaded canoes, prepared packs, and drew on credit from the traders the arms, ammunition, traps, and other items necessary for the long winter. On the chosen day the old men and the women and children slipped down the Rock in canoes and the able-bodied men turned their horses toward the hunting grounds.

Reassembling at their allotted area, the various bands of one or more families each settled down for uninterrupted hunting until the season of severe cold arrived. Then they congregated in the vicinity of the establishments of their traders, these hardy individuals having followed them to the hunting grounds. Attempting only a little hunting and trapping, the Indians waited out the worst of the winter snug in their winter lodges of mats and skins.

When the melting snows and mild breezes heralded the approach of spring, the encampments once more hummed with activity. Black Hawk joined one of the parties leaving to trap beaver, raccoon, and muskrats. With the others who remained behind, Singing Bird and the children prepared to go into sugar camp, a pleasant stop in the tribal itinerary. However, it was not of long duration, and the tribe soon reassembled at a rendezvous on the Mississippi to return to the village, settle with their trader, and begin the cycle again.

Over a period of a century and a half the Indians had become completely dependent upon the white trader.[6] Although Black Hawk, like any other Sac or Fox hunter, would have hotly denied the term, he was essentially a hireling of the fur companies. For the warrior, independence was a thing of the past. Without the articles supplied by the trader he could not have existed. Arms, ammunition, traps, cooking utensils, knives, blankets—all were obtained by Black Hawk and his fellows in return for their peltries. The tobacco he smoked and frequently the pipe in which he smoked it, the paint which adorned his face, and the wampum which he used as jewelry as well as a medium of exchange, came from the indispensable trader.

Over the years the Sacs and Foxes had dealt with French, Spanish, English, and American traders. Following the War of 1812 the Americans gradually supplanted their competitors, as John Jacob Astor's American Fur Company profited by Congress' exclusion of foreigners from the Indian trade.

Most of the transactions between the Indians and the traders involved credit. The improvident Indians seemed incapable of operating on any other basis. This situation satisfied the trader, as it gave him a hold on the hunter and helped insure

[6] Thomas Forsyth to Lewis Cass, October 24, 1831, Photostat WHS.

that furs came to his post instead of that of his competitor. Although the debts stimulated the diligent Indians, the shiftless were consoled by the certainty of receiving credit for the next hunt, whether or not they had cleared their old account.

In 1806, Lewis and Clark estimated that the Sacs and Foxes, reputed to be the best hunters on the Mississippi and Missouri, brought $10,000 worth of furs annually to their traders.[7] By 1831 the trade had increased until Farnham and Davenport, the agents of the American Fur Company at Rock Island, who had practically a monopoly on the tribe's trade, could report that each year they invested capital ranging from $33,000 to $60,000. In the seven years preceding 1831 their total credits amounted to $137,000; $53,500 was still uncollected in 1831.[8]

Normally, Indian traders considered doubtful a debt not paid the first year. They termed desperate one unpaid for two years.[9] To be sure, there was one successful method employed whenever possible to collect old debts. This was to have them written into treaties. Thus, annuities might be applied on the debts, or the government might assume them in partial consideration for a land cession. Living for the moment, the Indians were more concerned with obtaining traps and powder for the next hunt than with the disposition of their land twenty years in the future. Each fall the Sacs and Foxes went into debt outfitting for the winter hunt and added to that debt by small purchases throughout the winter.

Under the prevailing credit terms the Indians could amass a considerable debt quite simply. In the late 1820's, Farnham and Davenport were marking up 25 to 50 per cent on such principal items of trade as blankets, and more on such minor items as brooches, playing cards, and mirrors. These same ar-

[7] *American State Papers: Indian Affairs*, I, 711.
[8] Russell Farnham and George Davenport to the Secretary of War, November 22, 1831, Photostat WHS.
[9] Henry R. Schoolcraft to Lewis Cass, October 24, 1831, L. F. Stock Transcripts in the possession of the State Historical Society of Wisconsin (hereafter cited as Stock Transcripts).

ticles, when sold to the Sacs and Foxes for cash, were marked up only 12.5 to 25 per cent. Nor was this the only source of profit. When the Sac and Fox hunters brought in their beaver, muskrat, raccoon, deer, and other skins, which constituted the principal part of their trade goods, Farnham and Davenport credited them with an arbitrary valuation on the furs, estimated to be 25 to 50 per cent below the St. Louis rate. Canoes, maple sugar, and meat were purchased at similar discounts.

Despite this apparently more than comfortable margin, the traders rarely became rich at the expense of Black Hawk and his fellows, although their parent firm, which supplied the trade goods and marketed the furs, frequently did. Farnham and Davenport had heavy expenses. When the Indians visited their posts, they expected and received rations. In times of famine, which were alarmingly frequent among the Indians, this became a serious drain. Also, traders found it politic to humor visiting hunters and their families with small gifts of tobacco, needles, thread, and flints.

Although Black Hawk did not realize the actual role he played for the American Fur Company, he did realize the importance of the trader in his way of life. A relationship had developed between the two parties which had no counterpart among other white-Indian relationships. Frequently taking wives from among the sisters or daughters of influential braves or chiefs, the traders enjoyed the unrivaled confidence of their customers. The Indians consulted them on their relations with other whites and with the United States government. Although members of war parties had an unsavory record for indiscriminate murder, no Sac or Fox ever separated one of his traders from his hair.

As a rival to the trader for influence with the Indians, the United States relied upon the Indian agent. Depending upon the experience and ability that he brought to his position, the agent could be a real asset to the tribe to which he was assigned and an able representative of his nation's interests, or an extremely ineffectual link between the two diverse peoples. Political appointees though they might be, the agents on the frontier of the Old Northwest during this period, with few exceptions, performed their functions in a reasonably efficient manner.

The role of mediator between Indians and whites was no sinecure. It required an individual with the wisdom of Solomon to resolve the multitude of intratribal, intertribal, and white-Indian conflicts which occurred. Year by year the line of settlement encroached upon the Sac and Fox hunting grounds and increased the possibility of clashes. Both Indians and whites appealed to the agent for justice. The complaints of the whites usually dealt with stolen livestock and dismantled fences, forced levies of food and drink, and, occasionally, beatings and scalpings. From the Sacs and Foxes came tales of trade frauds, invasion of hunting grounds, stolen horses, and, occasionally, beatings and murders.

Presumably, the treaties between the United States and the Indians provided for an equitable settlement of grievances. Courts dealt with the guilty parties, whether white or Indian, and compensated for property damage. In practice this system exhibited many weaknesses, such as the Indians' reluctance to testify in court. A general prejudice against red men made it unlikely that a jury of frontiersmen would find a white man guilty, and guilty Indians were difficult to apprehend. However, it is apparent that the white claimant fared much better than his red counterpart. The law of the white man did not prove to be an adequate fence around the property and rights of the Indian.

Governor Harrison, as the first governor of Indiana Territory, had ample opportunity to experience the difficulties and embarrassments which were the lot of any government administrator on the frontier. The resourceful young governor solved the problems arising out of Indian-white relations in a manner which endeared him to his white constituents if not to his red children.

A Dutch Immigrant's View of Frontier Iowa
ROBERT P. SWIERENGA

IN 1848 a young Dutchman named Sjoerd Aukes Sipma wrote a letter to his relatives and friends in the Netherlands in which he described his new life in Pella, Iowa. Sipma was one of approximately eight hundred Dutch immigrants who came to Iowa in 1847 and settled the community of Pella. Literate, but with a meager education, Sipma nevertheless described in great detail the economic and social conditions in the new Dutch settlement. His letter has properly been called a "priceless document" as Sipma included full descriptions of many aspects of pioneer life.

Sipma's letter also touches on other considerations. Aside from the valuable information about early southeastern Iowa, he allows us to see our society through the eyes of a foreign observer. Many such foreign writers as Alexis de Tocqueville and Harriet Martineau offered penetrating insights into American behavior and attitudes in the first half of the nineteenth century. Even though Sipma offers a far more limited account, his letter provides a fresh, delightful view of two cultures.

Perhaps the most significant observation we can make about Sipma's experience is that he did succeed in the New World. His goal was to purchase land and this he was able to do after repaying the funds he had borrowed for his passage to the United States. Eventually he became a prosperous farmer and as such he typifies the concept of "The Agricultural Ladder." How would Sipma's account of early Iowa contrast with letters written by native Americans who underwent similar experiences?

A DUTCH IMMIGRANT'S VIEW OF FRONTIER IOWA

Edited with an Introduction by
ROBERT P. SWIERENGA
ASSISTANT PROFESSOR OF HISTORY
CALVIN COLLEGE, GRAND RAPIDS, MICHIGAN

Dr. Swierenga, a graduate of Calvin College and Northwestern University, recently received his Ph.D. degree from the University of Iowa and is in his second year of teaching at Calvin College. He uncovered this 1849 pamphlet while engaged in research on the voting patterns of the Dutch immigrants in Iowa in the decade prior to the Civil War.[1] His interest in the local Hollanders derives from his own Dutch ancestry and from three years he spent teaching at the Pella Christian High School.

In August of 1847 a group of approximately eight hundred travel-weary Dutch immigrants reached the site of their future home in northeastern Marion County, Iowa. The new colony, called Pella (after the classical Greek "city of refuge" of that name where the Christians fled upon the destruction of Jerusalem, 70 A.D.), had its inception in religious and economic difficulties in the Netherlands, stemming from a schism in the state-supported Dutch Reformed Church in 1834 and a series of agricultural disasters in the 1840's.[2] Under the

---

[1] Robert P. Swierenga, "The Ethnic Voter and the First Lincoln Election," *Civil War History*, XI (March, 1965), 27-43.
[2] Excellent accounts of the Dutch migration to Iowa are in Jacob Van Der Zee, *The Hollanders of Iowa* (Iowa City: State Historical Society of Iowa, 1912), and Henry S. Lucas, *The Netherlanders in*

leadership of the Reverend Mr. Henry Peter Scholte, a group of seceders met at Utrecht in 1846 and formed the "Netherlandish Association for Emigration to the United States of North America" to assist needy compatriots who wished to escape economic disasters and a mild persecution from government officials.[3]

Sjoerd Aukes Sipma, author of the following letter, here published for the first time in English, was one of the Netherlanders who migrated to Pella under the auspices of the association. Born into a large lower class family in Bornwerd, a city in the province of Friesland, and recently married, Sjoerd saw little economic opportunity in his homeland. With his bride and several other penniless Friesian seceders, he was sponsored by a local benefactor and fellow immigrant, Hierke Ypes Viersen. Working briefly for Scholte and Viersen and then for an unidentified American farmer living on the southern outskirts of the settlement, the Sipmas prospered and within two years managed to repay their 202 guilder ($81.00) debt to Viersen and purchase a small twenty-five acre farm from the local school fund commissioner. Soon Sipma was buying and selling land extensively. In the next two decades his name appeared in the Marion County deed record books no less than forty times as either the grantee or grantor of local real estate. Eventually in the late 1860's when Pella became overcrowded and land prices soared, Sipma and a few others spearheaded the drive to open a new colony in Sioux County in northwestern Iowa where government land was yet available for homesteading. Sipma's granddaughter, Mrs. Lillian Top, still lives in Orange City, the hub of the new settlement.

In the letter the author frequently mentions the "association," which refers either to the Dutch immigrant organiza-

America; Dutch Immigration to the United States and Canada, 1789-1950 (Ann Arbor: University of Michigan, 1955).

[3] The only biography of Scholte is Lubbertus Oostendorp, *H. P. Scholte, Leader of the Secession of 1834 and Founder of Pella* (Franeker, Netherlands: T. Wever, 1964). For a copy of the rules of the Netherlandish Association, translated into English, see Henry S. Lucas, "A Document Relating to Dutch Immigration to Iowa in 1846," *Iowa Journal of History and Politics*, XXI (July, 1923), 457-465.

tion noted above or to the Pella colony, depending on the context. References to the "Far West" denote the Middle West. Sipma's Friesian nationality also bears mention. Although the members of the association were Netherlanders, a few such as Sipma were from the Dutch province of Friesland. Among themselves the Friesians commonly used their own dialect, which is related to, but distinct from, Dutch. Friesians also claimed a long national history of their own, gloried in their separate ethnic identity, and were careful to preserve it. To other Dutchmen they often seemed a rustic and clannish people. According to the late Professor Henry S. Lucas, lifelong student of the Dutch in America, a distinct Friesian community existed a mile north of the town of Pella, which became known as the Vriesche Buurt ("Friesian Neighborhood").[4] Sipma himself, along with a few other Friesians, settled four to five miles southeast of Pella, but in his letter he displays a similar ethnic consciousness when he mentions that his wife mended clothing "for Gosse J. de Vries and Geert Dykstra [both Friesians] and also for a Hollander." He also states that the local Friesians, as a group, declined to participate in the business meetings of the immigrant association.

Whether or not this ethnic consciousness had anything to do with Sipma's obvious dislike of Scholte is a moot question. Certainly opposition to Scholte's leadership of the colony arose from many quarters and for various reasons, not all of them very clear.[5] In any case, the accusation that immigrant leaders used their positions for personal aggrandizement is a common one, and was also leveled against the leader of an English settlement in Clinton County, Iowa, as well as against the leader of the Dutch colony at Holland, Michigan.[6]

---

[4] Lucas, *Netherlanders in America*, p. 185.

[5] In the Pella *Blade*, April 6, 1865, an "open letter" discussed the charges against Scholte at some length. See typed copy in Henry P. Scholte Papers, Central College Archives, Pella. See also Swierenga, "Ethnic Leader," pp. 40-43, for evidence that the colony had turned against Scholte's political leadership by 1860.

[6] The charge against the English leader, George Sheppard, is related in his letter to the Iowa Emigration Society (Hull, England), on August 15, 1850, in Grant Foreman, "English Emigrants in Iowa," *Iowa Journal of History and Politics*, XLIV (October, 1946), 416. The

SJOERD AUKES SIPMA

This letter initially was the response to a request by Sipma's family and friends in the Netherlands, many of whom were prospective immigrants, for factual information about life in the Middle West. Sipma earlier had written a brief letter which, to his surprise, was published by a Dutch editor eager to capitalize on a keen interest in America among the Netherlanders.[7] Basking in his unexpected fame and prompted by requests for more detailed information, Sipma again took pen in hand, this time specifically for publication. The resulting document is priceless today, not only for illustrating

criticism of the Michigan leader, Dr. Albertus C. Van Raalte is noted in Albert Hyma, *Albertus C. Van Raalte and His Dutch Settlements in the United States* (Grand Rapids, Michigan: Wm. B. Eerdmans, 1947), pp. 182-184.

[7] *Brief van Sjoerd Aukes Sipma aan de Ingezetenen van Bornwerd* ... (Dockum, Netherlands: B. Schaafsma, 1848).

BELANGRIJKE BERIGTEN
UIT
PELLA,
IN DE VEREENIGDE STATEN
VAN
NOORD-AMERIKA,
OF TWEEDE BRIEF VAN
Sjoerd Aukes Sipma;
VAN DAAR GESCHREVEN AAN DE INGEZETENEN
VAN
BORNWERD,

WAARIN VELE BIJZONDERHEDEN, BETREFFENDE DE HOLLANDSCHE VEREENIGING IN DEN STAAT JOWA, DE LEVENSWIJZE EN DE GEWOONTEN DER AMERIKANEN, BENEVENS VELE NUTTIGE WENKEN VOOR HEN, DIE NAAR DE VEREENIGDE STATEN WILLEN VERHUIZEN, VOORKOMEN.

VOORZIEN MET EENIGE AANMERKINGEN DOOR

N. N.

GEDRUKT
BIJ DE WED. B. SCHAAFSMA, TE DOCKUM.

1849.

the pathos that immigrants experienced in the process of being uprooted but also for giving an excellent picture of pioneer life in central Iowa. Although the author admits to being uneducated and his style is an unpolished, rural Friesian vernacular, yet as a reporter his legacy to posterity is immense. For those interested in ethno-cultural aspects of American history, the document has an added bonus in that it reveals various facets of cultural conflict between native and foreign-born and even among the foreign-born themselves, conflicts which were endemic in American life.

R. John Vander Borgh, a native of the Netherlands and recently a student at Calvin College, assisted in the preparation of this translation of Sipma's tract, extracted from one of the few remaining copies of the original pamphlet, which is now located in the archives of the State Historical Society of Iowa, Iowa City. The text is complete except for the deletion (noted by elipses) of irrelevant personalia in the opening and closing paragraphs. An extraneous preface and ten footnotes added by a Dutch editor are also deleted. Capitalization, punctuation, and paragraphing have been altered where necessary to assist the reader, but many pronouns without antecedents have been left as is.

Pella, September 26, 1848

To my Relatives, to all the Farmers and
to the School Teacher at Bornwerd:[8]

Dear Friends,

We received your letter after it had been on the way for forty days and from it we learned that all our closest relatives are still in the land of the living and in good physical health. . . .

I shall begin now to answer your questions even though I will not be able to express myself in the most effective man-

---

[8] The school teacher referred to here and throughout the letter is likely Jelle Pelmulder, who in 1856, followed Sipma to Pella. Pelmulder,

ner. I am not an educated person but simply a laborer, even as you have known me to be in Friesland, and besides that, I am not expert enough in the English language to be able to discern everything adequately. Just the same, I am quite willing to answer you as best I can. I will begin by giving you a description of the state of Iowa.

You must not pronounce the word as if it were a Dutch word. It is an English word and is pronounced as ai-o-wa, in three syllables. On the east Iowa borders the Mississippi, on the south the state of Missouri, on the west the Missouri River, while the Indians mark its borders to the north. Indians also inhabit most of the land west of the Missouri River. Ten years ago there were no whites in Iowa yet. At that time the Indians were the only inhabitants here.[9] Only three years ago the state of Iowa was accepted into the United States. The state is about one hundred thousand quadrate or square miles and counts nearly one hundred thousand souls.[10] One mile here is twenty minutes walking distance. The state is divided into counties. Thirty counties have been surveyed, and according to the Americans there are to be sixty of them.[11] The counties are divided into townships, each county has sixteen townships.[12] The townships are divided into sections, each township has thirty-six sections, and each section in turn has 640 acres. Every section number sixteen of each township in Iowa is considered school property. In each county there is a person who sells the school property and places the money at interest. The teachers are paid from

with sipma and a few others, later led the movement to plant a new Dutch settlement in Sioux County in northwestern Iowa. See Lucas, *Netherlanders in America*, pp. 34ff.

[9] White settlement in Iowa began legally in 1833, fifteen years rather than ten years before Sipma wrote.

[10] The total land area of Iowa is only 56,280 square miles and the total population according to the state census of 1847 was 117,954. Sipma's 1848 estimate of 100,000 is probably about 35,000 too low. In 1849, Iowa's population numbered 152,148. These census figures are taken from a population table appended to *The Census Returns of the Different Counties of the State of Iowa for 1859* (Des Moines, 1859).

[11] Iowa eventually had ninety-nine counties.

[12] There are many exceptions to this general rule. Some Iowa counties, such as Tama and Linn, have as many as twenty townships and some, such as Van Buren and Henry, have only twelve.

this interest, each according to the numbers of pupils he has.

The state of Iowa is very fertile, the soil is exceptionally good. So far as I know there is about three or four feet of topsoil and beneath that a sort of reddish clay. The topsoil is black. At a few high spots in the forest the subsoil is sandy. The Americans, who come from almost every other state, say that they have never seen a state which is as convenient for transportation as Iowa, since this state is bounded by the great Mississippi River on the east and intersected from the west by three large rivers, which empty into the Mississippi at various places. It would therefore be easy to build canals. Besides this, railroads could be built quite easily since there are no mountains in this state.

You must not get the impression, however, that the land here is as flat as in Friesland because then it would have no drainage system. The land is hilly, but the hills are not so steep as to prevent farming. In fact, as a general rule the hills provide the best arable soil. Here one can also find level areas of about two hours walking distance, there are no forests on these places. These fields are situated midway between the rivers and are drained toward either side. Most of the wooded areas are found by the rivers. Incidentally, I have not seen a single area of land which cannot absorb water the way God has planned it. Approximately in the center between the rivers the land is higher and this we call a ridge. From this ridge there are small rivers, called creeks, which run through valleys and into the bigger rivers. The river farthest south is the Des Moines, then we get the Skunk River, and finally the Iowa River. In this state there is much more prairie than wooded areas. There are not as many trees as one could wish for. In the first place, because a great deal of lumber is needed for building; then there is so much needed to fence the land, and finally because there is always a great need for fuel. However, if a person uses common sense there is always plenty. After all, one need not go about it as carelessly as the Americans.

During the winter the prairies are burnt off to get new and better grass for the cattle. The burning causes forest fires at times, which sometimes burn for weeks. Not only does all the dead timber burn, but also nearly all the surrounding trees. Moreover, the young trees suffer so much that it rarely happens that even one reaches its full growth.

I cannot acquaint you with the different types of wood we have here because I simply do not know enough about trees. I do know this though, that most of it is oak. We have about seven or eight different types of oak, also linden and walnut trees. The wood is very hard and durable. Because of its tendency to split, oak wood is used exclusively for fencing. The trees are cut into eleven foot lengths after which they are split and used to fence the land.

I am not going to write much about the animal kingdom. As a rule the cattle here are not as heavy as in Friesland, and as far as I can see, this is caused by the fact that they are left on their own during the winter. Calves are not placed in the stable and no colts are taken inside, so livestock suffers terribly. For the rest I cannot detect much difference in the livestock. I am not familiar with wild animals other than wolves, deer, and snakes. The snakes are not very large, about three to four feet long. I have already killed some of them. In the more populated areas of this state, they are almost extinct. Rats are not common here but we have plenty of mice and even bedbugs although I have not seen any yet.

Now I shall tell you something about the plant kingdom. We grow more varieties of crops and vegetables than in Friesland. Some of these are oats, barley, buckwheat, wheat, rye, peas, beans, kohlrabi, cabbage, kale, and all kinds of vegetables, which I cannot explain to you because I cannot find names for them. Rapeseed, horsebeans, and big [lima] beans which the state did not have before, have been imported by the association.[13] In the spring wild flowers change from one color to another and cover the entire field. This is the time when the fields are covered with the most beautiful yellow lilies.[14] There is also a kind of flower which looks like

---

[13] Sipma listed only the common names for these vegetables. Since usage varies considerably, he may have had other vegetables in mind than the ones given here.

[14] There were no wild "yellow" lilies in Iowa. A likely specimen is the abundant orange Turk's Cap.

tulips but is somewhat smaller and entirely white; like tulips it also grows from bulbs.

Flax, hemp, and mustardseed are grown here and corn in great quantities. Those who have about fifty to sixty acres of workable land usually have about forty acres in corn since this crop is harvested during the winter and does not demand much work. One cannot enjoy the wild fruit which we have here. Wild applies are not good for food, wild grapes stay small and are as sour as vinegar. Wild plums are good and plentiful here; blackberries and hazelnuts are also plentiful and good to eat. In some years the hogs are tremendously fattened by them. I stop with this subject now as I think I have said enough about that.

Now I will write something about the poverty and riches of the inhabitants here. There is very little money in this state as yet; one is not rich because of his money. But there are many people who are rich in land, people who own hundreds of acres, yes and sometimes thousands of acres.[15] There is very little poverty here, for those who want to work [as common laborers] can make just as good a living as farmers. Orphans who have lost their parents at an early age and who thus cannot support themselves are taken into the homes of relatives. They are expected to stay with their relatives until they have reached the age of twenty-one. It is considered a terrible shame if children leave their parents before the age of twenty-one, that is, if the parents have plenty of work for them. When the children have reached the age of twenty-one, they are considered on their own.

The taxes which we have here are the following: one cent (2½ [Dutch] cents) per dollar (2 guilders, 50 [Dutch] cents) must be paid on everything one possesses. In the spring a man comes around to make a list of our possessions. Taxes must be paid on all livestock, cows, horses, sheep, and hogs, on everything more than half a year old. Everyone must make

---

[15] My study "Pioneers and Profits: Land Speculation on the Iowa Frontier," (Ph.D. dissertation, University of Iowa, 1965), disclosed that in thirty-three counties of central Iowa alone, over one thousand individual buyers each entered more than one thousand acres of government land at the local land offices (p. 55).

his own appraisal. Land that is fenced in and broken is appraised at about four dollars per acre, and on every hundred dollars worth, one dollar must be paid; the same applies to all the silver, gold, and loose money which a person has. Even on every hundred dollars worth of household goods one dollar must be paid. One must also pay a penny per dollar on the value of a pocket watch and a clock. On the same basis, the land which is appraised at four dollars per acre has a tax of four cents per acre. Money received from rent also is taxed one dollar for every hundred dollars. Thus, on all the things a person owns, the tax is one dollar per hundred dollars. All male persons over twenty-one must pay a poll tax; for those who are able-bodied fifty cents is the required amount. This year I am required to pay sixty cents to the tax collector. Taxes do not extend to anything else other than what I have mentioned. Every other thing, such as licenses, is tax free.[16]

The number of people here rises steadily. Almost every day two or three families travel through the Association. Some families remain but others move further west. The farmers profit greatly from the increased number of newcomers because of the fact that these people, who have practically no possessions, must buy everything during the first two years. If this were not so, the farmers could not make much, as we have as yet no means of transportation. If all merchandise had to be transported to the Mississippi from here, farmers would go bankrupt because it takes forty hours for the goods to be driven down to the river. If the wagoners take the goods, the cost is seventy-five cents per hundred pounds. However, when the Des Moines River is navigable for steamboats, and within three years this project is expected to be completed up to this area, then it is quite certain that the rates will be somewhat less, about sixty-five cents per hundred pounds.[17]

---

[16] The meaning here is unclear. License fees are themselves a tax.
[17] The Des Moines Navigation Improvement Company was established in 1846 to make the Des Moines River navigable as far upriver as the Raccoon Forks in Polk County. The construction costs were to be met by a federal land grant, donated on August 8, 1846, which ultimately

About five years ago the first white people came to Marion [County]. My boss told me that at first it was difficult for these settlers. They could not sell anything at that time because there were no other people here except Indians and these resided here by the hundreds. The Indians use wildlife as their food, such as hares, rabbits, wolves, dogs, snakes, and pigs.[18] They only grow two kinds of crop, corn and white beans. The field work is left entirely to the women. They have to do the planting and harvesting and they have to get firewood form the forests, while the men do nothing but huntting. Last fall we had about fifty of them here in Pella—men, women, and children. We met them one Sunday as we came back from church. Those people looked plump, fat, and healthy. One could not tell whether or not they harbored hatred against the white people. When the first white people came here, the Indians certainly had the upper hand, but they have always conducted themselves peaceably. I will now end this topic.[19]

As I have said before, the first white people could not sell their goods and in order to get their necessities they had to drive a hundred miles to the nearest store. They had to drive just as far to get their wheat and corn ground at the mill. Eggs sold for fifty cents a bushel. At that time it was a hard life for these people but now they are making a substantial living. Now we have in this area two mills which grind grain, two saw-mills, two brickkilns, a pottery, and enough stores.

Most of the Americans still live on claimed land. Each has about three to four hundred acres. I presume you know what I mean by a "claim" — settling on an unsold piece of land

totaled 1,161,513 acres according to the *Report of the Department of the Interior*, 1907, Vol. I, p. 148. For an account of the ultimate failure of this project see Roscoe L. Lokken, *Iowa Public Land Disposal* (Iowa City: State Historical Society of Iowa, 1942), ch. ix.

[18] Sipma may be under the mistaken impression that wild boar were indigenous to Iowa. He may also have intended to mention deer instead of pigs.

[19] By 1848 the various Iowa Indian groups had ceded to the United States all but their land in the northwest corner of the state. Most tribes removed further west but some straggler groups remained behind and roamed about as vagabonds.

without buying it. For a claim to be legal, a person must file it with the government and this costs each member of the family a half dollar.[20] A claim may not consist of more than 320 acres[21] and the right of claim lasts for a year, after which it becomes accessible to anyone, unless the claim has been bought by the person who has settled on the "claim" land. But nobody seems to be concerned about this because one helps the other to retain or to get a claim. They just go to the woods, cut down some posts, set them up on the corners of their claimed land, and that's that. Then, if someone buys such a claim, which is anyone's privilege according to the law, it will be to his disadvantage.[22]

It happened during this summer that we had a man here who, after having bought his own claim, also desired to have his neighbor's claim. He went to the government and bought two hundred acres of land which actually belonged to three of his neighbors. As can be understood, those people were very angry. The news traveled everywhere and people went to this man several times to persuade him to withdraw his claim, but he refused. Just a few days ago, when I was coming home to eat, I saw an army of people coming in the distance on wagons and on horseback. They were letting their flags wave freely, singing, whistling, and blowing their horns. I wondered what this meant. I asked my boss what this was all about and he told me that they were going to force this man to surrender his land. He also went along with the crowd himself, as well as all the other Americans. They went to the man's house but he was not at home; he had taken flight. They searched for two days and two nights but could not find him. Now the people really got angry — there were about two hundred men altogether — because since he stayed away,

[20] The Preemption Act of 1841 provided this right to any person over twenty-one, or to any other person at the head of a family. The fifty cent fee is paid by each claimant. (U.S. *Statutes at Large*, V, 455-456.). Often each member of the family over twenty-one would file his own claim.

[21] The maximum claim allowed under the Preemption Act of 1841 was 160 acres, but by neighborhood consensus, Iowans often claimed twice or three times that amount.

[22] A claim could be "jumped" legally only if the claimant failed to comply with the law, such as by not residing on his claim.

they thought that the man refused to reason with them. Then they began to carry out mischievous acts. The horse stable and a nearly-filled corn crib were put on fire. Fire was also set to about fifteen logs to be used for fencing; these logs were right beside his house. They also killed a few pigs. It seems as if the man heard this news, because he sent messengers who returned the land as well as the title deed. The government does not furnish a bill of sale, as is common among individuals, but rather they give a deed of property, and then it does not matter how many people use the same deed, as long as the valid deed can be presented. Thus it happened and every one returned home. This is the way one operates when someone tries to buy land which is held by a claimholder.[23]

When there are a sufficient number of inhabitants in a county, then the government begins to sell the land publicly. We have had two such sales here already this summer at the home of my boss, as he happens to be a notary public.[24] At such sales one does not try to take advantage of the other. When they come to these sales, the one person will say to the other, "This is my land where I live and I want to keep it." Then this person buys it from the government for the fixed price of a dollar and a quarter; it is never sold for less.

Now I am going to tell you a few things about the American way of life. The people live in block or preferably log-houses. For this purpose the straightest and finest trees are sought out in the forest. Some people cut the logs square, while others do nothing to them. Just as in Friesland, one

---

[23] The writer has described the famed "Majors' War." See William M. Donnel, *Pioneers of Marion County, Consisting of a General History of the County* . . . (Des Moines: Republican Steam Printing House, 1872), pp. 50-57. The Marion County claim club was organized on August 19, 1848, seemingly in direct response to the alleged claim-jumping of Jacob H. Majors. See *ibid.*, pp. 42-49. Claim clubs were often used as a facade to shield petty land speculation by club members, as Allan G. Bogue has conclusively proved in his "Iowa Claim Clubs: Symbol and Substance," *Mississippi Valley Historical Review*, XLV (September, 1958), 231-253.

[24] All "Congress land" in Marion County was sold at the land offices at Iowa City and Fairfield. Therefore, Sipma here is likely referring to school land which was sold locally by the respective township boards of supervisors.

builds a better home than the other. Most houses are eighteen feet long and sixteen feet wide; there are smaller but also larger ones. Only heavy logs are used and these are locked together at the corners. This four-cornered building is usually built eight to eleven logs high. The roof is not very steep and is covered with a double layer of shingles so that it is leak-proof. Two doors are put in, one opposite the other, and usually on both sides of each door is a window. The chimney is generally built of rocks found in the forest but some people use prairie sod. Here in the forest is plenty of rocks and also coal.[25] For furniture they have a beautiful clock, a mirror, a beautiful bed, and the best quality of bedding. Most people have a little chest under their bed to keep valuables. I am writing about only one bed, but there are those who have two or even three, depending on the size of the family. Tools for every day use, and also the clothes, are all hung up on the walls. Americans do not have barns. The log house, which I have described, is the only building on three or four hundred acres of land. There is, however, a stable for horses and also a shed for sheep to protect them from wolves during the night; there is also a shed for corn.

The other grain is usually threshed by machine. There are people who go around with such a machine, just as in Friesland with a rapeseed canvass.[26] For payment they receive one-tenth of the grain. The farmer also must provide seven or eight workers. Americans do not carry on much dairying, usually they have only two or three cows for their own use. The calves suck the cows, not because the cows will not give milk otherwise, but to make the cows come home by themselves. During the day the calves are tied up and when at night the cows get home, they are tied up and milked. Then the calves are untied so that they can suck the cows during the night. When a cow calves, they do not look after it and

---

[25] The general vicinity of Pella contained some of the richest coal veins in Iowa. Mining has been part of the local scene since frontier days.

[26] Rapeseed is a plant similar to a mustard plant which was useful for its oil. A rapeseed canvas was generally 125 feet square and was spread out on a piece of cleared ground in the middle of a rapeseed patch. On it the seed was threshed by a cylindrical block pulled by horses.

it is not brought to the house. It has to take care of itself. During the first fourteen days the milk is no good; then it is all for the calf. Americans claim that sheepmilk is no good for people either. Last year my boss had two sheep whose lambs died. I told him that these sheep had to be milked. "No," he said, "that milk is no good." I said, "Sheep milk is good for me, and I can milk them." "You may milk them," he said, "but the milk is no good." We are still milking them and the milk is just as good as in Friesland. When a horse gets a colt nobody concerns himself about it; and that goes for hogs too. Everything must go its own natural way.[27]

Americans do not need very many tools to work their land. Sixty acres of land can be easily cultivated by one man, two horses, and two oxen. The land is plowed once a year. The corn is cleaned of weeds by means of small cultivators; the other grains are sown and harvested, and this is all there is done to that. The winter wheat is always sown early and at present it already colors some fields green. We have finished plowing and seeding for this year.

Now something else. As far as eating and drinking is concerned, Americans are very particular. The dinner table is set with a white table cloth and dishes which have just been washed in warm water. Three different courses are always served, with as much wheatbread and bacon as one desires. Coffee is also served at every meal, usually with sugar.[28] After the meal the leftovers are gathered in the table cloth and are given to the dogs.

American women are terribly lazy. They do nothing but prepare food and drink. They never mend their clothes; they wear them until they become rags and are not fit to wear anymore; and then they buy new ones. They also do not like to walk. When they have to visit a neighbor-lady once in a while, they must have a horse. All the women know how to ride a horse. My boss, his wife, and their two children—one

---

[27] This and the following paragraphs clearly illustrate the different opinions on animal husbandry, family life, and the role of women, held by foreign-born overagainst native-born citizens.

[28] Sugar was regarded in Friesland as well as in other parts of the Netherlands as a luxury beyond the reach of the working man.

Courtesy Martha Lautenbach

Painting done by an unknown artist depicts the birth of the first girl in Pella, February 7, 1848. She was Nellie Kramer, born in a log cabin belonging to the LeCocq family. Note calf (lower left), chickens, and other animals in the scene. Early Dutch farmers brought their young stock inside for protection against the elements.

two-years old and the other three-weeks old—all ride on one horse. The women ride horseback sideways, and then spur the horses as fast as they can go. The women wear their hair loose. Otherwise, fashions are about the same as in the cities of Friesland. Men's clothing differ very little from ours. Whiskey-drinking is scandalous here.

I was asked whether we still have good land around here at a reasonable cost for settlers. To this I can only answer in the affirmative. There is still plenty room here for all Friesland. Within the association one can yet get a great deal of land, and even more outside of it. Also, someone asked me whether a person can be certain of a good living here. This is a somewhat more difficult question because I do not want to mislead anyone if I can help it. I am not sure when the transportation problem will be solved, but if it remains as it is now, and everyone gets his land cultivated, then we are bound to run into difficulty with the grain. As of now, because of the multiplying population, no grain needs to be shipped. Even though the price of grain is not high, farmers can still make a fair living. Farmers here need very little money, only to pay their labor wages and taxes; whatever they need from the store can be paid for with grain.

Some people want to know how much a good farm of two hundred pondematen [Dutch measurement] would cost and also what the initial cost would be for clearing and breaking the land if such would be necessary. I will try to explain this in every detail as well as I can. For one-fourth of a section — a so-called quarter-section — or 160 acres, which is exactly two hundred pondematen, one has to pay the government two hundred dollars. One dollar as you know is two guilders and fifty cents in Dutch currency. A dollar has a hundred cents just as your guilder, but when I speak of cents now I mean American cents. For so much land, I say, two hundred dollars must be paid to the government if there is no claim on it. There is a claim on most of the good land in this area, but the majority are willing to sell their claim. If one wants to buy, something must be paid for the claim deed, often a half dollar per acre, sometimes more, and sometimes a little less. With such a large amount of land, one must have no less than forty acres of woodland, but land which is claimed usually has plenty of timber.

First of all a house has to be built. If one wants to build a loghouse, he can get the logs from the forest and for fifty dollars he can build himself a home. A brick house can also be built. Bricks can be bought at four dollars per thousand. These bricks are slightly larger than in Friesland. Lime is not expensive, but I am not sure as to how much it costs. A well has to be dug which would take three men three to four days to complete. Stones for this purpose can be taken from the woods. The men earn fifty cents per day plus board. Next, rails must be made to fence off the land because we cannot dig ditches here. The rails are cut from one's own forest and these are prepared for one dollar per hundred. In order to fence in forty acres completely, one needs seven thousand rails and usually a whole field like this is done all at once. Then the rails must be hauled to the field, but a person can do this with his own ox team. With two oxen and a wagon one man can normally haul about 150 to 200 rails per day, if it is not too far. After this the rails have to be placed on top of each other and this does not take much work. A person can place seven to eight hundred rails a day

Now the field is fenced and ready to be broken. This is again done by someone else. There are men here who will break prairie for others. This is always done with oxen, usually eight or ten in front of the plow, and costs $1.50 or sometimes $2.00 per acre. Now the land is ready for farming. If the land is broken in the spring, corn is almost always planted. If the land is broken in the fall, either oats or summer wheat are sown. The latter will usually ensure a better crop than the former. Forty acres of land are now ready and that is enough at first. If the farmer has a hired man or laborer, then he has little to do himself and can easily add ten acres every year. After the first field has been fenced in, the remaining land can be fenced in with less expense because no new rails are needed between the two pieces of land. All that has to be done is to set the fences out farther.

On this land which is ready, two horses are needed. One could get by with one but two are better. Also needed are two oxen, a wagon, at least three plows, and a good harrow. A good workhorse can be bought for forty to fifty dollars, two good oxen plus a yoke for forty dollars and a very good new wagon for sixty to seventy dollars. A second-hand wagon usually costs about thirty to forty dollars. Plows are not expensive. They are made in the cities and can be bought here for six to nine dollars. I do not know the price of a good harrow. Americans usually make them themselves entirely out of wood. A harness for two horses costs about twenty dollars if purchased new.

Now I have told the price of different things so that every one of you can figure out what it costs. As far as I know I have not yet given you the cost of cows, sheep, and hogs. A person can handle as much livestock of this sort as he wishes, even if he has only one acre of land. The land which is not fenced in is open to all people, and there are at least ten acres of unbroken land to every one that is broken. A cow can be bought for ten to fifteen dollars and this includes the calf. A sheep costs a dollar fifty or two dollars while a good sow with seven, eight, or nine young ones, amounts to anywhere from four to six dollars. Such a farm as I have just described can be expected to give a substantial living but it cannot be expected to give one much profit. One can also settle nearer to the Mississippi where there is still plenty of land available. Prices are much higher there but transportation of course is much better. I cannot tell you more about this.

Now I am going to give you the average price of grains as they are sold here at present. Corn is twenty cents per bushel, wheat fifty cents, oats fifteen cents, white beans forty cents, and potatoes twenty cents. These are the products most commonly grown here. There are still other crops but there is no market for them. I have been asked how much interest a person can obtain in America. That varies quite a bit. The minimum is 6 per cent and the maximum is 10 per cent. The government here in Iowa loans at 7 per cent at present.

Also I have been asked how much of an annual income one needs here for an average-sized family to have a decent living. I am going to let you answer this out for yourself because I cannot figure out someone else's household costs. I will write you what everything costs individually and then each of you can figure it out for yourself. First of all, let me say that a pound is lighter here than in the Netherlands. One pound here is four Dutch ounces. Wheat flour costs two cents per pound, buckwheat flour one and a half cents, and corn meal around half a cent. If a person buys the grain and takes it to the mill himself, the cost is less. Women here bake their own bread and this is quite easy to learn. Dried bacon costs three to three and a half cents per pound; fresh bacon costs two cents. You probably know already the price of potatoes and beans, but perhaps you are not yet familiar with the bushel. A bushel of wheat weighs sixty pounds and a bushel of beans weighs sixty-five pounds, I cannot say more about this either. Rice is priced at eight to ten cents, coffee beans at ten cents per pound. Tea is some what more expensive here than in Friesland. Sugar costs seven to ten cents, salt two and a half cents, tobacco twelve and a half cents, soap five cents, and syrup ten cents per pound. I do not know the exact price of [edible] oil but it is more expensive than in Friesland. I think I have now mentioned most of the products needed in a family. I am not sure as to the price of clothes. As far as I know, cotton costs ten to twenty cents per yard. The yard is longer here than by you. Three American yards equal four Dutch yards. Wool clothing is not used to a great extent here and it is more expensive than in Friesland, and even then, it is not near as good. Shoes cost about one to two dollars and are not as good as yours. I think this will do. I have already written about taxes which are very low.

Now I am going to write something about religion and school life. There are many denominations in the United States, but they all have equal privileges. Not one minister is paid by the government. Every congregation, regardless of its denomination, must pay its own minister. I do not know how it is in the most populated cities, but here in the Far West our preachers cannot make a living from their office as minister. Most of them around here are both farmer and preacher. Everyone has the freedom to preach.

The government, however, is concerned with educating the youth. I do not know the situation in the states that were settled first, but in these new states of the west one thirty-sixth piece of land [section sixteen] is sold to finance the education of the youth. The money received from the sale of this land is placed at interest and teachers get their yearly salary from this money, each according to the number of pupils he has. Since the teacher's salary is not an adequate means of livelihood, teachers also farm in addition to their teaching. Anyone who wishes can teach. Here in this state the knowledge of the English language is necessary. We have two teachers in the association at Pella and both give instruction in the English as well as the Dutch langauge. The state of Missouri has both French and German schools, but I am not certain whether a knowledge of the English language is required there. In Missouri there are many French and Germans, but the climate is not healthy there.

I dare not advise anyone to come to the United States to be a teacher and expect a substantial living here, unless he came along with a group of colonists from the Netherlands who would keep him as their teacher, and that in addition he could be certain of a salary from the government over here. Anyone who can speak and write English fluently, however, can make a respectable living here in some other way, but he should not come to the Far West. He should stay in the big cities where he can find office work, no matter where he goes. I spoke to someone about this who is better acquainted with this, and he told me that anyone who had a knowledge of the English, German, French, and Dutch languages and came to the United States, could figure on having a very good living here. I cannot say much more about this. But I almost forgot, Teacher, that your wife could certainly earn a great deal of money in the big cities. We had with us several tailors and seamstresses who stayed behind for some time in St. Louis and they made money there like water. Tailoring in the cities is very expensive. Enough said about this.

Will a blacksmith who knows his trade well, be able to make a living? He cannot count on an adequate income merely from his trade. If a blacksmith wants to be self-employed, he must go to the city where he will be able to make a good living. A blacksmith can also make a good living here but he has to be a farmer and a blacksmith at the same time. In this area we need farmers and laborers.

Someone wanted to know how the future would look if he came to the United States with a capital of eight to ten thousand guilders. I would have to answer that he would be able to make a better living here than in Friesland. As a lender a person can make more money here than in the Netherlands. Money carries a heavy interest. The lowest is 6 per cent and when there is a lack of money, 10 per cent is paid. The school property in Marion County brings 9 and 10 per cent. Let us take the minimum interest for example, that is, 6 per cent. After deducting the tax [of 1 per cent], you still have 5 per cent left of the interest. There are no more taxes for anything else, except for your gold, silver, and household goods, and a half dollar poll tax. There are no taxes to support the poor or on real estate and personal possessions other than what I have mentioned.

I have told you about the prices of other products. Compared to the taxes and cost of living in the Netherlands, one could live twice as cheap here. When a person moves to the city some products are more expensive, but other things again are cheaper. I think I have said enough about the buying and breaking of land. Those who come to these western states should, in my opinion, buy government land which is still unsettled, rather than place their money at interest. After buying it, the land can be left alone just as it is until there are buyers who are interested in it. There are many people in America with money who do exactly that. In Iowa we have speculators who five years ago bought large areas of government land in the eastern part of our state at $1.25 per acre. These people are now selling it again for ten dollars or more. This is much better than tying up your money at interest. In short, if a person comes to the United States with such a large amount of cash, he need not doubt for a minute but that he surely will have a very substantial living.

I have gathered from the letter I received that my relatives and the citizens of Bornwerd are under the impression that there is some disagreement between H. Viersen and myself since I do not work for him. I shall tell you the reason for this. I wrote you how many men a farmer with forty acres of land needs. H. Viersen did not get land that was still wild. Scholte bought about thirty-six claims. These had to be entered first [at the land office]. P. and H. Viersen received one claim together; two-thirds went to H. Viersen and P. Viersen received one-third.[29] Of this claim, eighty to ninety acres were fenced in and cultivated and everything had already been harvested except the corn. There were two houses on this property and considering that it was an American farm, it was in good condition. H. Viersen had one hired man and another laborer besides me, and P. Viersen had three hired men, so the work on the place was just about finished. Consequently Viersen told us that we could all come to work for him whenever he had work to do, but he would not have work for us all the time. So he gave us the opportunity to look

---

[29] H. Viersen is the H. Y. Viersen who advanced money for the Sipma family's transoceanic crossing. P. Viersen is Pieter O. Viersen, H. Y.'s brother. Both were fellow Friesians who came to Pella with Sipma in the initial colonization group. See Lucas, *Netherlanders in America*, pp. 165, 185, 669.

for work someplace else. Each one had to look out for himself. I always had steady work, and I worked for Scholte even before Viersen came here. This is the reason why I do not work for Viersen anymore. But there is no ill-will between us. We still live in the same friendly way as we did when we left Friesland. My feelings were hurt, however, when we never heard from our relatives in the letters received from Friesland, but I never said anything about it to him. And now I understand from your letters that you did not hear about us either from the letters you receive in Friesland. Twice he told me that he wrote a few things about us and this is the reason I did not write back any sooner.

You also wrote me about the rumors which seem to be spreading among you that the immigrants lost money because of [Albertus C.] Van Raalte.[30] This is not true; no money has been lost. I was also asked how much it cost me to reach my destination. As yet I cannot tell you exactly because no one has received the bill from Scholte. But I will write you as much as I know about it. It cost me five guilders and eighty-one cents from Dockum to Amsterdam, and the food at Amsterdam for the ocean voyage cost forty guilders and fifty cents. Now I am going to tell you what I heard from someone else. The ocean voyage cost 45 guilders per person and the trip from Baltimore to St. Louis $11.50 per person, at their own expense. But each person was allowed to take along one hundred pounds of baggage at no charge. If the baggage weighed more than this, however, one had to pay $1.50 for each additional hundred pounds. From St. Louis to Keokuk cost one dollar per person, and ten cents for every hundred pounds of weight. Finally, from Keokuk to Pella the transportation came to one dollar per person and seventy-five cents for each hundred pounds of weight.

For traveling expenses from Amsterdam to St. Louis, as

---

[30] The Reverend Dr. Van Raalte was the leader of the initial Dutch colony in the midwest, founded in February, 1847, at Holland, Michigan. The source of the allegations against Van Raalte circulating in Bornwerd is unknown, but the rumors may have been planted by overzealous Pella colonists who at the time were bidding against the Michigan settlement to attract the new colonists from the Old Country. See *ibid.*, pp. 91-92, 187.

you already know, I paid 202 guilders in advance. For the trip from St. Louis to our destination Scholte had not paid anything from the money we had already made available to him, but each had to pay for himself. At Baltimore Scholte arranged for some Jews to take us to St. Louis for the above mentioned sum of money. This normally would cost no more than seven or eight dollars per person, but we paid $11.50. We were about fourteen hundred people.[31] I think I have paid about fifty guilders too much. I do not remember how much I spent on meals during the trip through America, but that did not cost me very much. Now you know a little about this and once the account is settled I can tell you the costs more precisely.

You wanted to know about my relationship with the Dutch association and I can only write that it is good; it could not be better. I have many good friends among them but the Friesians seem to stick together the most. Now I will give a few details about the association. As to religion it is fairly good. A large building was built in Pella where school is held during the week and church services on Sunday. Catechism is held there on Saturdays for the children, while the men who reached to the age of discretion have catechism from eight-thirty to ten o'clock on Sunday mornings. At ten o'clock the sermon is preached. At one-thirty o'clock in the afternoon is catechism again, this time for the womenfolk, and at three o'clock another sermon. We do not have a preacher here like you have in Friesland and the church is ruled by elders and deacons. Scholte is one of the elders. Five of them preach on Sundays and take turns conducting the services.[32] There is one thing which I do not approve of — and

---

[31] To avoid having his colonists victimized by unscrupulous travel agents who were known to prey on bewildered immigrants, Scholte after much effort and investigation, contracted with some Jewish businessmen in Baltimore to transport his group to St. Louis. Despite Sipma's charge, it appears likely that Scholte's careful planning reduced rather than raised the transportation costs.

[32] Unlike the typical Dutch Reformed congregation, the religiously independent Scholte insisted on an undenominational church with a lay brotherhood much akin to John N. Darbey's Plymouth Brethren Church. Darbey's strong influence on Scholte is demonstrated in Oostendorp, *H. P. Scholte*, pp. 162-169 and *passim*.

there are many others who also think this way — and that is that the festive days such as Christmas, New Year, Easter, Ascension, and Pentecost are not celebrated anymore. There is no sermon on these days and everyone does his daily work as he sees fit. Not everyone, however, follows this custom. They defend their position by saying that there is no commandment in the Bible that requires it and furthermore they claim that these festivities were introduced by the Roman [Catholic] church. Be that as it may, I cannot go along with this opinion. Church worship then is the only good thing around here; in the other things Scholte acts very improperly.

As you know, when we were still in Friesland we had to pay in advance for our traveling expenses and the land which Scholte was going to buy for the whole association. When we arrived at St. Louis, he thought that several farmers should go with him to help him choose what seemed the most favorable land. He admitted that he was not as qualified to make a judgment concerning land as some of our farmers. Scholte then bought land bordering two or three townships, situated between the Des Moines and Skunk rivers, forty hours west of the Mississippi.[33] Pella is located midway between these two rivers which are about four hours from each other.

There were about thirty Americans who had claims on this land and Scholte bought all of these claims because no Americans were to remain with us. For these claims he paid altogether too much, but for the land he gave no more than $1.25 per acre [at the land office]. He bought for the whole association and then the claims were to be divided. There were a good many who wanted to do that because then they were immediately put in possession of everything. Scholte bought the claims with the condition that the Americans must leave behind horses, cows, pigs, sheep, plows, harrows, wagons, etc. Those who had paid most money in advance received the claims and Scholte told them what the price was. It was expensive but of course they received everything with

---

[33] Scholte and a wealthy friend, John Armstrong Graham, mayor of Keokuk, entered 16,600 acres of land, all in Townships 76 and 77 North, Range 18 West. By a special act of the state legislature, in January of 1848, these two townships were combined into one and called Lake Prairie. See *Laws of Iowa,* 1848 (Extra sess.), p. 16.

HENRY PETER SCHOLTE

it. They were so ignorant that they gladly accepted it from Scholte. They put too much trust in him and later their stupidity became evident. For one claim he charged $400 too much, for another 5, for another 6, yes, he even asked up to $700 more for the claims than what they had cost him. Thus this man operates. Rather than fighting like a father for his children, he is out to fill his own purse.

H. Viersen also experienced this; he paid 2000 guilders too much. It has already become known how much Scholte himself paid. The Americans who had lived on the claims came to visit their successors once in a while and so the people found out to the last cent what Scholte had paid. The other land buyers who did not receive claims had to pay $2.25 per acre; this was also one dollar too much. It is now thought that we are not going to receive any extra money back from what we have paid for our trip. So he also makes about twenty guilders from every person in this respect and even more from some. As yet not one has received the title deed for his land, even though the money was already paid in advance in the Netherlands! There are some people who are after him, and they want him to give an account and hand out title deeds for the land. But he does not seem to care at all. I think we have reached the point where he will be challenged to appear before the American judges.[34] He, himself, is justice of the peace in Pella but this does not matter because the Americans sometimes give us instructions.

At this point you can probably understand why there is so much discord and confusion in the association; not so much among the people themselves, but toward the officers of the association. There are a few who are on the side of Scholte and do not want to hear anything unfavorable about him. These perhaps expect to share the booty with him.[35] The Americans keep an eye on him constantly. They say that he is making everybody poor. Not so long ago an American said, "You left the confines of a ruling monarch in order to live in a free land, but you yourselves have taken along a monarch who devours you."[36] The fact is that those who have not ad-

---

[34] The local church censured Scholte for his recalcitrant attitude toward the colonists but apparently no legal steps were taken as the deeds were eventually distributed. See Oostendorp, *H. P. Scholte*, pp. 168-169 and the Marion County deed record books. In 1849 Scholte issued the first deeds, forty-one in number, covering nearly three thousand acres. On eighteen deeds, totaling 1220 acres, the consideration recorded was only $1.25 per acre, the exact price which Scholte had paid for the tracts at the land office. On twenty-three deeds, totaling 1723 acres, the average consideration given was $2.36 per acre. These involved improved tracts for which Scholte had purchased both the original squatter's claim and the government's title. This analysis of the deed records indicates, therefore, that Scholte did not take advantage of his colonists.

[35] Although Scholte seems to have dealt honestly with his colonists, he certainly tried to invest his rather substantial inherited wealth wisely. In the 1850 manuscript federal population census his net worth is listed at $20,960. In 1860 this had increased to $40,000. At his death in 1868 Marion County Probate Court records list the value of his personal property at $20,000. In addition he owned 115 town lots in Pella and Knoxville worth a minimum of $100 each and 2,646 acres of land worth a minimum of $5.00 per acre or $13,230 for a total net worth of about $45,000.

[36] This comment portrays political overtones. Living on the outskirts of the Pella colony among native Americans who were staunch Democrats, Sipma had obviously accepted their rhetoric concerning Scholte, an ardent Whig advocate. See Swierenga, "The Ethnic Voter and the First Lincoln Election," 30 and *passim*.

vanced any money for land are better off because he can take no more from these people than the balance of their traveling expenses.

In Pella there are nearly forty houses I think. Building lots are quite expensive. On each acre there are three lots; that gives sufficient space. Such a piece of ground, if on the main street, which is also the state highway, costs $100.[37] On the other streets they are much cheaper. Many lots have been sold because every farmer wanted to have a house in town.

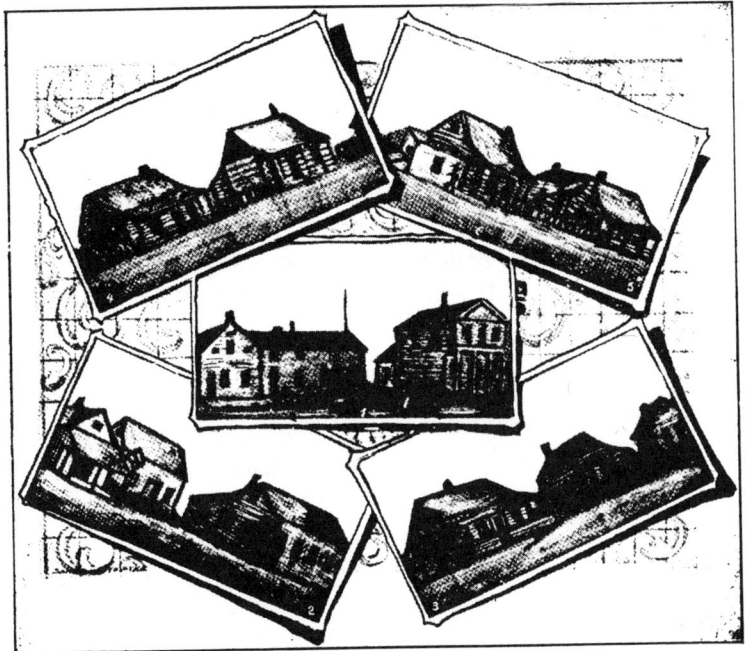

Scenes around the Garden Square in Pella—1847.

During this summer they have platted another town within the association on the Des Moines River. Scholte has made it known that this town will be open to Americans as well as to Netherlands — in Pella no Americans are allowed. The new town is called Amsterdam, but I heard that so far only one

[37] This is the present highway number 163.

lot has been sold there.[38] Pella could have been quite a fair-sized city if Scholte had only allowed Americans to settle there, but as it is now, the association remains about the same size. We do not number as many souls as when we left the Netherlands.[39] There are bad rumors about Scholte all over the United States and that is why most Netherlanders go to the state of Michigan, including quite a number of people who first intended to go here when they left the Netherlands.

The colony in Holland, Michigan, consists of between seven and eight thousand souls.[40] There are also Dutch people who settle in Iowa but who refuse to join the association. There are also many Dutch people south of the Des Moines River, but they were already there when we arrived.[41] In the last two months many Netherlanders came to this state and settled close to the Mississippi.[42] It seems as if the whole state of Iowa is no good with Scholte operating the way he does but there is plenty of room here outside of the association. This soil here is excellent; it slopes well and we have no mountains. The water is delicious and I never tasted such good water in Friesland. The air is healthy. The summer is a little

---

[38] With the failure of the Des Moines River navigation project, Amsterdam, which had grown into a modest village by 1850, gradually became a ghost town. Today only one building remains.

[39] Sipma is in error concerning the exclusion of native Americans from Pella. Although Scholte refused to sell farm land within the settlement to native Americans, the Pella leader did sell city lots to Americans. Indeed, from the beginning the city always contained a nucleus of non-Dutch citizens, many of whom were businessmen and proprietors. And the population growth of the community was steady — 75 newcomers arrived in 1848, 250 in 1849, and 600 in 1850-1854. By 1857 the settlement numbered about 2,000 people and covered an area of approximately one hundred square miles. Of the twenty-one stores in Pella at the time, Americans operated seven, or one-third. See Lucas, *Netherlanders in America*, pp. 187-188, 194-195. Cf. Donnel, *Pioneers of Marion County*, pp. 139-155.

[40] This is a gross exaggeration. Early in 1849, Isaac N. Wyckoff, of Albany, New York, visited the Michigan settlements and counted 630 houses and a population of only about three thousand. See Lucas, *Netherlanders in America*, p. 254.

[41] This likely refers to the more than one hundred Dutchmen who had settled in St. Louis. *Ibid.*, p. 332.

[42] A substantial Dutch settlement developed in Keokuk, with smaller groups in the Iowa river towns of Burlington, Muscatine, and Davenport. *Ibid.*, p. 333.

warmer than in Friesland but the nights are quite cool so that one can rest comfortably. This summer there was not one day that I could not work because of the heat and I have been so healthy that I have not been sick a single day.

Beukema said that you lose weight in America but this is not all the case.[43] All of the Hollanders and Friesians here are plump. During this summer all of the people in the association have been very healthy. I suppose the climate in Michigan is also healthy but the Americans tell us that the soil is not as good. There is also much more forest which of course costs more money and labor to clear. The soil there is sandy and the topsoil is of a reddish cast. Transportation is much better there but that can be improved here as well. The government has surrendered all the uneven numbered sections of land along the Des Moines River, five miles southward and five miles northward, to make the river more useful. This land is now being sold and the proceeds will be used to make the Des Moines River navigable. This is done by erecting dams or levies.

We still live in the same house as when I wrote my previous letter[44] and I still work for the same man.[45] I have already given him my word to work for him until March of next year. The first two months, as I wrote before, I received eight dollars per month but now I earn ten dollars per month for the entire year, winter as well as summer, and free quarters and fuel besides. Fuel is not expensive here but it costs quite a bit yet to haul it out of the forests. However, I do not have to worry about that. I do haul the wood from the forest all right but this is on the time of the boss. Because I work for him we share the fuel together. There is no peat here. The only fuels are wood and coal. Nothing but wood is used for the fireplace and there is plenty of that. I would not want to trade it for peat either because then it takes too much time starting the fire. During the winter Americans start the fire twice a day, in the morning when they get up and in the evening when the sun goes down. When there are two menfolk

---

[43] I have not been able to identify this Dutch immigrant.
[44] See footnote 7 above.
[45] This man, a native American, I have not been able to identify.

at home, they help each other and haul pieces of wood as large as they can carry. Trees are cut into pieces of about four feet in length and without a trim job are put directly on the fire. When it is cold the fire then burns brightly all night.

We work here from sunup to sundown throughout the whole year. In the morning we sleep until sunup. Then I feed the horses, milk the cows, and chop as much wood as we both need for one day. Then we have our first meal. It is customary here to eat three times a day. After breakfast I work until twelve o'clock when we have our second meal. At one-thirty I again go to work until sunset. This is typical all year long. The [working] days are long in the summer but short in the winter for then we always sleep until sunrise. It is not customary here to use a light in the morning.[46] I have no free board. I have to pay for that myself.

The houses are so close to each other that if we set foot outside our house, we could step right into the next one. We have many happy experiences here together. They are all very nice people. At first we could not understand each other; we always had to make signs with our hands. When I first went to work, my boss had to go along to point things out with his finger. Sometimes we nearly split laughing because he could not understand me and I could not understand him, but now we can talk with each other well. The Americans who live around here tell me that I speak English quite well, and sometimes they use me as their interpreter when they are with Hollanders that they cannot understand. I cannot tell you how profitable it has been for me to be able to live among the American people so soon. Now I learn the English langauge, earn good money, and am never pushed to do my work. Whenever it rains or is wet I do not have to work. Americans are terribly afraid of rain. I think that about one-third of the laborers from the association now work for Americans because there is not much money in the association. Scholte has all that. Most people have invested all their money in land and now they have nothing to work it.

I am renting an acre and a half from my boss for three dol-

---

[46] This was a typical custom in the Netherlands.

lars, or two dollars per acre, and then he has to plow it; otherwise the rent would be less than this. We grow for ourselves such things as peas, beans, potatoes, carrots, and turnips. We always have more than enough. And wherever we have not planted vegetables, we have corn for fodder for our hogs. At present we have eight hogs, one of them is a brood-sow. If we have a little luck with these, we will soon not have to buy any more bacon. We have no other cattle and hogs yet. If did not seem advisable to us to get a cow this summer because I was employed full-time. You have to run after a cow too much and besides we get plenty of milk from the two sheep of my boss. We did not have to do this because of a shortage of money as you can readily see from what I wrote about my earnings. My wife also earns quite a bit. She sews for two hired men of Pieter Viersen, Gosse J. de Vries and Geert Dykstra, and also for a Hollander; for this each pays eight guilders per year.[47] She also spins quite a bit. We buy the wool for twenty cents a pound and we sell the yarn for seventy to eighty cents. It is a good thing that we brought a spinning wheel along because they cost five dollars here.

I almost forgot to write how much a dairy farm earns. Actually I have so many things to write about. Butter during the summer is worth six to seven cents per pound and ten cents per pound during the winter. Cheese until now has brought six to seven cents. This summer a shipment was sent to St. Louis and after subtracting the expenses, the producer received about the same price which I have just mentioned. At the moment another shipment is on its way, and it is believed that the profit will be somewhat higher than before. We make nothing but cream cheese here since the price of butter and cheese is the same. When cheese brings seven cents per pound, dairying is better than farming, but we lack a good quality of grass around here. The prairie is destroyed by too much grazing and mowing. When a few cows have grazed on one piece of land for four or five years, then the prairie grass disappears and nothing but weeds will grow there. Americans do have some tame grass, but it is not the

---

[47] Sipma here distinguishes between Friesians (de Vries and Dykstra) and Hollanders.

right kind. I can best compare it to what we call "mollestaarten" in Friesland; it grows as tall as oats. We have clover here alright, but almost nothing but red clover. . . .

Pieter Viersen, Gerrit Van der Weit, and we live four to five miles southeast of Pella while the other [H.] Viersen lives one mile northwest of Pella. Gerrit Van der Weit bought a claim of forty acres of prairie and five acres of woodland for twenty-five dollars from an American. The greater part of this amount he can earn by working for it. But he still has to pay the government for the land. He has a loghouse there which he built himself. Last spring he had six acres broken and he grew corn on this. He had to harvest this rather early because his fences were so poor that the oxen and cows broke in. They are quite content and are healthy and able to make a good living. But last fall, when they lost their children, Van der Weit was ailing for a long time.

Courtesy Martha Lautenbach

The H. Viersen log cabin northwest of Pella was among the first homes built in the community.

Pieter Viersen sold his part in the place which he shared with H. Viersen. He bought another claim here — actually not a claim because the land is paid for — of 160 acres of prairie and sixty acres of timber, for $450. Seventeen acres have been broken and fenced in. This is better than to buy from Scholte. Now he lives on a rented place nearby. For rent he pays one-third of the grain. His new farm is in Mahaska County. The association land is in the northern part of Marion County. Mahaska County lies to the east of Marion County. This winter he wants to build a house on his land. A daughter was born to them this summer and at present they are all healthy. The other Viersens in Pella are also healthy and since I wrote my last letter not one of the Viersens has died.

If there are Friesians who plan to migrate to America, I am not quite sure how to advise them as to where they might settle. There is room everywhere for immigrants to settle. In the state of Michigan, in Illinois, in Wisconsin, and in Iowa; everywhere there is plenty of space. But let me advise you, do not join any association in the Netherlands as we did; travel at your own expense and do not turn your money over to others. In this way you will certainly save many guilders. The cheapest and quickest way is to travel via New Orleans. At New Orleans you can go right on to St. Louis without having to transfer all of your goods, for only $2.25 per person. I do not know what the cost of each hundred pounds of freight would be, but surely not more than fifty cents. If you start the trip in the spring, then I would advise you not to travel by way of New Orleans, because it is too hot for comfort there in the summer. If, however, you plan your trip for the fall, I would suggest that you travel by way of New Orleans for the reasons mentioned above. There you cannot see that many new and wonderful things anyway.

Friesians, my recent compatriots, I dare freely to invite all of you to come to the United States. Luxury and pomp are not to be found here, but a simple farmer's occupation. Do not expect to gather riches here in the Far West, but you can be sure of a substantial living without doing much work. A laborer who is willing to work hard can within a matter of a few years buy himself a small farm. But a person who comes here with money certainly has a head start. I only wish my whole family were here, for then I would know for sure that they would have a good living, if they would be healthy. But there is likely no possibility for them to come, unless some well-to-do immigrants from your area would be willing to take another family with them.

Citizens of Bornwerd, I only wish that you could help Ritske and his family in some way or another to come here, especially since he wants to come here so badly.[48] I would really appreciate it if some people in your neighborhood who plan to migrate would share with some other people of your village the expenses for this family. I think that it would cost, all in all, about 500 guilders for this family to come here. But do not count on H. Viersen; I do not think that he would help laborers to come over here.

When we left, my sister, Ytje, also showed some desire to come to America. If this is still the case, and if there is someone who would take her along at his own expense, then I pledge myself as surety for her in case she cannot repay the traveling expenses. No more of my brothers and sisters had a desire to migrate to America when we left. I do not know how it is now but I certainly wish they were all here. I may be far away from you but my thoughts are often with you.

Now a few words to you, my old father, if you are still alive.[49] For you to come here is perhaps not advisable since you would probably succumb on the journey. They were a few older people who left with us, but almost every one of them has descended into the grave. Two of them, however, had the privilege to see Pella. During the last days of their life, they rejoiced in the fact that they had brought their offspring to America. Of course it was only for a short while, for now they already rest in the dust.

Departing from you, beloved father, was very hard for me, even harder than I let on. But I suppose it was still harder for you to say good-bye to your nearest of kin so suddenly.

---

[48] Ritske was one of Sjoerd's brothers.
[49] Sjoerd's father, Auke Sipkes Sipma, was at this time a respectable, old man of eighty-five years of age.

But really, dear father, we did not leave to get away from you as you know very well, but it was to go to a land where by working hard we could hope to find a better living than in Friesland. And we really have not been disappointed because, if we remain healthy, we will be able in a few years to start our own farm, which we would never have been able to do in Friesland. And then to live on one's own land! Even now we already have a better living. We can eat the best bacon and meat three times a day, and we save money besides. What a contrast to Friesland! There is not one who by moving to America does not make more in his own trade than the common laborer over there. If we had stayed in Friesland, we would probably have suffered poverty within a few years. If you think seriously about all these things, beloved father, you need not be sorry at all that we left Friesland. Of course you never advised me against going and this was always very encouraging for me. We seldom spoke much about it, because really, it was so hard to think of parting. But I am still happy that I left Friesland behind. It must certainly be a blessing for you, beloved father, to receive reports from us now and then, and to know that we are in a much better land and that your children are well, even though we may never again behold each other's faces. I would like to be with you, father, and be near all my brothers and sisters, but I do not wish to live in Friesland again. Oh, father, may our names be written in the Book of Life, of which we know something on this side of the grave. In the hereafter we will again see each other in the heavenly Jerusalem where there will be no sorrow nor weeping, and all our tears will be wiped away. This is the prayer of my heart for you and for our whole family....

I do not know whether I have now answered all your questions adequately, but I have done my best. If I have not properly answered some of your questions you had better write to me again. I have written nothing about the mutual affairs of the association because we are not concerned with this. When there is a meeting in Pella concerning some matter or another, it is open to everybody, but none of the Friesians go there because we know enough about the association by now....

I am going to let you decide what you want to do with this letter. We thank all those who make it possible to send letters and in this way give us the privilege of sending and receiving letters from our relatives. I also thank you, Teacher, for being willing to go through all the trouble of copying my letter and sending it to our relatives in Engwierum. Whenever I can do something for you, let me know. Write as much and as often as you wish....

Sjoerd Aukes Sipma
Jantje DeVries

The People Come
ALLAN G. BOGUE

IN 1833 the federal government opened the Black Hawk Purchase for white settlement. Located in the easternmost part of the Iowa Territory and comprising approximately one-third of the present state of Iowa, the area had been taken from the Sac and Fox Indians as punishment for their part in the Black Hawk War. The opening marked the first significant movement of whites into Iowa and thus signaled the beginning of the pioneer era in the Hawkeye State.

One historian who has written extensively about Iowa in this period is Allan Bogue. In his book, *From Prairie to Cornbelt*, Bogue discusses the full range of agrarian experiences in both Illinois and Iowa during the mid-nineteenth century; as such his book represents one of the most thorough studies available of nineteenth century Iowa agriculture. Reprinted here, the second chapter of that book describes the population moving into Iowa and Illinois in the first half of the 1800s. In his examination of these early settlers, Bogue first considers their motivations in moving to Iowa and then assesses their personal characteristics. The result is a concise treatment of background information on the first settlers moving into Iowa and Illinois. Combining statistical data with actual case studies, Bogue presents the prelude for further study of Iowa's earliest pioneers; his material should also prepare students to better understand the pioneering experience itself.

From Allan G. Bogue,
From Prairie to Cornbelt
(Chicago: The University of Chicago Press;
© 1963 by The University of Chicago),
pp. 8–28.

CHAPTER I

The People Come

Until the 1830's few settlers entered the regions of Illinois that were dominated by the prairies. In 1830 there were six or more inhabitants to the square mile in but two irregularly outlined strips of territory in the state. One of these was based on the Ohio and stretched up the Wabash Valley almost to Danville. The other extended along the Mississippi from the Cape Girardeau area to a point midway between the mouth of the Illinois River and Quincy, projecting inland to include the lower third of the Kaskaskia and Illinois river valleys and the intervening country. North of Knox and Peoria counties, in this same year, there were more than two residents to the square mile only in the Galena lead region. In the interior of eastern Illinois, settlers were few as far south as modern Richland County.[1]

By 1840 there were fewer than two persons to the square mile only in the Grand Prairie counties of Livingston, Ford, Champaign, and Iroquois, together with the southern portion of modern Kankakee. Contiguous counties from Stephenson in the north to Christian in the south, however, still claimed only two to six persons to the square mile. At this time, settlers were increasing in the Illinois Valley, spreading out in a semicircle from Chicago, and moving rapidly into the northern tier of Illinois counties. Here was forecast the final pattern of settlement in northern Illinois. Pioneer farmers reached the interior prairies of northcentral and northeastern Illinois last among all the regions of the state. Lacking adequate water transportation and presenting many problems of adaptation to the farmer, these prairie counties waited for their full quota of settlers until the 1850's and thereafter.

We can deepen our understanding of the settlement process in northern

---

[1] The basic accounts of settlement in Illinois are: Arthur C. Boggess, *The Settlement of Illinois, 1778-1803* (Chicago Historical Society's "Collection," Vol. V, [Chicago, 1908]); William V. Pooley, *The Settlement of Illinois from 1830-1850* (University of Wisconsin Bulletin, "History Series," Vol. I [Madison, 1908]). The appropriate volumes of the "Centennial History of Illinois" include useful summaries of the settlement process; see particularly the maps in Solon J. Buck, *Illinois in 1818* (Springfield, 1917), p. 59; Theodore C. Pease, *The Frontier State, 1818-1848* (Springfield, 1918), pp. 4, 174, 384; and Arthur C. Cole, *The Era of the Civil War, 1848-1870* (Springfield, 1919), pp. 16, 330.

Illinois by comparing the number of farm units reported in various counties in the census years from 1850 onward with the totals of 1900. In 1850 Du Page and McHenry counties, but one county removed from Lake Michigan, reported 56 and 70 per cent of the farm units of 1900. Among the

Fig. 2.—The counties and major rivers of Illinois

counties of the Rock River Valley, Boone, in the northern tier, reported 68 per cent; De Kalb, 32 per cent; and Whiteside but 14 per cent of the 1900 totals. On the northern edge of the Military Tract, Bureau and Knox counties had slightly more than 20 per cent of the farm units which those counties contained in 1900. The census marshals of Champaign and Livingston counties in the Grand Prairie could find only 4 and 6 per cent of the number of farm units reported by their successors in 1900. The percentage in Edgar to the southeast of these counties on the Indiana line was 38.[2]

If settlers were slow in coming to northern Illinois, the counties of that region filled up rapidly once the full tide of settlement reached them. The pioneers usually needed only twenty or thirty years to open up a number of farms equal to the totals of 1900. Boone County indeed, had reached this figure by 1860 and surpassed it by 8 and 6 per cent in 1870 and 1880. For most counties of northern Illinois, the totals of 1900 represented a decline from maximums, which had been reached by the 1870's. Champaign and Livingston counties, indeed, reported 16 and 23 per cent more farm units in 1880 than in 1900. The farm-making era in the Grand Prairie had definitely ended by 1880.

Settlers crossed the Mississippi during 1833 to establish themselves in the lands acquired by the federal government from the disgruntled Sacs and Foxes in Iowa during the previous year — the Black Hawk Purchase. The river routes provided by the Mississippi and Missouri rivers and their Iowa tributaries shaped the early patterns of settlement in the state. The pioneers fanned out from the Mississippi and penetrated the Des Moines, Iowa, and Cedar River valleys particularly, so that by 1860 the population of the state was concentrated in eastern Iowa, and in the Des Moines Valley as far west as Polk County, seat of Des Moines. Settlement in interior counties between the Des Moines and Mississippi rivers, like Grundy, Tama, and Poweshiek, lagged behind that in the counties both to the east and along the Des Moines River. Meanwhile settlement was radiating from the southwestern counties along the Missouri. In 1870, however, the interior counties between the Des Moines and the Missouri were still being settled, and population was thinly scattered in the northwestern corner of the state generally. Indeed, the population density in Hancock, Ida, and the four northwestern counties of the state was still less than six residents to the square mile.[3]

In a study of the Iowa population, published in 1930, Professors Harter and Stewart, of Iowa State College, concluded that the agricultural settlement of Iowa was complete by 1890.[4] At that date there were more than

[2] These percentages are based on analysis of the county agricultural returns given in the printed federal agricultural censuses, 1850–1900.

[3] Cardinal Goodwin, "The American Occupation of Iowa, 1833 to 1860," *Iowa Journal of History and Politics*, XVII (January, 1919), 83–102; William L. Harter and R. E. Stewart, *The Population of Iowa; Its Composition and Changes: A Brief Sociological Study of Iowa's Human Assets* (Iowa State College of Agriculture and Mechanic Arts, Bull. 275 [Ames, 1930]). There is a series of excellent maps based on the township population figures given in the state censuses of 1856, 1867, and 1875 in G. B. Schilz, "Rural Population Trends of Iowa as Affected by Soils" (unpublished Ph.D. dissertation, Clark University, 1948), pp. 67, 68, 69. See also Clare C. Cooper, "The Role of Railroads in the Settlement of Iowa: A Study in Historical Geography" (unpublished M.A. thesis, University of Nebraska, 1958).

[4] Harter and Stewart, *op. cit.*, pp. 13–14.

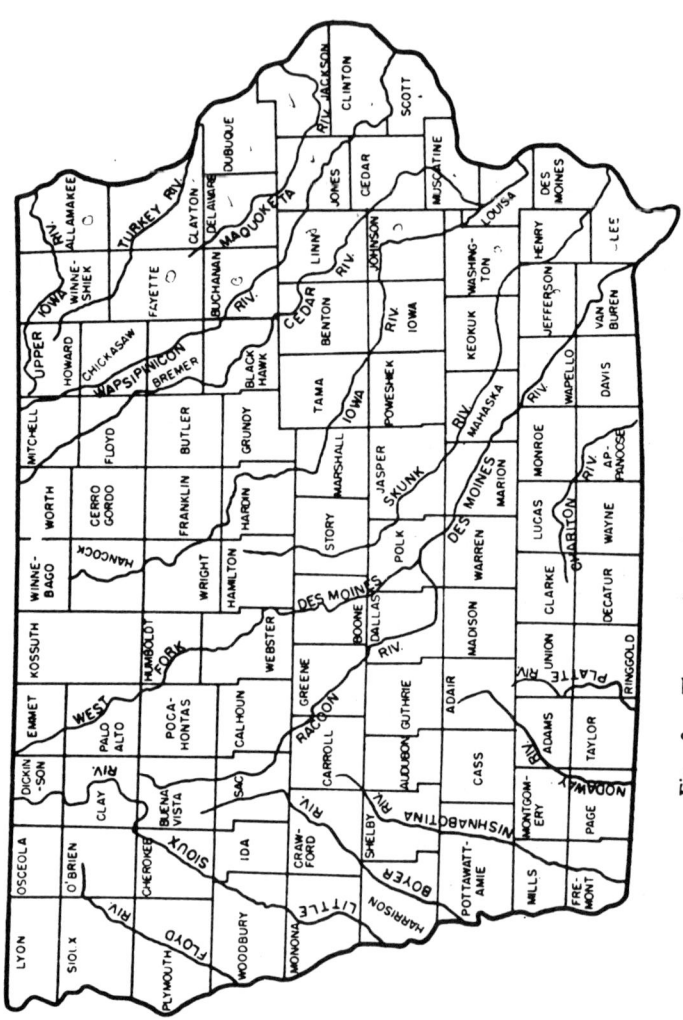

Fig. 3. — The counties and major rivers of Iowa

fifteen people to the square mile in all the ninety-nine counties of Iowa. But, even if a population of that density was all settled on the land, it still provided rather sparse settlement. Except in the oldest sections of the state, most Iowa counties reached their largest total of farm units about 1900, after which a decline began, similar to that experienced in northern Illinois a generation earlier.

It is a striking fact that large areas of a region, now considered to be particularly productive, should have remained unsettled so late in the nineteenth century. While great stretches of northwestern Iowa and the Grand Prairie in Illinois lay in virgin sod, settlers were pushing deep into Kansas and Nebraska. Lack of transportation facilities in interior Illinois and Iowa explains this paradox in part. Navigable rivers, canals, and later railroads not only carried many farm-makers to their destinations in the west but promised markets for the settlers' produce. A recent study, however, shows that settlement lagged for some years after the railroad had arrived in the counties of west, northwest, and west north-central Iowa.[5] As in the Grand Prairie, there was much wet prairie in these sections of Iowa, calling for additional outlays of capital by pioneers before a satisfactory tilth could be achieved. Many a settler turned his back on the potential riches of the Wisconsin drift to gamble five years of his life trying to win a free homestead in the sandhills of Nebraska. In reality a very complex combination of factors controlled the flow of settlement into any particular locality. Transportation routes and facilities, potential markets, the quality of the land, real or imagined, location in relation to older settlements, and the state of the settling-in process there — all had important effects upon the development of new areas.

The Indians but little impeded the flow of settlement into northern Illinois and Iowa. In general, the federal government purchased the Indian title in these regions long before settlers were ready to move in. That unfortunate compound of tragedy and comedy, the Black Hawk War of 1832, occurred when a small number of squatters encroached upon the cornfields of the Sac and Fox in the lower Rock River Valley. Here the Indians were living at the sufferance of the federal government on lands ceded earlier to the United States. At the time many miles of unsettled territory separated the lower Rock River Valley from the Illinois settlements to the south and the lead diggings of the Galena region to the north. The Potawatomis, the Chippewas, and the Ottawas ceded the last major tracts of Indian land in northern Illinois during 1832 and 1833.

A minor land cession in southeastern Iowa for the benefit of the mixed-blood descendants of the Sac and Fox Indians, the Half-Breed Tract, dates from 1824. Federal officers cleared the Indian title from the remainder of the state in a series of major treaties between 1832 and 1851. In less than thirty years the Sacs, Foxes, Potawatomis, Chippewas, Ottawas, Omahas,

[5] Cooper, *op. cit.*, pp. 136–38.

Iowas, Otos, Missouris, Winnebagos, and a number of bands of Sioux relinquished all their rights in Iowa.[6] One incident in the relations between Indian and Anglo-American may have retarded settlement in northern Iowa briefly. This occurred in the spring of 1857 when a group of renegade Sioux, led by Inkpaduta, killed some thirty members of a tiny community at the Okoboji Lakes and Spirit Lake.[7] But the settlers at the lakes were one hundred miles beyond the major settlements in the upper valley of the Des Moines. The massacre probably deterred the flow of pioneers into northwestern Iowa less during the next few years than did the depression of 1857.

Occasionally, settlers did congregate along the boundary line of a new purchase in Iowa, waiting for the opening. This behavior was not so much evidence that the lands in older areas were completely occupied as it was of the speculative bent of the "sooners," who coveted the best waterpower and townsites and the choicer timberlands of the new region. Such a rush occurred in Wapello County on May 1, 1843, and this county, according to one observer, was literally settled overnight.[8] The census figures of 1850 and 1860 tell a different story. Wapello County reported only 36 per cent of its 1900 farm total in the census of 1850 and but 40 per cent ten years later.

If Indians and Indian title little impeded settlement in the prairie triangle, neither did the land survey and sale policies of the federal government. Although in some regions, particularly in portions of Illinois and eastern Iowa, settlers did precede the federal surveyors, these forelopers could organize claim clubs to protect their holdings, and the federal surveyors were seldom long in arriving.[9] The large amounts of land purchased at private entry subsequent to the public auctions at all the prairie-land offices in Iowa and Illinois suggest that the settlers did not press hard upon the available supplies of land in the early years of settlement.

Table 1 shows the state or country of birth of the members of the more

[6] The basic details of Indian land cessions appear in Charles C. Royce, *Indian Land Cessions in the United States* ("Bureau of American Ethnology, 18th Annual Report, 1896–1897" [56th Cong., 1st sess.; House Doc. 736 (Washington, 1899)]), and Charles J. Kappler, *Indian Affairs, Laws and Treaties* (57th Cong., 1st sess.; Senate Doc. 452 [Washington, 1903]). See also Grant Foreman, *The Last Trek of the Indians* (Chicago, 1946). The most useful recent treatment of the problems of the Sac and Fox Indians is by William T. Hagan, *The Sac and Fox Indians* (Norman, 1958).

[7] Thomas Teakle, *The Spirit Lake Massacre* (Iowa City, 1918), and Dan E. Clark, "Frontier Defense in Iowa, 1850–1865," *Iowa Journal of History and Politics*, XVI (July, 1918), 315–86.

[8] William Dewey in *Prairie Farmer*, May, 1844, p. 117.

[9] The following contain material of relevance: Allan G. Bogue, "The Iowa Claim Clubs: Symbol and Substance," *Mississippi Valley Historical Review*, September, 1958, pp. 231–53; Margaret B. Bogue, *Patterns from the Sod: Land Use and Tenure in the Grand Prairie, 1850–1900* (Springfield, 1959), chap. i; Theodore L. Carlson, *The Illinois Military Tract: A Study of Land Occupation, Utilization and Tenure* (Illinois Studies in the Social Sciences," Vol. XXXII, No. 2 [Urbana, 1951]), pp. 49–53; Roscoe L. Lokken, *Iowa Public Land Disposal* (Iowa City, 1942), chaps. i and ii. A comprehensive study of the federal land surveys is badly needed.

important state and national groups in Illinois and Iowa in 1850 and 1870. In both years individuals born in Ohio, New York, and Pennsylvania were numerous in the two states. The figures of 1850 reflected also the large migration of settlers from southern states to Illinois and Iowa. Of the ten States contributing the largest numbers of their sons and daughters to Iowa, five were southern, and undoubtedly the parents of many of the Iowans born

TABLE 1A
MAJOR GROUPS BY NATIVITY: ILLINOIS

1850		1870	
Native-Born			
1. New York	67,180	1. Ohio	163,012
2. Ohio	64,219	2. New York	133,494
3. Kentucky	49,588	3. Pennsylvania	98,614
4. Pennsylvania	37,979	4. Indiana	86,807
5. Tennessee	32,303	5. Kentucky	67,702
6. Indiana	30,953	6. Tennessee	47,523
7. Virginia	24,697	7. Virginia	35,733
8. N. Carolina	13,851	8. Missouri	30,872
9. Vermont	11,381	9. Massachusetts	22,156
10. Massachusetts	9,230	10. Vermont	18,515
Foreign-Born			
1. Gr. Brit. & Ir.	51,647	1. Germany	203,758
2. Germany	38,160	2. Gr. Brit. & Ir.	192,951
3. Brit. N. Am.	10,699	3. Brit. N. Am.	32,550
4. France	3,396	4. Sweden	29,979
5. Norway	2,415	5. Norway	11,880
Illinois population	851,470	Illinois population	2,539,891

TABLE 1B
MAJOR GROUPS BY NATIVITY: IOWA

1850		1870	
Native-Born			
1. Ohio	30,713	1. Ohio	126,285
2. Indiana	19,925	2. New York	79,143
3. Pennsylvania	14,744	3. Pennsylvania	73,435
4. Kentucky	8,994	4. Illinois	65,390
5. New York	8,134	5. Indiana	64,083
6. Virginia	7,861	6. Wisconsin	24,309
7. Illinois	7,247	7. Virginia	19,563
8. Tennessee	4,274	8. Kentucky	14,176
9. Missouri	3,807	9. Missouri	13,831
10. N. Carolina	2,589	10. Vermont	12,204
Foreign-Born			
1. Gr. Brit. & Ir.	9,734	1. Germany	66,162
2. Germany	7,152	2. Gr. Brit. & Ir.	65,442
3. Brit. N. Am.	1,756	3. Norway	17,907
4. Holland	1,108	4. Brit. N. Am.	17,554
5. France	382	5. Sweden	10,796
Iowa population	192,214	Iowa population	1,194,020

in Indiana were southern-born. Numerically, the southerners were a much more important element of the population in both states in 1850 than in 1870.

Yankee, Buckeye, Yorker, Hoosier, and Kentucky "hoss" did not, of course, settle evenly throughout either of the states. The sons of Kentucky, Tennessee, and Virginia settled in southern Illinois and southeastern Iowa particularly. They contributed less to the settlement of the northern prairies in Illinois than did other groups. Especially important in central Illinois were the natives of Ohio and Pennsylvania, while the New Yorkers and New Englanders were most strongly intrenched in the northern section of the state. The southeastern two-fifths of Iowa especially attracted the Ohio-born. New Yorkers and Pennsylvanians settled all along the Iowa side of the Mississippi, but ultimately more of the latter lived in southern Iowa than did those born in New York.

By 1850 considerable numbers of European immigrants had arrived in both Illinois and Iowa. In 1870 slightly more than 20 per cent of the residents in Illinois were foreign-born, and in Iowa the percentage was just under 18 per cent. English-speaking foreign-born from Great Britain and Ireland and from the provinces of British America formed a group larger than that of any other foreign nationality in both 1850 and 1870. Of the British subjects from overseas, one out of every two was an Irishman in 1850, and two out of every three had come from the Green Isle in 1870. Much more striking to the native Americans than the English-speaking immigrants were the Continental-born, with their alien tongues. Natives of the German states made up the major group among them at first, and by the 1860's, Scandinavian elements were also important. The foreign-born settled particularly in central and northern Illinois and throughout the northern half of Iowa, with concentrations extending farther south along the Mississippi in both states. If the Germans, British, Irish, and Scandinavians predominated among the foreign-born of Illinois and Iowa, most of the nations of western Europe contributed in some degree to the settlement of these prairie states.[10]

[10] There is, of course, a very considerable literature dealing with the foreign-born groups. The major relevant works here are: Theodore C. Blegen, *Norwegian Migration to America: 1825–1860* (Northfield, 1931) and *The American Transition* (Northfield, 1940); Thomas P. Christensen, *A History of the Danes in Iowa* (Solvang, 1952); Albert B. Faust, *The German Element in the United States: with Special Reference to its Political, Moral, Social and Educational Influence* (2 vols., Boston, 1909); John A. Hawgood, *The Tragedy of German-America: The Germans in the United States of America during the Nineteenth Century and After* (New York, 1940); Carlton C. Qualey, *Norwegian Settlement in the United States* (Northfield, 1938); Carl Wittke, *The Irish in America* (Baton Rouge, 1956) and *We Who Built America: The Saga of the Immigrant* (New York, 1939); Jacob Van Der Zee, *The Hollanders of Iowa* (Iowa City, 1912). Of the journal literature, the following should be noted particularly: Leola N. Bergmann, "Scandinavian Settlement in Iowa," *Palimpsest*, XXXVII (March, 1956), 129–60, and "The Norwegians in Iowa," *ibid.*, XL (August, 1959), 289-68.

Native Americans from the same state were inclined to settle close to each other. Such bunching was even more pronounced among the Continental-born. Webster, Montgomery, and Page counties, in Iowa, ultimately contained large concentrations of Swedes; in Winneshiek, Allamakee, and Story counties, the Norwegians gathered particularly, and Marion and Sioux counties attracted the Dutch. The foreign-born did not include more than 30 per cent of the population in any Iowa county in 1900, but such statistics are somewhat misleading. To the census-takers, the children of immigrants, born in the United States, were, of course, native-born. In thirty-nine of Iowa's counties in 1900, the foreign-born and their children constituted more than 50 per cent of the population.[11] More important, census statistics may give a misleading impression of the relative numbers of foreign-born farm operators. In Hamilton County, Iowa, for instance, in 1880 the foreign-born made up one-third of the county's population. The manuscript census, however, showed that almost half the farm operators in the county were foreign-born.[12]

We can, of course, make too much of the tendency of members of particular cultural groups to settle in close proximity to each other. The list of nativities in most middle-western counties during the nineteenth century was a long one. Swede rubbed shoulders with German, and he with a Norwegian neighbor perhaps, and they must all deal with the native American. If the latter were all Yankees to the Continental-born, they were certainly not in the eyes of each other. Nor, we can agree, was there complete cultural solidarity among the foreign-born groups if we recall the varied heritages of the German states or the internecine animosities among the Irish.

Historians have suggested many reasons which prompted residents of the older states to come "bag and baggage" to the Illinois and Iowa frontiers. Those who had failed in the older communities, the small farmers who desired more land and could not meet local prices, the farm laborers who wished to be their own masters, the sons who found no farm units awaiting them as they came of age — all these were ripe grain for the western harvest. The swings of the business cycle shook others loose from old surroundings. Regional factors supposedly played their part as well in promoting migration. Writers have pointed to the exhausted soils of the Atlantic states, the competition of western grain, wool, and meat, revulsion against the slave system, and the unrewarding prices of southern staple crops. Illinois or Iowa "fever" fed also on the collapse of internal improvement schemes in Ohio and Indiana and on crop failures and disillusionment with the land in the unglaciated or less fertile portions of these states.[13] In the western states, also, one

[11] Harter and Stewart, *op. cit.*, p. 30 (Fig. 15).
[12] *Census of Iowa for 1880 . . . with Other Historical and Statistical Data . . .* (Des Moines, 1883), p. 216; Allan G. Bogue, "Pioneer Farmers and Innovation," *Iowa Journal of History*, LVI (January, 1958), 32.
[13] Pooley (*op. cit.*, chap. iii) has had an important influence on most subsequent historians. Ray A. Billington, *Westward Expansion: A History of the American Fron-*

writer discerned at work a "general law which seems to have always been fundamental in the westward movement." [14] This, explained William V. Pooley, was the tendency of the younger generation in pioneer areas to move onward to new frontiers.

Intensifying the influence of such factors were letters from friends and relatives who had found success in the western territories and states or conversations with other migrants who had returned for visits or to wind up their affairs. Newspaper accounts and the advertising of land-grant railroads and other large holders played their part as well. The improved roads and the canal systems built during and after the 1820's facilitated migration, as did the expanding services of the steamboats on the lakes and western rivers. Finally, the railroad provided the middle-western pioneer with transportation so speedy and convenient that it would have seemed miraculous to his counterpart of 1780.

Varying somewhat among the European states, a complexity of circumstances set the immigrant tide flowing to the United States as never before during the 1840's and 1850's.[15] Some of the new Americans came, remembering poor crops, absentee landlords, and onerous taxes. Others had chafed under political, legal, or religious grievances. Still others had been set free to migrate — willingly or unwillingly — by the operation of agrarian reforms or changing patterns of agriculture. The unpredictable ebb and flow of economic life had brought others to their decision. Most spectacular, of course, was the migration triggered by the rotting desolation in the Irish potato patches. Least easily explained, perhaps, was the very considerable migration to America of Englishmen or that of residents in the provinces of British North America. The motives of such emigrants were doubtless very similar to those of the native-born Americans who resolved to move west in this same period.

Many circumstances helped to keep the streams of immigration flowing from abroad. Playing a part was the advertising of some American states, including Iowa, the unofficial efforts of American railroads with land to sell and traffic sheds to build, and the assistance given by foreign philanthropists and local and national agencies of foreign governments to indigents who wished to migrate. The decision of the British parliament to abolish the navigation laws fostered competition in the North American trade and

tier (2d ed., New York, 1960), chap. xiv, presents an up-to-date summary of the causes of migration into the Lake Plains. See also Goodwin, *op. cit.*, and Dan E. Clark, "The Westward Movement in the Upper Mississippi Valley during the Fifties," *Mississippi Valley Historical Association, Proceedings,* VII (1913–14), 212–19.

Early writers overstressed the significance of depressions in causing migration. Although economic distress may have conditioned individuals to migrate later, it is quite clear that migration to the frontier slowed down sharply in depression years. Compare, e.g., the rate of population growth in Iowa during the late 1850's with that of the prosperous early 1850's in the *Census of Iowa for 1880...* , pp. 202–3.

[14] Pooley, *op. cit.*, p. 350 [64].

[15] Marcus L. Hansen, *The Atlantic Migration* (Cambridge, 1940), pp. 199–306.

helped to keep fares at a reasonable figure. The introduction of steam power and American and British sanitary legislation finally made the sea-crossing a pleasant interlude in contrast to the late forties, when famished Irish peasants rode the fever ships west from Irish ports and Liverpool. But most important probably were the "America letters" which poured into the old European communities, telling of the good life in America. Frequently printed in the old country newspapers, such testimonials from old friends or acquaintances carried a conviction that the advertising of land-grant railroads could hardly equal.

It is always difficult to determine the relative importance of the various factors which promote migration. Revulsion against the southern institution of slavery probably played little part in the thinking of the settlers of Illinois and Iowa. If many southerners joined the flow of pioneers across the Ohio from Virginia, Kentucky, and Tennessee after 1800 because they loathed the "peculiar institution," it is strange that they showed so much attachment for the South and its institutions later. Many residents of southern Illinois hoped indeed to legalize slavery in the 1820's.[16] Although the foreign-born flocked to the Middle West in much greater numbers than to slave territory, it was, no doubt, largely because of the location of the major immigrant ports and interior transportation routes rather than from a conscious effort to avoid the South. Substantial numbers of Germans did go to Missouri and Texas.[17] As for Pooley's law, it is the kind of generalization that must be tested against census data before we can accept it completely.

Whatever the combination of reasons which brought the settlers, native-born or foreign, to Illinois and Iowa, they hoped to improve their circumstances in life by moving. Such ambitions, of course, differed in degree. Note the contrast in tone between the letters of Edwin Terril, a hopeful Iowa capitalist, and Ephraim G. Fairchild, a tenant farmer of the same state. From Jasper County in 1848 Terril wrote:

> Since I last wrote to thee I have sold my farm and moved far back westward and settled entirely among the squatters and have become a squatter myself. . . . I have cleared about five hundred dollars since I have been here and my prospects at present are quite flattering. I am now building a saw mill. . . . I am also engaged pretty largely in speculating in land.[18]

[16] Pease, *op. cit.*, pp. 70–91.

[17] Historians have made much of the Germans' antipathy toward slavery (for a review of the problem see Hawgood, *op. cit.*, pp. 50, 123, 130, 134–136, 195, 238, 243–53). Professor Hawgood modified earlier estimates of the significance of the Germans in the antislavery controversy, but he may still have given them more than their due. In an unpublished paper, "Notes on Population and the Decline of the Democratic Party in Iowa, 1850–60," Mr. George H. Daniels has presented evidence to show that the Germans in that state remained opposed to the Republican party in 1860 to a much greater extent than is usually supposed.

[18] Edwin Terril to Walter Crew, Hanover, Virginia, February 24, 1847 ("Terril Papers," Iowa Department of History and Archives, Des Moines, Iowa).

From Jones County in 1857, Fairchild told his family in the East:

> i think that I can plough and harrow out hear without being nocked and jerked about with the stones as I allways have ben in Jersey . . . if Father and Mother and the rest of the family was out here . . . they would make a living easier than they can in Jersey.[19]

Joseph Morton explained emigration fever somewhat differently in 1830, writing from his home in Hatborough, Pennsylvania:

> Since our visit to the west 3 years ago . . . [your brother Charles] . . . has been uneasy and dissatisfyed, he is tired of working days work, wishes to get to farming. Land & rents are so high in our section of country that there is nothing to be made at the business here. . . . Living here has become so high & the people so penurious & selfish as to render life a burthen instead of a pleasure. We have therefore come to the conclusion to remove to the West provided Charles should succeed in getting a situation.[20]

To Benjamin Harris of Springfield, Ohio, in 1840, the decision to emigrate involved deciding whether he should settle down and nurture the $6,500, accumulated in seven years of cattle-droving, in Ohio where land was selling for $35 an acre, or go elsewhere. "I concluded," he later wrote, "we would come back to Illinois and live in a cabbin where we could get Eight hundred Acres and have 3500 left better land and a chance to get all the land we might want to buy in the future so we told our friends we would go to Illinois and grow up with the country."[21] For some it was hard to explain their decision in such concrete terms. Henry Eno wrote to his father in New York from Fort Madison, Iowa, in 1837:

> You have doubtless received ere this a letter I wrote from Peoria informing you of my intention of leaving there for this place. I am afraid you will think that I am feeble minded in leaving a place that offered me so many advantages and with which I was so well pleased — but I am still of the opinion that I shall better myself.[22]

Many historians have dwelt upon the cultural traits of the native-born and foreign groups that shared the task of developing the lands of the Middle West. Following the lead of Frederick Jackson Turner, William V. Pooley suggested that the southern-born stock moved northward through southern

---

[19] Ephraim G. Fairchild to his parents, April 9, 1857, in Mildred Throne (ed.), "Iowa Farm Letters, 1856–1865," *Iowa Journal of History*, XVIII (January, 1960), 40.

[20] Joseph Morton, Hatborough, Pa., to George R. Morton, Sanduskey City, Ohio, November 6, 1830 (quoted through the kindness of Mrs. Charles M. Ellsworth, Iowa City, Iowa).

[21] B. F. Harris, "Autobiography," p. 18 (quoted in Margaret B. Bogue, *op. cit*, p. 79).

[22] Henry Eno to Stephen Eno, Pine Plains, New York, March 11, 1837 ("Eno Papers," Special Collections Department, Library, State University of Iowa, Iowa City, Iowa).

Illinois in three stages. First came the hunter pioneers content to till "little clearings in the timber until succeeded by the small farmer, who, in turn, was succeeded by a third class, the more substantial farmer in search of a permanent location."[23] But, in the Yankee conquest of northern Illinois, the hunter pioneer played little part, thought Pooley. No specialist in the use of rifle and hunting knife was needed there to prepare the way for the oxen and farming implements of the New Englander and his cousin once removed from New York. To Pooley, central Illinois was a cultural battleground where "the southern stream . . . met the stream of northern settlers in a contention for the timber lands" and "gave way to the more energetic northern people who took up the land."[24] Yankee determinist that he was, Pooley cheerfully recorded another victory for energy and progress. Questioned by T. C. Pease in the *Centennial History of Illinois*, the theme of cultural conflict was revived in more sophisticated fashion by Richard L. Power in 1953.[25]

The explanation for the failure of the southerners to participate more fully in the conquest of the Illinois prairies probably lies in the mechanics of migration rather than in the theme of cultural conflict. The flow of emigrants from any particular region was anything but constant. From their earliest beginnings, American communities have sent out as well as received. In the early years of community growth inflow exceeded outflow. At some point, perhaps a generation and a half after settlement, the number of those leaving to make a new beginning or a first start elsewhere swelled to considerable volume and some years later declined. Such emigrants did not all seek the same destination. First one region then another might beckon most strongly. Cultural ties and animosities might modify the process; they seldom controlled it. This is not to deny, however, that cultural differences did add spice to life in the prairie communities. Consider the undertones of malice, ridicule, and envy in the following passage from the history of Allamakee County, Iowa.

Makee Ridge, as it was afterwards called, had among her earlier settlers a large per cent from Maine, and being shrewd, prudent, and enterprising Yankees they soon grubbed out, fenced in, broke up, and cultivated farms, built themselves frame houses which they painted white, made a turnpike road through the village one mile in length and were so far ahead of the surrounding country in style and improvements that they soon were dubbed by the settlers who came in from Hoosierdom, with the sobriquet of Nobscotters, and the ridge with the name of Penobscot, and this name like the lingering fragrance of the faded rose hangs round them still.[26]

[23] Pooley, *op. cit.*, p. 309 [23].
[24] *Ibid.*, p. 420 [134].
[25] Pease, *op. cit.*, p. 7; Richard L. Power, *Planting Corn Belt Culture: The Impress of the Upland Southerner and Yankee in the Old Northwest* (Indianapolis, 1953).
[26] Ellery M. Hancock, *Past and Present of Allamakee County, Iowa: A Record of Settlement, Organization, Progress and Achievement* (2 vols.; Chicago, 1913), p. 275.

A number of historians have studied the role of the immigrant in the settlement of the Middle West. Particularly, have they examined the Continental-born, and to a lesser extent the Irish. After painstaking analysis of settlement in a number of Wisconsin counties, Joseph Schafer concluded that there was "a poetic element in the intensity with which . . . [the Germans] . . . pursued the ideal of creating permanent homes on the land, a point in which they differed from the Americans."[27] The Scandinavians would have an even more emotional regard for the land than did the Germans because they came from countries "where land-hunger was more acute than in Germany."[28] In a recent study of the Irish in the United States, Carl Wittke maintained that, "the Irish in Wisconsin, in contrast with German and Scandinavian farmers in that state, were likely to buy and sell several times before settling down permanently."[29] Marcus L. Hansen suggested that the immigrants were "fillers in" who sensibly avoided the labors of the pioneer for which they were untrained, and preferred instead to buy improved farms from the native Americans who moved on to new frontiers.[30] Here again is the suggestion that the Continental immigrants were less mobile than the native-born Americans once they had chosen a place to put down roots.

However accurately Dr. Schafer may have described the behavior of the German settlers in Wisconsin, they, and the Scandinavians as well, settled on many an unimproved prairie section in Illinois and Iowa. So rapidly did the immigrants move into many prairie counties that it was utterly impossible for them to have found enough native Americans willing to sell out. No doubt Professor Wittke was correct when he stressed the Irishman's liking for the city, but anyone who has examined the population census rolls of northern Illinois and eastern Iowa also knows that many prairie farmers gave Ireland as the country of their birth.

How old was the pioneer? What particular paths had led him to the prairies of Illinois and Iowa? How long, once settled, did he stay in the new western community? To the student of agricultural history these questions all have more than antiquarian interest. If the settlers were young, they would perhaps prove more adaptable, more adept, at meeting the challenges of the new environment than the members of an older group. If they came from the next adjacent state, but recently settled, they were perhaps better prepared to face the tasks of settlement than if they had made the long jump from Massachusetts or North Carolina. We are by no means certain of the effect which cultural homogeneity has in shaping community relations, but information about agricultural practices may well have spread

---

[27] Joseph Schafer, *Wisconsin Domesday Book*, Vol. II: *Four Wisconsin Counties* (Madison, 1927), p. 118 (quoted without page reference in Hawgood, *op. cit.*, p. 31).
[28] Hawgood, *op. cit.*, p. 32.
[29] Wittke, *The Irish in America*, p. 65.
[30] Marcus L. Hansen, *The Immigrant in American History* (Cambridge, Mass., 1942), 76.

more rapidly in communities settled by pioneers with a common heritage. If most settlers moved on again after but a few years in a pioneer community, it may have taken longer for the farmers there to secure a firm understanding of the difficulties of managing local soils or to solve other farm problems linked to the local environment.

Ultimately, we will be able to answer some of our questions about the pioneers with great certainty. Only industry and eyes capable of searching faded manuscript census pages — or worse still their microfilm replicas — are required before we can generalize safely about the age of the settlers. Ten years, however, represented a sixth of a man's life, and the federal census-taker recorded only the state or country of his origin, neglecting periods of residence in other regions before settlement in Iowa or Illinois. The census data, therefore, can provide us with only partial knowledge of the wanderings of the pioneers. Collected in hundreds of county histories, of course, are thousands of biographical sketches of middle-western pioneers. Unfortunately, the sketches are not always reliable or complete, and their proud subjects were not representative of the county population as a whole. The ne'er-do-well and eccentric found scant welcome in the pages of the county "mug books." But, if our sources are incomplete, we can still cast some light on the demography of the middle-western pioneers.

Bureau County lies in the north-central portion of Illinois at the upper bend of the Illinois River. Some 120 miles to the west and slightly to the south in the lower Des Moines River Valley is Wapello County, Iowa.[31] In 1850 Bureau County contained some 23 per cent of the number of farms there in 1900, while in Wapello the figure was roughly 36 per cent. Both counties clearly were in a pioneer stage. The average or arithmetic mean age of 1,155 farmer householders in Wapello County was 42.3; that of 1,161 farmer householders in Bureau County was 38.8 (see Table 2). Seventy-three per cent of Wapello's farmers were thirty-one years of age or more. Of the farm householders in townships in three other widely separated Iowa counties, 78, 64, and 55 per cent fell in the same category in the first federal census year after organization.[32] Evidently, the pioneer was a mature man, and the boy settler and his child wife were rarities. Actually, the 990 Bureau farmers who had children living with them reported that 1,648 of them were born in states other than Illinois, as compared to 1,790 born within the state. The "typical" pioneer of the counties studied was apparently a married man between the ages of twenty-

[31] The material presented concerning Bureau County, Illinois, below is drawn from the writer's analysis of the manuscript population censuses of that county for 1850 and 1860. With one exception, Wapello County statistics are drawn from Mildred Throne, "A Population Study of an Iowa County in 1850," *Iowa Journal of History*, LVII (October, 1959), 305-30. The Wapello statistics in Table 2 were prepared for me by Dr. Throne.

[32] The townships were Springfield, Cedar County; Hamilton, Hamilton County; and Warren, Bremer County.

TABLE 2
Age and Nativity of Farmers in Bureau, and Wapello Counties in 1850

BIRTHPLACE	BUREAU		WAPELLO	
	Number	Average Age	Number	Average Age
New England:				
Connecticut	28	43.5	3	48.6
Maine	20	44.6	6	37.3
Massachusetts	87	43.0	12	45.8
New Hampshire	41	41.4	8	44.6
Rhode Island	21	36.8	..	...
Vermont	66	40.4	9	40.5
	263	41.8	38	43.2
Middle States:				
Delaware	10	37.0	5	43.6
New Jersey	22	45.8	16	48.9
New York	165	37.85	53	42.9
Pennsylvania	125	39.0	114	42.6
	322	38.8	188	43.3
Northern Ohio Valley:				
Illinois	7	25.0	19	26.7
Indiana	29	28.0	126	29.5
Ohio	152	32.8	241	33.7
	188	31.8	386	31.9
Interior South:				
Alabama	1	40.0	3	34.3
Kentucky	49	37.5	174	37.9
Missouri	..	...	2	24.0
Tennessee	22	36.8	67	36.2
	72	37.3	246	37.3
Seaboard South:				
District of Columbia	1	46.0	1	50.0
Georgia	2	47.0	1	50.0
Maryland	16	46.3	22	49.4
North Carolina	14	48.3	61	43.4
South Carolina	3	48.3	7	46.7
Virginia	89	40.0	156	43.9
	125	42.1	248	44.4
English-speaking foreign-born:				
England	41	39.7	10	40.4
Ireland	61	40.3	14	40.7
Scotland	10	40.0	1	
Canadas	4	29.5	2	49.5
	116	39.7	27	41.2
Continental foreign-born:				
Denmark	1	38.0	..	...
France	1	52.0	2	43.0
Germany	72	39.8	9	38.4
Holland	..	...	9	39.5
Sweden	..	...	2	35.0
Switzerland	1	40.0	..	...
	75	39.9	22	39.0
Total	1,161	38.8	1,155	42.3

five and forty-five who had started his family before he moved to the Illinois or Iowa frontier.

When considered as a group, the settlers of the Middle West did apparently have a unique age structure. If the midwestern prairies had attracted a cross-section of the general population, the age structure should not have changed substantially over time. The percentage of farmers over forty years of age rose perceptibly during the first twenty or thirty years in the three Iowa townships mentioned earlier. In a study of the Iowa population published in 1930, Professors Harter and Stewart of Iowa State College discovered that Iowans in general were older in those areas of the state that had been settled longest, youngest in those regions that had been settled for the shortest period of time.[33] We can say, therefore, that, although the pioneer farmers were older than some historians have believed, they were probably younger than the farm operators remaining in the communities from which they migrated and definitely formed a younger group than would be found a generation later in the communities which they were helping to build.[34]

Table 2 also shows that the ages of the farmers in both Bureau and Wapello counties in 1850 were apparently related to their states of nativity. New Englanders and farmers who were born in the states of the Seaboard South were on the average considerably older than the farmers who had been born in the Ohio Valley states of Indiana, Ohio, Kentucky, and Tennessee. In Bureau County, for instance, 263 farmers of New England birth were forty-two years of age on the average. The average age of 152 farmers born in Ohio was only thirty-three, while in both Bureau and Wapello counties the Hoosier farmers were younger still. The farther the middle-western pioneer of native origin was from the state of his birth, the older he tended to be. Although older than the Ohio Valley group, the foreign-born farmers were somewhat younger than the New England contingent.

The manuscript federal censuses do not tell us directly of the way stations through which the American emigrant passed on the journey from the state of his birth to the Illinois or Iowa prairies. His children's states of birth, however, do reveal some of them. Unfortunately, we cannot be sure just how much of the story the birthplaces of children provide in any one case. Of the 970 native-born farmers in Bureau County in 1850, 838 did have children living at home. The birthplaces of these children provided

[33] Harter and Stewart, *op. cit.*, pp. 16–17.
[34] Professor James C. Malin was the first western historian to interest himself in pioneer demography in a serious way. He interpreted his findings to show that the frontier population was simply a cross section of the population at large. However, his statistical studies of Kansas farm operators actually showed that, as in Iowa, the average age of farm operators increased for some time after a community was begun (*The Grassland of North America: Prolegomena to its History* [Lawrence, Kan., 1947], p. 289).

skeletal migration charts for their parents. Only 10 per cent of the Ohio-born farmers listed children born in states other than Ohio or Illinois. Somewhat more than half of the farmers born in Virginia and Pennsylvania had resided in states other than Illinois and the state of their birth. The New England– and particularly the New York–born farmers had apparently migrated more directly than had those from Pennsylvania or Virginia. Since the New England–born farmers were in general older than most of their neighbors, children born to them in the earliest years of marriage might have already left home by 1850. The census data showed that 66 per cent of the family men among the Bureau County farmers had lived in another state, approximately 30 per cent had lived in two other states and 0.5 per cent revealed residence in four states in addition to Illinois.

The stopping places of the New Englanders had usually been New York, Pennsylvania, Ohio, or another New England state. Ohio and Pennsylvania served as the main routes of the New York–born. Pennsylvania and Virginia natives had sojourned for the most part in Ohio, although some of the latter had lived in Kentucky or Indiana at one time. As we have seen, the Bureau County pioneers of 1850 brought at least 1,648 children with them. To a considerable extent, migration to the new settlements was a family movement. If some had neither wives nor children to accompany them, and a few thankfully left theirs behind, the majority of settlers brought them along; society on the agricultural frontier was a family society.

Of the 1,115 farmers present in Wapello County in 1850, only some 39 per cent were there ten years later. Of the 1,161 farmers in Bureau County in the same year, 38 per cent remained in 1860. Some of the missing farmers had, of course, died. But, if the farmers of 1850 in these counties were mature, they were not extremely aged. Many of them were undoubtedly living elsewhere in 1860. "Those who stayed" in Wapello County, wrote Mildred Throne, "were more prosperous than those who move on."[35] This was also true in Bureau County. The 438 farmers of 1850 who remained there in 1860 had real estate valued at $1,317 on the average in 1850. The 723 who had disappeared by 1860 reported real estate in 1850 worth only $1,006. In her study of Wapello County, Throne did not compare the ages of those who stayed with those who left. In Bureau County there was no clear-cut relationship between age and persistence.

The Continental-born, some historians believe, were more persistent than the native-born farmers. Table 3 does not show this to have been the case in Bureau County, although it does reveal that the English-speaking foreign-born were the most persistent of all groups in that county. The 72 Germans, however, were highly mobile. The southern stock supposedly were pre-eminently the "movers" among the native-born. It was true in Bureau County that the settlers from Kentucky and Tennessee were the least persistent of all groups. We should remember, however, that the

[35] Throne, "A Population Study," *op. cit.*, p. 321.

Germans and the natives of the interior South were present in relatively small numbers.

TABLE 3
ORIGIN AND PERSISTENCE, BUREAU COUNTY, ILLINOIS

	Number Farmers	Persistence, 1850–60 (Per Cent)
Great Britain, Ireland, British North America	116	46.5
New England	263	45.6
Middle States	322	36.9
Seaboard South	125	34.4
Northern Ohio Valley	188	34.0
European Continent	75	28.0
Interior South	72	23.6
	1161	37.7

TABLE 4
FARM OPERATOR TURNOVER in FOUR IOWA TOWNSHIPS *

	1850		1860		1870		1880	
	No.	Per Cent	No.	Per Cent	No.	Per Cent	No.	Per Cent
Crawford Township:								
Group 1	66	100.0	21	31.8	11	16.6	7	10.6
Group 2	..	....	94	100.0	35	37.2	23	24.5
Group 3	..	....	..	....	141	100.0	36	25.5
Union Township:								
Group 1	81	100.0	35	43.2	22	27.2	11	13.6
Group 2	..	....	84	100.0	41	48.8	25	29.8
Group 3	..	....	..	....	149	100.0	44	29.5
Hamilton Township								
Group 1	..	....	50	100.0	28	56.0	14	28.0
Group 2	..	....	..	....	64	100.0	30	46.9
Warren Township:								
Group 1	..	....	28	100.0	12	42.9	7	25.0
Group 2	..	....	..	....	163	100.0	72	44.2
Continental-born †	..	....	..	....	102	100.0	47	46.1

* The counties were Washington, Davis, Hamilton, and Bremer.
† The Continental-born group consisted mainly of natives of the German states with a few French men and Swiss as well. This group was included in Warren township, Group 2, as well as being placed in a separate category.

Based on manuscript population and agricultural census rolls, Table 4 shows the turnover of farm operators in four Iowa townships between 1850 and 1880. The farmers represented in this table differed from those in the Bureau and Wapello County studies in that they had all made agricultural census returns. Both the Wapello and the Bureau County statistics included a group of "farmers without farms" who described themselves as farmers but who evidently had no farm businesses of their own at the moment. By considering only the farmers who had made an agricultural census return in the townships, we restricted ourselves to those who had made a commitment to their community. In the table the new farmers of each census year stand separately. In Crawford and Union townships we could test the s⸝ing power of groups of farmers present in 1850, 1860, and 1870. Settled later, Hamilton and Warren townships provided figures for only the twenty year period between 1860 and 1880.

Table 4 shows that a high proportion of each new group of farmers dropped out early, leaving a core of much more persistent men. Among the ten groups of new farmers in the four townships, the farmers of 1860 in Hamilton Township showed the highest degree of persistence — 56 per cent of them remained there ten years later. The new farmers of 1870 in Crawford Township were least persistent, with only 26 per cent of them remaining after a decade. A considerable group of Continental-born farmers, mostly Germans, entered Warren Township during the late 1860's. Of the members of this group 46 per cent were still there in 1880.

Many historians have followed Turner in accepting the three-stage formula of agricultural settlement, and with even fewer qualifications than those of William V. Pooley. The hunter-farmer or squatter gave way with alacrity, in this interpretation, to the small farmer who obtained title to the land from the federal government and who in turn yielded with few exceptions to the man of property and substance. That there were hunter-farmers and "rolling stones" on the margins of settlement we cannot doubt. But the persistence of a substantial nucleus of settlers from the first census and the fact that all new groups of farmers behaved similarly, whatever the age of the community, force us to qualify the Turnerian formula.

Let us turn from the faceless statistics of Table 4 to discuss the life of one pioneer in Davis County, Iowa. Stephen L. Saunders was born in Pennsylvania in 1813. The family moved to Ohio when Stephen was nine. At the age of twenty-one he went to Michigan, and two years later he married in Indiana. His wife died shortly, leaving one daughter, and in 1837 Saunders went to Iowa. When he crossed the Mississippi, he counted a "York sixpence" as his only capital. After a year in Van Buren County, he worked for the government briefly in the Indian Service at Council Bluffs. Leaving this job, he returned to Van Buren County, joined his parents, who sold their claim, and moved with them to Davis County, still Indian land and unsurveyed. Here they staked out claims, including a number for "friends" in Ohio. A United States marshall arrested young Saunders at this point for trespassing on Indian lands. Fined for the offense, he enjoyed a period of custody by the United States Army, whose officers he found to be "genial, hearty fellows" and "talented drinkers." During 1844 he married again and was still living on his original claim when the county history appeared in 1882. At that time he owned some 1,200 acres, including the home farm of 430 acres, "well improved, with good buildings and orchard." [36]

Until he came to Davis County, Saunders had indeed been a rolling

[36] State Historical Company, *History of Davis County, Iowa* . . . (Des Moines, 1882), pp. 653–54.

stone. Few had better claim to the title of squatter there than did he. But in Davis County the rock stopped rolling and displayed a real talent for gathering moss. Stephen Saunders' career was probably more colorful than most — few settlers crossed the Indian boundary line or fell into the custody of the United States Army. But too many other early comers showed his persistence, once located, for us to dismiss the squatter or early settler simply as a man who left for new surroundings when the first ring of neighbor's axe came floating down wind.

Saunder's story allows us also to qualify our discussion of migration patterns. Had his daughter by his first marriage been living with him in 1850, we could have classified him as a man who had lived in two states, in addition to Iowa. As we know, he had actually resided in four other states, and in Iowa at least had lived in three different localities. Much reading of biographies in the county histories suggests that Stephen Saunders was more than ordinarily mobile as a young man, but he was certainly not unique.

"Book Farming" in Iowa, 1840–1870
MILDRED THRONE

IOWA AGRICULTURE underwent many changes between 1840 and 1870 but, as Mildred Throne indicates in this selection, Iowa farmers were generally not receptive to "book farming" methods. During the mid-1800s several movements were underway to convince Iowa farmers that they should practice more scientific farming methods and breed better livestock. Farm journal editors, weekly newspaper editors, and farm agricultural society members all worked diligently to persuade Iowa farmers that they should upgrade their methods. Old ways died hard, however, and even after thirty years farmers had made few changes in tillage methods other than to make use of more mechanized equipment.

Even though this selection centers around the adoption of "book farming," author Throne presents considerable information about agricultural attitudes and practices in mid-nineteenth century Iowa. Mirrored through the crusades of the farm journals and the weekly newspapers are the actual methods used by Iowa farmers and the reasons why.

Unfortunately Iowans were not atypical in their behavior as they shared their inefficiencies and wasteful practices with most other midwestern farmers. In so doing they revealed their acceptance of the "Ideology of Abundance," the belief shared by so many Americans that their country's natural resources—whether land, minerals, or timber—would never be exhausted.

"BOOK FARMING" IN IOWA
1840–1870
By Mildred Throne

" 'Book farming! away with your book farming,' says an individual solicited to subscribe for an agricultural journal, 'I want no books to teach me how to raise wheat, corn, and potatoes; I can raise as good crops as any of my neighbors, who seem to be filled with agricultural books and papers, and still gaping for more.' " Such was the attitude of the majority of Middle Western farmers toward the "better farming movement" of the mid-nineteenth century. To them the editors of agricultural journals were men "with silk gloves on," men "too lazy to work for a living," and they would have nothing to do with them or their ideas.[1] Since the time of Jefferson and Washington, farmers aware of the importance and necessity of soil preservation, crop rotation, and fertilization had preached and practiced scientific husbandry, to the best of their knowledge. Learned agricultural societies of the late eighteenth century had spread this knowledge to a select few, but the methods of the average American farmer remained little different from those of the European peasant of the Middle Ages.

Conquering the prejudice of conservative, "old fogy" farmers was a long, uphill task. Early in the nineteenth century a new impetus was given improved agriculture by "a gentleman farmer" of Pittsfield, Massachusetts, Elkanah Watson, who, in 1807, exhibited two Merino sheep in the public square. This show of livestock, so modestly begun, became an annual event out of which grew the Berkshire Agricultural Society. This society, organized in 1810, was different from the earlier types, which had sought to improve agriculture by scientific reasoning. It gave the farmer something he could understand: a view of the actual results of better methods; a view which aroused a desire for emulation and competition.[2] A beginning had

---

[1] *Northwestern Farmer*, 1:190 (July, 1856); 2:374 (October, 1857); Bloomfield *Democratic Clarion*, Dec. 7, 1859.

[2] Wayne Caldwell Neely, *The Agricultural Fair* (New York, 1935), 43–6, 49-50, 64; Percy Wells Bidwell and John I. Falconer, *History of Agriculture in the Northern United States,1620–1860* (Washington, 1925), 187.

been made in the fight against prejudice and ignorance; "book farming" would come later.

By the mid-nineteenth century other forces joined with agricultural societies to further the cause of better farming. Agricultural journalism had its beginning in Baltimore in 1819 with the publication by John Stuart Skinner of *The American Farmer*. Edmund Ruffin in 1851 gave credit to farm journals for whatever progress American agriculture had made to that date.[3] The weekly newspapers of the Middle Western market towns were also active in furthering "book farming," and farmers' clubs added their demands for better farming. What were the methods against which these forces battled, and what were the remedies suggested?

In Iowa, after the first decade or two of "pioneering," a general type of farming can be observed. The average farm was a combination of prairie and small patches of woodland. The farmer planted corn, wheat, oats, and a few other small grains. He raised pigs, a few cattle of doubtful lineage, and possibly some sheep; his work-cattle consisted of a yoke or two of slow-footed oxen or several nondescript horses. His farm buildings left much to be desired. By the 1860's he may have planted a small orchard, and he had a number of the latest agricultural implements — steel plows, reapers, mowers, corn shellers, and, in some cases, a few planting tools. In fact, his machinery was well in advance of his methods which were usually those of his father and grandfather. His farm, in spite of careless cultivation, produced a large surplus which he sold at the nearest town.

Grain alone could not support the Iowa farmer and his family, however. His only means of converting that grain into a product which could be taken to market easily and which would yield a good profit was to feed it to his livestock. Corn sold for 75 cents on the Atlantic seaboard in 1853, but at Burlington it brought only 18 to 20 cents.[4] The cost of shipping grain to the Atlantic was prohibitive, but cheap Iowa corn could be fed to hogs and cattle which could be driven to market and sold at a profit. As early as 1847, J. A. Pinto, secretary of the Danville Township Farmers' Club, urged the club members to pay more attention to the production of cattle and hogs, as the "most lucrative business" in which a farmer could engage.[5]

[3] Albert Lowther Demaree, *The American Agricultural Press, 1819–1860* (New York, 1941), 39–86 passim.

[4] *Iowa Farmer and Horticulturist*, 1:32 (June, 1853); 1:34 (July, 1853).

[5] *Iowa Farmers' Advocate*, 1:85 (December, 1847).

The increasing production of corn, plus the presence of plenty of hungry livestock, made such a system inevitable.

Almost from the first opening of the territory, hogs were important to the Iowa farmer. Between 1840 and 1870 the number of swine on Iowa farms increased from just over 100,000 to almost 2,500,000.[6] Increase in quality was not as noticeable as in quantity, however. Some few farmers raised Poland China, Suffolk, Berkshire, and other breeds, with the Poland China the most popular.[7] But when any hog taken to market would sell at around five cents a pound, the incentive was not to breed better animals but rather to make them heavier by feeding them plenty of corn. When packers later began to distinguish between types of hogs, and to pay better prices for better stock, improvements in breeds resulted.

A few farmers, as early as the 1840's were importing blooded cattle, particularly Durhams, or Shorthorns as they were sometimes called. A "Shorthorn Herd Book" was published in 1858, as part of the *Report* of the State Agricultural Society. Only 97 thoroughbred cattle were listed, the majority owned by Timothy Day of Van Buren County, by the Ohio Stock Farm in Butler County, and by H. G. Stuart of Lee County. A year later the "Herd Book" listed 171 Shorthorns and 43 Devons, the latter owned by James Weed of Muscatine County, C. D. Bent and Franklin Kimball of Johnson County, and a few scattered breeders in Poweshiek, Jones, and Jackson counties.[8] These figures, compared to the 540,088 cattle of all kinds on Iowa farms in 1860, indicate that thoroughbred cattle were still very much in the minority.[9] This was inevitable, since cattle were pastured in common on the unfenced prairies. There was thus little or no selection in breeding, even had there been a desire to keep the better strains pure. Only the well-to-do farmers, who could afford to fence their herds, were able to import and develop fine cattle.

Methods of cultivating the grain to feed this stock were changing slowly, largely because of the introduction of new farm machines rather than because of better tillage. The first farmers had hacked the corn into the unbroken prairie sod, or, if available, a huge breaking plow had been used

[6] *1836–1880 Iowa Census*, 360. The actual figures are: 104,899 in 1840; 2,409,679 in 1869.

[7] *Iowa Agricultural Report, 1857*, 227-8; *Report of the Commissioner of Patents, 1850*, 356.

[8] *Ia. Ag. Rept.*, 1858, 443–68; 1859, 424–61, 462–8.

[9] *1836–1880 Iowa Census*, 350.

to turn the tough sod while the farmer or his sons followed, dropping the seed corn by hand, or sowing wheat and oats broadcast. Once the sod was broken and a crop raised, further plowing was done with cast-iron sheathed plows, until John Deere "made his first steel plow from a saw blade." The cast-iron plow in common use when the first settlers moved into Iowa did not scour well in the rich prairie soil. Thus, the steel plow was a great boon to Iowa farmers. By 1850 Deere was producing 1,600 plows a year; by 1852 his enlarged plant turned out 10,000 annually.[10]

Threshers, mowers, and the McCormick or Manny reapers made their appearance on Iowa farms in the fifties. Corn planters and wheat drills, on the other hand, were not so widely used; the Middle Western farmer did not at once appreciate the value of planting tools, where the immediate results were not so evident as with the steel plow, the thresher, and the reaper.[11] The Pennock wheat drill, for instance, first patented in 1841, gained popularity slowly.[12] In 1858, Renchelor and O'Daniels were agents for the drill in Mount Pleasant; in an effort to increase its use, they offered to take as their pay "the increase over the common method of sowing, off of forty acres."[13] Where used, the drill was found satisfactory, but its acceptance by farmers was slow. One reason for this was that the drill needed a well-pulverized soil for proper operation; this plus the fact that broadcast seeding was easier, cheaper, and just as satisfactory in the rich prairie soils of Iowa and the Midwest made the drill more of a luxury than a necessity in wheat raising.[14] Corn planters, both the hand-operated and the horse-drawn riding type, had been introduced by the 1860's, and some few farmers were using them. According to the publicity released in 1867, fifteen hundred of the walking type had been sold in Iowa that year, and 416 of the riding type. Since there were 116,292 farms in Iowa in 1870, it is obvious that the number of farmers using corn planters was proportionately very small.[15]

Shelter, both for livestock and for farm machines, was extremely primi-

[10] Bidwell and Falconer, *Agriculture in the Northern United States* . . ., 283; Leo Rogin, *The Introduction of Farm Machinery* . . . (Berkeley, Calif., 1931), 33.
[11] *Ia. Ag. Rept., 1857*, 213, 225, 229, 236, 243, 267, 438.
[12] Rogin, *Introduction of Farm Machinery* . . ., 192-3.
[13] *Ia. Ag. Rept., 1858*, 257.
[14] Fred A. Shannon, *The Farmer's Last Frontier: Agriculture, 1860–1897* (New York, 1945), 131.
[15] *Ia. Ag. Rept., 1867*, 222, 226; *1836–1880 Iowa Census*, 244.

tive for several decades on the Iowa frontier. In 1856 the cost of the "necessary sheds for cattle and horses" for a small farm of eighty to one hundred acres was estimated at about $100.[16] "J. A. D." of Des Moines County, in 1858, asked a farm journal editor for advice on the problem. "We here have straw stables, rail corn cribs and muddy hog pens. Who can describe the best arrangement for avoiding these inconveniences, without an expense that will frighten us in these times?"[17] Although the eastern counties had, by 1858, been settled for almost two decades, the national business depression of this period made it difficult for many farmers to make the needed improvements which, in the normal course of events, they should have been making by that time. There were exceptions, of course. Davis County reported in 1858 that, "notwithstanding the stringency of the money market," the farmers of that region had, in the past year, built one hundred new houses and over thirty barns, in addition to other improvements.[18] But the severe winter of 1858-1859 caused a large loss of cattle, and agitation for better shelters became widespread.[19] As with other features of Iowa agriculture, improvement was talked and planned, and in some cases carried out, but as a general rule it was more an ideal than a reality. Most cattle found shelter in the woods or in the lee of a strawstack, and most machinery was left out in wind and weather, to rust and become useless within a few years.

Railroads were being built across Iowa in the late fifties and early sixties; many farmers looked to them for expanded markets which, they hoped, would result in better farming methods, as Iowa farmers began to compete with eastern agriculturists. Although some improvement may have resulted from the demands of the new and fast railroad transportation, progressive farmers still found grounds for criticism. The "pioneer" was the worst offender, in the eyes of progressive farmers. L. D. Morse of Wapello County believed that agricultural methods in the country would improve when the pioneers, "who flee from *rats* and Railroads," had moved on.[20] The farmers of Wapello County were using the same methods which had

[16] Nathan H. Parker, *Iowa Handbook for 1856* . . . (Boston, 1856), 160.
[17] *Emery's Journal of Agriculture*, 2:23 (July 1, 1858).
[18] *Ia. Ag. Rept.*, 1858, 238.
[19] *Albia Republican*, May 18, 1859; *Washington Press*, May 11, 1859; *Bloomfield Democratic Clarion*, April 20, 1859.
[20] *Ia. Ag. Rept.*, 1858, 418.

worn out the soil of their eastern farms: neither manuring nor a "systematic rotation of crops" was practiced. In fact, with some farmers "from four to eight successive crops of corn from the same ground, without any manuring," was common.[21] M. L. Comstock of Des Moines County found that farmers had fallen into "two errors of vital importance. . . . The first, is that prairie soil does not need draining; the second, that it cannot be impoverished." Heaps of manure were often left by the bed of a stream, where they sent their "enriching salts dancing away in their merry course toward the Gulf of Mexico."[22] The farmers of Lucas County, according to Dr. Isaac Kneeland, used careless and wasteful methods. Cattle and hogs were not sheltered; wheat was often sown on last year's cornfield without plowing. When the farmer did plow his fields, he turned over too shallow a furrow. Almost all farmers were in debt for more land than they needed, and did not "properly cultivate what they have fenced."[23] Similar stories were told in other localities. With so much land almost for the taking, it was hard to convince the farmer that he should limit his acreage, that he should preserve the fertility of his soil, or that he should provide shelter for his stock.

Such were the conditions of Iowa agriculture in the decades before 1870. The Iowa soil, after only some thirty years of cropping, was already beginning to show signs of exhaustion in some areas, or at least of decreasing fertility, in spite of the agitation of "book farmers." But certain areas reported improvement due to the constant work of agricultural societies, farm journals, newspapers, and farmers' clubs.

Agricultural societies and yearly fairs were important factors in spreading the gospel of better farming in Iowa. The leading spirits of these organizations and exhibitions were not always primarily farmers. Editors, doctors, lawyers, and businessmen, together with a few well-to-do and educated farmers, were the officers, and on them fell the work of organization and management. There were exceptions, of course, but as a rule the townspeople directed the societies and fairs, and the farmers enjoyed them. This role of the businessman of the small towns of the Middle West in sponsoring and furthering improvements in the business of farming is a factor which should not be overlooked in studies in agricultural history. Editors of local papers devoted much space to farm news and to propaganda for

[21] *Ibid., 1857*, 439.
[22] *Ibid.*, 244.
[23] *Ibid., 1859*, 318.

"book farming"; agricultural journals were edited by townsmen; and in Iowa the leaders in the campaign for an agricultural college came primarily from the urban centers.

Christian W. Slagle, a lawyer of Jefferson County, was active in founding the State Agricultural Society in Iowa; Joshua M. Shaffer, a physician of Keokuk, was for many years the secretary of the State Society; the first president was Thomas W. Clagett, lawyer, judge, and editor of Keokuk. Two other presidents were Peter Melendy, fine stock breeder and politician, and George G. Wright, lawyer, Chief Justice of the Iowa Supreme Court, and United States Senator. Josiah B. Grinnell, preacher and politician, was long active in the affairs of the Society, while Benjamin F. Gue, politician and editor, was one of the sponsors of the bill to found a State Agricultural College. William Duane Wilson, editor of the *Iowa Homestead*, was a leader in the Agricultural Society and in the movement for the State College and Farm; Dudley W. Adams, horticulturist and prominent Granger of the 1870's, was from the first prominent in agricultural societies, both county and state. James W. Grimes, lawyer and United States Senator, was always interested in agriculture and was, for a time, horticultural editor of the *Iowa Farmer and Horticulturist*. Mark Miller, editor of the *Northwestern Farmer* and the *Iowa Homestead*, was long active in the campaign to improve farming methods. Leading farmers in the agricultural societies were Timothy Day of Van Buren County, pioneer breeder of Shorthorn cattle in the state; James Weed of Muscatine, a breeder of Devon cattle; Suel Foster, horticulturist of Muscatine; and H. G. Stuart, stock breeder of Lee County.

Men such as these, in the state at large and in the counties, sponsored societies and fairs, edited farm journals, and constantly urged the betterment of Iowa farming methods. It is to them, together with Coker F. Clarkson and Henry Wallace in the later decades, that much of the credit is due for what little "book farming" was practiced in the years before the State Agricultural College at Ames took over the leadership in scientific farming and agricultural education.[24]

[24] For biographies and sketches of these men, see Benjamin F. Gue, *History of Iowa* . . . (4 vols., New York, 1903), 4:48, 111-12, 186-7, 239-40, 245, 496-7; William Salter, *The Life of James W. Grimes* . . . (New York, 1876); Luella M. Wright, *Peter Melendy* . . . (Iowa City, 1945); Charles E. Payne, *Josiah Bushnell Grinnell* (Iowa City, 1938); *Portrait and Biographical Album of Muscatine County, Iowa* . . . (Chicago, 1889), 210-12; David C. Mott, "William Duane Wilson," *Annals of Iowa* (third series), 20:361-73 (July, 1936); *Dictionary of American Biography*, 1:56.

The first efforts to form agricultural societies in Iowa during the forties had been abortive; no real progress was made until the fifties. The *Prairie Farmer*, which began publication in Chicago in 1841, at once urged that the farmers of the new territory make plans for agricultural fairs.[25] Some local exhibits were actually held as early as 1841; and the territorial legislature passed acts to encourage agricultural societies in 1838, 1842, and 1843.[26] Louisa and Van Buren counties later claimed the distinction of having held the first agricultural fair in the state: Van Buren in 1842, and Louisa in 1850.[27]

Whatever the origin or location of the "first" fair, the more settled counties of Iowa, under the stimulus of state funds, were developing local societies and holding exhibits by the early fifties. A law passed by the General Assembly in 1853 had provided that each county should receive a sum equal to the amount it could raise, the sum not to exceed two hundred dollars, and the *Iowa Farmer* expressed the hope that this law would speed the formation of county societies.[28] Whether because of the encouragement of the legislature, or the natural result of the development of the region, or the activity of certain leaders, by the middle fifties most of the organized counties in Iowa had formed societies and were holding yearly fairs.

The farmers came out of curiosity, at first. Almost all the counties report a small first fair, but growing interest and attendance.[29] The usual procedure was to hold an exhibit of cattle, grain, and fruit at the county seat, possibly in the courthouse yard, where modest premiums of a few dollars or subscriptions to some farm journal were given. Either the society then raised money and bought land, or some public-spirited member would offer a tract of five or ten acres as a site for subsequent fairs. This plot was fenced and sheds built; very soon, with the increasing interest in horse racing, a

---

[25] *Prairie Farmer*, 1:88 (November, 1841); 1:93 (December, 1841); 2:13 (February, 1842).

[26] Earle D. Ross, "The Evolution of the Agricultural Fair in the Northwest," Iowa Journal of History and Politics, 24:448 (July, 1926); *Laws of Iowa Territory, 1841*, Chap. 126; *Revised Statutes of the Territory of Iowa, 1842-'43*, Chap. 6; Myrtle Beinhauer, "The County, District, and State Agricultural Societies of Iowa," *Annals of Iowa* (third series) 20:50-51 (July, 1935).

[27] *Iowa Farmer and Horticulturist*, 1:40 (July, 1852); *Ia. Ag. Rept., 1857*, 410-14; *1858*, 364-6.

[28] *Laws of Iowa, 1852-54*, Chap. 45; Beinhauer, "The County, District, and State Agricultural Societies of Iowa," 53; *Iowa Farmer and Horticulturist*, 1:4 (May, 1852).

[29] *Ia. Ag. Rept., 1857*, 231, 249-51, 333-4; *1858*, 197-8, 324, 381.

track was laid out and a grandstand erected. On the two or three days that the fair was held, provided there was no rain, people would come from all over the county, some few to show their stock and produce, others merely to see what their neighbors were doing.[30]

By the late fifties many counties reported increasing interest in better farming as a result of the fairs. In spite of the constant complaint that, in general, farming methods were very poor, the fairs were breaking down conservatism and opposition to change. A farmer who saw better corn raised by careful selection of seed was encouraged to try his hand at the same process. If he saw fine Durham cattle or Poland China hogs, and the attention and interest they aroused, it was only natural that he would want to own better stock himself. Lee County reported in 1857 that "nine-tenths of the shorthorns introduced into the county, since 1852, were induced by the interest created by our exhibitions."[31] The same result applied to horses and hogs, to crops, and to tillage. Wherever a county society became firmly established, and fairs were held regularly, good results were reported. Mahaska County had "great improvements . . . in nearly every department of agricultural operations"; Keokuk County farmers were learning how to improve their methods; farmers in Mills County "flocked in from all directions" to the fairs; Monroe, Henry, and Davis also made reports of good progress.[32] The secretary of the State Agricultural Society observed in an optimistic vein in 1857: "That the method of cultivation has undergone a very great improvement in the last few years. . . ."[33]

A study of the reports of county secretaries for this same year, however, does not bear out his optimism. The recurring complaints were that the farmers cultivated too much land and that they cultivated that poorly, "stirring only a few inches of the top of the soil. . . ." Jasper County reported "a slovenly system of farming," while most of the newer counties in central and western Iowa told the same story. So much rich and fertile land was available that the farmer's chief interest was to cultivate as much as possible, rather than as well as possible.[34]

[30] Ibid., 1857, 335, 371, 426-8, 441-2, 444; 1858, 306-307, 324.
[31] Ibid., 1857, 337.
[32] Ibid., 230, 256, 354, 372; 1858, 295, 324; Sigourney Iowa Weekly Democrat, Apr. 15, 1859.
[33] Ia. Ag. Rept., 1857, 1.
[34] Ibid., 215, 237-8, 272, 283-4, 288, 369, 402-403.

Iowa's agricultural methods were no better and possibly no worse than the general over-all picture of Midwestern agriculture at that time. The worst features can be attributed to the exigencies of opening a new country. The secretary of the Adams County society reported in 1858: "The county being new, our farmers have necessarily devoted all their energies to increasing the number of acres cultivated, rather than to scientific agriculture."[35] There is no doubt that the local societies were to have a most beneficial effect upon agricultural practices, however.

A factor often ignored or not understood was that, in 1860, intensive agriculture as preached by the more progressive eastern farmers would not have been profitable or practicable in Iowa or in the other new sections of the Middle West. With cheap land, expensive labor, and low prices for grain and livestock, intensive agriculture, draining, and manuring were luxuries which the Iowa farmer could not afford. That the result was a rapid depletion of the soil does not alter the fact that in the mid-nineteenth century better farming was not economical. In the 1860 federal census of agriculture this problem was discussed at length: "High farming involves high prices. The system of cultivation and manuring which is profitable in Great Britain would not be remunerative in the State of New York, because labor is higher and produce lower, and the system which is profitable in New York might not be advantageous in Iowa." The improvement of farming methods is "simply a question of profit and loss. . . . We shall farm better as soon as such improvement is perceived to be profitable and necessary."[36]

Nevertheless, active county groups in Iowa continued to agitate for improvement of farming in spite of the logic of dollars and cents, and the movement grew for a state society. The county fairgrounds at Fairfield were offered as the site for the first State Fair, which was held in 1854. It was estimated that 7,000 to 10,000 people attended, coming from all the settled parts of the state, many camping on the way. A second fair was also held at Fairfield in 1855, attended by some 13,000 to 14,000 farmers.[37] Awards were made in thirty-two classes, ranging from Durham and Devon

[35] *Ja. Ag. Rept., 1858,* 196.

[36] *Eighth United States Census, 1860: Agriculture,* vii, ix.

[37] *Iowa Farmer and Horticulturist,* 1:22 (June, 1853); *Ja. Ag. Rept., 1855,* 3-4; *1874,* 486; Ross, "Evolution of the Agricultural Fair in the Northwest," 24, 50; Neely, *Agricultural Fair,* 96.

cattle, "Thorough Bred Horses," sheep, swine, farm machinery, grains, and fruits to breads and preserves, "sculptural marble," needlework, paintings, flowers, and "miscellaneous." Most of the premiums in the cattle shows were taken by Timothy Day of Van Buren County, others going to "a son and cousin of 'old Tim' also of the name of Day." The show of hogs was "meager, considering the amount of capital invested in Swine"; only ten grain entries were made because the fair was held too early for full crop maturity; only nine entries were made in the class of "Farm Machinery," whereas there "should have been a hundred." [38] All in all, however, these two fairs were a good beginning for a society which was to play a large part in the improvement of Iowa farming.

One of the regular features of the early fairs was an address by the president of the society or by some prominent farmer. At Fairfield in 1855, D. P. Holloway gave a typical address, filled with praise and advice to farmers, and leavened with a proper number of jokes. After noting the progress made in farming and stock breeding, he touched on a wide variety of subjects, urged government aid to agriculture, better farm representation in Washington, and tariff protection for farm products. Speaking of a problem already beginning to disturb agriculturists — the migration of the young men to the cities — he reminded them that "God made the country, and man made the town." On the subject of better husbandry, he told the story of the preacher who went through the neighborhood, praying at the fields of his parishioners, but at one field of an indolent and careless farmer he refused to offer up a prayer. "Ah, my friend," said he, "there is no use of praying here — *this field needs manure.*" [39]

Plowing matches were popular features of the early fairs, and aroused considerable interest. Plots of one-quarter acre were laid out for each contestant, and his work was timed. At the 1857 fair the average time was 55 minutes per acre — the shortest time being 48 minutes, and the longest 61 minutes. Here again the spirit of the times is manifest: the emphasis was on fast rather than on thorough cultivation. Few machines were shown at the earliest fairs, largely because of the difficulty, before the introduction of railroads, of transporting heavy equipment.[40]

Premiums at the fairs ranged from $1.00 to $15.00, and, as at the

[38] *Ja. Ag. Rept.*, *1855*, 14, 19, 28, and 7-31 *passim*; Keokuk *Gate City*, Oct. 13, 1855.
[39] *Ja. Ag. Rept.*, *1855*, 35–43 *passim*. Quoted material on p.42.
[40] *Ibid.*, *1857*, 26-7; *1859*, 63.

county fairs, subscriptions to some farm journal were also given. These journals, several of which were published in Iowa, are another phase of the campaign to improve farming methods. According to a student of the agricultural press in America, the progress of agriculture in the years before 1860 was due "in part to the educational impetus of the farm press together with other agencies such as agricultural societies, clubs, and fairs."[41] The policies of the editors were manyfold, not the least of which was the breaking down of old superstitions and prejudices against "book farming." They supported all progressive movements and all new inventions, they encouraged experimentation, and they reported at length all new methods of cultivation and of livestock breeding.[42]

The *Prairie Farmer*, which began publication in Chicago in 1841, was well patronized by the more progressive Iowa farmers. In 1842 the editor announced, under the heading "IOWA FOREVER!" receipt of the first Iowa subscription, from S. S. Carpenter of Keosauqua.[43] Thereafter agents in all the counties were rapidly appointed to secure subscriptions. Iowa farm journalism soon made its appearance. *The Iowa Farmer's Advocate* was published in Burlington for about a year, between 1847 and 1848, and was then merged with the *Valley Farmer* of St. Louis. *The Iowa Farmer and Horticulturist*, published at Burlington in 1853, the *Northwestern Farmer and Horticultural Journal*, at Dubuque in 1856, and the *North-Western Review*, at Keokuk in 1857 are some of the other Iowa farm journals of the early period. The *Iowa Farmer* and *Northwestern Farmer* were combined in 1860, and in 1862, at Des Moines, Mark Miller, editor of the *Northwestern Farmer*, started publication of the most important of the early Iowa farm journals, *The Iowa Homestead*.[44]

The goal of the farm journal editors was the same as that of the leaders of the agricultural societies — better farming. Their articles discussed new ways of plowing and cultivating, various breeds of livestock, types of seed to use, care of orchards and vineyards, the advantages of the various kinds of grasses, and the necessity for fertilizing the fields. The

---

[41] Demaree, *American Agricultural Press* . . ., 231.

[42] *Ibid.*, 39–86.

[43] *Prairie Farmer*, 2:96 (November, 1842).

[44] *Iowa Farmers' Advocate*, 1:189 (December, 1848); letter of Hosea B. Horn, *Annals of Iowa* (first series), 2:91 (April, 1863); *Northwestern Farmer*, 5:66 (February, 1860); C. R. F. Smith, "The Iowa Homestead," *The Palimpsest*, 11:230 (June, 1930).

Northwestern Farmer carried an article each month on the work the farmer should be doing at that season. All journals had special departments for the farmer's wife, complete with recipes, sewing instructions, and short stories. The advertising columns were filled with news of the latest farm machinery, advertisements for seeds, for the local nurseries, and — from the more settled areas — of farmlands for sale. The editors warred constantly against the conservatism of the average farmer; they printed editorials or letters from farmers on this theme. A correspondent from Wisconsin wrote to the *Northwestern Farmer* in 1856:

> Book farming is a subject which is often named by a certain class of agriculturists in connection with an off-hand slang, hurled as it were, at all who seem to be interested in agricultural progression, and improvement. Even to this day we see many that are clinging tenaciously to the "ways their father had" without even a thought as to there being a possibility of improvement upon the old method to which they seem fairly fastened.[45]

In 1857 "E. B. C." of Linn County added his comments to the subject:

> There is, perhaps, no class of people more tenacious in their ideas in regard to the improvements of the day, than the farmer. The old way of ploughing and reaping suits him so well, that he thinks it the only right way of farming. Talk to him of acquainting himself with the elements of his soil, that he may know what crops it is best calculated to produce, and he will tell you, it is all moonshine, or something equally absurd; and thus content himself that, "whatever is, is right," and thus continue to plod along in the old way, envious perhaps of his neighbor that raises more from fifty acres, than he does from double the amount of land, simply, by having the views and experience of others, combined with a systematic course of labor.[46]

Newspaper editors were also advocates of better farming. They filled their farm columns with glowing tributes to the Iowa soil, with suggestions for improving husbandry, and with reprints of agricultural articles from eastern papers and journals. Since their readers were mostly farmers, editors made constant efforts to appeal to this class, and in the early days accepted produce in payment for subscriptions. Newspapers carried agricultural columns, or "Farmers' Corners," and the editors constantly urged the

[45] *Northwestern Farmer*, 1:190 (July, 1856).
[46] *Ibid.*, 2:374 (October, 1857).

farmers to write "for their papers." [47] Some few responded to this request, and now and then a lively exchange would appear.

In 1859 "K" wrote to the Bloomfield *Democratic Clarion,* urging farmers to read more agricultural papers and to hold meetings for discussion of the best ways of farming. The editor added a paragraph endorsing these suggestions and asked for more comments from farmers. The result was a letter bristling with anti-book-farming sentiments. The editor took the blast quite seriously and assured his readers that he printed the letter because his columns were "open to all," and not because he agreed with this "radical and ultra old fogy farmer." The "radical" commented on the suggestions of "K" that farmers read agricultural journals:

> Now this all looks well enough on paper, but what will one gain by reading the Northwestern Farmer or any other agricultural paper got up by men with silk gloves on, who don't know a potato from a saw log unless it is cooked. The first thing you will find like enough in one of these papers, is a pair of Bantam (or some such name,) chickens, about the size of a sore finger, and fit for nothing but to look at. As for my part I would not give a copper for a chicken that cannot scratch for a living, and roost on the fence all winter without freezing their toes off.
>
> Then, perhaps, the next thing you will see is a pair of great fat lazy hogs — called Suffolk or Chester White, or some other big name, that Mr. Kimball, at Iowa City, has for sale at $10 a pair — with a long chapter on their history and habits and remarks on *hogs* generally, though they always call them *porkers.* Now, what use have we in this country for Suffolk hogs, or any other hog that can't root?— I tell you these Suffolks wont do — turn them into the woods, or out in a dog fennel lane to get a living, and they will lay in a fence corner until they starve to death. What we want here is a hog with a nose to him so that ho [sic] can root; legs so that he can climb a hazel bush, and hair on him to keep him from freezing; such a hog as this you can turn out at four months old to take care of himself, and if he is of any account, will live without a shelter, and outrun the dogs, and average 200 pounds at 18 months old, with very little trouble — in short, Sir, we want an *active* thorough-going hog that can take care of himself.

[47] Burlington *Iowa Patriot,* June 20, 1859; Burlington *Hawk-Eye,* Oct. 30, 1845; Sigourney *Keokuk County News,* Oct. 20, 1860; Burlington *Wisconsin Territorial Gazette,* June 2, 1838; Mount Pleasant *Home Journal,* March 17, 1859; Bloomfield *Democratic Clarion,* Nov. 30, 1859.

Then there are pictures of the "Cotwold" sheep, that will shear 16 pounds of wool and turn out 200 pounds of mutton — that you can cook with two sticks of wood, and all that kind of thing, but they have got to be sheltered in houses and taken care of like babies, or they will die off; so they are not fit for much but to make pictures of after all.

Then you will find long chapters on posies and verbenas, and Sunflowers, and all kinds of flummydiddles for flower pots for women and children to play with, but for no earthly use except mere show, and after you get through with all these you will find long chapters on building barns and cow stables, and hog houses, and all such stuff. Just as though we didn't know that a thousand dollars invested in a barn could be put out at 25 per cent. interest, and that people could stack their hay or small grain out of doors, or that a rail fence or jack oak thicket was a good enough shelter for cattle and hogs, besides, who wants to be at the trouble of cleaning out cow stables, and having great piles of manure in his way. Now this is the kind of thing a fellow will learn from these books on farming, and farmers are gone crazy with new fangled notions, and before long everybody will have to build fine barns and nice fences, and raise posies and sunflowers, and all such trash, or leave the country. As for my part, I'll show 'em that they can't train in an

OLD SEED CORNER [48]

The letter was answered in a later issue of the paper, but the reply was more an attack on the possible unsavory reputation of "Old Seed Corner" than a refutation of his opinions on farming.[49] With that, the debate died down. It serves, however, to point up in perhaps a too highly colored light the opinion of many farmers on scientific farming. It was this attitude against which the agricultural societies, the farm journals, and the newspapers fought and were to fight for many years to come.

A fourth movement for better farming — perhaps the most effective because it reached more farmers — was the agitation for the formation of local farmers' clubs. Fairs brought agriculturists together only once or twice a year; a farmers' club brought intimate discussion of farm problems and questions almost to the farmer's dooryard. These local clubs, more or less long-lived, were formed in various places throughout the state. As early as 1847 such a club was reported in Des Moines County; "Another

[48] Bloomfield *Democratic Clarion*, Dec. 7, 1859.
[49] *Ibid.*, Dec. 21, 1859.

Farmer's Club" was announced in 1848. A "Farmer's Festival" was held at Washington in 1857, "to inaugurate the manufacture of sugar and molasses," where premiums were also offered for the best crops, and for breads, butter, and pies.⁵⁰ The meetings of these clubs were usually held at the township schoolhouses during the winter, the farmer's slack season, and many attended who did not go to the fairs or read the agricultural papers. The discussions often encouraged the farmer to read some of these papers, and many a farmer began "to realize that there were other people who lived in the world besides his grandfather."⁵¹ The clubs subscribed to several farm papers and passed them around among the members. In this way some of the "prejudice against 'book larning' " was being dissipated.⁵²

A typical call for a farmers' meeting appeared in an Albia paper in 1865:

> We call attention to the meeting at the Court House Friday evening, and invite all that can possibly, and feel any interest in the cultivation of fruit trees and shrubbery, to come to the meeting. Some branch of Agriculture or Horticulture, perhaps both, will be discussed in an entertaining lecture by persons of experience. It is also proposed on that occasion to permanently organize an agricultural club, and make arrangements for establishing a library in connection therewith, so that members may, at trifling expense, avail themselves of such valuable information upon these important subjects — too much neglected by all.⁵³

A farmers' club was organized at Oskaloosa in February of 1865. A Henry County club was suggested by the Mount Pleasant paper, which also promised to publish the proceedings of each meeting for the benefit of all. "The experience of a New York farmer is not as valuable to you as that of an Iowa farmer," the editor reminded his readers, in urging their support of the club. The county already had two such groups, one bearing the name of "Progressive Farmers' Club."

> They now have about fifty members, and hold weekly meetings, at which subjects of interest to stock raisers, Agriculturists and Horticulturists are discussed. Thus far, we are told, the meetings have proved highly interesting and beneficial. — They are also

⁵⁰ *Iowa Farmers' Advocate*, 1:69 (November, 1847); 1:93 (January, 1848); Washington *Press*, Dec. 2, 1857.
⁵¹ *Ja. Ag. Rept., 1859*, 11.
⁵² *Ibid.*, 11; *Iowa Farmers' Advocate*, 1:69 (November, 1847).
⁵³ Albia *Weekly Union*, March 30, 1865.

> collecting a Library, and have already about fifty volumes of appropriate works. This is a most commendable move, and we hope to hear of similar organizations in all parts of the County.[54]

These are only examples of the many farmers' clubs being formed throughout Iowa at this period. Some of them were forerunners of the Granges of the 1870's; others continued their independent existence and their avowed purpose of education and entertainment.

These clubs attempted to improve agricultural practices by discussion and by providing agricultural journals and books for the members. Their importance in this respect can be seen as early as 1861 in a notice by William Duane Wilson regarding the "patent office seeds" which he had for distribution. The Patent Office at Washington had, since the late fifties, furnished seeds to local editors and to secretaries of agricultural societies, in the hope that these individuals would distribute them, either for agricultural or political purposes, to the farmers of their localities. The recipients of this governmental largess were supposed to report on the success or failure of the seeds, but few bothered to do so. The Lucas County Agricultural Society, in 1859, urged that such seeds be given only to the best farmers, "as their votes could not be changed by such bribes," and they would be the ones most likely to give full reports on the results.[55] Wilson proposed "a more efficient plan."

> I have determined, therefore, at least this year to supply first, Agricultural Clubs which have an efficient organization, when I am informed of the same by the Secretaries and their post office address. Second, County Agricultural Societies when notified by the Secretaries thereof, that they want them. Third, to reliable individuals who may write to this office for them, in the order their applications are received.[56]

The chief work and interest of the clubs, however, remained in the discussion of practical farm problems. The subjects discussed were legion. The farmers of Warren County were interested in bringing new manufacturing and new capital to their county. They also sought a remedy for the "present exorbitant railroad charges" and debated the question of the "best representation of the working class in our Legislature." Jefferson County farmers

[54] Mount Pleasant *Home Journal*, Feb. 17, Nov. 3, 1865.
[55] *Ja. Ag. Rept.*, *1859*, 317.
[56] Keosauqua *Des Moines News*, Feb. 23, 1861.

were interested in wheat, cattle raising, the improvement of agricultural societies, buttermaking, corn raising, profits in orchards, and haymaking. The ever-present problem — how to make farming more profitable — was likewise discussed several times and at great length.[57]

Mahaska County had a club of "live farmers," but there were a number of "old fogies" in the county who would have nothing to do with them. "They say 'book farming' is a humbug, and that agricultural papers are a nuisance, got up by a set of sharpers to swindle honest men out of their hard earned substance, and that they are *too poor to patronize such scamps.*"[58] The prejudice against scientific farming was still alive.

The evils against which these various forces battled were, as has been pointed out, the natural outcome of pioneer conditions. A Burlington editor, as early as 1844, suggested that the time had arrived when the farmers could pay more attention to scientific agriculture.

> In the early settlement of the territory, subsistence was by necessity, wrung from the soil in the simplest and least artificial manner. The demand was not for stock of particular breeds but for any kind, that would furnish the staples of labor and sustenance, but with the increase of means has come also an ability to make improvements in every department of the calling, and superadded to this, as we doubt not, the inclination.[59]

Other evils, more deep-rooted, were the natural inertia of many farmers, their refusal to change, and a lack of education which made many of the principles of scientific management incomprehensible mysteries. To offset prejudice and ignorance agricultural education was already being agitated. In 1858, at the session of the Seventh General Assembly, Benjamin F. Gue, Robert A. Richardson, and Ed Wright had sponsored a bill for the establishment of a State Agricultural College and Farm. The bill passed, a board of trustees was appointed, the site in Story County selected, and the Farm opened. Passage of the federal land grant for agricultural colleges in 1862 aided the struggling institution, but it was not until 1869 that the College was opened to students.[60]

But before the State Agricultural College could take over the leadership

[57] Fairfield *Tribune*, April 16, 30, Dec. 24, 1885; Dec. 2, 16, 1886.
[58] *Prairie Farmer*, 43:272 (August 24, 1872).
[59] Burlington *Hawk-Eye*, Dec. 19, 1844.
[60] Earle D. Ross, *A History of the Iowa State College* . . . (Ames, 1942), 16ff.

in the better farming movement, that is, for the thirty years between 1840 and 1870, the fight for improved methods was almost entirely a matter of individual and group effort in the various communities. The College would re-emphasize what agricultural societies and editors had long preached. It would have the advantage, however, of these thirty years of propaganda. What had been accomplished? Had the untiring work of these groups and individuals borne any fruit in the state as a whole, or had their work been confined to a few like-minded and progressive farmers? Were Iowa farming methods "better" in 1870 than in 1840, and if so, whose is the credit?

One source of answers to these questions is the *Report* published annually by the State Agricultural Society, beginning in 1854. For the first few years these volumes are somewhat sketchy, being mostly accounts of the annual fair. But with 1857 they take on an increased value, both for the farmers of that era and for the historian of the present. Aside from the record of the State Fair and the activities of the Board of the Society, the books contained essays on farming in its many phases and reports from each county which had a local society and fair. These *Reports*, thus, give a running account of changing farming conditions over the years.

One conclusion is at once evident. Whereas almost all counties report growing improvement in breeds of livestock, few report improved methods of tillage. The Woodbury County secretary wrote in 1859:

> With a soil as rich and fertile as is ours, the great practical study of the farmer is not with reference to enriching the soil, but rather to the adaptation of seeds and modes of culture to the soil. . . . Care as to the rotation of crops has never been practiced with us. Some fields have been planted in corn for 12 years, and it must be owned, with more than average success. It has not been established by our experience that rotation in our soil and climate is essential to success.[61]

In Allamakee County, in 1857, a similar report was made: "Farmers generally sow to suit their own circumstances, without regard to roatation [sic] of crops, and generally have a fair yield."[62] The Belle Plaine Union Agricultural Association, consisting of Benton, Tama, Iowa, and Poweshiek counties, reported no rotation of crops in 1868, since "Many seem

[61] *Ja. Ag. Rept., 1859*, 416.
[62] *Ibid., 1857*, 197.

to have imbibed the erroneous idea that the strength of the soil is inexhaustible."[63] Evidence of soil exhaustion begins to show up in some county reports, however. In Decatur County in 1857 wheat averaged 20 bushels per acre, while corn averaged 75; thirteen years later, in 1870, the wheat average had fallen to 9 bushels, that of corn to 40, although it must be noted that this was a year of a bad infestation of "chintz" bugs.[64] Allamakee County farmers, in 1857, averaged 20 to 25 bushels of wheat and 70 bushels of corn per acre; in 1868 the wheat average had fallen to 15 bushels and corn to 40.[65]

Floyd County, in 1863, reported there was "Too little attention . . . to the economy and use of manures." By 1868, however, things had changed. "The manure from the stables is more generally spread upon the land, and the eye can everywhere detect its effects."[66] In Jackson County, in 1857, the plowing methods consisted of "skimming the ground"; by 1870 the county secretary reported that "Farming is done with more method and on a more improved plan than in former years. Deep fall plowing is the motto of the farmer, and the farmer's cry of 'The land is rich enough,' is not so often heard."[67]

Cattle were increasingly important in the farm economy in these years, and interest in improved breeds was growing, although the great majority were still "grades" and "scrubs."[68] Distance from market, plenty of wild grass, and large crops of corn made cattle raising profitable, especially in the more isolated western counties. But a general desire to improve the breed of the stock was lacking, although both newspapers and farm leaders never tired of pointing out to farmers the advantage of better breeding.

On the other hand, hogs were increasing not only in number but also in quality. In 1857 Marshall County farmers had paid little attention to improvements in hogs, but by 1870 Chester Whites had become the favorite. "The merchant vies with the farmer," wrote the county secretary, "and

[63] *Ibid.*, *1868*, 341.
[64] *Ibid.*, *1857*, 232; *1870*, 441.
[65] *Ibid.*, *1857*, 195; *1868*, 329.
[66] *Ibid.*, *1863*, 389; *1868*, 370.
[67] *Ibid.*, *1857*, 281; *1870*, 463.
[68] Council Bluffs *Bugle*, Dec. 26, 1867; Fontanelle *Adair County Register*, June 16, 1870; *Ja. Ag. Rept.*, *1867*, 9; *1868* 13-14.

the banker with the merchant in efforts to produce the best breed of hogs."[69] Davis County was "*some on Hogs*," although the majority were still of the "old, long legged, sharp-nosed, slab-sided, fence despising races." In 1857 no hogs were raised in Decatur County except for home consumption; in 1870 various types of improved breeds, such as the "Magee," Poland China, Chester White, and Berkshire were "generally disseminated."[70] In 1865 A. G. Nye of Libertyville, in Jefferson County, contributed an essay on "Hog Raising" to the *Report* of the Agricultural Society:

> It has been a common practice with farmers in this county, as it is indeed in most new countries, to breed hogs without any regard to the connection of the families bred from, and to raise them upon the principle of "root hog or die." That this is to turn them out in to the woods or on to the prairies to get their own living, feeding them a little corn, just enough to keep them [alive] through the winter, and letting them root for a living through the summer, then shutting them up about the first of October to fatten, feeding about six weeks and then sending them to market. In this way we have succeeded in raising a good deal of snout and bristles but not much pork. A better practice is however now pursued by most of the farmers of Jefferson county. The high price of pork having stimulated them to increase and improve their breed of hogs.[71]

In 1867 the secretary of the State Agricultural Society was optimistic about the general improvement in Iowa hogs. "Since this stock is the principal medium of converting the corn crop into cash," he reported, "any suggestion to improve the quality is seized upon with avidity, and the farmer who has not abandoned the common, and adopted the improved breed, must prove a rare exception."[72] Thus, by the late sixties, the "finer bloods" of swine were popular and much sought after in Iowa.[73]

These examples could be multiplied many times. The general refrain by 1870 was: better livestock, more attention to such adjuncts as fruit, sheep, sorghum, live hedges, and better barns and outbuildings for the cattle; but poor cultivation, little use of fertilizers, and not much attention

[69] *Ja. Ag. Rept., 1857*, 368; *1870*, 493.
[70] *Ibid., 1857*, 227-8, 232; *1870*, 441.
[71] *Ibid., 1865*, 358-9.
[72] *Ibid., 1867*, 10.
[73] *Ibid., 1868*, 361.

to rotation of crops nor to the deep plowing which was then considered essential to proper husbandry.

Thus it would seem that "book farming" had some successes to show for thirty years of propaganda, but also some failures. Several reasons can be cited. It is obvious that better livestock, particularly hogs, brought a more immediate return in money than did the slow and painstaking task of properly cultivating and feeding the soil. In these years the Iowa farmer was gradually moving toward the Corn Belt pattern of farming — corn, hogs, and cattle. Not only the pleas of the scientific farmers, but higher prices for better animals, can be credited with improvements in Iowa livestock between 1840 and 1870. Nevertheless, it was the scientific farmers who had led the way, for without their suggestions and examples, and the backing of editors and businessmen, the necessary knowledge for improving livestock would have been lacking, no matter what the desire might have been.

Another factor had changed Iowa farming methods radically, but whether for better or worse was a question. The decades from 1840 to 1870 saw many new farm machines invented and put into use. These machines enabled the farmer to cultivate more land with fewer farm laborers and to do it faster, but this very fact hurt the cause of scientific farming. Reapers, mowers, planters, the sulky or riding plow, and many other machines were admirably adapted to the level and rolling prairies of the Middle West. These machines did not increase yields, however, nor make for more scientific farming. Rather, "the tendency was more to wear out the soil than to improve it."[74] Intensive farming, urged by government bureaus and agricultural societies, was not furthered by the new machinery. "To reap with less manpower was the object chiefly in view."[75] The mechanical revolution in farming was, thus, in some respects the enemy of the scientific revolution in agriculture. A government report concluded that "The success and prosperity of the American farmer are due to the unbounded fertility of the soils, the cheapness of farm lands, and the privilege of utilizing modern inventions in machinery rather than to systematic organization and efficient farm management."[76]

[74] Shannon, *Farmer's Last Frontier* . . ., 147.
[75] William T. Hutchinson, "The Reaper Industry and Midwestern Agriculture," in Avery Craven (ed.), *Essays in Honor of William E. Dodd* (Chicago, 1935), 117.
[76] Quoted in Shannon, *Farmer's Last Frontier* . . ., 147.

Practically all Iowa counties, in their list of improvements during the 1860's, included the increased use of machinery of all kinds. Even here, though, many paid no attention to the proper care of this equipment. Expensive machinery was often left where it was last used, or where it would be convenient for use the next season, but meanwhile it was exposed to wind and weather. In this way farm tools wore out in two or three years. In Clarke County $300,000 worth of machinery had been bought in the two years before 1870, but few farmers understood how to care for this investment.

> Pass through the county and it is no infrequent sight to see a costly mower on the prairie just where the farmer concluded that if we had a mild winter he had enough hay cut. It is true that the "implement" will be handy to hitch to next haying but how long will it last exposed to sunshine, rain, or prairie fires, and is it paid for; other costly labor savers are remaining in the last ditch, others stacked against a breach in the fence. . . .[77]

This picture was not uncommon in the sixties. Farmers were growing prosperous during the war years, the demand for their produce was high, and new laborsaving machinery was offered on attractive terms. The farmer bought the machines, usually "on time," but had little knowledge of how to care for them, and often wore them out before they were paid for. He could "ride in his seat and do nearly all his work from April to October," wrote one enthusiastic booster, who added that "Labor-saving machinery is completely revolutionizing the work of the farm."[78]

Farming was indeed "revolutionized" during the decades before 1870, yet this very revolution was increasing the exhaustion of the soil. Practicing "book farmers" were too few to prevent the steady march of worn-out farmland, a march which had begun on the shores of the Atlantic and was steadily moving into the prairie lands of the Middle West. These same rich prairies tended to make farmers "lazy, careless and slovenly," according to the author of an essay on "General Farming" in the 1866 Iowa Agricultural Society Report. Some, who saw their fields producing less each year, gave up, sold out, and moved farther west, but those who remained — if they practiced soil conservation, sowed their pastures to tame grasses for their stock, and rotated their crops — obtained "good

[77] Osceola Republican, Dec. 1, 1870.
[78] Fontanelle Adair County Register, July 25, 1867.

results of their better system of tillage." "The truth is," continued the author, "it requires greater skill and genius to farm well and with success, than most people are aware of. Any ninnyhammer may be called a farmer, simply because he can plow, and sow, and reap, as his father did before him. But farming is a science that few persons well understand. It requires much thought, patience and skill, as well as hard muscle."[79] M. V. Ashby of Eddyville, in Wapello County, contributed an essay on "General Farming in Iowa" to the 1868 *Report* of the State Agricultural Society:

> General farming in Iowa . . . is a system of exhaustion. In every community our attention has been drawn to the careless manner in which farmers regard the manuring of their farms. They do [not] often manure their farms we admit, but while they do occasionally, we believe the extraordinary labor they force the soil to submit to, requires a corresponding return of some substance which will strengthen and support the soil while being so heavily taxed. In the cultivation of corn more land is used by farmers than they possibly can do justice to. This we find is general. Year after year fields are used without endeavoring to restore or strengthen what the crop has consumed. There are so very few exceptions to this rule that we do not consider them. It is notoriously general among farmers. . . .
>
> In the present *modus operandi* for sowing and planting, the rule in Iowa is to continue to sow and reap until there is, finally, a sowing but nothing to reap. . . .[80]

The western custom of moving the barn instead of the manure pile was ruinous to the Iowa soil, and it was this habit against which the agricultural leaders talked and wrote. A future governor of Iowa, Cyrus Clay Carpenter, told the Webster County Agricultural Society in 1869 that "unless the laws of nature have been repealed in favor of the Iowa farmer . . . those who come after us will find that the strength of a soil, now unequaled, has vanished into thin air beneath our feet. . . ." The farmer needed intelligence, not "main strength and awkwardness," said Carpenter. "As much as some men may belittle the idea of book farming, I tell you, intelligence in any business, tells upon its success."[81] Peter Melendy,

[79] *Ja. Ag. Rept., 1866*, 481, 483, 486.
[80] *Ibid., 1868*, 477-8.
[81] *Ibid., 1869*, 339-40, 343.

Suel Foster, William Duane Wilson, J. M. Shaffer, and a long list of others constantly echoed this plea for soil conservation.[92]

Unfortunately, all too many farmers had the attitude of the easterner turned Iowan who wrote home to the Barre *Gazette* in Massachusetts: he had seen "wheat and corn growing in fields where the same grains have grown fifteen or twenty years, with out the use of a particle of fertilizer," and although he "supposed that this could [not] be the case for an indefinite period . . . it will be long enough for the present generation to get rich and retire from the farm."[83] At the same time, in Montgomery County, the farmers considered manure a nuisance and usually burned their straw piles. " 'Our land is rich enough without it,' is the cry of too many," reported the county secretary. In Marion County the farmers built portable barns so that they could be moved easily when the manure became "too plenty for the comfort of stock." When manures were used for fertilizer, as in Madison County, it was done "more with a view of getting them out of the way than to fertilize the fields." The result, continued the county report, was a decline in yields of wheat and corn. In Jones County the farmers had all the laborsaving machines, but did no fertilizing.[84] Although more encouraging reports came from the older, eastern counties, the general picture of farming methods by 1870 was little better than that of 1840.

As the years passed, farm leaders came to realize that the solution lay not alone with the agricultural societies and farm journals, but in the movement for better agricultural education. Peter Melendy told the State Agricultural Society in 1868:

> We may, and no doubt to some extent have, awakened in the farmers who yearly come up to our fairs, a desire to enter into a generous competition for the greater improvement of their farms. We can not, however, teach the difficulty with and the remedy for a worn out, barren field, whose weather-beaten surface is a mockery to the most commendable zeal; we can not explain why the same acre will not produce good wheat through all the years, nor why manure seems thrown away in one place, and comparatively worthless in another. In short, we can not

---

[82] *Ibid., 1859,* 350–52; *1863,* 10-11, 96–102; *1864,* 224–6; *1865,* 38.
[83] Quoted in Fontanelle *Adair County Register,* July 25, 1867.
[84] *Ja. Ag. Rept., 1868,* 396, 414, 420, 429.

make plain what a farm is made of, nor of what are composed the crops yearly reaped from it. These things the farmer must learn elsewhere. An agricultural education is therefore essential to progressive farming.[85]

By 1870, then, it was evident that individual and group action and example were not enough — state-sponsored education was necessary to carry the knowledge of the few to the many. "Book farming" must be taught by the schools, not by speeches at county fairs. That the fairs and the farmers' clubs, the farm journals and local newspapers had contributed mightily to the campaign for better farming is undoubted, but their work had been preliminary only: it paved the way for the more active and more far-reaching work of systematic agricultural education in the schools. Agricultural societies and fairs would continue their work, and Iowa's famous farm journals, *Iowa Homestead*, *Wallaces' Farmer*, and *Successful Farming*, would enjoy wider and wider circulations: but Iowa farmers, in the future, would look to the State College at Ames for education, guidance, and "book farming."

[85] *Ibid.*, 56.

A Decade of Transportation Fever in Burlington, Iowa, 1845–1855
✣ GEORGE A. BOECK

PERHAPS IOWANS had little use for such economic institutions as banks in the 1840s and 1850s, but other kinds of economic facilities were vital to the state's development. The establishment of an adequate transportation system was imperative, for example, if Iowa was to continue expanding as an important agricultural region. Moreover, early-day merchants needed a means of transportation to ship goods to settlers in the surrounding countryside. As population increased in eastern Iowa, intense rivalries developed between the rapidly expanding river communities, and merchants competed vigorously for the business of the backcountry inhabitants.

The problems, considerations, and solutions involved in Iowa's transportation dilemma are considered in this article by George Boeck. He presents the community of Burlington as a representative area during the decade following 1845 when "internal improvements fever" had infected all small towns in Iowa. In an attempt to find an adequate solution, Burlington citizens turned first to river transportation, speculating about clearing the rapids along the Mississippi River between Burlington and Keokuk. A second consideration was to build plank roads which, for a time at least, appeared as a sound alternative. But, as in all communities, the final and most efficient system was the railroad, and by the end of the decade under discussion the citizens of Burlington had enthusiastically accepted the "iron horse" as the best solution to their dilemma.

Although a case study of one community only, Boeck's article provides excellent information and insight regarding many Iowa communities in the mid-1800s as they too attempted to solve their transportation problems.

From *Iowa Journal of History,*
Vol. 56, No. 2, April 1958,
pp. 129–52.

A DECADE OF TRANSPORTATION FEVER IN BURLINGTON, IOWA, 1845-1855

*By George A. Boeck**

Burlington and Brighton, Council Bluffs and Centerville, Des Moines and Deedsville — towns of Iowa, towns of the Middle West, towns of America. The map is freckled with them. They grew to be giants, they withered and died, they held their own. They had the same aspirations and fears, they shared common experiences, they fought one another with the same weapons. This is a chapter in the life of one town, Burlington, and a decade of transportation fever, a malady from which few towns were immune. Burlington in itself has but slight intrinsic interest, but as a representative community its story is of great importance. What it experienced was experienced by countless other towns; therein lies its significance. What was happening in Burlington was happening in the other towns of Iowa, Wisconsin, and Minnesota; it had already occurred in Ohio and Pennsylvania; it was yet to occur in the still younger areas of the West. This representative quality and the implications it holds for the larger state, regional, and national picture should be kept firmly in mind as the Burlington effort is related.

The Mississippi River between Iowa and Illinois does not afford many natural sites for settlement. Where it does, however, early communities took hold and grew, reaping the benefits which that great artery of trade presented. The Mississippi was to the river towns as the Atlantic to the eastern seaports, vital to their early existence, shaping their character, and directing their orientation. Beneficent and destructive, placid and turbulent, sparkling and muddy, the river made its presence constantly felt. For the men of the early river towns the River was omnipresent.

One such town, Flint Hills — named for the bluffs which rose for a hundred feet above the river — was marked by nature for settlement. At a single point the bluffs retired before the river, leaving a bottom area suffi-

*George A. Boeck is assistant professor of history at The College of St. Catherine, St. Paul.

ciently high for a business district surrounded by a crescent of hills suitable for residences. When settlement was authorized in the Black Hawk Purchase in 1833, Flint Hills was occupied immediately. From the outset it showed promise of becoming one of Iowa's leading towns. In an early account of the Wisconsin Territory, Lieutenant Albert Lea noted that Burlington (the older, more picturesque name Flint Hills had been changed) contained some 400 inhabitants and that choice lots were selling for $1,500. The Lieutenant concluded that Burlington, the county seat for Des Moines County, must necessarily capture the trade of a large and fertile back country, since it was the only convenient site for a settlement between the Chacaqua (the present-day Skunk) and Iowa rivers.[1] In addition to its natural advantages, Burlington was fortunate in that it was not only the seat of one of the two huge counties created in the Black Hawk Purchase, but territorial capital as well. This was undoubtedly a stimulus to the town in this early period; the sale of public lands in 1838, for example, brought 2,000 men to Burlington.[2] With a population of 1,200 in 1838, and 1,600 a year later, Burlington was the leading town of the Territory and had already acquired a superior attitude toward younger and smaller communities.

A town on the river could be but a temporary capital, however, and the future of Burlington lay in trade and commerce rather than in political administration. It was a port of entry to the most populous area of the Territory. Immigrants poured into Iowa at Burlington; every steamboat came loaded with settlers, and the Illinois shore reminded observers of an army continually encamped, despite the ferry's efforts to thin its ranks.[3] The young town's primary function during the 1830's was to supply the surrounding countryside with goods imported from older areas. In the late thirties her merchants were still importing pork, lard, butter, and bacon from Cincinnati. By 1840, however, a local merchant shipped 5,000 pounds of lard and several thousand pounds of bacon to New England, as well as several lots of beef to the South. The same season a Burlington editor watched scores of flatboats from Iowa, some built and loaded at Burlington, pass down the river.[4] The Territory was becoming an exporting region.

[1] Albert M. Lea, *Notes on the Wisconsin Territory; Particularly with Reference to the Iowa District, or Black Hawk Purchase* (Philadelphia, 1836), 36.
[2] Louis Pelzer, "Early Burlington," *The Palimpsest*, 15:249 (July, 1934).
[3] Burlington *Iowa Patriot*, Oct. 17, 1839.
[4] Burlington *Iowa Hawk-Eye and Patriot*, Apr. 2, Sept. 19, 1840.

The decade of the 1840's was marked by population growth, economic expansion, and growing rivalry with other towns. South of Burlington, at the southern tip of the Territory, was Keokuk, while to the north were the rival towns of Davenport and Dubuque. Burlington still relied on the river. In 1839 a local editor expressed satisfaction that the legislature was ignoring canals and railroads, which he felt led only to bankruptcy. His opinion was that railroads would not be needed in Iowa for the next twenty-five years, perhaps never. The wise policy was to work for better roads and improved navigation of the Mississippi.[5] The latter was a source of great frustration to Burlington. Thirty miles down the river were the "Lower Rapids" extending some twelve miles above the town of Keokuk and impassable for large boats during low water. Throughout the 1830's and 1840's Burlington's goal was to see this obstacle cleared. She complained bitterly that her farmers could not compete with those below the Rapids and that many of her staples could not be exported at a profit because of the increased freight costs imposed at Keokuk. Burlington citizens compiled statistics to show that in a single season the $100,000 in produce exported from Burlington lost 22½ per cent of its value at the Rapids and that the loss to her back country was $50,000 in a single year.[6] Long articles were written to demonstrate the practicability of the task of clearing the Rapids from an engineering standpoint, and politicians were praised or damned in proportion to their efforts to secure government aid for the project. Especially galling was the fact that Keokuk was benefiting from this greatest obstacle to Burlington's prosperity. Keokuk was an ambitious young town, advantageously located. Southernmost of the Iowa river towns, it commanded the entrance into the Territory from the south by way of the Mississippi. It also benefited from the Des Moines River which flows from the northwest across Iowa to the southeastern corner of the state, where it joins the Mississippi. This "Gate City" was already tapping the trade of the rich Des Moines Valley, which Burlington coveted, and an intense rivalry grew between the two towns. Burlington was convinced that Keokuk wanted to keep the "Gate" shut, monopolize the trade of the interior, restrict Burlington to a small back area, and watch her wither and perish.

In 1845 considerable enthusiasm developed in Burlington over a pro-

[5] Burlington *Iowa Territorial Gazette*, Nov. 23, 1849.
[6] Burlington *Weekly Hawk-Eye*, Oct. 30, Sept. 18, 1845. (Cited hereafter as *Hawk-Eye*.)

posed Memphis Convention of western and southern states which was called to discuss the development of those regions. Surely this great gathering would convince the government that the Rapids must be improved. Public meetings were held in Burlington, and prominent local citizens were chosen to go to Memphis. Augustus Caesar Dodge, influential Democratic politician; William B. Ewing, respected merchant; and James G. Edwards, well-known Whig editor, represented Burlington at the convention. Delegates from nineteen states and territories attended the meeting; John C. Calhoun of South Carolina presided as president, and John Bell of Tennessee and A. C. Dodge of Iowa served as vice-presidents.[7] The results, however, were negligible, and an embittered Burlington began casting about for other solutions to her problem. St. Louis was severely criticized for her lack of interest in the improvement of the Rapids, and the Burlington *Hawk-Eye* predicted that the Missouri metropolis would lose the trade of the Upper Mississippi to Chicago when that growing city connected the Lakes and the Mississippi by rail. The editor suggested that Burlington herself might one day have a railroad.[8]

By 1847 imports at Burlington amounted to 3,776 tons, while exports tototaled over 14,000 tons, chiefly corn, oats, wheat, flour, pork, and barley. Burlington merchants, claiming they had suffered losses of nearly $160,000 due to the Rapids, increasingly turned to the idea of a possible railroad connection with some line in Illinois.[9] This idea was hastened by reports of a proposed north-south railroad from Dubuque to Keokuk which would bypass Burlington. The Burlington editors naturally attacked this idea as impracticable. The Chicago and St. Louis markets were compared as to prices to the detriment of the latter. Burlington did not give up hopes for improvement of the Rapids; indeed, she continued to urge such projects and to send delegates to future Rapids conventions, but the seeds of railroad fever had been planted.

While the idea of a railroad to the east was beginning to crystalize, Burlington faced the immediate problem of her trade with the interior. Lacking waterways west, she depended on inadequate roads which became impassable in wet seasons. Impressed with the success of plank roads in the East, a group of prominent businessmen began urging the construction of

[7] *Ibid.*, Sept. 25, Nov. 27, 1845.
[8] *Ibid.*, Jan. 15, 1846.
[9] *Ibid.*, Sept. 23, 1847.

such a road from Burlington to Mount Pleasant, twenty-six miles to the west, the central point from which the surrounding back country sent its goods to Burlington. Plank roads had originated in Russia and came to the United States by way of Canada. They were constructed of long heavy planks which were laid on top of wooden "stringers" which were in turn set into a graded roadbed. This gave a smooth, fast surface over which horses could pull the heaviest loads in excellent time even in wet seasons. Like the eastern turnpikes, the plank roads were toll roads, and the cheapness and speed of construction were thought to be an advantage over the turnpikes. The difficulty and expense of keeping them in good repair, their disappointingly rapid deterioration by rotting, and the avoidance of the payment of tolls by users were to cause their failure, but for a time they seemed a panacea to solve the transportation problem. Introduced in New York in the mid-1840's, "plank road fever" momentarily swept the nation. By 1857 New York, Pennsylvania, New Jersey, and Maryland had invested $10,000,000 in plank roads.[10]

The fact that as early as January, 1849, articles began appearing in the Burlington papers describing the advantages of plank roads over macadamized roads and even railroads is indicative of the alertness of the town's citizens in seeking a solution to their transportation dilemma. In January of that year the editor of the Burlington *Hawk-Eye* expressed confidence that the twenty-six miles to Mount Pleasant would be planked and that the road would eventually be extended to the towns of Fairfield and Washington.[11] A public meeting in New London stirred up interest in the proposal. H. W. Starr, J. C. Hall, David Hendershott, T. L. Sargent, A. W. Carpenter, J. G. Foote, William Walker, and J. F. Henry were appointed to committees to have a route surveyed, to draw up a charter for a corporation, and to get subscriptions of stock with shares at $100 each.[12] Farmers were

---

[10] George Rogers Taylor, *The Transportation Revolution, 1815-1860* (New York, 1951), 30-31.

[11] *Hawk-Eye*, Jan. 11, 1849.

[12] *Ibid.*, Feb. 1, 1849. H. W. Starr, a member of the law firm of Grimes and Starr, was the key figure in the plank road movement and a director of the Burlington & Missouri River Railroad Company. J. C. Hall, well-known Democratic politician and member of the state supreme court in the 1850's, was also a B. & M. director. The other men were local merchants, except J. F. Henry who was a physician. J. G. Foote was a director of both the B. & M and the P. & O. railroads. A. W. Carpenter was a local jeweler and a B. & M. director.

told that every quarter section along the route of the road would increase in value by $250, and Burlington property owners were warned that if they wished to maintain the town's position as the "commercial emporium" of Iowa they must build the plank road immediately.[13] Articles of incorporation for the "Burlington and Mount Pleasant Plank Road Company" were adopted at a public meeting in February, and the price of shares reduced to $50. Fifteen thousand dollars was necessary for the company to become fully organized, and books were opened at Burlington, Middletown, New London, and Mount Pleasant.[14] When subscriptions did not come in as anticipated, the Burlington papers chided the property holders and suggested that perhaps the city should become a stockholder in the company to the amount of $10,000. The *Gazette* declared that a plank road would be of more importance to the city and to the county than a railroad and that if Burlington acted she could have a population of 10,000 within a short time. Those gold-hungry individuals afflicted with the "California excitement" were advised to stay home and seek the surer profits which the plank road would bring.[15]

In March, 1849, the city council discussed the possibility of obtaining a loan of $5,000 or $10,000 in order to buy stock in the plank road company.[16] Friends of the road wrote to the local papers declaring there was no risk involved; the earnings of the road would pay the interest on the loan and upon expiration of the loan in ten years the stock owned by the city would be par stock and command in the market the money to repay the loan.[17] A Mr. Sanders of Middletown kept track of traffic passing to

[13] *Ibid.*, Feb. 22, 1849.

[14] Prominent names among the organizers of the company included H. W. Starr, J. L. Corse, J. G. Edwards, Thomas Hedge, Prugh and Cook Company, W. H. Starr, Copp and Parsons Company, F. J. C. Peasley, J. W. Grimes, J. P. Sunderland, A. W. Carpenter, J. S. Schramm, J. F. Henry, J. Adam Funk, W. F. Coolbaugh, Silas Hudson, William Sunderland, J. F. Tallant, J. C. Fletcher, Charles Mason, W. H. Postlewait, J. G. Foote, E. E. Gay, T. L. Sargent, R. S. Adams, G. P. Kreichbaum, and J. G. Lauman. For a copy of the articles of incorporation of the plank road company, with the above names affixed, see *Deed Record Book No. 11* (Recorder's Office, Des Moines County Courthouse, Burlington, Iowa), 605-608. Information regarding the public meeting and the opening of the books is given in the *Hawk-Eye*, Feb. 23, 1849.

[15] Burlington *Iowa State Gazette*, Mar. 21, 1849 (cited hereafter as *Gazette*); *Hawk-Eye*, Jan. 18, 1849.

[16] *Hawk-Eye*, Mar. 22, 1849.

[17] *Ibid.*, Mar. 28, 1849.

Burlington and found it averaged 88 units per day. From this count he deduced that, at twenty-five cents per unit, the road would take in $8,030 per year or in seven years $56,210. The cost of the road to Middletown was estimated at $17,000 with interest for seven years at $11,900 and expenses for gatekeepers, etc., at $5,600; hence expenses would be $34,500, or $21,710 less than the earnings.[18]

Apparently this kind of reasoning was convincing, for the question of the city becoming an investor in the road was put before the people.[19] The local papers swung their support behind such a move, and in April, 1849, an overwhelming 294 votes were cast for a $10,000 loan proposal to only 46 against.[20]

At a public meeting in May, designed to whip up enthusiasm for the road, internal improvements were compared to the education of the individual: just as the brightest boy will be outstripped by his less able but better-educated neighbor, so will the most favorably located city lose out if it does not engage in improvements. Cincinnati was cited as an example of a city, less favored by nature than Burlington, which had made tremendous strides by improving its transportation facilities. At this meeting, T. L. Parsons, J. Adam Funk, E. D. Rand, H. B. Ware, and Silas A. Hudson were appointed to a committee to solicit subscriptions to company stock.[21] Later that month the "Burlington and Mount Pleasant Plank Road Company" was fully organized by the election of F. J. C. Peasley as president. W. F. Coolbaugh was chosen as treasurer, while T. L. Parsons, H. W. Starr, Charles Mason, and T. L. Sargent were elected directors of the company.[22]

---

[18] *Ibid.*, Mar. 29, 1849.

[19] *The Charter with Amendments Thereto and the Revised Ordinances of the City of Burlington* (Burlington, 1871), 113.

[20] *Ibid.*, 114; *Ordinance Book No. 1, 1835-1852* (Burlington City Hall), 131, 149; *Hawk-Eye*, Apr. 12, 1849.

[21] *Hawk-Eye*, May 10, 1849. Funk, Hudson, Rand, and Ware were all businessmen. Hudson had helped organize the Whig party in the Territory. Rand, a pork packer, became prominent in the Iowa lumber industry and was a director of the Plank Road Co.

[22] *Ibid.*, May 31, 1849. Parsons was a merchant and a director of both the Plank Road Company and the B. & M. Peasley was a banker and a B. & M. director. Coolbaugh was a merchant and banker; he was treasurer of the Plank Road Co. and later president of the B. & M. Mason, chief justice of the territorial and state supreme courts and later United States Commissioner of Patents, was president of the P. & O.

Arrangements were made at once to have the road surveyed and the section to Middletown put under contract. On July 4 the company broke ground on the edge of town. The cost of the road was estimated at $1,300 to $1,600 per mile; it would last from five to seven years. A meeting in November, 1849, announced that the whole line to Mount Pleasant had been marked out by T. L. Sargent and that the route from New London to Mount Pleasant would require no excavation or filling, with very little necessary from Middletown to New London. A dividend was promised before the next semi-annual meeting.[23] The company advertised for white oak, black oak, honey locust, or walnut planks eight feet (or sixteen feet) by three inches by ten inches and for stringers of the same wood thirteen feet by three inches by four inches, and local sawmills began cutting timber for the road.

The year 1850 was one of great plank road activity. In January one of the largest meetings ever held in Burlington overflowed the courtroom. Its object was to respond to the feeling in southwestern Iowa in favor of a connection with the Mississippi at Burlington by plank road or railroad. James W. Grimes presided, and James Clarke, J. L. Corse, W. H. Starr, J. G. Foote, W. F. Coolbaugh, J. P. Sunderland, and T. L. Parsons, acting as a committee, submitted resolutions that the road to Mount Pleasant was only a link in a chain of roads which was to diverge from that place to the Des Moines River. Keosauqua, Ottumwa, and Fort Des Moines were favored as connecting points. The meeting professed no hostility to the railroad projects being agitated in various parts of the state (although noting that railroads required government aid, which the plank road did not) and said that when the time came when a railroad was necessary it could be built on the plank road, thus making the plank road the commencement of a future railroad. Interest was expressed in getting the Peoria & Oquawka Railroad of Illinois to Burlington and also in a railroad from Burlington to Council Bluffs on the Missouri River. The committee also suggested that the city council submit the question of a second $10,000 loan to the voters and that the county commissioners consider the legality of subscribing to stock. W. H. Starr, J. G. Foote, W. F. Coolbaugh, James Clarke, William Walker, J. G. Edwards, and William Sunderland were appointed to committees of correspondence and subscription. The meeting closed after selecting twenty dele-

[23] *Ibid.*, Nov. 29, 1849.

gates to attend a forthcoming meeting of plank road promoters to be held at Keosauqua.[24]

Other towns were becoming interested in the plank road pioneering of Burlington. The Ottumwa *Courier* supported the project for a plank road to the Mississippi, suggesting that the road from Burlington to Mount Pleasant be extended to Ottumwa via Fairfield, Libertyville, Ashland, and Agency City.[25] A factor in the desire to connect with Burlington was the belief that she would one day have a railroad to Chicago. H. W. Starr and J. G. Foote of Burlington attended a meeting in Ottumwa which adopted resolutions agreeing with the *Courier's* suggestions.[26] Such plank road meetings became popular in southern Iowa. In February of 1850 Burlington sent sixty delegates and the Burlington brass band to an eight-county convention in Mount Pleasant. James Clarke was chairman, James W. Grimes was one of its permanent officers, and H. W. Starr addressed the delegates. The convention urged an extension of the Burlington road to Ottumwa, a road from Mount Pleasant across the Skunk River into Keokuk County, and declared that eventually the plank road from Burlington would become a railroad. It also approved the Peoria & Oquawka Railroad, a project which southern Iowa was watching with great interest.[27]

In the spring of 1850 a second $10,000 loan was authorized by the voters of Burlington, and there was talk of extending the road to Oskaloosa, with a branch to Brighton.[28] James W. Grimes was elected president of the plank road company, with W. F. Coolbaugh as treasurer, and T. L. Parsons, E. D. Rand, J. L. Corse, and J. K. Scott as directors.[29] An article in the Fort Des Moines *Star* commented on Burlington's "plank road fever" and said if

---

[24] *Gazette*, Jan. 30, 1850; *Hawk-Eye*, Feb. 14, 1850. The Sunderlands were in the milling business. W. H. Starr was a lawyer. Corse, a bookstore proprietor and a director of the Plank Road Co., was the father of J. M. Corse, the hero of Allatoona in the Civil War. Clarke was the editor of the *Gazette*. Grimes, of course, is famous in politics as the father of the Republican party in Iowa and (Senator John Kennedy's *Profiles in Courage* notwithstanding) as the most courageous and influential of the Republican Senators in the trial of President Andrew Johnson. Grimes was president of the Plank Road Co. and the key figure in the P. & O. project.

[25] *Gazette*, Jan. 30, 1850; *Hawk-Eye*, Jan. 31, 1850.

[26] *Gazette*, Feb. 13, 1850; *Hawk-Eye*, Feb. 14, 1850.

[27] *Gazette*, Mar. 6, 1850; *Hawk-Eye*, Mar. 7, 1850.

[28] *Ordinance Book No. 1, 1835-1852*, 149; *Gazette*, Mar. 28, 1850; *Hawk-Eye*, Mar. 21, 1850.

[29] *Gazette*, June 5, 1850; *Hawk-Eye*, May 30, 1850.

Keokuk did not look out, Burlington would capture the trade of the Des Moines Valley. Anticipating this, the Keokuk *Register* announced that a company had been organized there with a Keokuk and Des Moines Valley plank road in mind. Burlington replied with a meeting at Dodgeville to consider a road north from Burlington to Louisa County to Wapello and Virginia Grove. The Dodgeville meeting, presided over by A. W. Carpenter and addressed by H. W. Starr and David Rorer, passed resolutions in favor of such a road. Three weeks later the Burlington papers reported that the "Burlington and Louisa County Plank Road Company" had drawn up articles of incorporation and that a "Burlington and Toolesboro Plank Road Company" had also been organized to connect Burlington with Toolesboro at the mouth of the Iowa River.[30] By the end of 1850 the Mount Pleasant plank road was completed to Middletown, and it was hoped that by the following June the wagons would be able to roll all the way to Mount Pleasant on plank.

The "plank fever" continued to rage unabated throughout 1851. In February a meeting was held in Benton Township to aid the proposed road from Burlington to Virginia Grove. Grimes and Rorer were selected to draft new articles of incorporation, and William Sunderland was appointed to a committee to open books for the company.[31] The Burlington city council discussed borrowing $50,000 to invest in plank roads and bridges, and delegates were sent to Illinois, where a "Burlington and Warren Plank Road Company" was organized with Luke Palmer and T. D. Crocker on its board.[32] This road was to run across the bottoms opposite Burlington and facilitate bringing the valuable Illinois trade to the river. In Fairfield a "Fairfield and Mount Pleasant Plank Road Company was established, and Burlington citizens gave encouragement to the president of the company when he came to their town seeking subscriptions.[33]

Burlington editors commented on the activity in the interior, where they saw branches springing up everywhere, all eager to connect with Burlington.

---

[30] The Des Moines and Keokuk editorials were reprinted in the *Hawk-Eye*, Nov. 14, 1850. The Dodgeville meeting and the reports of new road companies were cited in the *Gazette*, Sept. 4, Oct. 9, 10, 30, 1850; *Hawk-Eye*, Oct. 5, 31, 1850. David Rorer was a lawyer of state-wide reputation. He drew up the B. & M. charter and later became a C. B. & Q. lawyer.

[31] *Gazette*, Feb. 5, 1851; *Hawk-Eye*, Feb. 6, 1851.

[32] *Gazette*, Feb. 12, Mar. 12, 1851; *Hawk-Eye*, Feb. 13, Mar. 13, 1851.

[33] *Gazette*, Mar. 19, 1851; *Hawk-Eye*, Apr. 24, 1851.

The towns of Toolesboro and Deedsville had initiated movements to link with the Burlington roads. Lowell organized a Burlington and Lowell road which was to bridge the Skunk River, and a meeting at Lowell urged the citizens of Danville, Baltimore, Jackson, Salem, Pleasant Ridge, and Marion townships to hold similar meetings. A "Mount Pleasant, Trenton, Deedsville and Brighton Plank Road and Bridge Company" was formed, and Burlington invested $2,000 in the venture. Grimes, Starr, and Coolbaugh were appointed commissioners to open books and solicit subscriptions for a "Brighton and Richland Plank Road Company."[34] The voters of Burlington approved by a 90 per cent majority a loan of $10,000 for the Virginia Grove road and $5,000 for bridging Skunk River.[35]

The St. Louis papers watched with admiration the whirlwind of activity in Burlington, noting her growth of "astonishing rapidity" and the large scale of her internal improvements. A brilliant future was predicted for her, when, flanked on all sides by plank roads and commanding the trade of the interior, she was to become the depot for one of the richest regions of the Northwest. Impressed by the new spirit and prosperity of the young city, "a few years ago a trading post," the *Missouri Republican* urged St. Louis to follow Burlington's example.[36] The Burlington editors were grateful for the publicity which they felt was well deserved in view of the liabilities which their citizens had cheerfully incurred.

A willingness to increase these liabilities was demonstrated by a petition presented to the city council asking the city to subscribe to the Burlington and Warren road in Illinois which was to bring to Burlington all the immigrants heading for southeastern Iowa as well as the trade of Illinois. The city council approved, and at a special election in June of 1851 a large majority voted in favor of a $5,000 loan by the city to the Warren road.[37] At the same time, interest was being shown in Illinois for a plank road from Springfield to Burlington.

---

[34] These developments were reported in the *Gazette*, Feb. 12, 26, Mar. 12, Apr. 23, 1851; *Hawk-Eye*, Apr. 24, 1851; *Ordinance Book No. 1, 1837-1855* (Burlington City Hall), 188; *Charter With Amendments* . . ., 122.

[35] *Gazette*, Mar. 5, 1851; *Hawk-Eye*, Mar. 6, 1851; *Charter With Amendments* . . ., 119, 122; *Ordinance Book No. 1, 1835-1852*, 181, 188.

[36] *Hawk-Eye*, May 15, 1851.

[37] *Ibid.*, May 15, June 5, 1851; *Gazette*, June 4, 1851; *Charter With Amendments* . . ., 117; *Ordinance Book No. 1, 1835-1852*, 161, 180; *Journal of the City Council, 1850-1853* (Burlington City Hall), 168.

Like the cholera which afflicted Burlington in the same years, the plank fever was intense and brief. It began in 1849; 1851 was its climactic and indeed its final year. In that year Burlington kept its attention on the steady progress of the Mount Pleasant road. In May readers were treated to a description of a local editor's ride to Middletown in Iowa's first "Omnibus" at the respectable rate of eight miles per hour.[38] By the end of the year the road to Mount Pleasant was finished, and a happy celebration was held in Mount Pleasant in December commemorating the successful completion of "the first major public improvement West of the Mississippi."[39] In a sense, it was an anticlimax. The primary task was finished, and the people were proud and satisfied with their work. But brief as the period had been, new forces had arisen to divert attention from plank roads to a new and more exciting mode of transportation.

Even as the plank road to Mount Pleasant was completed, Burlington turned with enthusiam to railroad promotion. As early as the Memphis Convention of 1845, Burlington had observed the projects to connect the Lakes and the Mississippi and had at that time warned St. Louis that she was to suffer for not cooperating in the Rapids improvement. The work of Chicago and Galena promoters had awakened Burlington's interest in railroads. In the fall of 1847 half a million dollars had been subscribed to this road; in two years Burlington would be as close to Chicago as to St. Louis.[40] A few months later the citizens of southern Iowa were urged to take steps to get a railroad connection from Burlington to intersect the Illinois and Michigan Canal and later the Michigan Central Railroad to the Atlantic. Eastern capitalists would take stock in such a venture, they were told. The Keokuk Rapids were used as an argument for the eastern connection, and the possibility of a railroad from the Des Moines Valley to Burlington and eastern markets was suggested.[41] The "utopian scheme" of a proposed Dubuque-to-Keokuk road was dismissed as foolish in a time when east-west roads were needed. The Dubuque-Keokuk road was characterized as an excessively expensive route crossing innumerable rivers and traversing seven counties which averaged only twelve persons per square mile.[42] Nevertheless, the efforts of Keokuk, Davenport, and other towns worried Burlington.

[38] *Hawk-Eye*, May 29, 1851.
[39] *Ibid.*, Dec. 25, 1851.
[40] *Ibid.*, Nov. 25, 1847.
[41] *Ibid.*, Jan. 20, 27, 1848.
[42] *Ibid.*, Dec. 28, 1848.

Until late in 1849 Burlington could do little but stir up interest in railroads and talk bravely about the dreadful fate Keokuk would suffer when eastern roads touched Iowa above the Rapids. A specific focus was lacking until Peoria and Oquawka proposed a line between their towns in Illinois. This caused an immediate reaction in Burlington. The local papers applauded the idea and suggested that eastern capital could be attracted only if the road were extended to Burlington, where it could tap the best part of the state. James W. Grimes, Evan Evans, J. P. Sunderland, Henry Ware, J. G. Edwards, Levi Hager, William Ewing, Dr. Ransom, James Clarke, John Hollingsworth, and John Armstrong were appointed delegates to get the Peoria road to build to the Mississippi opposite Burlington.[43] Unfortunately, thin ice on the river prevented the trip to Knoxville. The following month, however, Burlington held its plank and railroad meeting. While most concerned with the plank road to Mount Pleasant, this meeting expressed "deep interest" in the Peoria railroad, suggested that the plank road could be the basis for a future railroad west, and declared its willingness to join with Keosauqua in petitioning Congress for a land grant to aid a Burlington to Council Bluffs railroad.[44] (Keosauqua had previously sent out a circular to the towns of Illinois and southeastern Iowa, urging cooperation in asking Congress for a grant of land to build a railroad from Burlington via Mount Pleasant, Keosauqua, Bloomfield, and Centerville on the old Mormon Trail to Council Bluffs.) The plank and railroad convention was followed by railroad meetings at Keosauqua, dominated by H. W. Starr, J. L. Corse, and J. F. Abrahams, and at Monmouth, Illinois, with Grimes, Rorer, Coolbaugh, and Dr. J. F. Henry attending.[45]

Railroad promotion was catching on in Iowa. Ottumwa's interest in connecting with the plank road at Mount Pleasant was due in part to the belief that a railroad from Peoria would extend to Burlington. Promoters of the Dubuque and Keokuk road sent two leading citizens to Congress in behalf of their road, and Burlington showed some concern lest all the land granted might be given to this company.[46] Davenport as well as Keokuk came under

---

[43] *Gazette*, Dec. 19, 1849; *Hawk-Eye*, Nov. 1, Dec. 13, 20, 1849.

[44] *Hawk-Eye*, Jan. 31, 1850; *Gazette*, Jan. 30, 1850.

[45] *Hawk-Eye*, Feb. 21, 1850; *Gazette*, Feb. 20, 1850. J. F. Abrahams owned a bookstore in Burlington and served as secretary of the B. & M.

[46] *Hawkeye*, Jan. 31, 1850; *Gazette*, Jan. 30, 1850.

editorial fire from Burlington. The Davenport papers, in response to a query from Iowa City, had replied that as soon as they completed a road to connect the Mississippi with the East, they would take all the stock necessary for a road to Iowa City. The *Hawk-Eye* called the Iowa City project "one of the small humbugs of the day" and with heavy sarcasm said that doubtless Davenport would take all the railroads in the country under her special care and patronage.[47]

In February, 1851, the editors at Burlington reported that the Illinois House of Representatives had amended the act incorporating the Peoria & Oquawka Railroad to allow a branch to come to Burlington. They hoped, said the editors, within two years to "hear the iron horse opposite us."[48] This was the first indication that Burlington would really get the connection with Illinois. A public meeting met immediately and after being addressed by Grimes, Starr, and Rorer recommended that the city invest $75,000 in the Peoria road.[49] This made a great impression on the interior. The Fairfield *Ledger* declared that "the enterprise of [Burlington's] citizens is proverbial," and that Fairfield had better deal with her instead of Keokuk, where "they stand with their hands in pockets waiting for the railroad to be built to their door."[50] Ottumwa, admiring the "sleepless vigilence [sic], untiring perseverence, liberality and enterprise of [Burlington's] businessmen," which would make her the "Emporium of Iowa," advised Keokuk to follow her example before it was too late.[51] The people of Burlington approved the $75,000 loan by a vote of 598 to 46, and in April, 1851, books of the P. & O. Railroad were opened in Illinois and in the office of Grimes and Starr in Burlington.[52] Grimes and Starr were among the many prominent plank road people who were also leaders in the railroad movement. By May 22 a subscription committee reported that between $40,000 and $50,000 had been raised. A week later the figure had reached over $79,000 by individual subscription. Among the heavy subscribers were H. W. Starr, Grimes, F. J. C.

---

[47] *Hawk-Eye*, Oct. 10, 1850.
[48] *Ibid.*, Feb. 13, 1851; *Gazette*, Feb. 19, 1851.
[49] *Gazette*, Feb. 19, 1851.
[50] Reprinted in *Hawk-Eye*, Mar. 13, 1851.
[51] *Ibid.*, Feb. 19, 1851.
[52] *Ordinance Book No. 1, 1837-1855*, 183; *Hawk-Eye*, Mar. 6, Apr. 3, 1851; *Gazette*, Mar. 5, 1851. For an enthusiastic letter from Grimes to his father describing the "great railroad and plank fever" in Burlington, see William Salter, *Life of James W. Grimes* (New York, 1876), 30.

Peasley, Luke Palmer, E. D. Rand, A. C. Dodge, W. F. Coolbaugh, Charles Mason, A. W. Carpenter, William Ewing, J. S. Schramm, Dr. Ransom, David Rorer, Lyman Cook, Thomas Hedge, Enos Lowe, and John David, all investing from $500 to $2,000. More impressive is the fact that over 150 men subscribed in Burlington.[53] Keokuk congratulated Burlington and, referring to the low bottom land opposite her, said she was fortunate that about seven miles of the route could be run by steamboat. To this rather good hit the Burlington editor could only admit that the water had indeed reached five miles on the contemplated route and suggest that this providentially showed them how high to build the road.[54]

Once secure in the belief that a branch of the P. & O. Railroad would come to Burlington, the attractive idea soon arose that Burlington should replace Oquawka as the main western terminus of the road. This was given formal expression when a railroad meeting, held in Burlington on May 7, 1851, resolved that the road should proceed in a straight line from Monmouth to Burlington.[55] When information arrived a week later that Henderson County (Oquawka) had rejected a $50,000 loan to the road, this attitude was strengthened. A short time later, Grimes, Dodge, Corse, and Mason returned from a P. & O. meeting in Knoxville with the encouraging news that the road would be built directly from Monmouth to Burlington. Grimes and Mason were elected directors at that meeting.[56] Oquawka objected to this plan to build to Burlington first and leave the main trunk to Oquawka until later. Yet, $155,000 had been raised at Burlington, while Oquawka and Henderson County had contributed nothing. In their corporate capacity, Burlington had loaned $75,000, Peoria $75,000, and Warren County $50,000 to the road. Individual subscriptions totaled $80,000 at Burlington, $32,000 at Peoria, $22,000 at Farmington, $40,000 in Warren County, and $41,000 in Knox County. A total of $415,00 had been raised for the P. & O. in Illinois and Iowa.[57]

Despite the valiant work by Burlington, a call went out from the company

[53] Hawk-Eye, May 22, 29, 1851; Gazette, May 28, 1851. Schramm, Hedge, David, and Cook were merchants. Lowe was a local physician. Cook and Hedge were B. & M. directors.

[54] Hawk-Eye, June 12, 1851.

[55] Gazette, May 7, 1851.

[56] Hawk-Eye, June 26, 1851; Gazette, June 25, 1851.

[57] Hawk-Eye, June 26, 1851; Gazette, May 28, 1851.

for more subscriptions. The president declared an additional $100,000 was needed before work could begin, and Grimes pledged that Burlington would raise another $25,000.[58] Apprehension was allayed when the "glorious news" arrived that fifty miles of road from Burlington to Peoria had been put under contract. Grimes and Mason brought the news back from a meeting of the directors of the P. & O., and at a mass meeting at the Methodist church the factual report of the two directors was received with roars of approval which "the most brilliant oratory could not have elicited."[59] The *Hawk-Eye* proclaimed, "this forever fixes the destiny of Burlington and leaves no doubt as to the future Commercial Metropolis of Iowa."[60] By December of 1851 contracts for the entire road were closed, the route located, and grading begun.

As work progressed with painful slowness on the eastern and western divisions of the road it became increasingly clear that for Burlington the real objective was no longer Peoria. The emergence of a Chicago to Quincy line which was to cross the P. & O. forty-five miles east of Burlington turned Burlington toward Chicago via Galesburg rather than Peoria. Late in 1852 Judge Charles Mason reported that Burlington would reach Galesburg and intersect the Central Military Tract road (to Chicago) in 1853.[61] In June of 1853 the stockholders of the P. & O. met and arranged for a connection with the Central Military Tract road at Galesburg and for a road from Peoria to Logansport, Indiana. The Burlington papers predicted travel to the Atlantic via Chicago in six months and by way of Peoria in one year.[62] By December, 1853, the *Gazette* editor had advanced the Galesburg deadline to May of 1854; he insisted however that the road was progressing well and described his ride on the locomotive "Burlington" at thirty miles per hour.[63] The ride must have been of short duration, for a month later the locomotive was running only five miles. In March, 1854, J. G. Foote

[58] *Hawk-Eye*, Sept. 4, 1851; *Gazette*, Sept. 3, 1851.
[59] *Gazette*, Oct. 8, 1851.
[60] *Hawk-Eye*, Oct. 9, 1851.
[61] *Gazette*, Nov. 24, 1852. Burlington's shift from Peoria to Chicago is an episode in the larger drama of the creation of the C. B. & Q. system by the Michigan Central group; the P. & O. was absorbed, as were several Illinois lines, by the eastern company. Richard Overton expertly pieces the story together in his *Burlington West* (Cambridge, 1941).
[62] *Gazette*, June 22, 1853.
[63] *Ibid.*, Dec. 7, 1853.

returned from a directors' meeting in Peoria and reported that the "feeling of jealousy" between the two ends of the line had been resolved and that there was now every disposition to favor the work at the western end and to furnish all the materials to complete the road to Galesburg.[64] By June only twelve miles had been completed, and at the end of the year there were still ten miles of "staging" necessary on the line near Monmouth. By this time, however, the end was in sight, and preparations for a railroad celebration were begun. On March 1, 1855, the *Gazette* editor took another trip by locomotive. This time he could see another engine working its way west assisted by a hundred Irishmen.[65] A week later the road was completed, and Burlington was in direct connection with Chicago.

The Keokuk papers, continuing their steady flow of editorial venom, observed that a "ricketty [sic] branch of a Railroad has been constructed into the swamps opposite Burlington," and that it was unlikely that an accessible terminus could be had within seven miles of the city half the time.[66] The *Gazette*, although noting that any rise in the Mississippi that would stop cars seven miles from Burlington would make the "rats" leave their holes as high up as Second Street in Keokuk, preferred to publicize the "immense change" in business caused by the railroad.[67] The editor urged a public ceremony to advertise the city and its road, and in June, 1855, a large Illinois delegation arrived (from Chicago not Peoria) to share Burlington's first railroad celebration.

Despite the plank road to Mount Pleasant, many in Burlington realized the need for a railroad into the interior, one which would connect with the road to Peoria and eastern markets. Often when discussing the Peoria road this prospect was mentioned. The promotion of railroads within Iowa was very competitive. The Dubuque and Keokuk road was especially resented in Burlington; it was considered a "rope with which to strangle the river towns between these points."[68] The formation of a Davenport road designed to run westward to Iowa City and eventually to the Missouri River was also a challenge to Burlington.

Even as the last miles of the road to Mount Pleasant were being planked,

[64] *Ibid.*, Mar. 8, 1854.
[65] *Ibid.*, Mar. 7, 1855.
[66] Reprinted in *ibid.*, Apr. 4, 1855.
[67] *Ibid.*, Apr. 4, May 2, 1855.
[68] *Ibid.*, Nov. 24, 1853.

the desire for a railroad of their own was translated into action by leading businessmen in Burlington. By January, 1852, they were ready for formal incorporation of the "Burlington and Missouri River Railroad Company," the object of which was "to construct and use a Railroad extending from Burlington to the most eligible point on the Missouri River."[69] Their immediate goal, however, was to build to some point on the Des Moines River and thereby capture the trade of the Des Moines Valley.

Building a plank road was one thing; a railroad was quite another. The latter was enormously expensive to construct. The towns and counties along the route would contribute, of course, but the real solution in financing the road, it was felt, lay in a large congressional land grant to the company. Unfortunately, the proposed east-west roads at Davenport and Dubuque had the jump on the other roads, and it was necessary to persuade the state legislature to change its policy favoring grants only to these two lines. For a year Burlington lobbied and propagandized incessantly against the "state policy" favoring the two roads, demanding equal favors to all and equating her own interests with those of the whole state.[70] In the end, the Burlington position prevailed, as Grimes led the fight in the Iowa legislature which committed that body to four east-west lines, of which Burlington was one.[71] The Burlington papers congratulated themselves for annihilating in twelve months the old policy which would have "cut her off from the rest of the state" and trumpeted their victory over the "designing speculators and . . . political hacks" who had sponsored the "Ram's Horn" road between Keokuk and Dubuque.[72]

[69] Most active among the B. & M. incorporators were: J. F. Tallant, Charles Mason, William Endsley, David Rorer, James W. Woods, J. C. Hall, Lyman Cook, William Sunderland, H. W. Starr, J. P. Sunderland, G. P. Kreichbaum, A. W. Carpenter, W. F. Coolbaugh, George Frazee, F. J. C. Peasley, J. F. Abrahams, J. Copp, T. L. Parsons, J. A. Funk, R. S. Adams, J. Pierson, T. D. Crocker, J. G. Foote, Levi Hager, J. C. Fletcher, Thomas Hedge, J. M. Swan, J. G. Law, D. Denise, J. G. Lauman, and J. S. Schramm. For a complete list of the original incorporators, see *Mortgage Book No. 5* (Recorder's Office, Des Moines County Courthouse, Burlington, Iowa), 429; W. W. Baldwin, *Corporate History of the Chicago, Burlington and Quincy Railroad* (Chicago, 1921), 129; W. W. Baldwin (comp.), *Documentary History of the Chicago, Burlington and Quincy Railroad* (3 vols., Chicago, 1928-1929), 2:4-7.

[70] *Gazette*, July 7, Aug. 4, Nov. 24, 1852.

[71] Mildred Throne, "The Burlington and Missouri River Railroad in Iowa," *The Palimpsest*, 33:8 (January, 1952).

[72] Burlington *Weekly Telegraph*, Jan. 15, Mar. 12, 1853. (Cited hereafter as *Telegraph*.)

Nothing was accomplished during this interlude, and further disappointments were in store for the B. & M. promoters. For one thing, there was serious doubt as to the legality of counties taking stock in railroad ventures. A bill before the legislature authorizing such action failed, and Governor Stephen Hempstead refused to call a special session to clarify the issue.[73] Also, despite the victory regarding the Iowa legislature's recommendations to Congress concerning land grants, Congress proved a disappointment. Other roads were no more satisfied with the four roads recommended than Burlington had been with the earlier arrangement. The B. & M. promoters watched impatiently as various land bills came before Congress, as more and more roads sought to share in a land grant. At one point Representative John Letcher of Virginia, having found more than one hundred such bills on the docket, felt compelled to protest against this unseemly rush to the public trough. Representative Bernhart Henn of Iowa explained that actually many of the applications were for the same road; that he, for example, had filed twenty for one road. Letcher retorted that his friend, Representative Williamson R. W. Cobb, had admitted that Alabama had no less than five distinct grants before the House and asked how many there were from Iowa. When informed that Iowa had in fact submitted petitions for fourteen different roads, the gentleman from Virginia asked, "Mr. Speaker, is that not modest for a young state! [Laughter] No more than fourteen!"[74] The lobbying activities carried on by this multiplicity of roads made it difficult for any land bill to get through Congress.

Finally, as 1853 wore on, the B. & M. people adopted the attitude that it was useless to depend on Congress and determined to go ahead with the road.[75] The towns in the interior which had participated in Burlington's plank road project were eager to share in the benefits which the railroad would bring. In March, 1853, the Fairfield *Iowa Sentinel* declared that although at first they were undecided between Keokuk and Burlington, they had determined to aid the Burlington railroad. (The *Gazette* rather un-

[73] *Gazette*, Mar. 23, Apr. 27, June 29, July 6, 1853; *Telegraph*, Apr. 2, 30, May 21, June 4, 1853. For a discussion of the difficulties involved in the taking of stock by counties and cities, see Earl S. Beard, "Local Aid to Railroads in Iowa," IOWA JOURNAL OF HISTORY, 50:1-35 (January, 1952). The B. & M. backers eventually decided to ignore the disputed legality of such investments and proceed with the road in the hope that the issue would be favorably resolved in the interim.

[74] *Gazette*, Mar. 8, 1854.

[75] *Telegraph*, Mar. 26, Apr. 30, 1853.

graciously responded that Fairfield had at last found out on which side its bread was buttered.)[76] A railroad convention held at Fairfield in April of 1853, with Des Moines, Henry, Jefferson, Wapello, Decatur, and Marion counties represented, resolved that the wants of the country required a railroad from Burlington to the Missouri River, that the legislature should legalize counties taking stock, and that county judges should appropriate funds to survey possible routes.[77] In the same month, railroad meetings at Salem, Agency City, Keosauqua, and West Point, declaring their desire to be on such a route, offered financial aid.[78]

Amid the flush of enthusiasm concerning the new road west, a prophetic sobering note was sounded in the local papers regarding finances. The city's indebtedness on bonds was said to be $112,000 with interest at $8,880 plus city script at $10,000. Revenue from licenses, wharfage, etc. amounted to $2,880, leaving a balance of $16,000 to be paid by taxation. The city assessment was $1,500,000 which at the maximum of one per cent yielded $15,000 in taxes; minus delinquents, it meant about $11,000. Hence the editor warned, even with maximum taxation, there existed a deficit of about $4,000. The railroad men felt that once in operation the road would pay for itself and that the city assessment would greatly increase so that a tax of one mill on the dollar would be sufficient. They had asked for a loan of $6,000 to meet the interest on railroad bonds. The *Gazette* said that since the interest came due before provision could be made to meet it by taxation, perhaps the loan was necessary, but expressed the hope that it would not be repeated. Declaring that in times of railroad excitement caution was needed, the editor stated that he did not condemn the policy of the city taking railroad stock as it had, but urged that after this loan it would be better to face liabilities manfully and not threaten the future by contracting more debts.[79] With predictions of a population of 10,000 in five years, railroad meetings throughout southern Iowa endorsing the B. & M. road, and even eastern papers declaring that the Burlington railroad would be the course of a great trunk Pacific railroad, such cautious advice was unusual — and unheeded.

The cooperation of friends along the route was not enough to finance

[76] *Gazette*, Mar. 16, 1853.
[77] *Ibid.*, Apr. 4, 20, 1853.
[78] *Ibid.*, Apr. 4, 20, 1853.
[79] *Ibid.*, Apr. 4, 1853.

the road, and the land grant had not been secured. Therefore, logically and indeed inevitably, the company sought eastern aid in financing the B. & M. The Michigan Central people agreed to build the road, with the condition that $600,000 would be subscribed in Iowa, $450,000 by counties, and $150,000 by private individuals.[80] In this way the road could be built to the Des Moines River.

The quota for Des Moines County was $150,000, and in July of 1853 the county judge issued a proclamation calling on the people to decide whether or not to take the stock.[81] A meeting hastily called in Burlington recommended that Des Moines, Henry, Jefferson, and Wapello counties vote for the loans. The meeting had also declared that John W. Brooks of Detroit and others were ready to put "millions" in the road but that, knowing of the prejudice which existed everywhere against monopolies, they would not be willing unless the people were with them.[82] Grimes, Rorer, Browning, Hall, and others spoke throughout the county for the loan. A meeting that summer reported that the $450,000 had been taken by the counties and that $50,000 in private subscriptions was left to be taken in Des Moines County.[83] In July, John W. Brooks was elected president of the company and his townsman, James F. Joy, became a director; thus began a process of gradually increasing control of the B. & M. by eastern influences.[84] The same month Henry Thielson and a band of engineers of the Michigan Central arrived in Burlington to begin surveying. In August, 1853, the Michigan Central applied to the city council for a portion of submerged land on the edge of the river, proposing to spend $1,500,000 reclaiming it from the river and erecting depots, warehouses, and shops to make Burlington the point of manufacture and supply for the needs of the B. &. M. Railroad, the Central Military Tract in Illinois, and the Lyons & Missouri River road. The city leased the ground to the company for ninety-nine years on condition that the company raise the ground, locate their depot there, and begin work on the B. & M. Railroad within one

---

[80] *Telegraph*, July 9, 1853; *Gazette*, Sept. 21, 1853.

[81] *Telegraph*, July 9, 1853; *Gazette*, July 6, 1853.

[82] *Gazette*, July 13, 1853.

[83] *Ibid.*, Aug. 24, 1853.

[84] *Telegraph*, July 9, 1853; *Gazette*, July 6. 1853. The B. & M., like the P. & O., soon lost its local character and was swallowed up by the powerful C. B. & Q. interests.

year.[85] This news convinced Burlington that she was to be the Queen City of the Upper Mississippi. In December the *Gazette* optimistically reported that Brooks of Detroit was expected shortly to arrange for the speedy completion of the road.[86] In the spring of 1854 a meeting of the board of directors decided that the road was to run from Burlington through Middletown, New London, Mount Pleasant, and Fairfield, to Agency City.[87] Later Ottumwa was added. The *Gazette* said the "agony is over." The western road was located, in May the contracts for the first 75 miles were advertised, and the work began.[88]

The agony was not over, but Burlington had the beginning of her railroad to the Des Moines Valley. The prevailing climate of opinion in Burlington during the years described was one of optimism and urgency. The key to the future lay in the expansion of internal improvements. It is difficult adequately to convey the spirit of grandiose expectation with which the town regarded its projects, nor the concomitant anxiety that other towns might somehow outstrip Burlington in the competition. Improvement of the Rapids, the plank road, the railroad, each in turn was to make Burlington the St. Louis or the Cincinnati of the Upper Mississippi, and they could do the same for others if the citizens did not support such undertakings.

The financing of such programs was an acute problem. Capital was always lacking in young areas, and Burlington, a town of only a few thousand people, had to strain every nerve to maintain the race. When possible, money was raised by private subscription, but when necessary the city subscribed in its corporate capacity, borrowing on its future and incurring a sizeable indebtedness. While proud of their local efforts, aid from the government was accepted and even demanded; there was no revulsion against internal improvements at federal expense from Whigs or Democrats in Burlington. This is not to say that partisan politics were not involved in the transportation schemes, but political criticism was usually directed against parties for not aiding them vigorously enough.[89] Also, despite a strong

[85] *Telegraph*, Aug. 13, 1853; *Gazette*, Aug. 10, 1853.
[86] *Gazette*, Dec. 7, 1853.
[87] *Ibid.*, Mar. 29, 1854; *Telegraph*, Mar. 25, 1854.
[88] *Corporate History of the C. B. & Q.*, 30; *Gazette*, Mar. 29, Apr. 26, 1854; *Telegraph*, Mar. 25, 1854.
[89] David Sparks describes the relationship of internal improvements and politics in Iowa in "The Decline of the Democratic Party in Iowa, 1850-1860," IOWA JOURNAL OF HISTORY, 53:1-30 (January, 1955).

tradition of suspicion against corporations, banking, and monopoly in Iowa, aid from "eastern capitalists" was eagerly sought. Nevertheless, the primary responsibility for success or failure rested with the people at the local level. In these early years there was apparently only one way to deal with a public question, whether it was internal improvements, a cholera epidemic, a lecture series, or organizing a charitable society. Standard procedure was to call a public meeting, adopt and publicize resolutions, and appoint committees to carry out the work at hand. From the newspapers of the time one gets the impression that a chief source of diversion and entertainment came from attending public meetings.

A well-defined, cohesive, and rather sizeable group of merchants and professional men spearheaded every project with public ramifications. With an almost monotonous regularity the same names appear in connection with innumerable Rapids, plank road, and railroad events. There were merchants such as J. F. Abrahams, R. S. Adams, A. W. Carpenter, Lyman Cook, W. F. Coolbaugh, J. Copp, J. L. Corse, Evan Evans, J. C. Fletcher, J. G. Foote, J. Adam Funk, E. E. Gay, Levi Hager, Thomas Hedge, Silas Hudson, G. P. Kriechbaum, J. G. Lauman, Luke Palmer, T. L. Parsons, W. H. Postlewait, E. D. Rand, T. L. Sargent, J. S. Schramm, J. P. Sunderland, William Sunderland, J. F. Tallant, William Walker, and Henry B. Ware. M. D. Browning, T. D. Crocker, A. C. Dodge, George Frazee, James W. Grimes, J. C. Hall, Charles Mason, David Rorer, H. W. Starr, W. H. Starr, J. P. Wightman, and James Woods were lawyers. J. F. Henry, Enos Lowe, and S. S. Ransom were doctors, and James Clarke and J. G. Edwards were editors. F. J. C. Peasley was a financier, and Henry Moore was a building contractor.

Possessed of imagination and courage, these men led the way. They invested in transportation projects, but their primary contribution was more significant than the money they risked. Their chief role was a promotional and educational one. They sacrificed large amounts of their time to put their objectives across. They organized and managed meetings, they served on committees, they incorporated companies, they attended distant conventions, they scoured the countryside pleading, cajoling, threatening, and opening vistas of a great future to the farmers and townspeople of southern Iowa. An examination of such a group would be a fascinating study in leadership in itself.

There is enough data available concerning most of these leaders to justify drawing a tenative composite portrait of the group. The average member was a surprisingly young man; in 1850 he was probably still in his late thirties. Despite his youth he had been a resident of Burlington for some ten or eleven years, a long time considering the life of the town. There was an equal chance that he came from New England, the mid-Atlantic states, or the South, with New England holding a slight edge. He was most likely to be a merchant, although lawyers were very active in his group also.[90] Unlike his modern counterpart of one hundred years later, he was truly a "self-made" man; there had been no niche waiting for him in his father's (or father-in-law's) business when he came to Burlington. He had probably begun by clerking in a store, saved his money, gone into business for himself, and succeeded — all in a decade. He was a Democrat or a Whig (this group was equally divided politically) and active in local and state politics.

It would be naive to suppose that these men were not motivated by self-interest, but one receives the favorable impression that they thought not in terms of immediate returns on their investment *per se*, but rather of a long-range program. They were working for their town and their region; this in turn would benefit them — but it would also benefit everyone else. They were not thinking of a safe return on their money but rather of visions of a metropolis of the future which they were creating. It was a great competition in which they were engaged, and they exhibited a keen thirst for the game. It led them to incredible notions which never materialized for their town. But if Burlington did not become a St. Louis, neither did it remain an Oquawka, and this is largely due to the efforts of those who early saw the need for transportation improvements and worked indefatigably to convince the community of their necessity. Largely to them goes the credit for the benefits, and the burdens, which such projects brought. It should be reiterated that their experience was not an isolated one. They were but typical of similar groups in countless other communities. They, and others like them elsewhere, were the first victims and subsequent carriers of the "internal improvements fever."

[90] Of the forty-seven leaders listed above, well over 50 per cent were merchants, about 25 per cent were lawyers, and the rest were scattered among other professions — editors, doctors, contractors, etc.

Politics and Society in Sioux City, 1859
ROBERT EDSON LEE

THE FOLLOWING SELECTION by Robert Edson Lee raises significant questions about American frontier communities. His study centers on Sioux City in 1859, but many of his observations have a wider frontier application. Although frontier communities have traditionally been characterized as devoid of legal institutions, lacking in social or intellectual refinement, and full of bawdy elements, early Sioux City proves something of an exception to these generalizations.

All too often writers have referred to "the frontier" as opposed to *specific frontiers*. Ray Billington in his book, *Westward Expansion*, described six frontier zones—fur traders, cattlemen, miners, pioneer farmers, equipped farmers, and the specialists of the urban frontier; each had distinct characteristics and represented a different stage in the development of society. In similar fashion, Lee reminds us that it was impossible to broadly generalize about the "frontier line" as well as the makeup of frontier communities.

Yet another consideration raised by Lee is that we know far less about the town or urban frontier than we do about agrarian frontier living. His study helps to fill in one more piece of that puzzle. Regardless of these considerations, Lee paints a colorful portrait of local boosterism, political shenanigans, and typical boastfulness of the American pioneer.

POLITICS AND SOCIETY IN SIOUX CITY, 1859
By Robert Edson Lee*

The frontier is commonly defined as the line drawn through regions with a population of two to six inhabitants per square mile. The region to the west, with a population of less than two people per square mile, is said to be "beyond the frontier." In Iowa in 1860 the frontier line was roughly a straight line drawn from Council Bluffs northeast to Mason City.[1] Beyond this line, the student of history pictures a wilderness; east of it, a neat and ordered patchwork of emerging farms and towns settled by eager, strong, individualistic, staunch pioneers somewhat starry-eyed with the concept of Manifest Destiny. To such a student, the early newspapers of Sioux City present a problem. For instance, in January, 1859, the firm of Heineman & Gumbert, Sioux City, was forced out of business to satisfy debtors; the advertisement for the sheriff's sale lists an extraordinary collection of merchandise: tooth brushes, bear's oil, dirk knives, overshoes, garters, stocks, neck shawls, artificial flowers, gauntlets, large mirror, long boots, vests, bed ticking, sardines, moccasins, feather dusters, ink stands, calicoes, mousdelaine, marsailes, mantillas, fans, bracelets, playing cards, fish hooks and lines, thimbles, jewsharps, fancy soaps, powder flasks and horns, umbrellas, violins, pocket diaries, buffalo robes, fox and wolf skins, glove stretchers, pocket pistols and revolvers, fancy furs, veils, and about one hundred items more.[2] This list uncovers a cultural complexity not fitting to a town a hundred miles beyond the frontier. This does not sound like the wilderness.

It would seem that the "frontier line" is a term of convenience. No such fence row, marching steadily westward, existed in fact. The actual frontier was a fluid thing. Spearheads of settlement surged out beyond the line to military forts or along military roads or up the navigable rivers. Such settlements scarcely waited for surveyors or economic pressures from

---

*Robert Edson Lee is a doctoral candidate in American Civilization at the State University of Iowa.

[1] William J. Petersen, "Frontiers of the Pioneers," *The Palimpsest*, 32:55-6 (January, 1951).

[2] Sioux City *Eagle*, Jan. 15, 1859.

behind or the giving way of Indian lands to the west. Rumors of gold made towns of a thousand overnight. Land speculators platted cities on likely sand bars along the bends in major rivers. Although the frontier line was but approaching western Iowa in 1860, there were by then settlements in nearly every future state to the west.

Consider the western border of Iowa in 1860, the "frontier." Indians to the north prevented movement up into the Little Sioux River region. Settlements at the far south were involved in the slavery controversy and border warfare preliminary to the Civil War. In between are outfitting stations for western emigrants, some of which flourished (Omaha and Council Bluffs) and others which were to fail (Pacific City, Iowa). Some settlements were contact points for the northwest fur trade. There were islands of stranded Mormons. There were towns whose only development was ghostward. The actual frontier line in 1860 included communities which had existed for thirty years and lands which would not be occupied for thirty years more. Homogeneity of character cannot be assumed. Generalizations about such a frontier must be very general indeed.

A case in point is Sioux City, in Woodbury County on the Missouri River. After studying its origins and, through its newspapers, its culture while it was still west of the frontier line, what generalizations can be made about frontier characteristics — the reputed violence on the frontier, the equality of opportunity, the individualism, the idealism, the political liberalism, the personal freedom, the absence of social castes?

Sioux City's origins lie in French-Canadian traders who built cabins in 1848 and 1849. In December, 1854, Dr. John T. Cook arrived; ostensibly he performed his duties as the government surveyor, but privately he was looking for a townsite to be developed by his newly formed Sioux City Townsite Company to which Senators Augustus C. Dodge and George W. Jones had subscribed the summer before. In 1855 Cook and the real estate promoter Daniel Rider bought out the squatters at Sioux City, and Dodge and Jones worked in Washington to secure the United States Land Office for the city — a Land Office that was to sell about one-eighth of all the land in Iowa (this at a time when there were but two log cabins at Sioux City). In March of 1856, with the help of a keg of whisky on election day, local settlers voted to have the county seat moved to Sioux City from the rival Sergeant's Bluff. In June, 1856, the first steamboat stopped at Sioux City. With the Land Office, the county government, and river transportation assured, the town began to grow. Four hundred people had arrived by the end of 1856 — government officials, land speculators, bankers, lawyers, merchants, and confidence men.[3]

One of the land speculators was John F. Charles who has left us a vivid picture of frontier conditions. He arrived in December, 1856, in a blizzard, and spent the night at the two log cabins that formed the Hagy House or Western Hotel, nicknamed "The Terrific." A dozen men were clustered around a stove, one of them with an umbrella raised to keep off the blowing snow inside the cabin. The men were "a hard-looking set . . . dirty and ragged, but talked chiefly of their real estate sales and of the money they had made." Charles slept that night under a buffalo robe with the future postmaster, and nearly froze to death.[4]

Newspapers soon followed. In the spring of 1857, Seth W. Swiggett and his printing press arrived by river from Cincinnati, Ohio, and began (July 4, 1857) publishing the Sioux City *Eagle* as an independent paper. Down river at Sergeant's Bluff, Francis M. Ziebach, printer from Lewisburg, Pennsylvania, published the *Western Independent* beginning in August, 1857. But since Sioux City grew and Sergeant's Bluff did not, Ziebach closed down the one paper and opened up another, the Sioux City *Register*, beginning July 22, 1858. The two papers, the *Eagle* of Swiggett and the *Register* of Ziebach, ran in competition for over a year, until October, 1859, when Swiggett sold out to Ziebach. Together, the one paper measuring the truth in the other, they give a fascinating and unusual picture of life beyond the frontier.[5]

The reputation of the frontier for lawlessness is well known. What can be found in these papers to support this claim? The editors dwell almost lovingly on the circumstances of crime. A Mr. Wiley of Woodbury County stabbed George Hubbell three times in the back with a dirk knife; in the same month it was reported that two men in Omaha who had stolen four horses were removed from jail and hanged.[6] A savage fight occurred across the Missouri in Dakota Territory; the Frenchman Lefleur survived

[3] Iowa Writers' Program, W. P. A., *Woodbury County History* (Sioux City, 1942), passim.

[4] Frank Harmon Garver (ed.), "Reminiscences of John H. Charles," *Annals of Iowa* (third series), 8:408 (July, 1908).

[5] *History of Woodbury and Plymouth Counties* . . . (Chicago, 1891), 160-61; "Francis M. Ziebach," *Annals of Iowa* (third series), 17:238 (January, 1930).

[6] Sioux City *Eagle*, Jan. 8, 15, 1859.

various blows of an axe which nearly cut off his right arm and his jaw.[7] A man in Jasper County quarreled with his wife, struck her down with an axe, cut her throat with a razor, severed her head and legs, and then in despair hanged himself.[8] The editor of the Omaha *Nebraskan* was "cowhided" on the street by the wife of a maligned gentleman; opinion was that the editor deserved it.[9] It is not that the crimes were so frequent but that the treatment of them was matter-of-course.

The crimes reported took place anywhere but in Sioux City itself. A Sioux City alderman had shot and killed a political opponent in 1858, but this seems to have been the exception; the town was not riotous in spite of its red-light district along the waterfront, the "Sudan."[10] Even New Year's Eve was reported as quiet: "Little drunkenness was manifested, and the few who did resort to intoxication for enjoyment, did so when darkness concealed their orgies."[11] When a New Hampshire newspaper reported that "The steady drink of the Sioux City people is whiskey, and they take to it very kindly," the editor of the *Register* retorted: "The facts are, there is less liquor drank in Sioux City than in any other town of its size in the west; there is but one place where liquor is sold as a beverage, and it is a rare occurrence indeed that a drunken man is seen in our streets."[12]

Another way to soft-pedal home conditions was to point out how much worse conditions were elsewhere. An editorial on "The Mines! The Mines!" had this to say:

> All of the accessories to vice will doubtless soon obtain a footing in the anriferous region. Gambling hells, low groggeries with all their accompanying vices, are as sure to spring into existence there as is the excitement to attract a heavy emigration. . . . Comfort and personal security are two of the non-essentials to success in border life, and need not be anticipated in a region where the only inducement to emigrate is to gratify a lust for gold.[13]

[7] Sioux City *Register*, Feb. 3, 1859.
[8] Sioux City *Eagle*, Feb. 19, 1859.
[9] *Ibid.*, Mar. 26, 1859.
[10] *Woodbury County History*, 62, 66.
[11] Sioux City *Register*, Jan. 6, 1859.
[12] *Ibid.*, Feb. 17, 1859.
[13] Sioux City *Eagle*, Jan. 22, 1859.

A correspondent in Nebraska Territory wrote back: "The weather is delightful, the air pure, the water good, whiskey high, game plenty, fiddles in demand, squaws pretty and affable, and no man was ever known to die a natural death in this country."[14] It seems natural that the mining camps would attract vice; it is also natural that the young town of Sioux City would attract fur traders and army men and river men, all noted for a penchant to violence. What is hard to comprehend is the high moral tone and the high society which the newspapers reported instead.

Lyceum lectures were given every week throughout the winter. A dancing school was formed. Tableaux were the fashion at local parties: "A pleasing feature, which is becoming popular at private social gatherings, are the tableaux conceived and executed by young ladies and gentlemen. They are generally of a serio-comic nature and afford much amusement, and are harmless in their results. The actors in some which we recently witnessed were quite *au fait* in their parts."[15] The Sioux City String Band was established. Prizes for the county fair were announced in the categories of oil painting, pastel, crayon, water color, pencil work, and engraving. A "Pike's Peak Ball" was advertised to be followed two days later by a "Grand Musical Ball." In regard to a "brilliant party" of one hundred, an editor wrote: "Had some of our eastern people, who think the citizens of the frontier are little better than semi-barbarians, been present on this occasion and seen the beauty, grace and intelligence of the ladies, and the gallantry of the gentlemen . . . they would have good cause for changing their opinion."[16] It should be emphasized that this was in 1859, when there were no paved streets or sidewalks in the town ("Weather item: Mud! Muddy! Much mud, a heap," or "A slight fall of rain is needed to make the mud really interesting.")[17] and in a region where a man could be lost in an April blizzard a mile or two outside of town. Urban pretensions are surely as important a factor as violence on the frontier. Distinct social castes are in evidence here to contradict ideas of social equality.

The social life is all the more remarkable when we consider the business character of Sioux City. Enterprise was everywhere, community spirit was limited. Large salaries had been voted to the city officials, but not enough

---

[14] Sioux City *Register*, Feb. 3, 1859.
[15] Sioux City *Eagle*, Jan. 22, 1859.
[16] Sioux City *Register*, Jan. 13, 1859.
[17] *Ibid.*, Mar. 24, 1859; Sioux City *Eagle*, Apr. 16, 1859.

taxes were levied so they could collect these salaries. When spring floods swept away all the bridges across the Floyd River, nothing could be done about rebuilding them. What is wanted in Sioux City? asked one editor. More public spirit and less selfishness. "When we are visited by strangers let us treat them liberally and kindly, and not as though they were considered legitimate prey to be skinned and fleeced." [18]

The commercial life of Sioux City ebbed and flowed with the Missouri River, moving from freeze to flood. The town cheered when the first steamboat of the 1859 season arrived on April 9th with one hundred tons of freight and with cigars to relieve a local tobacco famine. Corn and potatoes were shipped out, and an editorial noted a hard economic light: "We are beginning to assume the character of exporters as well as importers, and just as soon as our exports exceed our imports, just that soon may we expect to witness better and easier times." Times were hard in Sioux City in 1859, partly as an aftermath of the Panic of 1857. The city's future was uncertain. The population fell to 767 in 1859 because of the exodus to the Colorado gold mines and did not number in the thousands until long after the Civil War.[19]

Sioux City was no boom town, thanks to the Panic of 1857, the Colorado gold rush, the Civil War, the Indian raids in the 60's, and the drainage of settlers into the Dakotas. The population was predominantly male and extremely transient. Civic duties were ignored; in the municipal election of 1859 only 156 men voted. There was fear that the entire population would leave for the gold mines or, once the Dakota lands were opened, that they would move off there. There was a strong feeling that the town would die unless a railroad could be built, and a frank admission that they were dependent on the federal government for assistance. But there was confidence, too. "Sioux City is bound to go ahead; hard times can't stop her progress." [20]

In line with this get-ahead spirit, there were numerous efforts to secure more people in the west. Much of the optimistic mood and motivation of the time is made clear in the editorial, "The Time to Come to the West." The time to come was obviously now, for property could be had at a low

[18] Sioux City *Eagle*, Feb. 12, 1859.

[19] *Ibid.*, Apr. 16, 1859; *Iowa Historical and Comparative Census, 1836-1880* (Des Moines, 1883), 606.

[20] Sioux City *Eagle*, Apr. 9, 1859; Sioux City *Register*, Feb. 17, Mar. 3, 1859.

cost, emigration to the gold mines and the opening of Dakota Territory would increase the demands for local produce, and "by industry and frugality a home and a fortune may be acquired by the poorest." It was a country unsurpassed for beauty and healthfulness, so free from epidemic diseases there had not been a single death in Sioux City for several months. "There is room, health, wealth and happiness for all who may come in the illimitable west — let all who can come!" [21]

But it was obvious that the emigration was going straight on through to the Nebraska gold mines, as they were called (it was Nebraska Territory, but this was the Cripple Creek strike in Colorado). The papers faithfully reproduced the letters from the gold fields, wildly speculative though they were. The editors cautioned restraint, but as spring came, all they could do was to urge a northern route across Nebraska so that Sioux City could outfit the emigrants. Then the rush was on. The town's only barber left. The daguerreotype man left. The printer of one of the newspapers deserted, and the editor and his "devil" had to publish the paper themselves. At least 10 per cent of the town population had left before April.[22]

So the newspapers sought to halt the exodus by ridiculing the reports from the mountains in terms reminiscent of Mark Twain. "The Wheelbarrow Man" reported that anything left in Cherry Creek for twenty-four hours would be turned to gold. "It is so strange — so marvelously, wonderfully strange, that men can scarcely credit their own senses; and yet it is every word of it true — just as true as some of those gold stories published in some of the papers in Kansas and Missouri." He proceeded to turn to gold his wheelbarrow, pistols, knives, stew kettle, candlesticks, and a dead Indian. Another report was solemnly published that the miners were greatly discouraged because they were compelled to dig through four feet of solid silver before they could reach the gold.[23]

The gold rush was national. Far too many people went out, not enough gold was found, and the starving men who returned attacked the wagon trains of westbound gold-seekers. Twenty thousand people at the Rockies by July, reported one newspaper, and not one in five hundred was making good wages. The gold rush was a humbug, someone charged, to draw people

[21] Sioux City *Register*, Jan. 27, 1859.
[22] Sioux City *Eagle*, Apr. 2, 1859.
[23] *Ibid.*, Mar. 12, 1859; Sioux City *Register*, Mar. 24, 1859.

out of Kansas and keep it out of the Union until after the elections. "Come to Iowa" instead of the mines was the final call.[24]

The whole affair has much to show in regard to the type of person who went west and his motivations. The gold fever was surely enough to unsettle Sioux City, but on top of this came the national break-up of political parties. Considering how recently Sioux City had been settled, considering the preoccupation of the people with get-aheadism and the general exodus to the mines, surely there would be little interest in politics. On the contrary!

Woodbury County, solidly Democratic in 1854 (with 23 voting), voted Democratic until the national election of 1860. In the gubernatorial election of October 13, 1857, the Democratic candidate Benjamin M. Samuels received 144 votes and the Republican Ralph P. Lowe, 125 votes. In the next election for Governor, October 11, 1859, the Democrat Augustus C. Dodge received 163 votes, the Republican Samuel J. Kirkwood, 132. The Republican strength in the county was located in the towns of Smithland and Sergeant's Bluff; Sioux City voted Democratic two to one. In the presidential election of 1860, Woodbury County gave 129 votes to Lincoln, 117 to Douglas, 5 to Bell, and 8 to Breckinridge. It would thus seem that Woodbury's Republican strength in the 50's was mostly a result of defection from the Democratic party, in line with the general Democratic decline throughout the state, and not so much a result of sympathy with the National Republican platform.[25]

The Sioux City *Register* of F. M. Ziebach backed the regular Democrats. Seth W. Swiggett's *Eagle* was avowedly independent, but Swiggett operated as a Bolter within the Democratic party in 1859. The Republicans tried to buy his support in that year; in August he was reported as nearly ready to be bought, "providing satisfactory arrangements can be made to compensate him for the Sacrifices he will necessarily have to make, as a democrat, by taking that course," but "Knowing the character of Mr. S. I would suggest that a very paltry Sum would be no inducement to him." These plans fell through, however, and Swiggett sold out to his opposition, Zie-

[24] Sioux City *Eagle*, May 28, June 4, 1859.

[25] *Census of Iowa . . . 1867* (Des Moines, 1867), 232; Sioux City *Register*, Oct. 13, 1859; *Census of Iowa . . . 1869* (Des Moines, 1869), 263; David S. Sparks, "The Decline of the Democratic Party in Iowa, 1850-1860," Iowa Journal of History, 53:30 (January, 1955).

bach, in October, 1859. The next year he reappeared with a Republican paper, the Sioux City *Times*, which lasted just through the national election (March 16, 1860, to November 16, 1860).[26] The power of the press is indicated. In 1859, both papers supported the Democratic ticket, but in 1860 one paper had gone over to the Republicans. The county's vote moved at the same time in the same direction.

The statistics give little indication of the real political intrigue and attitudes toward politics, but newspaper editorials do. Swiggett was the more aggressive editor, quick to scent out corruption, vituperative in his editorials. He was "out" and Ziebach was "in," allied with what Swiggett called the "clique" — the members of the original Sioux City Townsite Company and two new members, the Register of the Sioux City Land Office (S. P. Yeomans) and the postmaster. Swiggett watched Ziebach like a hawk and was quick to announce any irregularities. In February of 1859 a treaty was signed with the Yankton Indians which would open the way to settlement of the Dakotas. Ziebach and four other men slipped out of town to make illegal land claims, and Swiggett wondered loudly why. In the maneuvering before the city election in April, 1859, Swiggett announced that Yeomans had just sold Ziebach city lots at a nominal sum, and concluded, "The Zebra [Ziebach] is being rewarded for his servility."[27]

Meanwhile, as Ziebach discovered, the "independent" Swiggett was attempting to secure for himself Yeoman's position. Word was sent to Washington that Swiggett was a Bolter, a "political hybrid." Swiggett was dropped and Yeomans reappointed to the Land Office. Swiggett's comment on the affair took this form: "We ain't quite done yet. Look out! Keep your eyes skinned! You don't know where you will get hit next time!" Two weeks later he continued his invective against Ziebach: "Poor cur, we pity you; but you are so sunken and depraved that we fear pity will have but little effect for good on you, and we are therefore induced to give you an occasional kick." He added that Ziebach was a pimp for a little clique, and, "His downcast sheepish look, and averted eye, when he meets an honest man, is proof that a corrupt and wicked heart lies concealed beneath

---

[26] John W. Charles, Sioux City, to C. C. Carpenter, Mar. 28, 1859; E. H. Edwards, Sioux City, to C. C. Carpenter, Aug. 20, 1859, *Cyrus Clay Carpenter Papers* (State Historical Society of Iowa, Iowa City); *History of Woodbury and Plymouth Counties*, 161.

[27] Sioux City *Eagle*, Mar. 5, 29, 1859.

the ugly and loathsome exterior."[28] This type of journalism, common throughout the country at this time, was no doubt motivated as much by a desire for increased circulation as it was by political convictions.

In the same issue, Swiggett smelled a rat in the approaching municipal election. The central committee of the Democratic party announced that it would not name its city candidates until the Saturday preceding the election. Swiggett yelled "anti-democratic" and "dark lanternism" and went to work. Hints of what happened came out afterward. The regular Democrats met on the Saturday afternoon, April 2, 1859, in a blizzard, self-confident but few in number. Once the meeting was opened officially, the Bolters (and Swiggett) appeared in a body and with their majority forced the official party to name their own candidates — but voted the next week for the successful reform candidates of the Citizens' party. Ziebach stormed: "Where is the Republican that would condescend to such meanness?" Swiggett sat back and said calmly: "Election is over; what will come up next to excite and interest?"[29]

Swiggett's whole approach to local politics is instructive. On the local level it was a game, a sport, an entertainment. The only discernible issue was the demand of the Citizens' party to elect city officers who would volunteer to serve without pay (since tax money to pay salaries could not be collected anyway): "We are not choice as to the politics of our officials, so that they will do something for the City," wrote Swiggett.[30] Ziebach and the regular Democrats were more conservative than Swiggett and the Bolters.

On the national level, the Bolters were for Douglas and the regular Democrats for Buchanan, but both were numerically too small to count for much in the state Democratic party. Ziebach complained that the Democratic state convention was run by the eastern Iowa politicians, and naturally it would be.[31] Woodbury County's state representative was elected from an eight-county district in 1859; the state senator was named from a twenty-three county district.[32] However, both the Republican and the Democratic parties recognized the growing importance of the "western slope" and nomi-

---

[28] Ibid., Mar. 12, 26, 1859.
[29] Sioux City *Register*, Apr. 7, 1859; Sioux City *Eagle*, Apr. 9, 1859.
[30] Sioux City *Eagle*, Mar. 19, 1859.
[31] Sioux City *Register*, Apr. 21, 1859.
[32] *Census of Iowa* . . . *1867*, 201, 203.

nated a Lieutenant Governor and a Supreme Court judge from that area, but from Pottawattamie County, not Woodbury. Even Swiggett complained that the Democratic nominee of the Woodbury County district for the state senate, John F. Duncombe of Fort Dodge, was too far away from Sioux City.[33] The frontier had little voice in state politics.

Indeed, Ziebach complained of the general apathy: "In this warfare of personal interests and animosities, local matters have been everything, while state and national questions have received but a meager consideration."[34]

The question remains whether Woodbury County politics was controlled by the townspeople or by the farmers. In spite of the strong suspicion that Ziebach's "clique" and Swiggett's Bolters controlled the local situation, there is at least talk that each individual on the frontier controlled his destiny. A visiting judge in a Lyceum address had this to say: "The Farmer has little time to spare to engage in Politics, and sometimes from that fact is said to be conservative, or to use a recent term, he is regarded as an Old Fogy in politics. But let Political Demogogues [sic] once swerve from a true line of policy, and they soon find that the Farmer is the government."[35] However, since in 1859 some 68 per cent of Woodbury County's population lived in Sioux City, it can be inferred that at this time the town dominated the county, politically, although centers of Republicanism in two smaller towns were growing.

In 1859 and 1860 the Democrats controlled Woodbury County, even though the state of Iowa was now voting Republican. The Bolters voted the Democratic ticket in the fall of 1859 because, as Swiggett made quite clear, the Republicans had refused to include a single Bolter on their slate of local officials.[36] Swiggett, however, said nothing against the Republicans on the national level. That effort was entirely Ziebach's. He called the Republicans disorganized and fanatical. He fulminated on "Slavery Aggression" and spoke of popular sovereignty as the "grand safeguard of freedom and the grand opponent of slavery," and he called Republicanism "Niggerism."[37]

Although Sioux City in 1859 sent delegates to the state convention of

[33] Sioux City Eagle, Aug. 6, 1859.
[34] Sioux City Register, Jan. 6, 1859.
[35] Sioux City Eagle, Mar. 19, 1859.
[36] Ibid., Sept. 24, 1859.
[37] Sioux City Register, Jan. 13, Feb. 10, Mar. 24, 1859.

the Republican, the Democratic, and the Temperance parties, probably the Democratic delegate represented the will of the majority. If so, the majority from this particular frontier town was conservative. The Democratic platform resulting from the state convention at Des Moines, June 23, 1859, may indicate local stands on political issues: (1) reaffirmed the 1856 Democratic stand in favor of states' rights; (2) approved self-government in the Territories; (3) favored territorial popular sovereignty on slavery; (4) asserted the supremacy of the Supreme Court; (5) opposed nullification; (6) favored a tariff for revenue only, but with "incidental protection"; (7) desired the acquisition of Cuba; (8) called for land grants to build a Pacific railroad; (9) favored a homestead act. Resolutions were also passed in regard to state policy: (1) lower taxes; (2) more white immigrants; (3) against cheap Negro labor in the state; (4) against the non-segregation policies in Iowa schools; (5) for the exclusion of freed Negroes from Iowa; (6) for the repeal of the state constitutional provision requiring Negro education; (7) for the liberalizing of present prohibition laws; (8) for the revision of the expensive school system.[38] What is significant is that neither the *Eagle* nor the *Register* complained about any item on this platform, and, as has been noted, the majority in Sioux City and Woodbury County voted the Democratic ticket on October 11, 1859. This must remain a vexing problem to one who believes in the political liberalism of the frontier.

The Democratic platform reflects typical frontier demands — land grants for railroads, a homestead act, lower taxes — and the typical concept of Manifest Destiny. It is a foregone conclusion that our two newspaper editors will reflect an interest in the unlimited expansion of the United States. Pride, boastfulness, self-confidence, and independence of spirit can be read into the newspaper quotations given thus far. The patriotism was strong and rough-shod. "Our people are the most active and enterprising nation on the globe," wrote Ziebach, and elsewhere devoted a long editorial to urging a big navy to protect our expanding interests. Swiggett too displays an international interest on considering the admission of Oregon to the Union: "Further than this we do not propose to look at present, although we are aware that the eyes of Young America are looking eagerly toward Cuba, Nicaraugua [sic] and even at Mexico. It will not be at all surprising if all of these swell the number of American states."[39]

[38] Herbert S. Fairall, *Manual of Iowa Politics* . . . (Iowa City, 1884), 51-4.
[39] Sioux City *Register*, Jan. 20, Feb. 24, 1859; Sioux City *Eagle*, Mar. 5, 1859.

In order to define the frontier spirit, consider Swiggett's editorial on "Democracy." To him democracy meant the rights of the people: "Not the rights of individuals; not the rights of the cast [sic], or class, or section, but the rights of all including each." What were these rights? "The full recognition of each one's claim, the unfettered development of each one's faculties, the unrestricted enjoyment of each one's rights." This can be translated as Jacksonian Democracy with its emphasis on individualism, equal opportunity to get ahead, and a laissez faire attitude concerning government. The history of the democracy Swiggett traces back to Jefferson, "the great founder and originator," but the Jacksonian caste is evident. Note that this is Swiggett and not Ziebach — whose paper, party, and principles were probably more representative of the time and place than Swiggett's. Ziebach is obviously more conservative — "In politics, our faith is DEMOCRACY — our Platform the CONSTITUTION" — and he believed in "correct and well tried political principles — adhering strictly to party usage."[40]

One last extended quotation sums up the complexity, the richness, the boastfulness, the humor, and the realism beyond the frontier. It is an editorial published by Seth Swiggett and not credited by him to anyone else. Whether he wrote it himself, or borrowed it from another paper, is not, however, as important as the fact that he published it with approval as an expression of pride in America, a pride which flourished on the frontier as strongly as anywhere else. Whatever the origin of the piece, it is equal to the best of Davy Crockett or Mark Twain. It is entitled "Our Country."

> There is not the least shadow of doubt about the matter — ours is emphatically, undeniably, incontrovertably, positively, comparatively and superlatively, a great and glorious country. The annals of time furnish nothing to compare with it; Greece was'nt [sic] a circumstance; Rome was "no whar;" Venice could'nt [sic] hold us a candle; while all the modern nations sink into insignificance before our country. It has longer rivers and more of them, and muddier, and deeper, and they run faster, and go farther, and make more noise, and rise higher and fall lower, and do more damage than anybody else's rivers. It has more lakes, and they are bigger and clearer and deeper than those of any other nation. It has more cataracts, and they fall further, and faster, and harder, and roar louder and look grander than all other cataracts. It has

[40] Sioux City *Eagle*, Sept. 10, 17, 1859; Sioux City *Register*, Oct. 20, 1859.

more mountains and higher ones, and more of 'em, and they are harder to get up and easier to fall down than any other mountains. It has more gold, and it is heavier and brighter, and worth more than the gold of other countries. Our railroad cars are bigger, and run faster, and pitch off the track oftener, and kill more people than all other railroads. Our steamboats are longer, and carry bigger loads, and "bile their busters" oftener, and captains swear harder than in any other country. Our men are bigger, and longer, and higher, and thicker, and faster, and drink more whiskey, and chew more tobacco, and spit further, stick their heels higher, and do anything else more and better and oftener than men in all other countries combined. Our ladies are prettier, dress finer, spend more money, break more hearts, wear bigger hoops and shorter dresses, and kick up the deuce generally to a greater extent, than all other ladies. Our politicians can spout louder and lie harder, make gas faster, dodge quicker, turn oftener, make more noise, and do less work, than anybody else's politicians. . . . Our children squall louder, grow faster, and get too big for their trowsers [sic] quicker than all other children.

It is a great country! It is the cornerstone of nations; it is the top of the pile, the head man of the heap, the last button on the coat, the crowning jewel of the diadem, the capitol of the column, the last link in the chain, the observed of all observers. It will eat up the fat ones. When all other nations are numbered among the things that were, it will just be rejoicing in its strength. It will kick all other nations out of existence. It will lick them up as a cow licketh salt. It has now thirty-three States, and "more a comin." It covers more territory than all other nations. And finally, it has louder thunder, faster lightning, bigger hail and colder ice, than can be found in any other part of the habitable globe. Hurrah for this pro—di—gi—ous constellation of free States! Hang a man that wouldn't praise his own.[41]

The mixture of pride and parody in Swiggett's editorial — whether original or not — indicates that a complex civilization existed beyond the Iowa "frontier" in 1859. Undoubtedly the conditions of life were crude, and violence was virtually unchecked. But there is every indication that socially, the frontier pretended to be civilized. This study indicates a greater conservatism socially and politically than the student of history has usually found. The point seems to be the complexity — that one should think twice before making generalizations about life on the "frontier."

[41] Sioux City *Eagle*, Aug. 27, 1859.

The Decline of the Democratic Party in Iowa, 1850–1860
DAVID S. SPARKS

THE DECADE of the 1850s was a tumultuous one for the American nation and as David Sparks points out in the following essay it was also a chaotic period for Iowa Democrats. Maintaining political control from the time Iowa acquired statehood, the party of Jackson retained supremacy until the election of 1860.

In analyzing the decline of the Democratic Party, Sparks believes that previous interpretations were too simplistic and that the Democrats' defeat was far more complex than traditionally presented. In the 1850s Iowa Democrats not only faced such divisive issues as slavery and expansion, but perhaps equally important they consistently failed to get national party leaders to respond to their local needs; requests for internal improvements, railroad land grants and free homesteads went largely unheeded and resulted in a split between the local party and the national party leadership. Thus the internal split coupled with discontent over national party leadership led to the downfall of the Iowa Democrats.

The traditional view that the Kansas-Nebraska dispute caused the decline of the Iowa Democrats is reviewed, but Sparks believes that many other issues were involved as well. Thus the author takes the major national issues of the 1850s, examines the reaction of Iowa Democrats to these issues, and in doing so answers the question—what effect did these have on the demise of Iowa's Democratic Party?

THE DECLINE OF THE DEMOCRATIC PARTY IN IOWA, 1850-1860

By David S. Sparks*

The political revolution of the 1850's in the United States has very properly attracted long and serious study by historians. The death of the Whig party, the division of the Democratic party, and the birth of the Republican party certainly prepared the way for the greatest crisis in their history, as Americans tried to settle by armed force what they had been unable to solve by the art of politics.

Political developments in Iowa during the critical decade following 1850 were of much the same pattern as in all the states of the Old Northwest. Originally Democratic as a result of the party preferences of the first settlers, Iowa soon contained a lively Whig opposition. While the two parties shared town and county offices throughout the state, the Democrats managed to keep control of the constitutional conventions of 1844 and 1846 as well as the territorial and early state legislatures and the executive offices. Iowa Whigs shared the national experience of their party and gradually died out after the presidential campaign of 1852. The Democrats held on a little longer and despite defeat in 1854 managed to remain an organized opposition until the Civil War reduced them to a corporal's guard. Although the Republicans first campaigned as such in 1856, all those elements later making up the party had previously worked together to elect James W. Grimes on an "Opposition" ticket in 1854.

Most studies of Iowa politics during the 1850's have quite naturally concentrated on the Republicans.[1] These studies have carefully detailed Re-

---

*David S. Sparks is assistant professor of history at the University of Maryland.

[1] Louis Pelzer, "The Origin and Organization of the Republican Party in Iowa," IOWA JOURNAL OF HISTORY AND POLITICS, 4:487-526 (October, 1906); Frank I. Herriott, "A Neglected Factor in the Anti-Slavery Triumph in Iowa in 1854," Deutsch-Amerikanische Geschichblatter, Jahrbuch der Deutsch-Amerikanische Historische Gesellschaft von Illinois, 18-19:174-335 (1918-1919); Frank I. Herriott, Iowa and Abraham Lincoln (Des Moines, 1911); Kenneth F. Millsap, "The Election of 1860 in Iowa," IOWA JOURNAL OF HISTORY, 48:97-120 (April, 1950); David S. Sparks, "The Birth of the Republican Party in Iowa, 1848-1860" (Ph.D. thesis, unpublished, University of Chicago, 1951); Edward Younger, "The Rise of John A. Kasson in Iowa Politics, 1857-1859," IOWA JOURNAL OF HISTORY, 50:289-314 (October, 1952).

publican interest in halting the expansion of slavery. They have examined Republican promises for free land, higher tariffs, and a Pacific railroad. They have analyzed Republican leadership, party conventions, campaign strategy, and the party's fate at the polls. Much has been learned about the methods and objectives of Iowa politicians and their supporters during a very critical period. In one respect, however, our understanding of this vital time in Iowa politics remains quite deficient. In concentrating on the positive story of the rise of the Republicans, historians have failed to explore the negative side of the story — that is, the decline of the Democrats in Iowa during the 1850's. Is it not as pertinent to question why men abandoned their earlier allegiance to the Democrats as it is to ask why they turned to the Republicans? Certainly it is true that many Iowans looked upon a vote for the Republican party during the 1850's as no more than a protest against their own Democratic leadership. To a surprising degree the Republican party of the 1850's in Iowa was a temporary refuge for men whose political roofs had fallen down around their ears. It is clear that a thorough understanding of the birth of the Republican party is dependent upon some understanding of the division and decline of the Iowa Democrats which took place in the decade of the 1850's.

The defeat of the national Democratic party has usually provided the chronology and pattern for the brief examinations which the state parties have received. In this process considerable attention has been given to the effects of the Kansas-Nebraska bill, "Bleeding Kansas," the Lecompton Constitution, and the Dred Scott Decision, and, as a result, Democratic decline and defeat is usually dated from 1854. Professor Nichols' brilliant study[2] of the disruption of the national Democratic party begins only in 1856. For Iowa, at least, such emphasis and chronology are misleading. By accepting the national story as the matrix for the Iowa pattern, we distort the early history of the Republicans and the reasons for their success as well as the causes for the "disruption" of the Democratic party in Iowa.

A close examination of the Democratic party in Iowa shows a party so seriously torn by factionalism and so thoroughly at odds with the national party leadership that it was on the verge of collapse before 1854. The party press, county and state conventions, and most of the party leadership were regularly divided into two or more warring camps. Even in the halcyon days between 1846 and 1850 factionalism was a serious problem. A

[2] Roy Franklin Nichols, *The Disruption of American Democracy* (New York, 1948).

persisting conflict with the national party leadership revolved about the problems of slavery and the needs of the state for internal improvements, railroads, and homesteads. The significance of this story of the Iowa Democrats is that it pushes back in time the division and decline of the state organization. This, in turn, reduces the concentration on slavery as the question which destroyed the Democrats and places greater emphasis upon the more "normal" frictions within the party. If further study of the Democratic party in Iowa and in other states of the North tends to bear out the results of this brief review, then we must continue our revision of the causes of the political crisis of the 1850's and the Civil War that followed.

Iowa's first settlers were Democrats by a ratio of nearly two to one. Throughout the territorial period and during the first years of statehood the Democrats clearly controlled state politics. Both William W. Chapman and A. C. Dodge, delegates from the Territory of Iowa to the Congress from 1838 to 1846, were frontier Democrats. The territorial legislature was in Democratic hands, and the first state governors were Democrats. The constitutional convention of 1844 was made up of fifty-one Democrats and only twenty-one Whigs.[3] A similar constitutional convention in 1846, with a total membership of thirty-two, contained twenty-two Democrats and ten Whigs.[4] Iowa's first Senators were Augustus Caesar Dodge and George Wallace Jones who served in the Senate until 1855 and 1859 respectively, while one lonely Whig shared the honors with the Democrats, representing Iowa in the House of Representatives during the first seven years of statehood.[5]

The hegemony of the Democrats in the early political life of Iowa was the direct result of the way in which the land was settled. The earliest settlers came into Iowa from the south by way of the Mississippi and Missouri rivers. This stream of migration flowed into Iowa and spread out along the Missouri border, into the Des Moines River Valley, or on up the Mississippi. As in Ohio, Indiana, and Illinois,[6] the new settlers from the

[3] Benjamin F. Shambaugh, *The Constitutions of Iowa* (Iowa City, 1934), 123.

[4] *Ibid.*, 189.

[5] The Whig was Daniel F. Miller who only won his seat after a congressional investigation ordered a special election to resolve the issue. See Louis B. Schmidt, "The Miller-Thompson Election Contest," IOWA JOURNAL OF HISTORY AND POLITICS, 12:34-127 (January, 1914).

[6] David Henry Bradford, "The Background and Formation of the Republican Party in Ohio, 1844-1861" (Ph.D. thesis, unpublished, University of Chicago, 1947); Roger Van Bolt, "Sectional Aspects of Expansionism, 1844-58," *Indiana Magazine of*

South were Democrats of the Jackson and Benton stamp. They had left behind them the landed gentry who owned slaves, filled the political offices, and who called themselves "broadcloth Whigs." Preferring woodland to the open prairie, these southern settlers took up land in the southern tiers of counties, on both sides of the Des Moines River, and up the Mississippi wherever woodland was to be found. The loyalty of these folk to the Democratic party was so strong that even the overwhelming popularity of Lincoln in 1860 did not win over Lee and Dubuque counties on the Mississippi; Davis, Appanoose, Wayne, and Decatur in the southern tier; or Wapello, Marion, and Boone in the Des Moines River Valley.

Iowa's early Democratic leaders came from among these southern settlers. Both in the House of Representatives and in the Senate there were to be found Iowans who were tied to the South by birth, education, or tradition. The father of Senator A. C. Dodge brought his slaves along with him when he migrated from Missouri to Wisconsin. Young Augustus was raised by a Negro mammy in the best tradition of the South.[7] Senator George W. Jones was bound to the South by ties which even the Civil War did not break. Born in old Vincennes, Jones was raised in Indiana. When he entered Transylvania University in Lexington, Kentucky, in 1821, Jones carried a letter of introduction to Henry Clay. Years later, in an eulogy to Clay, Jones harked back to his own youth and told how Clay was "the guardian and director of my collegiate days; four of his sons were my college mates and warm friends. My intercourse with the father was that of a youth and a friendly advisor."[8] During his college days Jones was also close to Jefferson Davis and to David Atchison, the "Hotspur" of the proslavery forces in Missouri. It was a letter from Jones to the President of the Confederacy in 1861 which led Lincoln's Secretary of State to order the imprisonment of Jones in December, 1861. Jones's Southern sympathies cost him several very uncomfortable months in a Northern prison, but even Secretary Seward could not prevent Jones's two sons from joining the Confederate service.[9]

History, 48:119-40 (June, 1952); John S. Wright, "The Background and Formation of the Republican Party in Illinois, 1846-1860" (Ph.D. thesis, unpublished, University of Chicago, 1946).

[7] *Congressional Globe*, 33 Cong., 1 Sess. (1853-1854), Appendix, 381.

[8] *Cong. Globe*, 32 Cong., 1 Sess. (1851-1852), 1638. For biography of A. C. Dodge, see Louis Pelzer, *Augustus Caesar Dodge* (Iowa City, 1908).

[9] John C. Parish, *George Wallace Jones* (Iowa City, 1912), 62.

The history of the Democratic party in Iowa prior to the Civil War is one of crumbling hegemony in which dissension led to division and defeat. One major source of Democratic difficulties was a growing divergence between the needs of the local party and the demands of the national party leadership. From the day that Iowa had entered the Union there had been signs that the local Democracy would find it difficult to support wholeheartedly the national platform. Even the large measure of agreement between the two on the issues of slavery and the status of the Negro in national life was sometimes threatened. Most Iowa Democrats were anti-Negro, indifferent to slavery in the South, and opposed to the entry of either into Iowa or the territories to the west. Most local party chieftains shared the national party's hope that slavery would never become an issue in national politics, but dissent cropped up even on this subject. The Germans, Dutch, English, and Scandinavians who came into Iowa in the 1850's regularly joined the Democratic party and just as regularly were openly hostile to the institution of slavery. They were not abolitionists but they were unwilling to see it spread.

Second only to slavery in the politics of the day was the issue of expansion. Iowa was thoroughly imbued with the spirit of Manifest Destiny. To most Iowans it mattered little whether settlers expanded north, west, or south, so long as territory was added to the national domain. Further, the enthusiasm of Iowans for the Mexican War indicated that they cared little whether it was peaceful expansion or conquest. Although President Polk's decision for war against Mexico was widely applauded, most Iowans soon were sorry that Polk had not lived up to his brave campaign slogan of "54° 40' or Fight" and had negotiated instead a settlement with the British in Oregon.

There can be little doubt that much of the early success of the Democratic party in Iowa was the result of its devotion to expansion. Unfortunately the Democratic advantage was soon neutralized by the introduction of the Wilmot Proviso in 1846, forcing the Democrats to take a stand on slavery whenever they tried to make political capital out of expansion. After the introduction of the famous Proviso, Iowa Democrats had either to advocate slave expansion or the expansion of free soil and were denied the pure joy of supporting simple expansion without reference to slavery. The result was to divide the Democracy in Iowa. Before the ink was dry on the Treaty of Guadalupe Hidalgo one faction of the party was ready to repudiate the administration if any further expansion of slave territory resulted from the defeat of the Mexicans. The possibility of demanding an indemnity of Mexico and taking part of her northern provinces as payment of such an indemnity provided grounds for further division in local Democratic ranks.[10] Loyal party men stood helpless while the Democrats' political capital evaporated in the growing controversy over slavery.

Iowa Democrats labored under even greater difficulties in the matter of the party position on internal improvements at federal expense. The local organization made repeated efforts to follow eastern and southern leadership and oppose internal improvements, but the needs of a frontier state were much too insistent. The obvious necessity for transportation of all kinds forced Iowa Democrats to break away from the national party policy and seek federal aid for river improvements and land grants for railroads. Even before Iowa had been admitted to the Union, Delegate A. C. Dodge had succeeded in obtaining from Congress a grant whereby alternate sections of the public lands, forming a strip five miles wide on each side of the Des Moines River, were set aside to aid the Territory in improving the navigation of the stream. With admission to the Union, Iowa increased its demands for such aid. Democratic Representatives William Thompson and Shepherd Leffler tried hard to have the improvement of the Des Moines and Rock River rapids of the Mississippi River included in the rivers and harbors bills of 1846 and 1847. The fact that they were not successful did not make President Polk's vetoes of the two bills any more palatable to Iowa Democrats. All through the 1850's Democratic administrations in Washington were able to bring a few local Democrats to heel on the matter of internal improvements, but the overwhelming majority of the Iowa party was stubborn and steadfast in its approval of internal improvements at federal expense.

Finally, a fourth issue seriously dividing Iowa Democrats during the antebellum period was land. A grant of free land out of the tremendous reservoir of the public domain was the dream of every western settler. By 1846 the dream had taken concrete form in the demand for a homestead law which would grant free land to those who would settle upon it. Undeniably popular in Iowa, the homestead idea ran into considerable opposition in the East and the South. When the eastern and southern leadership of the Democratic party regularly pigeonholed the homestead bills intro-

---

[10] Iowa City *Iowa Capital Reporter*, March 29, 1848.

duced into every Congress, Iowa Democrats could do little more than wring their hands and try to avoid the subject at home among their constituents.

The divisions in the Iowa Democracy over slavery, expansion, internal improvements, and land, as well as on several minor issues, were generally between two rather well-defined groups. One, usually labeled the "administration" group, followed the lead of George Wallace Jones in state politics. This group reached its peak of power under the Pierce administration. The other faction, the anti-administration Democrats, tended to follow the lead of Augustus Caesar Dodge, but his absence from the country as ambassador to Spain from 1855 to 1859 deprived this wing of the party of responsible leadership at the time it was most needed.

Genuine party politics came to Iowa in 1848. While politicians had been cutting their teeth on the preceding two-year struggle to elect United States Senators,[11] it was not until the first presidential election after statehood that all the platforms, conventions, and miscellaneous paraphernalia of a real campaign appeared in Iowa. The Democrats made a clean sweep of county, state, and congressional offices in the August election, and in November they carried the state for Cass in the presidential contest. The widespread rejoicing over the handsome victory was, of course, marred by the election of Taylor to the presidency, but there is little evidence that Iowa Democrats were much worried by the cracks which had appeared in the party armor during the canvass. The immense popularity of the Mexican War and the resulting land cessions had dictated party strategy. Democratic ownership of the Mexican War was defended against the Whig attempts to steal the credit. The Wilmot Proviso was castigated as a bald move to drag the issue of slavery into national politics, and Iowa Democrats were united in their belief that slavery was strictly a problem for the Southern states. A few editors shed a tear or two over the defection of Martin Van Buren, and at least one noted the danger to the Union involved in the Free Soil party, but most Iowa Democrats felt the local party was immune to the antislavery agitation of the Free Soilers. Van Buren was pictured as the candidate of a "long-heeled, wooly-headed, flat-nosed, runaway negro, mongrel whig disorganizing Convention!"[12]

[11] Dan Elbert Clark, *History of Senatorial Elections in Iowa* (Iowa City, 1912), 1-48.
[12] Iowa City *Iowa Capital Reporter*, July 19, 1848; Keokuk *Dispatch*, Sept. 2, 1848.

But the problem of internal improvements did give Iowa Democrats some trouble in 1848. Unable to sidetrack the issue they were forced to admit serious disagreement on the question. While President Polk had vetoed rivers and harbors bills in 1846 and again in 1847, Democrat William Thompson spoke for the majority of Iowa Democrats when he voted for the Petit resolution in the House repudiating the President's action.[13] Indeed, scarcely more than six weeks after the veto message was published, Representative Thompson was back at the old stand pleading for either a land grant or a cash grant of $50,000 from the federal government for the improvement of the upper Mississippi River. Even Whig editors sympathized with the local Democrats and admitted the futility of all efforts in the face of presidential vetoes.[14] In the course of the campaign Democratic editors went so far as to fabricate a sympathy for internal improvements on the part of Lewis Cass out of his voting record in Congress. But this fell flat, for the Whigs recalled quite readily the way in which Cass had refused to identify himself with the great Rivers and Harbors Convention in Chicago the previous July.[15] In the summer of 1848 the administration in Washington began to crack the party whip, for a few Democratic papers in Iowa reversed themselves and started to try to make a case for the Polk vetoes and the national party position on internal improvements. In such papers the President was pictured as the only barrier between a voracious East and a defenseless West, while the grants in rivers and harbors bills were likened to "a golden trumpet" for the East and a "tin whistle" for the West.[16] At least one Iowa Democrat went so far as to echo Polk's constitutional doubts and, at the risk of being laughed out of the whole Northwest, called the bills "unjust to other portions of the Union" because they appropriated "more than Half a Million of dollars to the improvement of 'Harbors' on the Lakes which as 'ports of entry' have no existence save on paper. . . ."[17] Fortunately for the local party, the campaign of 1848 was decided on the issues of expansion and slavery; on these the Democrats were united. Winning control of the state legislature in 1848 gave the Democrats the right to name two United States Senators. Such a handsome prize made the difficulties over internal improvements seem minor.

[13] *Cong. Globe,* 30 Cong., 1 Sess. (1847-1848), 59.
[14] Fort Madison *Iowa Statesman,* Feb. 5, 1848.
[15] Keokuk *Des Moines Valley Whig,* June 23, 1848.
[16] Burlington *Iowa State Gazette,* May 29, 1848.
[17] Bloomington [Muscatine] *Iowa Democratic Enquirer,* July 15, 1848.

The year 1850 was a good one for Iowa Democrats. Alone among the states of the Northwest, Iowa had no avowed Free Soilers in either the state legislature or in Congress.[18] In the gubernatorial contest Democrat Stephen Hempstead defeated Whig James Thompson by a comfortable margin. William Penn Clarke, the Free Soil candidate for governor, won only 575 votes out of a total of over 25,000. In congressional elections, too, the Democrats were victorious in both districts. This happy state of affairs largely resulted from the Democrats' firm support of the Compromise of 1850.

The efforts of Clay, Douglas, and Webster to find a method of keeping the question of slavery out of national politics were perfectly suited to the mood of Iowa Democrats. Just before the Clay resolutions were introduced in the Senate, the editor of the Dubuque *Miners' Express* was busy belaboring the Free Soil agitation of slavery so far from the home of the slaveowners.[19] With the introduction of Clay's compromise resolutions the *Miners' Express* and all other Iowa Democrats were given a focus for their efforts to halt the agitation of the slavery question.[20]

Meanwhile, in the Senate A. C. Dodge waded into the opponents of compromise:

> . . . when I read these bitter animadversions from the North and East upon what I regard as the patriotic exertions of the venerable Senator from Kentucky to pour oil upon the troubled waters, and listen here to the merciless denunciations which both he and his resolutions receive from my friend from Mississippi, I could not but feel for the Senator from Kentucky a sympathy which nothing in his past history had awakened in me.[21]

At the same time, Jones busied himself introducing petitions and resolutions in favor of the Compromise. In July he reported that "in a large correspondence . . . equal, perhaps, to that of any member of Congress — I have received from my constituents and friends *not one* letter which takes ground against the compromise bill." Jones was expressing the heartfelt sentiments of all Iowa Democrats on the subject of slavery when he cried, "Would to God that this Congress could so elevate itself above the passions

---

[18] Theodore C. Smith, *The Liberty and Free Soil Parties in the Northwest* (New York, 1897), 244.

[19] Dubuque *Weekly Miners' Express*, Jan. 30, 1850.

[20] *Ibid.*, Feb. 6, 1850.

[21] *Cong. Globe*, 31 Cong., 1 Sess. (1849-1850), 404.

and prejudices of the day as forever to give the quietus to this distracting question!"[22]

All through the summer of 1850 the Democrats of Iowa, following the lead of Dodge and Jones, pounded away at the need for concessions in order to preserve the Union. It was the spirit of the Wilmot Proviso which the Democrats had come to fear by 1850. Dodge called the Proviso "a mask from behind which abolition seeks to destroy the Constitution, and, as an inevitable result, the Union."[23] The party press, while admitting that some of the provisions of the Compromise were "not to our liking" (notably the new fugitive slave law), agreed that "every good citizen should overlook the little of evil that may result, and be satisfied with the vast amount of good to flow from a definite and permanent adjustment of questions which have always proved too much for American equanimity. . . ."[24]

Iowans were content, regardless of party, to follow the Democratic lead in accepting the Compromise, for as Dodge said, they wanted "to get the subject from before" them. Undoubtedly they would have echoed his thoughts when he said: "I am sick, sore, and tired of it; and therefore, though this measure is one that does not please me in all its parts, I shall swallow it in order to get the subject out of the halls of Congress. . . ."[25] The feeling that slavery was a question like a time bomb which might blow up the party and the Union was as prevalent among Iowa Democrats as it was in Washington. Local party meetings and conventions adopted resolutions and planks like the one passed in the Second Congressional District maintaining that "the continued and prolonged excitement" had been "kept up on the subject of slavery by designing demagogues in Congress and elsewhere for selfish and interested motives. . . ."[26]

But the prestige and power of the Iowa Democrats were greatly weakened in 1850 as a result of their acceptance of the fugitive slave law embodied in the Compromise. Both Dodge and Jones, in their efforts to win Southern support for the Compromise, had made statements which seemed a little strong to many of their Iowa constituents as well as to their enemies.

[22] *Ibid.*, Appendix, 1716.
[23] *Ibid.*, 1085.
[24] Bloomington [Muscatine] *Iowa Democratic Enquirer*, May 30, 1850.
[25] *Cong. Globe*, 31 Cong., 1 Sess., 1086.
[26] Muscatine *Iowa Democratic Enquirer*, June 13, 1850.

The Senators tried to allay Southern suspicions of Iowa's sincerity in support of the Compromise. For his part, Jones reminded his Southern colleagues in the Senate of his long residence in slave states and charged that the evils which Free Soilers and abolitionists described in such lurid detail were a better reflection of their fanaticism than of actual conditions of slavery in the South.[27] Dodge felt constrained to read to the Senate a state law of Iowa which prohibited the entrance of free Negroes into the state except under a $500 bond.[28] While such statements might serve to convince the South that a true compromise spirit prevailed in Iowa in 1850, they would live to haunt local Democrats for years to come.

Whatever the future might bring, the present belonged to the compromisers, and the fact that the Democrats possessed a monopoly of the pro-compromise votes in Congress was thoroughly exploited. The governor, both houses of the legislature, and both congressional districts remained Democratic in 1850-1851. The spirit of compromise was still supreme when the Whigs and Democrats began their spring maneuvers for the presidential campaign of 1852. The Whigs opened their February convention with a firm resolve that the Compromise of 1850 was a settlement of the slavery question "now and forever."[29] Together with the Democrats, the Whigs denied the concept of a "higher law" on the subject of slavery. Convening in April, the Democrats devoted four of the eight planks in their platform to singing the praises of the "final compromise." All Whig efforts to introduce other issues into the campaign came to nought when the Democrats refused to be drawn into a discussion of internal improvements, a new national bank, or distribution of the proceeds from the sale of public lands. Instead, the Democrats sat tight and expounded upon the virtues of their noncommittal candidate, Franklin Pierce. Pierce and the Compromise gave the Democrats a winning combination. This they knew, but there were more impelling reasons for the type of campaign they conducted in 1852.

The first of these reasons was the existence of a growing division in Democratic ranks both before and after the election of 1852. In Dubuque, the "Gibraltar of Democracy," the Jones wing of the party took umbrage at the nomination of Lincoln Clark for Congress from the Second District

[27] *Cong. Globe*, 31 Cong., 1 Sess., 1716.
[28] *Ibid.*, 1623.
[29] Keosauqua *Western American*, March 6, 1852.

and refused to print his name on the ticket when it appeared in the local party press. They gave out the startling information that Clark's name was not being printed because of the way in which "politicians" had become "despots" in the matter of making nominations.[80] A truce was subsequently worked out, however, and in the end Clark received the support of the Jones faction.

Perhaps Jones was a little extra touchy because he himself was a candidate for re-election. The traditional arrangement in Iowa decreed that the northern and southern halves of the state should share equally in political offices and privileges. This was especially true in the matter of senatorships. Since the term of A. C. Dodge, who was a Burlington man, ran until 1854, Jones and his friends assumed there would be no opposition to the right of Dubuque to name the new Senator and that Jones would be it. But opposition there was. Jones had apparently neglected to include a Burlington railroad project in a plea for federal land grants which he had introduced into the Senate,[81] and there was considerable talk in Democratic circles of ignoring the old north-south division of the spoils. It looked to Jones like the beginning of a move to throw him overboard.

There was quite clearly a concerted drive in several factions of the state party to defeat Jones, but most of it appears to have remained beneath the surface and confined to the professional politicians.[82] Jones fought back as best he could, putting all the pressure he could on the national party leadership to grant Iowa some railroad lands. In June he had written to the party's presidential nominee, Franklin Pierce, that he had "great fears for the success of our party in my own State if the Bill now before the House making a grant of land to the State of Iowa for the construction of certain Rail Roads in that State, be not passed."[83]

Jones was quite correct. The party was in serious trouble because of railroads. Iowa was displaying a positive mania for railroads in the spring of 1852, but the state was too sparsely settled to support, without federal aid, one-tenth of the railroads it envisioned. The fact that the national

---

[80] Dubuque *Weekly Miners' Express*, July 7, 1852.

[81] Parish, *George Wallace Jones*, 44.

[82] Clark, *History of Senatorial Elections in Iowa*, 52; Dubuque *Weekly Miners' Express*, Dec. 15, 1852.

[83] George Wallace Jones to Franklin Pierce, Washington, June 7, 1852, *Franklin Pierce Papers* (Library of Congress).

party refused to support federal expenditures of land or cash for such ventures put an intolerable strain on the state Democracy. Democrats in the House and Senate had been and would continue to be most diligent in their attempts to win federal support, but by the time some success was achieved by the land grant of 1856 the local party was too far gone to derive much benefit from it.

According to election returns in 1852, the Democrats had done fairly well. It appeared that local party leadership may have been overly pessimistic, for Pierce carried the state, the Democrats controlled the legislature and would choose the next Senator, and the party had won in both congressional districts. But balanced off against this impressive showing was the Free Soil vote now three times its 1848 total, with a sizeable portion of it coming from traditionally Democratic counties in the southeastern corner of the state. Also on the debit side was the continued split in Democratic ranks which was now completely in the open as the party caucus met to decide upon a successor to Jones. A bitter fight ensued. If James W. Grimes can be believed, the feeling was intense. He wrote to his wife, "Everybody is busy electioneering, some for one office and some for another, but the all-engrossing subject is the election of United States Senator. It has already been the subject of one bloody fight, and many more are anticipated."[34] The election of Jones was finally rammed through the Democratic caucus, but not until party loyalties had been strained to the breaking point in the case of many individuals.

If the years following the election of 1852 had presented no problems, the Democratic party in Iowa might have found a new basis for unity and patched up its many quarrels. But few parties in American history have been allowed a respite in which to thrash out their family troubles, and the Democrats of Iowa were no exception. Outside pressures on the party increased rather than lessened. The greatest of these came from the way in which the local party continued to be squeezed between the demands of a frontier state for internal improvements, railroads, and homesteads, and the national party's refusal to open the federal purse.

Throughout 1853 Iowa's railroad fever continued unabated. In October the *Enquirer* of Muscatine noted that every tier of counties was backing a favorite railroad, and several of them seemed sure that their projected road would become a link in the transcontinental railroad which all Westerners

[34] William Salter, *The Life of James W. Grimes* (New York, 1876), 31.

were eagerly awaiting.[85] A host of counties mortgaged themselves for years to come in order to purchase stock in railroad companies, many of which never laid a single mile of track in Iowa.[86] Examples of the extent of the fever can be found in virtually every issue of every newspaper published in Iowa during the summer of 1853. One issue of such a paper carried the news that Dubuque County had just voted $200,000 in bonds to promote the Dubuque & Pacific Railroad, while the city of Dubuque had come up with $100,000 more for the same road; Linn County was to vote the following week on a $200,000 bond issue for the Iowa Central Air Line Railroad; the Iowa Western Railroad had the support of Mahaska County to the tune of $60,000, Keokuk County for $25,000, Warren County for $10,000, Marion County for $50,000, and Muscatine for $55,000.[87] There was scarcely a businessman or politician in Iowa who did not have an interest in some railroad.

Iowa Democrats were naturally called upon to win the coveted land grants to aid construction. Both Senators Dodge and Jones supported a projected grant to the Davenport and Iowa City road as early as 1851. In February of that year Dodge introduced in the Senate a bill designed to secure public land for railroad use.[88] Dodge recognized that opposition from the South within the ranks of the Democratic party threatened to defeat the whole land grant movement. In an effort to head off such opposition he cited the deciding vote which the martyred Calhoun had cast in support of a land grant to the Illinois and Michigan Canal and argued that the Calhoun vote was an excellent precedent for southern Democratic approval of railroad grants.[89] Dodge and his friends succeeded in driving the bill through the Senate over Southern opposition, but the grant died in the House.

Jones was back in 1852 with his bill, "Senate Bill One, An Act to grant the right of way, and making a grant of land to the State of Iowa in aid of the construction of certain railroads in that State." Once again the bill passed the Senate only to be defeated in the House. To make matters worse for the Iowa Democracy, Senate Bill Three, "An act granting the

---

[85] Muscatine *Iowa Democratic Enquirer*, Oct. 20, 1853.

[86] Earl S. Beard, "Local Aid to Railroads in Iowa," IOWA JOURNAL OF HISTORY, 50: 1-17 (January, 1952.)

[87] Muscatine *Iowa Democratic Enquirer*, June 11, 1853.

[88] *Cong. Globe*, 31 Cong., 1 Sess., 392.

[89] *Ibid.*, 848.

right of way to the State of Missouri to aid in the construction of a railroad from Hannibal to St. Joseph in said State," passed both the House and Senate and became law just after the Iowa bill was defeated. Dodge and Jones might well have wondered if the national Democratic leadership was trying to destroy the party in Iowa. Whatever the purpose, Iowa's dreams of getting on the highroad to the Pacific were being regularly thwarted between 1850 and 1854 by opposition within national Democratic ranks.

It was the same need (and mania) for railroads which led Iowa into the embroglio of the Kansas-Nebraska bill. Land grants for Iowa railroads could be logically defended if such roads were to become part of the mainline of the Pacific railroad or if (and this was far more likely) they were to become feeders and distributors for the transcontinental line. Iowans also were very much concerned with the future of the territory on their western border. All past frontier experience indicated that Iowans would be the largest single group in the settlement of the Platte River country when it was opened. Iowa railroad men, real estate promoters, bankers, and politicians watched eagerly for the first sign that the new lands would be opened. During 1853 the Pierce administration had concluded a series of treaties with the Indian tribes in Nebraska and Kansas, and it was apparent that the trans-Missouri lands would soon be available for settlement, investment, and exploitation.

The story of Hadley Johnson illustrates the immediate interest of Iowans in the Nebraska country and explains their initial enthusiasm for the Kansas-Nebraska bill of 1854. A member of the legislature and a state politician of some note, Johnson had settled in Council Bluffs in the expectation that it would become the eastern terminus of the Pacific railway. In October, 1853, a vagrant Missouri newspaper fell into his hands. The paper carried the information that a group of Missourians, missionaries, and Wyandotte Indians were going to hold an election in the country across the Missouri River. While the Missourians were apparently making no claims for the legality of their election, Johnson became convinced that Iowans could not afford to be bested in any respect in the Kansas-Nebraska country. He quickly organized a group of "impromptu immigrants" numbering over 350 men who rowed over to Scarpy's Landing on the Nebraska side of the river in order to hold an election. When the vote was counted it was found that Johnson had received the endorsement of every man present for the office of "Delegate from the Provisional Government of Nebraska to the National Congress." After the Scarpy's Landing proceedings had been "ratified" by several meetings along the Iowa "slope," Johnson set out for Washington to join Senators Dodge and Jones in their efforts to prepare a new bill for the organization of a territorial government for Nebraska.[40] When Congress convened in December, 1853, Dodge again introduced a Nebraska bill which was promptly referred to Stephen A. Douglas' committee on territories. That committee went to work immediately upon it, reporting early in January. Within a few days the measure had been modified to include provisions for the repeal of the 36° 30' line of the Missouri Compromise and allow slavery to enter the Nebraska Territory, if the people there should vote for it. Now the fat was in the fire.

Too long has the defeat of the Democrats in Iowa been interpreted as resulting almost exclusively from the party's stand on the Kansas-Nebraska bill. According to this understanding, the Democrats were driven from power by an angered and aroused citizenry who could not stomach the "soft" attitude of the party on the subject of slavery. In this respect the role of the "Anti-Nebraska" Democrats has been carefully examined and emphasis placed upon their resistance to the introduction of slavery into the West. Without depreciating the significance of the Kansas-Nebraska bill and the slavery question in the decline of the Democrats and the beginning of the Republican party in Iowa, it can be shown that the story is far more complex and significant than has been believed.

There were at least five distinct problems or issues which the Democrats faced as the campaign of 1854 opened. Over and above these five concrete problems, discussed in both party councils and press, was a sixth one only dimly understood at the time. This latter problem, and probably the most fundamental one, was the lack of purpose in the national Democratic party. The youth and vigor of Jackson's day were gone; the glory of the Mexican victory had faded away. There was no reforming zeal or crusading fervor left in the party, no positive issue to which it was dedicated. A truly conservative party might well survive and prosper without any of these, but the party of Jackson had never been conservative. One finds no dedicated souls among the Iowa Democrats of this age. They were honorable, responsible, and diligent men, but such qualities rarely inspire an electorate.

[40] William E. Connelly (ed.), "The Provisional Government of Nebraska Territory," Nebraska State Historical Society, *Proceedings and Collections* (2nd series), 3:84-7 (1899).

The Democratic party in Iowa, as in the nation, was old and tired. Long in power (the Harrison and Taylor interludes had not broken the Democratic grip on the political life of the nation), the local party now contented itself with the small questions of office and favors. In addition to this basic problem of no positive purpose, the Democracy of Iowa was defeated in 1854 as a result of (a) the excessive factionalism we have seen at work earlier; (b) a record of failure to achieve the coveted federal lands and money desired by the entire Northwest; (c) a bad case of defeatism; (d) the temperance issue; and (e) the question of slavery and the Kansas-Nebraska bill.

The Democrats got off to an early start in the campaign of 1854, opening their convention in Iowa City on January 9. The date is of some consequence, for it is the day before the Kansas-Nebraska bill appeared in the Washington *Sentinel*, with the additional Section Twenty-one, which gave the first intimation that the Missouri Compromise line was in jeopardy. January 9, 1854, was almost two weeks before the famous White House conference in which the Democratic leadership decided to make an administration measure of the repeal of the Missouri Compromise. Thus signs of factionalism among Iowa Democrats in their January convention had nothing to do with the Kansas-Nebraska bill and the problem of slavery in the territories. As a matter of fact the only reference to the whole problem was the adoption of a simple resolution calling for the speedy organization of the Nebraska territory.

But that factionalism was present was evident in many of the actions taken by the convention. The resolution of thanks to the party's representatives in Washington was introduced but defeated. Such a vote of thanks was normally taken for granted; its defeat meant the party was in serious trouble. The finished platform was a collection of mild generalities including planks against monopolies and disunion and favoring the Declaration of Independence and the Constitution. After giving the Pierce administration a pat on the back, the convention did agree upon a general endorsement of the national party's platform of 1852, which had included approval of the Fugitive Slave Law, but no specific endorsement of that law was made. The platform was plainly a compromise affair between bitterly feuding factions. The knotty problem of banks was ignored as were the questions of railroad land grants and the homestead law. Nothing was said about the location of the state capital, one of the hottest issues of the day, nor did the rising temperance movement receive either encouragement or reproof. Silence was obviously considered the best alternative to agreement and unity.

The Democrats' failure to secure the much-coveted grants of land and money for homesteads, railroads, and internal improvements also hurt the party during the 1854 contest. The campaign started off ominously with the rejection of another homestead bill by the Eastern and Southern leaders of the Democracy. Piled on top of previous defeats, with no sign that the national Democratic leadership would ever relent and pass a homestead law, this defeat gave an air of futility to the actions of Dodge and Representative Bernhart Henn who had fought valiantly in both the Senate and the House for the measure.[41] There is, on the other hand, some indication that the homestead bill which Henn introduced in the House in December, 1853, became something of a handicap to the Iowa Democrats in the subsequent campaign. The Henn measure would have prevented several categories of foreign-born from deriving any benefits under the bill, and Iowa Germans were particularly sensitive to any discrimination at this time because of a rising tide of nativism in many communities in the state.[42] The Democrats were equally unsuccessful in securing land grants for railroads. Dodge and Jones continued to present the petitions of various Iowans for a grant to this or that railroad.[43] They made speeches[44] and spent a good portion of their time seeking support for the Iowa grants. The pressure on the Democrats on this score appears to have increased somewhat during the year because of a slump in railroad building, making federal grants seem imperative for their continued construction. The third plank in the economic platform of the Northwest also remained a stumbling block to the Democracy: federal support of internal improvements. When the Pierce veto of a rivers and harbors bill was announced, Iowa Democrats accepted it without a murmur.[45] It was not unexpected and certainly added to the sense of frustration plaguing the Democrats of the entire Northwest as they watched their economic program either ignored, defeated, or vetoed, and largely by their own party leadership in the East and South.

[41] *Cong. Globe*, 33 Cong., 1 Sess., 1127-8.
[42] Herriott, "A Neglected Factor in the Anti-Slavery Triumph in Iowa in 1854," 66-70.
[43] *Cong. Globe*, 33 Cong., 1 Sess., 159, 221, 273, 407, 1058.
[44] *Ibid.*, 357-8.
[45] Muscatine *Iowa Democratic Enquirer*, Aug. 17, 1854.

Democratic defeat in 1854 has been frequently attributed to overconfidence.[46] It would be more accurate to call it defeatism. Since the state legislature to be elected in the fall was the one that was to choose a successor to Dodge in the Senate, he was as much a candidate as other Democratic nominees in the state. In spite of his personal stake in the campaign, Dodge did not return from Washington, and his total public contribution to the canvass was a couple of joint letters which he and Jones sent to the Democratic press in Iowa. It is significant that when the Democrats were defeated, Dodge accepted an appointment as ambassador to Spain rather than return to Iowa and try to repair the damage the party had suffered. He did not return to the state until 1859. Jones's contribution was no more substantial. While not a direct candidate for office, he certainly had much at stake. Aside from participating in the joint letters with Dodge, he sat pat in Washington. When his term expired he followed Dodge's example and accepted the post of minister to New Granada and never returned to political prominence in Iowa. These are not the actions of men determined to hold their party together and turn back the vigorous challenge of their foes, but rather of men who had already lost a large measure of hope.

A fourth problem to give the Democrats trouble in 1854 was the "Maine Law agitation" as the temperance question was then labeled. Maine had recently adopted a law prohibiting liquor, and all the states of the Old Northwest seemed to be following suit and were in the midst of referendums on the issue. The temperance movement had been developing for some years in Iowa, but until 1854 it had remained outside of politics. However, late in 1853 several state temperance leaders came to the conclusion that the success of the crusade elsewhere warranted a bid for legislation in Iowa.[47] Accordingly, each of the parties was approached early in 1854. The Democrats refused to commit themselves on the subject, but the "Opposition" was receptive and adopted a platform plank in support of prohibition. In the course of the campaign Henry Clay Dean, the "stormy petrel of Iowa politics," tried to nail down the two gubernatorial candidates on the temperance question. In open letters to both Curtis Bates and James W. Grimes, Dean asked them to outline their position on the temperance issue

---

[46] Herriott, "A Neglected Factor in the Anti-Slavery Triumph in Iowa in 1854," 7; George Fort Milton, *The Eve of Conflict* (Boston, 1934), 173; Sparks, "The Birth of the Republican Party in Iowa, 1848-1860," 114.

[47] Dan Elbert Clark, "The History of Liquor Legislation in Iowa," IOWA JOURNAL OF HISTORY AND POLITICS, 6:68-70 (January, 1908).

and their course of action if elected. Although both Bates and Grimes replied that they would not veto a prohibition bill, it was well known throughout the state that Grimes was personally a temperance man, while Bates preferred either a license law or no legislation at all. Actually, neither party was united either for or against prohibition, although there is little doubt that the bulk of the temperance people were among the Whigs or "Opposition," while the majority of the Democrats wanted to leave the subject alone. As a result, while the question of prohibition divided both parties in 1854 to some extent, it divided the Democrats themselves even more. The aforementioned Henry Clay Dean became one of the most active campaigners in the state in behalf of Bates and prohibition.[48] This led to difficulties in towns like Dubuque, Muscatine, and Burlington, where the German population was high and the prohibition sentiment low. The Dubuque *Miners' Express*, a Bates paper, noted with an evident air of distaste the activities of "Henry Clay Dean the Temperance Brawler" and spoke of him as a *"raving* and *ranting* apostle of temperance."[49] In the Second Congressional District, James Thorington, a well-known temperance advocate, won the "Opposition" nomination and went on to defeat the popular ex-governor Stephen Hempstead.[50] After the election, editorial comment was in general agreement that temperance had been the vital issue in that District. Further evidence of the handicap which the liquor question imposed upon the Democrats may be deduced from the vote taken in April of 1855 resulting in the adoption of prohibition for Iowa. To a surprising degree the counties returning majorities against a prohibition law were the same counties voting Democratic in 1852.[51] But even the Democratic anti-prohibition counties contained very substantial prohibition elements which had weakened the party in the previous campaign.

Thus it is evident that the Democrats in Iowa might well have been defeated even if there had been no problem of slavery in the territories and no Kansas-Nebraska bill. Democratic factionalism in the local party, repeated defeats for the Northwestern economic program, defeatism, and troubles with temperance had thrown the party way off balance.

[48] Charles E. Snyder, "Curtis Bates," Iowa Journal of History and Politics, 44: 307 (July, 1946).
[49] Dubuque *Weekly Miners' Express*, June 28, 1854.
[50] Muscatine *Iowa Democratic Enquirer*, Aug. 31, 1854.
[51] State of Iowa, *Official Register, Executive, Judicial and County Officers of the State of Iowa, 1889* (Cedar Rapids, 1889), 207-208.

State Democratic leaders appear to have been quite as surprised by the storm of protest kicked up by the Kansas-Nebraska bill as was the national party leadership. They also seemed to share the view that the Missouri Compromise had been effectively repealed by the Compromise of 1850, even though that repeal was not explicit. All three of Iowa's Democratic representatives in Washington emphasized the virtues of expansion and thought the repeal of the 36° 30' line a small price to pay for the tremendous benefits that would follow. In his major speech in the Senate on the measure, Dodge predicted that the "settlement and occupation of Nebraska will accomplish for us what the acquisition and peopling of Iowa did for Illinois." He then explained that he had originally thought of creating a single territory to the west of both Missouri and Iowa but soon switched to support of the "establishment of *two* Territories; otherwise the seat of government and leading thoroughfares must have all fallen south of Iowa."[52] Obviously Iowa's interest in organizing the territories centered on the "seat of government and leading thoroughfares" (meaning railroads).

Bernhart Henn used a little more circumspect language, but his meaning was the same. In May he told the House:

> . . . it was the mission of our race to subdue the wilderness of the North American continent. . . . We have acquired possessions on the Pacific; we need roads thither to protect them! We have planted our banners west of the Rocky Mountains; we need American muscle to hold them aloft! Between us and them interpose Nebraska and Kansas. The sovereignty is ours — the possession must follow. By organizing these Territories, we have American law, *created by American will*, from the Atlantic to the Pacific. We have a safe conduit for our overland emigration. We have peace with the Indian tribes. We have increased commercial advantages, and increased wealth as a nation.[53]

Perhaps the trouble with the Democrats was that they were carried away by their visions of Manifest Destiny and simply could not imagine that anyone in Iowa would oppose a measure so lofty in purpose and so promising in its prospect of profits.

Senator Jones agreed with Dodge and Henn on the virtues of the Kansas-Nebraska bill. However, he seems to have sensed the danger in an open endorsement of the measure, for in his only Senate speech on the subject

[52] *Cong. Globe*, 33 Cong., 1 Sess., Appendix, 382.
[53] *Ibid.*, Appendix, 885-8.

Jones confined his remarks to an attack upon the Clayton Amendment.[54] This amendment, introduced by Clayton of Delaware, had its roots in the nativist sentiments gaining currency in these years. The amendment would have limited the right to vote and hold office in the proposed territories to citizens of the United States. This was contrary to the frontier experience, where a man's presence in the new community was all that was normally required to make him eligible for the suffrage and office holding. Jones, with long personal experience in frontier politics, knew that, regardless of Iowa's reaction to the bill as a whole, his foreign-born constituents would deeply resent the second-class status which the Clayton Amendment would create for them. Jones was also aware that the foreign-born Democrats in Iowa were already upset by the provisions of the homestead measure currently before the House, which had been introduced by Henn. And finally, by concentrating upon the Clayton Amendment, Jones was able to obscure his general approval of the Douglas bill. He was so successful in this last objective that the Whig press in Muscatine sternly accused him of "shirking the responsibility" when it announced the vote on the bill in the Senate.[55]

With few notable exceptions, opposition to the Kansas-Nebraska bill was as general among Iowa Democrats at home as approval had been in the Washington contingent. Both of the Democratic newspapers in Dubuque rejected the Douglas bill when it was first reported, but within a week they had reversed their stands.[56] Originally opposing the measure on the grounds that it would needlessly reopen the slavery question, they both laid their change of heart at the door of Douglas' speech. A search of the surviving files of Democratic newspapers fails to show another paper, either pro- or anti-administration, which approved the Kansas-Nebraska bill. A very revealing side light appears in the columns of the *Iowa Democratic Enquirer* of Muscatine. Late in 1853 H. D. LaCossitt had sold the paper with the understanding that he could send back to the new editors dispatches from the Washington scene. LaCossitt wrote a series of articles while in Washington during the Kansas-Nebraska debate. These articles were in support of the Nebraska bill, and the new editors of the *Enquirer* dutifully printed them. The *Enquirer's* editors then devoted several edi-

[54] *Ibid.*, Appendix, 779-80.
[55] *Muscatine Journal*, March 10, 1854.
[56] Dubuque *Weekly Miners' Express*, Feb. 8, 1854.

torial columns to explaining why they could not agree with their Washington correspondent and why they persisted in their rejection of the Douglas bill.[57] The foreign language press, largely Democratic, joined in the repudiation of the national leadership. Theodore Guelich, editor of *Der Demokrat* of Davenport, slashed out at the "despicable treachery" of Douglas and the administration. Guelich also made the rather acute observation that this bill simply revealed that the fundamental differences between the moribund Whigs and the divided Democrats had disappeared and that they were now being held together solely in the interests of office and spoils. He also predicted the rise of a new party that would put fresh spirit and purpose into American politics.[58]

The famous "Appeal of the Independent Democrats," penned in Washington by Salmon Chase, signed by Charles Sumner and four other abolitionists or Free Soilers, and so influential in wreckng the Democratic parties in Ohio and Illinois, apparently had little effect on Iowa Democrats. It was published by both the New York *Times* and Horace Greeley's *Tribune* and thus certainly received wide circulation in Iowa, but the fact that it was reprinted in only one newspaper in the state would indicate that the local politicians found it inapplicable to the Iowa situation.[59]

It is very difficult to determine the exact damage done to Iowa Democrats by the Kansas-Nebraska bill. In the flurry of Anti-Nebraska meetings which were held all over the state, Democrats did take part. They were present, along with "Conscience" Whigs, Free Soilers, Abolitionists, and Know-Nothings. The press of the day frequently observed that many men gathered outside of halls where Anti-Nebraska meetings had been called and waited to see the size of the crowd and the political complexion of those present before declaring themselves by entering the hall. Few prominent Democrats allowed their names to get into the press in connection with these meetings, and the correspondence of such men sheds little light on the subject. Most of the election returns of 1854 are no more significant, for they do not distinguish between those who left the Democratic party because of its record of failure and dissension and those who left only with the introduction of the Kansas issue. The victory of Democrat Augustus

---

[57] Muscatine *Iowa Democratic Enquirer*, Feb. 9, 16, March 2, 1854.

[58] Quoted in Louis Pelzer, "The History and Principles of the Democratic Party in Iowa, 1846-1857," IOWA JOURNAL OF HISTORY AND POLITICS, 6:205-206 (April, 1908).

[59] Ottumwa *Des Moines Courier*, March 2, 1854.

Hall over Rufus L. B. Clarke in the First Congressional District had greater significance than it had generally been accorded. As the Keokuk *Dispatch* observed:

> Mr. Hall was nominated as a Nebraska man; the Convention that placed him before the people, eschewing a timid policy, passed resolutions endorsing the great principles of popular sovereignty, contained in the Nebraska-Kansas Bill. . . . This demonstrates that our general defeat in Iowa was not caused by the Nebraska measure.[60]

The opinion of the *Dispatch* cannot be accepted without reservations, but it does help to redress the balance. It reminds us that the Democratic defeat in Iowa in 1854 was the result of a complex series of events, some of which, like the frustration of the Northwestern economic program, dated back to the Polk administration, and many of which were the result of a loss of purpose. Excessive factionalism, a defeatist attitude, divisions on matters like prohibition, the location of the state capital, and the constitutional prohibition on banking in the state were the symptoms of a sick party. Just as the healthy human body is host to bacteria and virus at all times, but sickens and dies only when the invaders exceed a certain number, so a political party can stand considerable dissension and many honest differences of opinion but will weaken and die if these things become excessive.

In the campaigns following the 1854 defeat the Iowa Democrats continued to be bothered by a variety of troubles. Throughout 1855 and 1856 the Know-Nothings showed considerable power; they found the Democrats particularly easy prey. It must be remembered that the main sources of Democratic strength in Iowa were the early settlers in the southern border and river counties and the immigrant elements concentrated primarily in the river counties. Here, the anti-foreign-born prejudices of the Know-Nothings were highly popular with many of the native-born and quite unpopular, naturally, among the immigrants. The Democrats were particularly anxious to stifle the Know-Nothing movement before it drove the German vote into the arms of the "Opposition." In a Democratic convention of the Eighth Judicial District of Iowa, comprising the counties of Jones, Clinton, Muscatine, Scott, Cedar, and Jackson, the only issue deemed worthy of a resolution was one taking a strong stand against the Know-

[60] *Keokuk Dispatch*, Sept. 13, 1854.

Nothings.[61] Muscatine Democrats followed suit some months later.[62] A Jefferson County Democratic convention provided a variation: as a preliminary to participation in the convention, each delegate was required to "rise in his place and give a pledge that he was a Democrat and had no sympathy with Know-Nothings."[63] Within a year the Know-Nothings had acquired a party press of at least five newspapers and apparently more voting strength in one year than the abolitionists had acquired in ten years. The relationship of the Know-Nothing movement to the decline of the Iowa Democracy was properly understood by the editors of the Muscatine *Enquirer*. These editors noted that the death of the Whig party and the divisions in the Democratic party had left many men without a political roof. Such men were ready to "go in for anything rather than the two old organizations." The real threat of the movement lay in the fact that many men found it the "readiest means to break up the old parties, with which they were dissatisfied."[64]

The Democrats were further demoralized in 1855 by the departure of A. C. Dodge for his position in Madrid, leaving the anti-administration wing of the party without experienced leadership. By 1856 the various "Opposition" elements had succeeded in forming a Republican organization in the state and carrying Iowa for Fremont, as well as winning both seats in Congress. Democratic reaction was feeble; rather than searching out the best candidates they might have nominated and trying to exploit the many mistakes made by the inexperienced Republicans, the Democrats continued to spend most of their energies on squabbling among themselves. In August, 1857, just six weeks before the gubernatorial contest, Jones wrote to former President Pierce, revealing the full extent of his party's collapse. According to Jones:

> I have had a great deal of correspondence with the present admintration [Buchanan's] relative to the offices in this state, all of which they intended to fill by other than my friends through the influence of the men in the state who went for Mr. Buch[anan] for the nomination in preference to yourself who they knew I preferred to all other men on earth. I distinctly gave them to under-

[61] Muscatine *Iowa Democratic Enquirer*, March 15, 1855.
[62] *Ibid.*, July 19, 1855.
[63] Charles J. Fulton, "Jefferson County Politics Before the Civil War," *Annals of Iowa* (3rd series), 11:437 (July, 1914).
[64] Muscatine *Iowa Democratic Enquirer*, Nov. 30, 1854.

stand that if men who had been apptd to office by yourself at the instance of my colleagues & myself were to be removed from office merely to gratify such fellows as [Thomas S.] Wilson, [Augustus] Hall, [Lincoln] Clark and the like — and their favorites were made to succeed them & I could not procure their rejection by the Senate that I would resign the seat which I hold there & allow another abolitionist like Mr. Harlan to be appted as my successor.[65]

Surprisingly enough, one of the factors which accounted for much Democratic embarrassment in other northern states in 1857, and which is normally credited with being an important factor in the decline of the Iowa Democracy, apparently had no effect. This was the famous Dred Scott Decision which, with its endorsement by the Buchanan administration, wrought havoc in some sections of the North. A careful search of the Iowa press reveals only an occasional announcement of the Supreme Court's decision and no political discussion of it at all. This is equally true of both the Republican and Democratic press in 1857. The Dred Scott Decision seems to have had no perceptible effect on the declining Democratic fortunes until it became a very minor issue in the 1860 presidential campaign.

The year ended with the Democracy split further by the Lecompton debacle. While Senator Jones endorsed the Buchanan approval of the proslavery Lecompton Constitution for Kansas, 90 per cent of the Democratic editors in the state supported Stephen A. Douglas' rejection of the Lecompton "fraud," and repudiated the leadership of Jones.[66] This situation persisted throughout 1858, culminating in a comic opera scene in Dubuque. Although Jones's term in the Senate was to expire in March, 1859, the legislature which was to choose his successor had been elected in 1857 and that election had been won by the Republicans, giving them the choice of the next United States Senator. Under these circumstances a senatorial nomination by the Democratic caucus would be honorific — an endorsement for past policies rather than a promise of future support. But Jones's support of Buchanan and the Lecompton Constitution gave his old rival, Thomas S. Wilson, an opportunity to repudiate Buchanan and reprimand Jones by taking from him the endorsement of the Democratic caucus in the legislature. The race between Jones and Wilson became heated and lasted

[65] George Wallace Jones to Franklin Pierce, Dubuque, Aug. 6, 1857, *Pierce Papers.*
[66] Muscatine *Iowa Democratic Enquirer,* January and February, 1858, *passim.*

long after it had become a statewide joke. Many editors likened the Dubuque wrangle to the famed feud between Shakespeare's Montagues and Capulets.[67] The upshot of the affair was that Benjamin Samuels was chosen to make the futile race,[68] his choice being interpreted as an emphatic repudiation of the Buchanan administration by the Iowa Democracy.[69]

With Jones out of the way in 1859, as minister to New Granada, and Dodge returning to the state to make the run for governor, the Democrats began to perk up. Stephen A. Douglas in the Senate gave the Iowa party and the entire Northwest a leader they could honestly follow. His emphasis upon popular sovereignty squared with the hopes and experience of Iowans. The Democratic Convention, remembering Dodge's long service to the party, his proven vote-getting ability, and his absence from Iowa during the 1856 fiasco and the Lecompton mess, nominated him by acclamation. His companions on the ticket included Thomas S. Wilson and two other prominent Douglas men. The usual resolution backing the national administration was stopped cold on the floor; for a time it looked as though Buchanan actually would be censured, but cooler heads prevailed. The finished platform was a straightforward statement of the Douglas position: it endorsed popular sovereignty; repudiated the Dred Scott Decision, together with the Supreme Court; called for the acquisition of Cuba, the building of a Pacific railroad, and passage of a homestead law; and condemned the move to reopen the African slave trade. On state issues the platform was a little more equivocal but not nearly to the degree that had become habitual during recent campaigns.

When the election was over in 1859, Iowans had chosen the taciturn Samuel Jordan Kirkwood over the fiery A. C. Dodge, but by a margin so slim that it gave Republicans cold chills. In a total vote of 110,048, Kirkwood won by a majority of only 2,964. It was a slight increase over the size of the Republican victory of 1857 but only a little more than half the victory Grimes had won back in 1854. While a county-by-county survey of the election showed that the Republicans had picked up five scattered counties which had been Democratic in 1857, it also showed that the Demo-

[67] Parish, *George Wallace Jones*, 49-52; Clark, *History of Senatorial Elections in Iowa*, 104.

[68] There is added evidence of the severity of the Democratic schism in 1858 in Mildred Throne, "C. C. Carpenter in the 1858 Iowa Legislature," IOWA JOURNAL OF HISTORY, 52:31-60 (January, 1954).

[69] Clark, *History of Senatorial Elections in Iowa*, 118-19.

crats had won back three of the counties voting Republican in 1857. An unimpressive two counties was the net Republican gain. In spite of the good showing Dodge had made, the fact that they had been defeated even behind their best vote-getter seems to have taken most of the starch out of the Democrats: if they could not win with Douglas and Dodge in 1859, what chance had they in 1860?

The February convention to choose delegates to Charleston was completely dominated by Douglas men who chose A. C. Dodge and Benjamin M. Samuels to head a delegation of eight. After reaffirming its 1856 platform, denouncing John Brown and his raid on Harper's Ferry, and voting a perfunctory thanks to the Buchanan administration, the convention instructed its Charleston delegates to cast their ballots as a unit for Stephen A. Douglas "so long as he should be a candidate before that body."[70] Ben Samuels played a prominent part in the Charleston drama, joining other Iowans who watched in dismay as the convention disintegrated.[71] Later, in Baltimore, there was not one dissident voice as Iowa delegates joined the Northwestern Democrats in nominating Douglas.

The Democratic ratification convention met in Des Moines on July 12. It was a dispirited crew and reached for straws to keep afloat. The first five resolutions of the meeting pledged allegiance to Douglas and adherence to the doctrines of nonintervention and popular sovereignty; the sixth was a plea for homestead legislation. Beyond that the convention sought to shift the discussion from national problems to local issues. Apparently working on the assumption that a flood of words might drown their troubles, the convention adopted seventeen more resolutions, making the final platform the longest in the history of the state.[72]

The overwhelming majority of Iowa Democrats either went along with Douglas or stayed home, but a small group met in Davenport on August 15 to promote the Breckinridge-Lane candidacy. This faction chose a full slate of presidential electors and adopted an ultra-Buchanan platform. The heart of the movement lay in Davenport and Scott County with some support coming from other river towns. This "National Democracy" had one lone voice in the Lyons City *Advocate*, but the enthusiasm that comes with a

[70] Louis Pelzer, "The History of Political Parties in Iowa from 1857 to 1860," IOWA JOURNAL OF HISTORY AND POLITICS, 7:216 (April, 1909).

[71] Owen Peterson, "Ben Samuels in the Democratic National Convention of 1860," IOWA JOURNAL OF HISTORY, 50:225-38 (July, 1952).

[72] Herbert S. Fairall, *Manual of Iowa Politics* (Iowa City, 1884), 54-7.

chance for victory was not there, and the moral fervor which usually characterizes a third party was missing.

Iowans never doubted that the Republicans had the state in the bag. On the one hand was the divided Democracy, fast losing its grip on the spoils and daily becoming more identified with the interests of the South. A long series of defeats in Iowa had left it without leadership or enthusiasm. The Republicans, on the other hand, were strong in their youth and popularity. The smell of victory was in the air, and ambitious men were hurrying to get aboard the bandwagon. A firm grip on the state patronage gave Republicans an ample supply of money and loyal workers at the grass roots level (in precincts or townships).[73] Senator Grimes, answering an inquiry from Abraham Lincoln concerning Republican prospects in Iowa, reported that the state would go Republican "by an increased majority."[74] Grimes thought the Democrats with their candidate Benjamin Samuels were waging a last-ditch fight in the First Congressional District to defeat the Republican incumbent, but even there Grimes was confident of victory. Grimes's report to Lincoln showed that he was far more concerned about the outcome in Pennsylvania and Indiana than in Iowa. He was right: in Iowa, Lincoln defeated Douglas by 70,000 to 55,000; Breckinridge and Bell each received just over 1,000 votes and less than 3,000 altogether.

The Democracy of Iowa had harvested the bitter fruit of years of division which went all the way back to 1850-1851. A bankruptcy of ideas and purposes had led to division between national and local parties and to dissension within the local party itself. The Democrats could not close ranks on the issue of prohibition. Local party chieftains were thwarted by the national leaders when Iowa's need for federal land or money grants was advanced. A general atmosphere of hopelessness and defeatism had replaced the old vigor of the Jacksonians. Offices and spoils had become a major concern of the party leaders as well as of the usual party hacks. The issue of slavery served to topple a badly weakened Democracy whose foundations had already crumbled as a result of bitter and long standing divisions. The 1860 crisis and the Civil War which followed merely empha-

[73] In July the *Iowa Capital Reporter* of Iowa City went over to the Republicans for a reported $500 plus a promise of county printing. J. Edward [H?]orce to Grenville M. Dodge, Iowa City, July 29, 1860, *Grenville M. Dodge Papers* (State Dept. of History and Archives, Des Moines, Iowa), Vol. I.

[74] James W. Grimes to Abraham Lincoln, Burlington, Oct. 1, 1860, *Abraham Lincoln Papers* (Library of Congress).

sized the depth of these divisions and prolonged their life. Democrats loyal to the Union had become first disgruntled Democrats and then had joined the Republican party because they had nowhere else to go.

Development of the Grange in Iowa, 1868–1930
MYRTLE BEINHAUER

TODAY IN IOWA the Grange is a relatively small farm organization. Four Iowa counties—Jasper, Poweshiek, Delaware, and Muscatine—presently have Grange units for a combined membership of 1,650. In the decade following the Civil War, however, the Grange experienced a high degree of success in the Hawkeye State. Large numbers of farm families joined the organization to make known their discontent with the country's economic and political systems as well as to seek social and educational advancement. Thus the Grange in Iowa mirrored the farm discontent evident throughout the entire United States. Faced with economic hardships which they believed were not of their own making, farmers banded into such organizations as the Farmers' Alliances and the Grange. They formed scores of third political parties throughout the Midwest and the South as well, most of which were shortlived.

Myrtle Beinhauer's article gives a lucid account of the Granger movement in Iowa. Beginning with the conditions that produced discontent, she then explains their growth and internal organization. Throughout the selection both the immediate and long range goals of the group are visible; cooperative buying would bring temporary economic relief but better rural living would also come through social and educational improvements. The Grange offered something for everyone and, as author Beinhauer concludes, perhaps added some color and excitement to the otherwise drab lives of farm people at that time.

Development of the Grange in Iowa, 1868-1930

By Myrtle Beinhauer[*]

Since Iowa is an agricultural state, it is understandable that early interest in the improvement of rural life and production was evidenced. Soon after Iowa Territory was created, the landowner turned his attention to the improvement of his status. The Territory was first open for settlement in 1833. By 1838, its First General Assembly passed a law providing for the organization of county agricultural societies.

The farmer showed continued interest in improving his product, his way of life, and his economic status. Throughout the years the Iowa farmer has organized and supported societies dedicated to the improvement of agricultural pursuits and the general welfare of the rural population. Predominately, in the early years of Iowa's development, these organizations emphasized improvement of the farmer's lot through education, but they could not avoid economic and political activities. Later, there appeared societies whose primary concern was the economic problems of the farmer, and still others which were basically political in nature.

The Origin of the Granger Movement

The second oldest agricultural society in Iowa is the Grange, which was founded in 1868.[1] This organization, having had its inception in Washington, D.C. among government officials, is national in scope and, when once started, it found hearty support in Iowa.

Conditions in the South gave rise to the Granger movement. After the Civil war the farmers of America, particularly those in the South, were suffering from hardships and losses. Because of their circumstances, President Johnson, in 1866, authorized the Commissioner

[*]Assistant professor of economics, Western Michigan University, Kalamazoo.
[1] The oldest is the Horticultural Society, founded in 1866.

of Agriculture to send a clerk through the South to procure "statistical and other information from those states."[2]

Oliver Hudson Kelley was selected for this mission. He not only noted the farmers' financial distress, but was struck by "their blind disposition to do as their grandfathers had done, their antiquated methods of agriculture, and most of all by their apathy."[3] Kelley pondered the situation of the southern farmers and initiated an organization for them based upon the Masonic Order of which he was a member. He interested some of his friends in the idea and, in 1867, seven men, "one fruit grower and six government clerks, equally distributed among the Post Office, Treasury, and Agricultural Departments," founded the Grange.[4] These men were: O. H. Kelley and W. M. Ireland of the Post Office Department, William Saunders and Rev. A. B. Grosh of the Agricultural Bureau, Rev. John Trimble and J. R. Thompson of the Treasury Department, and F. M. McDowell, a pomologist of Wayne, New York.[5] On December 4, 1867 they framed the constitution which was the official beginning of the National Grange of the Patrons of Husbandry.

The purpose of the Grange was the advancement of agriculture through education rather than through politics. With this idea in mind, the men begam organizing the farmers according to their new plan. At first progress was slow, but agricultural conditions were so deplorable that the farmer, nearly desperate, was ready to try almost anything to improve them, and before long the Granger movement was in full swing. In Iowa and the surrounding states, it was particularly successful. Dissatisfaction in the midwest was so great that the farmers of this region accepted the organization more readily than those of other sections of the United States.

[2] Solon J. Buck, *The Agrarian Crusade* (Vol. 45 of *The Chronicles of America Series;* New Haven: Yale University Press, 1919), p. 1.
[3] *Ibid.,* p. 2.
[4] *Ibid.,* p. 1.
[5] *Ibid.,* p. 4.

Causes for the Rise of the Grange

According to W. A. Anderson, in his article "The Granger Movement," there were economic, political, social, educational, and psychological reasons for the Grange's rapid growth in America.[6] Of these, the economic factors were the most vexing to the farmer, with his most bitter grievance against the railroads. The farmer must market his produce and, in an effort to secure better transportation facilities for his goods, he had supported the railroads, investing large sums in them. He was disappointed in his investment, for he did not receive dividends, nor were his shipping rates lowered.[7]

The railroads had their problems also. Traffic was not great, competition was keen and, in their effort to realize a profit, they discriminated in rates between various towns and customers. Persons shipping to distant points were charged lower rates than those shipping short distances. Thus developed the so-called "long and short haul" discrimination. Again, persons frequently shipping large amounts were given lower rates or, if charged the same rates, were given rebates. These practices incensed the farmer,[8] who was not a beneficiary. In addition, passengers were treated discourteously. Accommodations for them were inadequate, and the conductors and brakemen were rude to them.

The low price of farm produce caused by overproduction during the Civil war and the aftermath of the Reconstruction period contributed to the discontent. During the war between the states, farm products had been in great demand and their prices were high but, with the close of the war, the demand for these products decreased without a corresponding decrease in their production; so naturally prices fell. Martin, writing in the decade of the 70's, said, "One of the principal causes of the great distress prevailing among the farming in-

[6] W. A. Anderson, "The Granger Movement," *Iowa Journal of History and Politics*, Vol. 22. (January, 1924), p. 9.
[7] Solon J. Buck, *The Granger Movement* (Vol. 19 of *Harvard Historical Series;* Cambridge, Mass.: Harvard University Press, 1913), p. 294.
[8] Anderson, *op. cit.,* p. 5.

terest today is the low price which the farmer receives for his product."⁹

On the other hand, while the farmer was getting a low price for his products, the middleman was making handsome profits, or so it seemed to the unhappy farmer. Martin expressed the sentiment of the time when he said:

> Now the truth is, that of all the profits we have enumerated, (miller's, merchant's, and farmer's) that of the farmer is the smallest and the most unfair. It is not in proportion to that of the merchant or miller. He is robbed by the railroads in the first instance, and in the next place his price is kept down in order that the grain merchant and the miller may enlarge their profits.¹⁰

Depreciated currency was a third reason for complaint. Many farmers had contracted debts during the Civil war when prices were high and currency was inflated. These debts had to be paid with goods. With the return to peace, money began to appreciate in value which was equivalent to a decrease in prices. Naturally, if a product was worth only 50 per cent of its former value, it would require twice as much to pay a given debt. This meant that, while the dollar amount of the debt had not increased, the lower price of goods had the effect of increasing the indebtedness. Greater purchasing power was paid the creditor than he had loaned and, conversely, the debtor farmer repaid greater purchasing power than he had borrowed. With falling prices, it became increasingly difficult for the farmer to meet his obligations plus the seemingly exorbitant interest rates.

Finally, among the economic reasons for dissatisfaction were high taxes. To defray the cost of the Civil war, the government needed more money. Taxes rose. Theoretically, taxes on all property were increased during the period of strife, but in reality the farmer felt the burden most keenly because his property was

[9] Edward W. Martin, (pen name of James Dabney McCabe), *History of the Grange Movement* (San Francisco: National Publishing Company through A. F. Bancroft Company, 1873), p. 294.
[10] *Ibid.*, p. 295.

chiefly in land which was easily assessed. On the other hand, possessors of intangible property were able to avoid taxes on a large portion of their holdings since they could easily be concealed.[11]

The next group of causes of discontent among farmers, in order of importance, was the political. Anderson accredited this to the fact that the farmer was underrepresented in the legislature. To prove his point he stated that the farmers were represented by one legislative member to every 228,000 persons, while professional men were represented by one to every 10,800, and trade and industry by one to every 26,000.[12] It is the opinion of Buck that, at this period, the farmer was looked upon as a stable element whose vote could be depended upon for the party, and hence his interests received little consideration from the politician.[13]

The remaining causes of discontent, while seemingly minor, were nevertheless significant. Educationally and socially great differences existed between rural and urban populations. Rural communities were comparatively isolated and had fewer school facilities than the towns. Consequently, they did not enjoy the social and educational advantages of the urban districts, and they felt the apparent class distinction between themselves and their city cousins.[14] Psychologically, the extreme individualism of the farmer increased his discontent and dissatisfaction, but at the same time, it made him more willing to support an organization whose purpose was to better the then existing conditions.[15]

Growth of the Granger Movement in Iowa

With the farmers of the country so obviously disgruntled, the Grange found fertile soil, especially in Iowa, where agriculture was the chief occupation. Iowa claims the oldest Grange west of the Mississippi River,

[11] Anderson, *op. cit.*, p. 6.
[12] *Ibid.*, pp. 7-8.
[13] Buck, *The Granger Movement*, p. 36.
[14] Anderson, *op. cit.*, p. 8.
[15] *Ibid.*, p. 9.

that of Buena Vista, located about four miles from Newton.[16] This Grange came into existence when A. Failor of Newton, on May 2, 1868, sent the required $15.00 fee to Washington, D.C. and secured a charter for the Newton group.[17] This was soon followed by a second Grange, established at Pottsville October, 1869. Later that same year, Kelley himself organized a third at Waukon.

During the year 1870, largely through the efforts of General W. D. Wilson, nine more Granges were added, making a total of twelve such organizations in Iowa.[18] On January 12, 1871, representatives of these twelve local groups organized the Iowa State Grange with Dudley W. Adams, Master and General W. D. Wilson, Secretary.[19] At this time the enthusiastic members planned to organize the entire state into local Granges and to work through them to redress the grievances of the farmer. As a result of their ardor and activity, the number of Granges in Iowa reached thirty-seven by April, 1871; by the end of that year, 102 locals had been instituted.[20] Within another year, over one-half the Granges in the entire United States were in Iowa; of the 1,150 local Granges in existence, 652 were in Iowa.[21] This surprising development was revealed by Martin when he reported that, "the most remarkable growth was manifest in the state of Iowa, in which as many as eighty Granges per week were organized at one period of the present year [1873]."[22]

The following chart shows the singular growth of the Grange in Iowa.[23]

[16] Letter, F. L. Hummel, Master of the Iowa State Grange, to Myrtle Beinhauer, February 16, 1931.

[17] Anderson, *op. cit.*, p. 13.

[18] Buck, *The Granger Movement*, p. 49.

[19] *Ibid.*, p. 50. The State Grange held its first meeting after its organization meeting, September 14, 1871.

[20] Anderson, *op. cit.*, p. 13.

[21] *Ibid.*, p. 13.

[22] Martin, *op. cit.*, p. 410.

[23] Buck, *The Granger Movement*, chart between 58 and 59.

The Growth of Local Granges in Iowa, 1873-1874

Date	No. of Local Granges
May '73	1507
Aug. '73	1763
Oct. '73	1818
Mar. '74	1918
Sept. '74	1991

Another way to demonstrate the spectacular development of the Granger movement in Iowa is to compare it with the growth in other midwestern states as is done in the following table.[24]

The Growth of Local Granges in Midwestern States, 1873-1874

State	May 1873	Aug. 1873	Mar. 1874	Sept. 1874
Iowa	1506	1763	1918	1999
Minnesota	219	327	467	538
Missouri	245	483	1807	1976
Kansas	128	399	1073	1350
Nebraska	100	300	504	596
Illinois	431	562	1148	1503
Indiana	142	266	1502	1987
Ohio	47	80	594	1014
Michigan	24	40	284	496
Wisconsin	140	189	410	504
Dakota Territory	8	11	47	56

Philosophy of the Grange

The Grange, as organized, was a fraternal organization and, therefore, a secret society exclusively for the farmer. Its signs and its symbols played upon the imagination and, since social contacts of the farmer were few at the time of its origin, it filled a need of the period and became distinctly a farmer's club. Membership in the Grange gave a certain glamour and distinction to an otherwise drab existence. At its monthly meetings, the farmer forgot some of the dull monotony of his existence and eagerly participated in the ceremony and business of the organization.

[24] Anderson, *op. cit.*, p. 15.

Its purpose, as expressed in the declaration of the National Grange adopted at St. Louis in 1874, was:

> ... to foster mutual understanding and cooperation, to buy less and produce more in order to make our farms self-sustaining, to diversify our crops, to act together for our mutual protection and advancement, as occasion may require, to dispense with a surplus of middlemen and bring producers and consumers, farmers and manufacturers into the most direct and friendly relations possible[25] and to advance education among ourselves and our children.[26]

As has been implied, the Grange was composed of the local, the state, and the national Grange units. The local Grange was, of course, the smallest. Anyone interested in agricultural pursuits, male, 16, and female, 18, might become a member,[27] after having paid a membership fee of five dollars for men and two dollars for women.[28]

> The membership of the Order is confined to persons engaged in agricultural pursuits. This limitation is necessary as the success of the Order depends upon the unity of interests existing among its members. There must be a common object and a common incentive to attain the fulfillment of that object.[29]

A charter could be issued a local Grange when at least nine men and four women had pledged themselves to membership, that is, when there were enough persons to fill the offices of a local unit. These officers were Master, Overseer, Lecturer, Steward, Assistant Steward, Chaplain, Treasurer, Secretary, and Gatekeeper, filled by men, and Ceres, Pomona, Flora, and Lady Assistant Steward, held by women.[30]

Originally the subordinate Grange conferred four degrees:

[25] National Grange, *Declaration of Purposes*, pp. 1, 2 (Adopted at St. Louis in 1874).
[26] *Ibid.*, p. 4.
[27] Martin, *op. cit.*, p. 434.
[28] *Ibid.*, p. 434.
[29] *Ibid.*, p. 422.
[30] *Ibid.*, p. 423.

Degree	Men	Women
First	Laborer	Maid
Second	Cultivator	Shepherdess
Third	Harvester	Gleaner
Fourth	Husbandman	Matron

The members assure us that each rank was conferred with a beautiful, elaborate, and appropriate ceremony. Although the Grange was a secret organization, we have learned that the "ritual is intended to symbolize man in his upward progress toward a better and higher condition."[31] According to the philosophy contained in the ritual, man's moral and economic development are similar. Man began life as a barbarian. At first he lived by hunting and fishing and was often hungry, but gradually he learned that by laboring, by collecting flocks, and by tilling the soil, he could be assured of plenty. As a result, man began cultivating the soil. As the earth in its primitive state is unfit to bring forth products, so the mind of man without training is unfit to develop moral men and women. As the soil must be prepared to receive the seed, so the mind must be prepared to receive moral truths. Therefore, in the first degree, confidence in intelligent guidance, perseverance in overcoming difficulties, faith in his teacher and guide, and the lesson of fraternity were implanted in the mind.

In the second degree, emphasis was placed upon charity. Just as all soils do not yield the same quantity nor quality of a product, all men do not respond in the same way to their environment. The influences on human life are varied and the result is that human character is diversified. Hence, the members of the Grange were taught to be charitable to their fellowmen.

The third degree was that of the Harvester. After the seed had been planted and grown to maturity, harvest began. The members were assured that for every problem of life there is a solution which comes with the same regularity and certainty as the annual

[31] Smedley, *Manual of Jurisprudence and Co-operation of the Patrons of Husbandry*, p. 84.

harvest in the agricultural world if they will but wait for it. Consequently, they were taught to await patiently the solution of their problems and not let the mind go forth into the future seeking for evil, or anticipating darkness which may never materialize, or when confronted is easily overcome. "A well-balanced mind will look every difficulty which really presents itself, squarely in the face, and use all honorable and legitimate means to surmount it or put it aside; but a constant going out into the future to borrow trouble is unworthy."[32]

The lessons taught in these three degrees were designed to fit the individual for the high moral obligations of citizenship; so to be a Matron or a Husbandman was to occupy a position which could only be reached by study and appreciation of its character. The members learned that:

> ... trust and confidence in each other is essential to growth; that intelligent well-directed labor, a wise understanding of the laws of nature and their operation, are of vital importance and an absolute necessity ... that we are but the stewards of God's gifts, that we are to be wise in dispensing as well as earnest in gathering, and ... that only by intelligent action can we hope for success.[33]

"Having reached this point we come to comprehend our duty as neighbors, as parents, as friends and as citizens, together with our relations to our country."[34] Love of country was shown by participation in a variety of activities as an occupation, sports, and culture. Beautifying the home was studied. The Matron learned the training of the "immortal soul" of her child for "the responsibilities and duties of life."[35] The Golden Rule was taught. These teachings were designed to improve the moral life of the members and "when the principles of our Order are fully understood, when

[32] *Ibid.*, p. 92.
[33] *Ibid.*, p. 93.
[34] *Ibid.*, p. 93.
[35] *Ibid.*, p. 95.

its aims and its purposes are reached, wrong doing will scarcely be possible."[36]

By 1875 the ritual was revised to permit the locals to confer a fifth degree, Pomona, originally conferred by the State Grange and open only to Masters and their wives. This change was made because the State Grange met only once a year with only a few of the Masters present. Because of the infrequency of meetings and the small attendance, the membership felt "the enjoyments and instructions of the real work of the degree were in a great measure lost."[37] It was believed that on a local level more would participate; hence the change would be beneficial to both the individual and the organization.

A Pomona Grange could be organized after nine men and four women petitioned the secretary of the State Grange for such an organization. As originally planned all Masters and Past-Masters and their wives who were Matrons, were eligible to membership. In addition, fourth degree members were admitted to membership if, after examination by a special committee, they were found to be sufficiently versed in the ritualistic and unwritten work.

This Grange was to aid and to strengthen the subordinate Granges within its jurisdiction and to look carefully to their interests. Further, this unit was to try all members of the subordinate Granges within its jurisdiction for any offense or misconduct.[38]

Above the local was the State Grange, which could be organized when a state had a total of fifteen or more locals.[39] The membership of this group comprised the Masters and Past-Masters of the local Granges.[40] The

[36] *Ibid.*, p. 96.

[37] Martin, *op. cit.*, p. 436 (Constitution of the Grange, Article IX, Section 5).

[38] Smedley, *op. cit.*, p. 102.

[39] This is the requirement according to the national constitution adopted in 1873, but apparently this provision was not effective before that time because the Iowa State Grange was organized in 1871 with only twelve locals.

[40] Martin, *op. cit.*, p. 436 (Constitution of the Grange, Article IX, Section 5).

offices of the State Grange were the same as those of the local, but the officers were elected biennially instead of annually.[41]

Uniting all State Granges was the National Grange, which was composed of the Masters and Past-Masters of the State Granges.[42] This division also met annually and followed the same patterns of organization as the other units, with its officers elected triennially.[43] In 1930 the annual meeting of the National Grange was held at Rochester, New York with approximately 30,000 persons attending.[44]

The National Grange bestowed the sixth and seventh degrees. They were Flora (Charity), conferred upon the Masters of the State Granges and their wives who held the rank of Pomona; and Ceres (Faith), bestowed upon any member of the National Grange who had served one year.[45]

The Grange also had a Juvenile Division for children between the ages of five and fourteen organized in a manner similar to the adult branch of the Order.[46] Each Juvenile Division carried on its own secret work and had educational programs in which its members participated. The work of the division was under the direction of the young people themselves although supervised by an adult.[47] At their monthly meetings, just as at the adult meetings, parliamentary law, book reviews, and subjects of the day, as well as farm problems, were discussed. In this way, the Grange attempted to make better farmers and better citizens of the rural youth of the nation. All locals did not have a Juvenile Division but apparently records were not complete, for in a letter to the author, Mr. Hummel

[41] *Ibid.*, p. 433.
[42] *Ibid.*, p. 423.
[43] *Ibid.*
[44] Letter, F. L. Hummel, Master of the Iowa State Grange, to Myrtle Beinhauer, August 17, 1931 (Ms. form).
[45] Martin, *op. cit.*, p. 424.
[46] Letter, F. L .Hummel, Master of the Iowa State Grange, to Myrtle Beinhauer, February 16, 1931. (Ms. form).
[47] *Ibid.*

stated that in 1930 it was impossible to ascertain the exact number of Juvenile Divisions in Iowa.[48]

The entire Grange organization was supported by the membership fees collected by the local Granges, which were five dollars for men and two for women. The support of the State and National Granges is described by Martin in the following manner:

> The treasurer of the subordinate Grange is required to pay to the State Grange the sum of $1 for each man, and fifty cents for each woman initiated into the Grange, such payments being made quarterly. He is also required to pay a quarterly due of six cents for each member.
>
> Each State Grange is required to pay to the National Grange in quarterly installments, the annual due of ten cents for each member of the Order within its jurisdiction. The funds of the Order are guarded by a series of judicious regulations, and their proper administration is thus guaranteed.[49]

POLITICAL ACTIVITIES

The Grange filled a social and educational need, but from its inception, it was interested in the political and economic questions of the day. One of its more important activities in its early years was in connection with the railroads. Naturally, the question of transportation was important to the farmer. As has already been stated, the railroads discriminated between customers and points of shipment. They charged what the farmer considered unjust rates on farm produce. By 1864 the farmer was complaining loudly about these injustices and was asking that the state legislature regulate railroad rates. The Iowa General Assembly claimed authority to regulate railroad activity under the laws of 1856 and 1866[50] which stated that any company accepting a land grant would be subject to any regulation the legislature might place upon it. Consequently the Assembly made its first attempt to fix

[48] Letter, F. L. Hummel, Master of the Iowa State Grange, to Myrtle Beinhauer, August 17, 1931.

[49] Martin, op. cit., pp. 424-25.

[50] Laws of Iowa, 1856, Ex. Sess., Chap. I; Laws of Iowa, 1866, Chap. 137, Section 7.

railroad rates in 1866. This bill passed the house but was rejected in the senate.[51] By 1870 three rate bills had been passed in the house, but each was defeated in the senate.[52]

Feeling became so vehement that in 1870 and 1871 both political parties included the issue in their platforms, declaring the right of the state to control railroads and calling for the exercise of that right. Other attempts were made in 1872 to fix rates, but each bill met the fate of its predecessor. With continued failure the legislature was inclined to discontinue its efforts, but the Iowa Grange was persistent. During the special session of 1873, the Grange memorialized the General Assembly to enact a law "to protect the people from outrageous discrimination and exorbitant charges."[53]

During the summer of 1873, the Grange's demand for railroad regulation and agricultural cooperation resulted in the organization of the Anti-Monopoly party.[54] This party demanded that the state legislature fix the maximum freight rates of the railroads of Iowa, permitting them to compete below those rates.[55] In the fall, fifty of the one hundred legislators elected to the Iowa General Assembly were members of the Anti-Monopoly party, while seventy of them were members of the Grange. With this dominance of agricultural interest, the legislature found it possible to enact a bill, effective July 4, 1874, which divided the railroads of Iowa into three classes: A, those with gross earnings of $4,000 per mile; B, those with gross earnings between $3,000 and $4,000 per mile; and C, those with gross earnings of $3,000 or less per mile. A detailed rate schedule was given. Each company was to post classification and schedules of fares, and make an annual report to the governor of the state, giving its gross receipts.[56]

[51] Iowa Senate, *Journal*, 1866: 25, 495, 540, 661; Iowa House, *Journal*, 1866: 59, 184, 235, 290, 438-56, 517, 764.
[52] Anderson, *op. cit.*, p. 23.
[53] Buck, *The Granger Movement*, p. 169.
[54] *Ibid.*
[55] Martin, *op. cit.*, p. 513 (Platform Anti-Monopoly Party).
[56] *Laws of Iowa*, 1874, Chap. 68.

The railroads protested the law, claiming that the rates were too low for them to operate profitably. The law was not successful. The opposition of the railroad officials was so vehement and the administrative machinery so weak that the law was repealed four years after its passage.[57]

Even though the law was revoked its impact was felt in Iowa's economic philosophy. It was held constitutional by the courts. It established the principle that the state had the right to regulate business, and that, until congress acted, the state could regulate interstate commerce so far as its own citizens were affected.

While the railroad legislation sponsored by the Grange is its most notable work, the Grange sought other legislation. For example, it favored and helped to enact prohibition into law. For years it supported a state income tax for Iowa which was eventually passed. It worked for several years, though unsuccessfully, to make military training in the state college optional. Other measures it supported were the abolition of the county assessor and the popular election of the county superintendent of schools.[58] While this is not a complete list of the Grange's legislative program, it does give an idea of its scope.

The Grange set up a systematic organization for presenting its bills to the legislature. First, needed changes were discussed in the local Grange, and a resolution embodying these needs was sent to the state legislative committee located at the state capitol. If the issue was of nation-wide interest, the resolution was sent to the national committee at Washington, D. C. The Grange did not use the lobby extensively nor did it resort to propaganda campaigns in behalf of, or in opposition to, pending legislative measures. It merely sought to bring its viewpoint and desires before the legislators.[59]

[57] *Laws of Iowa*, 1878, Chap. 77.
[58] Letter, F. L. Hummel, Master of the Iowa State Grange, to Myrtle Beinhauer, August 17, 1931. (Ms. form).
[59] National Grange, *The Grange in Legislation*, p. 1.

Cooperative Enterprises

Following their avowed purpose "to foster cooperation," the farmers undertook cooperative buying and selling enterprises. Iowa was the first state in which Grange cooperatives achieved marked success.[60] The first cooperative effort of the farmer was the purchasing of large quantities of goods from the local dealers. Later a county agent was appointed who took orders for his community and, with growing success, a state agent was employed. The first agent was J. D. Whitman, appointed in 1872, who maintained headquarters at Des Moines.[61]

Through cooperative buying large amounts were saved the farmer. According to Martin, "It is safe to say . . . that the purchases have amounted to many thousands, and that not less than $50,000 have been saved to the farmers of the state, within a year in the purchase of plows and cultivators alone."[62] Not only were there savings on these implements, but large discounts were also received on other commodities. It is estimated that 40 per cent was saved on sewing machines; 20 to 25 per cent on parlor organs; 15 per cent on shellers; 20 per cent on wagons; $33\frac{1}{3}$ per cent on hay forks; and 25 per cent on implements. General Wilson, Secretary of the State Grange, thought that by 1873 two million dollars had been saved through cooperatives.[63]

By 1874 cooperative buying had reached its peak. It is estimated that for that year the volume of business transacted by the Grange reached the five million dollar mark.[64] It is remarkable that a new enterprise should have grown to this extent in two years. Especially is this development noteworthy because it was the first experience with cooperatives in Iowa. The

[60] Buck, *The Granger Movement*, p. 243.
[61] *Ibid.*
[62] Martin, *op. cit.*, p. 476.
[63] *Ibid.*, p. 477.
[64] This amount includes the amount of business handled both in buying and selling.

singular achievement of this new experiment for 1874 is shown in the following summary:[65]

PURCHASES AND SAVINGS MADE BY THE GRANGE COOPERATIVES IN IOWA 1874

Product Bought	Amount Paid	Per Cent of Saving
Farm implements	$225,000	27
Farm supplies	445,612	18
Lumber	107,000	15

Cooperative selling developed hand in hand with buying and, even before State Agent J. D. Whitman was appointed in 1872, one-third of all the elevators and warehouses in Iowa were owned by the Granges.[66] To market farm produce, agents were located at New York and Chicago. They received all the Granges' shipments and sold them at the best possible price. For their services these agents received a 1 per cent commission. From the following chart, showing the amount of produce sold by these agents in 1874, it is evident that the farmer had the utmost confidence in cooperative selling:

AMOUNT OF PRODUCE SOLD AND GAIN MADE THROUGH GRANGE COOPERATIVES IN IOWA 1874

Produce Sold	Amount Sold	Per Cent of Gain
Farm produce	$3,234,000	11
Livestock	1,021,200	12

It was also in that successful year of 1874 that the Grange cooperatives embarked upon a venture which was to herald their downfall. It was then that the National Grange, led by the enthusiastic E. R. Shankland of Iowa, conceived the idea of manufacturing farm implements.[67] Manufacturing establishments were set up in Iowa and in other midwestern states. Attempts were made to manufacture plows, binders, harrows, and other agricultural machinery.

[65] Anderson, op. cit., p. 40.
[66] Ibid., p. 36.
[67] Buck, The Granger Movement, p. 269.

For several reasons the Grange was unable to support such enterprises. First, it did not have enough capital to organize factories properly. Secondly, the market was too small. The Iowa factories could sell to Iowa farmers, but they could not sell to the farmers of other states for that was the market of the Grange manufacturing establishments of those states. The farmer used a machine several years. The number of farmers in Iowa was not increasing rapidly. Consequently, when the Grange factory had once supplied the farmer's needs, there would be little market for its product until the implements needed to be replaced several years later. In other words, the number of machines a factory could sell equalled the number of farmers in Iowa. Even then, each farmer was a prospective customer only once in approximately five years. Under these conditions, it is apparent that the market of these factories was too small to allow expansion of the plants or, for that matter, to cover costs. Thirdly, the farmer, to a great degree, needed to purchase seed and implements on credit. It was soon evident that the Grange manufacturing enterprises did not have sufficient capital to advance the necessary credit.

Because the factories did not have adequate capital nor income to meet the demands placed upon them, they failed. With their failure, faith was lost in all cooperative enterprises and the movement rapidly declined. Only three years after the inception of the cooperative movement, the Grange records stated that so few reports were made by the various business enterprises that it was impossible to make an accurate statement regarding the extent of their business, except that they had saved the farmer "many thousands."[68]

Although the cooperative efforts of the Grange were successful for a time and apparently saved large sums for the farmer, they were ultimately failures. In the first place, cooperative buying and selling required working together which was foreign to the independent

[68] Iowa State Grange, *Proceedings Sixth Annual Session*, 1875, p. 12.

spirit of the farmer who is first of all an individualist.[69] In the second place, many of the enterprises were not suitable for cooperatives. This was particularly true of manufacturing, as previously noted.[70] Third, the management of the cooperatives was in the hands of inexperienced persons whose frequent blunders caused large financial losses. Finally, the extensive credit needed by the farmer undermined cooperative buying and selling. The Grange at first insisted upon cash payments, while its competitors would sell on credit. When competition became too strong, the Grange was compelled to extend credit which, when once given, had to be continued. With the extension of credit and the resultant "bad debts," the financial condition of the cooperative system was greatly impaired.[71]

Although the cooperative efforts of the Grange ultimately failed, they were not without benefit. They resulted, temporarily, in large savings for the farmer and they showed the farmer that the hated middleman did perform beneficial and necessary services.

Noneconomic Activities

The Grange's opposition to the railroads and its cooperatives have without question, received most attention, but the Grange was also interested in educational and social pursuits, that is, in the general welfare of the community. This is in keeping with the organization's declared purpose "to educate and elevate the American farmer." The social activities were largely the monthly meetings and the annual Grange picnics which brought the farm families of a community together. Particularly was this important in the early period of Grange activity when recreation was scant and transportation difficult, forcing the farmer to stay home the greater part of the year. At these meetings, and especially at the annual Grange picnics, the members met to play, to gossip and to be entertained.

Education was also carried on through the programs

[69] Buck, *The Granger Movement*, p. 274.
[70] *Ibid.*, p. 274.
[71] *Ibid.*, p. 276.

of the monthly meetings. Here, public speaking, parliamentary law, subjects of the day and the latest books, in addition to subjects pertaining to farm life, were discussed. As a part of the educational feature, the subordinate Granges were asked to send crop reports to the secretary of the State Grange, who in turn gave these reports to agricultural papers for dissemination. The reports thus compiled were claimed by some to be more accurate than those published by the government.[72] In an attempt to aid in the education of children, equipment and magazine subscriptions were given to schools.[73]

The Grange was also active in charitable work. One of its early projects was to provide for 980 families made destitute by the grasshopper plague of 1873.[74] In later days, it provided toys for children's homes, gave dinners to the poor, presented fruit and candy to the sick, supplied beds for hospitals, and furnished hot lunches for needy children in schools.[75]

Decline of the Grange

From 1875, the prestige of the Grange diminished in Iowa. There are a variety of causes for this decline: first, the business failures of the cooperative enterprises; second, legislation which proved unwise;[76] third, reaction to the very rapid growth during the years of 1873 and 1874;[77] fourth, the rapid growth resulted in a large membership which it was impossible to maintain;[78] fifth, politicians and other "outsiders" who were interested in their own gains rather than in the promotion of agriculture, crept into the organization.[79]

The startling rapidity of the Grange's decline in Iowa is shown in the following table:

[72] Anderson, *op. cit.*, p. 45.
[73] National Grange, *The Grange and the Community.*
[74] Anderson, *op. cit.*, p. 46.
[75] National Grange, *The Grange and the Community.*
[76] Anderson, *op. cit.*, p. 46.
[77] Buck, *The Granger Movement*, p. 70.
[78] *Ibid.*, p. 71.
[79] Anderson, *op. cit.*, p. 49.

THE RAPID DECLINE OF THE GRANGE MOVEMENT IN IOWA
SHOWN BY THE DECREASE IN THE NUMBER OF LOCAL
GRANGES, 1875-1892

YEAR	NUMBER OF LOCAL GRANGES
1875	1838
1876	1018
1885	8
1886	15
1887	36
1888	40
1889	37
1890	52
1891	31
1892	25

By 1930 the Grange was still moderately strong and active in Jasper county where the movement originated, and in Mahaska county, but elsewhere in Iowa its influence had diminished. During the '30's it was far more active in the eastern states than in the midwest[81] where it was once dominate. This fact can probably be accounted for in two ways. First, the leadership in Iowa was not as competent as in the eastern states. True, the leadership in Iowa was efficient in the early period, but it gradually fell into less capable hands, while in the East it was retained by able men. Second, growth in memberhip in the Grange was phenomenal in Iowa. When growth of any organization is unusually rapid, it is difficult to continue that growth or even maintain its strength. Facilities cannot expand to meet the needs or interests of all. Consequently, there is usually a correspondingly rapid decline in the organization. Such was the case with the Grange in Iowa, whereas strength was maintained in the east where it had grown more slowly. Third, Grange cooperatives in Iowa far outnumbered those of any other area. With the failure of large numbers of these enterprises, support of the entire Granger movement was withdrawn.

[80] *Ibid.*, p. 48.
[81] Interview, Carl Kennedy, Assistant Secretary of Agriculture in Iowa, August, 1931.

In the East, with fewer business failures, reaction against the Grange was less violent.[82]

CONTRIBUTION OF THE GRANGE

There is no doubt but that the Grange rendered valuable service to the farmer, especially in the frontier days. It helped him to meet and to overcome many difficulties which were then confronting him. Specifically, it helped him to obtain legislative regulation of the railroad rates, which placed him in a more equitable position with respect to other shippers. Thus, he was able to realize greater benefits in the marketing of his crops.

Through education it encouraged him to increase his production and to broaden his life, and that of his family. It taught his wife to manage her household more efficiently and later, through the Juvenile Division, it taught his children to use to better advantage the opportunities which were offered them. When the Great Depression came, the Grange still felt that it had a great work to perform.[83] It hoped through its social, educational and legislative activities to make the farmer's home a more beautiful and profitable place in which to live.

[82] Interview, Carl Kennedy, Assistant Secretary of Agriculture of Iowa, August, 1931.

[83] Letter, F. L. Hummel, Master of the Iowa State Grange, to Myrtle Beinhauer, August 17, 1931.

The Story of Icaria
MARTHA BROWNING SMITH

ONE OF THE dominant themes in American history during the first half of the nineteenth century was the drive to reform society. The reform tendencies manifested themselves in many ways but among the most obvious were the attempts to remake society through the development of new, utopian communities. Some societies, like the Shakers and Oneidas, settled in the East, but many social experimenters looked to the frontier because of the availability of land and the absence of social structure. The average life span of most utopian communities was short, usually less than ten years. Reasons for the high rate of failure varied, but of primary importance were inadequate planning and lack of experienced leadership.

Iowa serves as an excellent focal point for the study of social experimentation since many utopian groups chose to locate in this region: German socialists settled at Communia, Hungarian noblemen at New Buda, German communalists at Amana, and French Icarians at Corning, plus many more. A few groups, like the Community of True Inspiration, or Amanas as they are more popularly known, succeeded, but most attempts failed within a short time. Others, like the Icarians, might be called semi-successful since they survived for about two generations and thus had the opportunity to develop their agricultural operations and implement their theories about communal living.

In this selection, Martha Smith is concerned with the story of the Icarian community in Iowa. She presents an informative account of the physical facilities, agricultural problems and practices, and general lifestyle of these nineteenth century communitarians. The article is also significant because the Icarians' difficulties in making sound decisions regarding land and settlement and their inability to resolve internal disagreements are reflective of the problems faced by countless other utopian societies throughout American history.

THE STORY OF ICARIA

By Martha Browning Smith

Mrs. Smith, a resident of Creston, Iowa, received her Master's degree from Northeast Missouri State College and is teaching in the Afton Public Schools.

In 1860 a group of French people of the Icarian Society established the community of Icaria near the present site of Corning in Adams County, Iowa. Icaria was perhaps the most typical representative of the rational democratic community as opposed to the religious groups concerned only incidentally with the solution of social problems.[1] With the Icarians their religion was the solution of social problems as advocated by Etienne Cabet. It was an attempt to realize the democratic communism of the Utopian philosophers;[2] therefore it was invaluable as an experiment.

According to the Greek legend, Daedalus was a skillful artist and inventor who built a labyrinth in Crete for King Minos. He and his son, Icarus, were then unable to get out, and in order to escape he made wings for himself and his son. In spite of his father's warning, Icarus, in his eagerness to escape, flew so high that the sun's rays melted the wax with which his wings were fastened, causing him to fall to his death. From this has been derived the present meaning of Icarian. Which, as stated in Webster's New World Dictionary, is "of, like or characteristic of Icarus; hence, too daring; foolhardy; rash."

This writer was unable to find anything as to how the people of the Icarian Society got their name, but it is easy to imagine how Etienne Cabet, who was exiled from France because of his writings, could be called an Icarian.

Etienne Cabet was a French lawyer who was the author of the popular *History of The French Revolution from 1789 to 1830*. He was also editor of the newspaper, *Le Populaire*, in which he advocated the rights of working people, and he also wrote many controversial pamphlets and books.

---

[1] Albert Shaw, *Icaria, A Chapter in the History of Communism*, London and New York, 1884, p. vii.
[2] *Ibid.*, p. viii.

ETIENNE CABET

He was sentenced to prison for an article in his paper; however, he was able to escape to London. While in exile he studied history and the Scriptures and continued his writings. He wrote "Vrai Christianisme" or "True Christianity" in 1840 and the novel, *Un Voyage en Icarie*, in which all follow Christian concepts of brotherly love as a solution to social problems. An English reviewer in 1848 wrote:

> It [*The Voyage*] has already gone through five editions — There is not a shop or stall in Paris where copies are not in readiness for a constant influx of purchasers—hardly a drawing-room table on which it is not seen.[3]

The above is evidence that Cabet's writings created quite a sensation in France. His book, *The Voyage*, told of an imaginary community, but against his protests people began to believe it. His disciples set up the cry, "Let us found Icaria!"

[3] *Ibid.*, fn. p. 18.

In 1847, in response to their cries, Cabet published an article in *Le Populaire* entitled "Allons en Icarie" ("Let us go to Icarie"). Thousands responded and America was chosen as the place to set up such a community. Cabet's announcement in the January 17, 1848 issue of the paper will be another feather in the cap of the Texan. He said that Texas was chosen as the place to go because it "presents the most advantages in health, temperature of the climate, fertility of soil, extent of country, etc."

On February 3, 1848, seventy picked men gathered at Le Havre, France to set out for Texas. Thousands of people came to bid them farewell. For the first time the song, "Partoons pour Icarie," was sung. Cabet then read a profession of faith and asked the seventy a series of questions. Each was answered with a loud chorus of "YES!" after which the crowd cheered. At that time it was expected that so many would be converted to Icarianism that a world-wide revolution would take place and "Equality, Liberty and Fraternity" would rule civilization.

The trip across the ocean was a pleasant one. The Icarian pioneers, dressed in their uniforms of black corduroy tunics and gray felt hats made the decks of the ship, *Rome*, sing with repeated choruses of their "Chant du Depart" — the new song, "Partoons pour Icarie."[4] Cabet had painted in their minds a pleasant picture of their new home in Texas. They had time on the boat to speculate about life in their new community. Cabet had assure them that they would have absolute title to one million acres by the banks of the Red River.

After landing at New Orleans they started up to Red River to their lands in Texas. When they arrived at Shreveport they were due for a big disappointment as the lands turned out to be more than 250 miles from the river with a wilderness of swamps in between.

Since it was necessary to go overland to reach the newlands, they had to purchase wagons and yokes of oxen. They found they had too much baggage; so some of it was left behind in Shreveport. To further their disappointment, they found that they did not have absolute title to any land; instead they had the right to homestead the land. Each person would receive 320

---

[4] Marie Marchand Ross, *Child of Icaria*, New York, 1938, p. 111.

acres of land, provided he had a cabin built on his land by July 1st. To make matters even worse they were unable to get adjoining sections. The State of Texas retained every other section, and the Peters Company, with whom Cabet had been dealing, retained half of each section. The accompanying diagram[5] of one township shows the way their holdings lay. The blank sections represent the holdings of the State of Texas, the blank half sections represent those retained by the Peters Company, and the shaded half sections show what could be held by the Icarian Domain.

It is easy to see the problems such an arrangement would present to a people with a communal type of life such as these people planned. They had a lot of courage, however, and dedecided to make the best of a bad situation. They built a community building on one of the half sections and were able to complete thirty-two cabins by the first of July.

Back in France, Cabet was making arrangements for the second group of men to start for Texas. This group, which was to have numbered in the thousands, was composed of nineteen men.

These nineteen men, under the leadership of J. P. Favard, arrived at New Orleans and set out to find the first group. They too were told of the location of the lands; so they set out in wagons for the last stretch of their trip. Some of the men died

---

[5] Shaw, *op. cit.*, p. 34.

of malaria on the way. When the remaining men finally reached the settlement they found that most of the settlers also had contracted the malarial fever.

It was expected that the women and children would soon arrive at New Orleans and begin the arduous trip out to their poor establishment. It was decided that the only possible thing to do was to return to New Orleans in time to prevent the women from starting the rest of their trip. The men knew that the few homes along the way would not be able to feed many, and no one was able to carry any provisions; therefore they decided to set out two or three at a time to make their own way as best they could. The money in the treasury was divided; and each man had six or seven dollars[6] which, with a gun and knapsack, were his only assets as he started the return trip.

Most of the men were able to reach New Orleans where they met the women. By this time several of their letters telling of the pitiful state of affairs had reached Cabet. He published excerpts form them in the paper and seemed in no way concerned; however he was finally persuaded to come to America.

When he arrived in January, 1849, he found the entire group living in two rented houses in New Orleans. By this time they had only money to last a few months if they returned to Texas. They stayed in New Orleans for a time, and exploring parties were sent out to search for a new location. Two hundred abandoned the group and took $5000 or nearly one third of the money with them. A few of these people remained in New Orleans, but most of them returned to France.

That spring (1849) they heard that the Mormons had left the town of Nauvoo which at that time had been the largest town in Illinois, having 15,000 population compared to 8,000 in Chicago. In March Cabet, with two hundred eighty, left on on a Mississippi River steamer for Nauvoo. By the fifteenth of March the migration of the Mormons was almost complete, leaving Nauvoo practically an empty town. The Mormons had left one man to act as agent in charge of their properties.

Cabet and his followers were able to purchase a large building to use as their community hall, a mill, a distillery and one or two homes. The rest of the buildings were rented.

[6] *Ibid.*, p. 36.

Although about twenty had died of cholera on the steamer, the rest did not give up their resolution to found Icaria. The community prospered for seven years at Nauvoo in spite of the fact that the people were "ignorant of the language, laws, customs and business methods of the country."[7] They were also hampered by their leader who "was rather a patriot, agitator and theorist than a practical business manager."[8]

More people were admitted, and at one time there were as many as 500 members. The community had every kind of industry and good schools. They also had a very good orchestra and gave amateur plays that were "as good as could be had."[9]

"Everyone seemed filled with enthusiasm for the cause but – –." Every year at their election day celebration on February 3, the history of the community would be given by Cit. Marchand.[10] As he would come to this phase of their life in Nauvoo he would be overcome with emotion at the memory of the trouble which broke out there.

Cabet, who was very elderly by this time, was becoming "dictatorial and unreasonably arbitrary."[11] He requested to be elected dictator for a term of ten years instead of president for a one-year term. The majority balked at this. A few upheld their leader for whom all still held much respect; however they would not allow him to become dictator. He wrote letters back to France telling of how badly he was being treated, and the people of France could not seem to believe the letters of the people of the community. He waged a regular war of secession and went to court to try to dissolve the society, but he did not succeed. He then left with one hundred eighty followers to found another community at Cheltenham, Illinois.[12] They took with them all of the account books and a large portion of the library.

Cabet died only a few days after their arrival at Cheltenham,

---

[7] *Ibid.*, p. 49.
[8] *Ibid.*
[9] Ross, *op. cit.*, p. 112.
[10] Cit. or Citoyen means man in French, and Cite. or Citoyen means lady. These people, mostly French, always used these terms to address or speak of the others.
[11] Ross, *loc. cit.*
[12] Cheltenham is now a part of East St. Louis, Illinois.

and the community only lasted about eight years. After its dissolution a few members came to join the larger group that had come to Iowa.

Shortly after Cabet and his followers had left Nauvoo, the remaining people began to make plans for their own future. A few were discouraged and left the group to return to France or to settle other places in America. The rest still held to their determination to follow the teachings of their former leader and to found an Icaria.

The community at Nauvoo reorganized with Cit. Gerard as the new president and Cit. Marchand secretary-treasurer. They had never considered Nauvoo as a permanent place, and of course most of their land and homes were only rented.

A few years before, Cabet had contracted to purchase 3115 acres of government land in Iowa. This land was located in Adams County and was to be paid for at $1.25 per acre. Very little of this had been paid; so the remaining principle with the interest at 10 per cent amounted to quite a heavy debt. But these people were still undaunted. Therefore, in 1856 it was decided to come to Iowa, and several of the men decided to go there as soon as possible to prepare for the families to come later.

On the first of January, 1857, there were 239 members of which eighteen were already in Iowa. The Icarians had about 275 acres in cultivation and had erected several log cabins. They brought livestock and farming implements from Nauvoo and purchased more in Des Moines.

In 1860 the families who remained in Nauvoo started across Iowa in covered wagons. The women and children encountered many hardships on the trail, but they continued on toward their new home. The little village of Icaria was built in a clearing of the woods bordering the Nodaway River a short distance from the present town of Corning in Adams County. The community had about thirty families at the time it was established in the early 1860's.

Their log houses were built from the trees they had cut to clear the land for farming. The homes were built without floors or windows. However, these people had a powerful determination to build their Icaria; and they worked together to found their "ideal and model society, based on the communist principles of equality, fraternity and liberty."[13] They worked with much enthusiasm and soon had a flour and saw mill built near the river and run by water from a dam which they built across the river. They could then saw boards to be used for floors in their cabins as well as for furniture. Wheat and corn could also be ground at the mill.

Their furniture was simple and was made from the fine black walnut trees from their own woods. Each cabin had beds, chairs, and a table; and some had a chest for clothing and a closet built into the cabin. Some had only pegs on the wall instead of a closet. These pegs were then covered with a muslin curtain.

After they could afford to buy windows, the Icarians traveled to the nearest town which was St. Joseph, Missouri. St. Joseph was about one hundred miles away, and the roads were almost impassable. It was necessary to go by ox team in order to bring back the windows and the necessary supplies. Later this trip was made twice a year, in the spring and in the fall. Their supplies such as flour, sugar, coffee, and salt were purchased in barrels.

The Icarians' first attempts at colonization in Iowa had met with so much trouble, in fact almost failure, that there were no births in the colony until the fall of 1864. The people of the colony were much interested in the little girl who was the first child to be born in their new home. "Even from a group of Iowa Indians who at that time had their camp in the woods nearby came a squaw with her papoose to see the new white baby and compare it with hers."[14] The little girl was Marie Marchand, the daughter of Cit. and Cite. A. A. Marchand. Cit. Marchand had been one of the first to come to the United States and had many times been an officer of the colony. This same little girl was to become the late Mrs. W. A. Ross, the author of the book, *Child of Icaria,* and many magazine and newspaper articles about her beloved Icaria.

As the Colony began to prosper the log houses began to change somewhat. The cracks were plastered with clay mor-

---

[13] Ross, *op. cit.*, p. 7.
[14] *Ibid.*, p. 8.

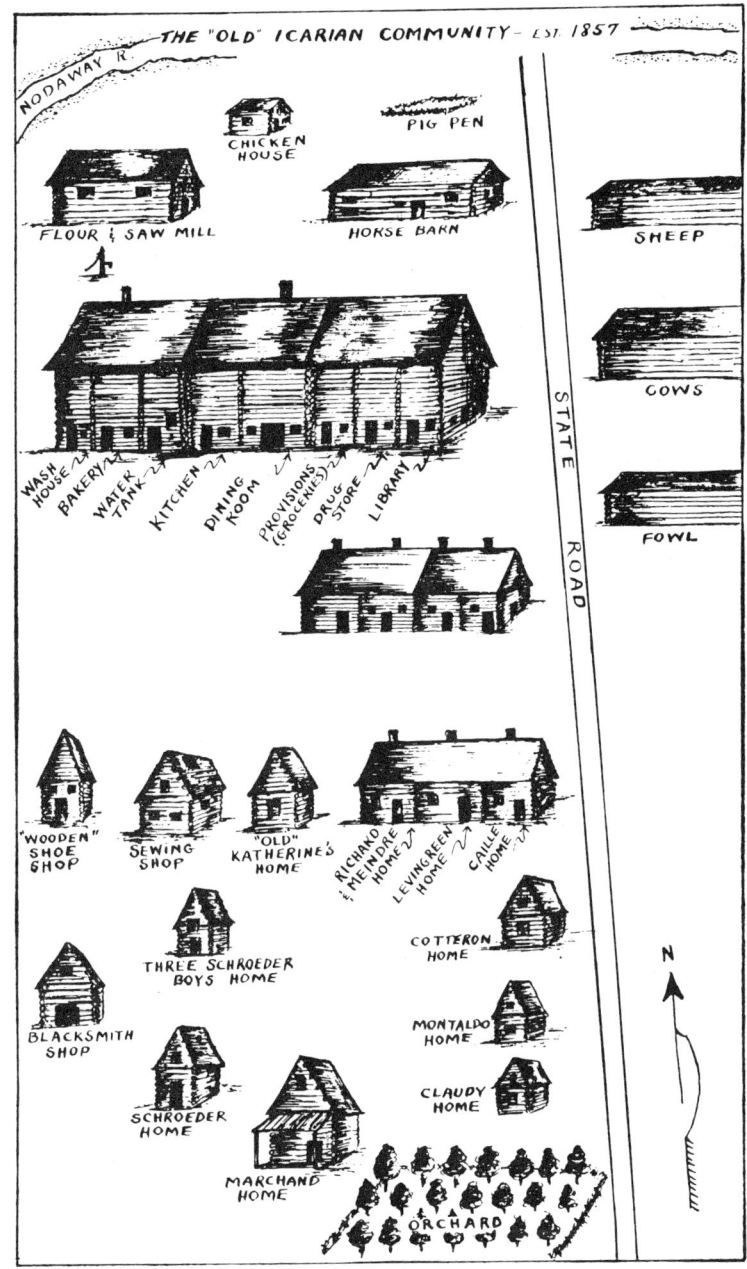

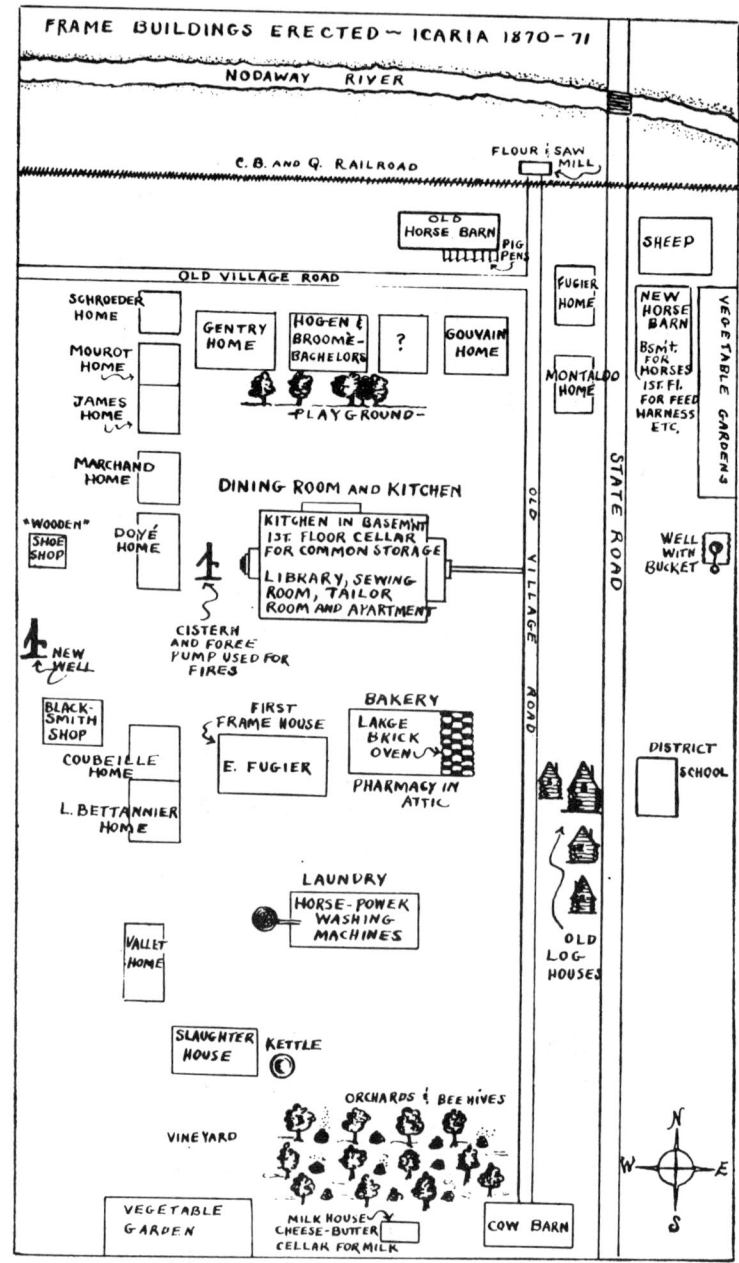

tar, the walls were whitewashed and windows were added. A typical cabin of this time would have a French window and a door in front with a small square window in the back. The women braided rugs to place on the floors and made muslin curtains to hang at the windows. However, the curtains were soon badly stained by the rain and snow which dripped in through the cracks between the logs. In the winter a small, square wood-stove stood in the center of the house for heat. It was removed in summer. Around the cabins lilacs and flowering shrubs began to appear as well as vines and currant and gooseberry bushes. Many of the yards contained cherry trees.

Several cabins were placed side by side and were for the common use of the community. These cabins contained the laundry, bakery, water tank, kitchen, dining room; and the store, the pharmacy, and the library. The supply of food such as barrels of brown and white sugar, coffee, dried apples, salt and everything that was bought in quantities for the colony was kept in the store.

After a time as the colony prospered, new dwellings were built on the same site and many of the log cabins were torn down. These new cabins were placed in rows facing each other with a rough street or road running between.

These people had their troubles also. There was no near market for their livestock so it had to be driven to Des Moines to be sold. One winter seventy-five hogs were driven to Des Moines, and when they arrived there it was found that the market price was one and three quarters cents per hundred weight. The men decided not to sell the livestock, so they drove the hogs all the way back to Icaria again. The animals were slaughtered and the meat was cured. The following spring the meat was sold to the army. At that time a ham or a shoulder would bring one dollar.

"Icaria was to be an experiment of owning land in common and self-government under socialistic theories."[15] All property was owned in common and under the control of the assembly and officers. The General Assembly consisted of all male members over twenty-one. Their officers were a president, secretary

[15] Maude Friman, "History of Adams County," Adams County *Free Press*, March 12, 1931.

and treasurer and three directors. There was a Director of Industry, a Director of Agriculture and a Director of Clothing. These officers were elected every year on the third of February. Every other year the constitution was to be reviewed and revised if necessary on that date.

The third of February was said to be "the grandest day of the year." A celebration was prepared months ahead for the coming anniversary of the day the first group of men left La Havre to establish an Icaria.

When the big day came the election would be held in the morning, a dinner at noon and a banquet in the evening. Many outside friends attended the evening banquet. After the meal they would sing, "Partoons pour Icarie," which was first sung as the men took the oaths and prepared to leave La Havre on that memorable February 3, 1848. This would be followed by special recitations by the children and many speeches and toasts.

The first of the speeches was given by Cit. Marchand, the only man still with them who had come over with the first group to Texas. He would give the history of Icaria from the first writings of Etienne Cabet in France and in exile in England to the present day life in Iowa. Perhaps this is one reason these people seemed so well versed in the background of the colony. The one other strictly Icarian holiday was the *Fete du Mais*. This occurred in the fall after the crops were harvested.

The laws provided that anyone leaving the community under the age of twenty-one would receive one hundred dollars and twenty dollars for each year of the age over twenty-one that was spent in the colony. Any new members were to bring one hundred dollars for the colony and sufficient clothing for one year. Any other money and valuables were to be turned over to the officers to be used for the good of the entire community. In addition, any money which they received from work outside the colony was to be turned into the treasury. Any money that the men who were in the service had at the time of their return was to be turned into the treasury as was the pension money that was received by two of the men. No compensation was to be given for services of any kind.

The Story of Icaria

The Fourth of July was a great day of celebration for young and old. On the eve the cooks could be found in the kitchen preparing all sorts of good things to eat. Others cleaned the large hall while the young people gathered vines and green boughs to make garlands to decorate the dining hall. Even the big fireplace was filled with greenery and wild flowers.

After a few years the town of Corning had a big Fourth of July celebration with a grand parade. The people of the French Colony usually went in five or six heavy farm wagons decorated with flags and bunting. One year all of the girls rode in one wagon. They were to be dressed in white with red and blue sashes. As the girls had no white dresses they wore a white waist and a white petticoat. The sash of red and blue bunting completed the dress. They wore straw hats of white wheat straw which they had made themselves. This in itself was quite a parade.

After the procession the Icarians did not take part in the other festivities. The children did not even visit the ice cream and lemonade stands. They remained grouped together, spreading their lunch on the grass and taking in what was going on around them as they ate. They did not fire fire-crackers or make any extra noise.[16] When they arrived home later in the afternoon, a banquet was soon spread which was enjoyed by all the Icarians as well as the many neighboring friends who never failed to attend. At night a grand ball was held. This was sometimes preceded by a play in French.

The late Mr. Jules Gentry, who lived on his farm near the old site of Icaria, told of one Fourth which he remembered. In the later years there were not enough young men to do the field work in the summer; so it was necessary to hire other young men to do part of the work. The boys of Icaria worked right along with the hired men but were not paid anything. When the Fourth came along, Jules told his father that the boys wanted to celebrate like the hired men were planning to do; so Mr. Gentry proposed to the Assembly that each of the young men who were doing the field work that summer receive one dollar. As this was contrary to the entire teachings of Cabet, it was not passed. Jules had seven cents so he walked

[16] Ross, *op. cit.*, pp. 34-35.

to Prescott to celebrate anyway. When asked how he had gotten the seven cents, he said that there was one hired hand who hated to do the milking. His turn to milk came every second Sunday, and at that time he would pay Jules to do it for him. He paid him ten cents for milking five cows in the morning and again in the evening. Jules was glad to do it for the precious spending money.

Although the men worked where ever they were needed, most of the men had definite jobs. For example, Cit. Mignot was the wooden shoemaker and Cit. Mitchel Bromme made the leather articles such as harness. Cit. Cotteron was the blacksmith and Cit. Caille was the regular baker, although the baking was done at times by Cit. Marchand.

Game was abundant and the men did a great deal of hunting. They had made molds into which they poured melted lead to make their own shot and bullets. They also did a great deal of trapping. In addition to beaver, muskrat and raccoons, they trapped many prairie chickens and rabbits, a few wolves and coyotes.

The women's work was divided. The women worked in pairs and each week would have a different job. They took turns with the cooking, each doing it for one week. The men did the cooking on Sunday.

The laundry was done together. The women sorted the clothes and the men did the washing. The women then separated the clothes into baskets for each family to take to their home to dry. This was facilitated by marking each piece of clothing with a number, one number being assigned to each family. In the case of the men who lived alone, the other women took turns taking care of their laundry and the mending of their clothes as well as the cleaning of their rooms. Women with children under two were exempt from chores outside the home.

The cooking was done in the central kitchen, and all of the families were together in the large dining room.

The dining room was used for many other purposes. On every other Saturday night an opera was presented. Since the nearby town of Corning was just getting started, the people there had no organized entertainment; therefore they attended many of the operas and plays that were given at the colony as well as the many dances.

The young girls learned to sew, embroider and knit. The girls usually knitted all of the socks and stockings for the family, and they also did the marking of the clothing. Cit. Marchand taught all the girls to braid hats for their families. Later these hats were sold to the neighboring farmers, and the money they received was used to buy hats for the citoyennes from the shops in Corning.

By 1876 matters began to look better. That year they planted 250 acres of corn, 100 acres of wheat, five acres each of potatoes and sorghum and had a strawberry bed of one and a half acres.[17] The large mortgage on the land had been paid off, and the people had approximately $60,000 in assets. They had conveniences that certainly were not in evidence during the early 1860's. They even had a few luxuries besides. With the new houses that had been built and the little gardens around them, the colony began to take on a new look. It was decided to build a new common refectory. They had been using the first log one which was aged and beyond repair. It was also a little small with the new members who were joining the community.

Masons and carpenters were employed to aid in the construction of this building. It took months to do the excavating, lay the foundations and build the walls of the basement which were made of stone. This basement was to be used as the common kitchen as well as a cellar for storing the winter vegetables. They had a large variety including parsnips, salsify, turnips, carrots and potatoes. They also had plenty of their big cream cheeses as well as barrels of wine, vinegar and sorghum molasses stored there. From this list, one would assume that the noon meal must have been very similar to our main meal of today. For their evening meal there was always onion soup.

An amusing incident is told regarding the soup kettles. It seems that one of the influential citizens of Corning who was also a political aspirant wanted to give a big oyster supper. There was no place in Corning large enough to handle it; so

---

[17] Shaw, *op. cit.*, p. 86.

he decided to have it at New Icaria. Everything seemed fine until the soup was tasted. It had been prepared in the large kettles that had been used solely for onion soup. It is said that the stew tasted most like onions than oysters.

The first floor of the new refectory was one large hall except for one end which was partitioned off for service. In this end section was an elevator to bring the food up from the kitchen. It also contained work tables and cabinets for bread and dishes. The rest of the main floor was where the daily meals were served. The hall was also used for the weekly business meeting of the Assembly. Operas and plays were given there as were the dances and indoor games.

The second floor was not finished at that time. When it was finally completed, part of it was made into rooms for the Valet family who had just arrived at the colony with their four children. This apartment covered about one quarter of the floor space, and the space across the hall from it was used for the library. The remaining half was used as the common sewing and tailoring shop. They had a very good library consisting of approximately two thousand volumes. When the colony finally disbanded years later, many of these volumes were given to Judge Horace Towner, and at his death they were given to a museum in Omaha.[18]

At first the same long tables and benches that had been in the old dining hall were used, but later new tables were made. A fine cabinet maker, Cit. Coubeille, made round, drop-leaf tables of the beautiful black walnut wood from their own trees. They then purchased chairs of solid wood and painted them. A German family by the name of Schroeder had come to the colony soon after its beginning in Iowa. Cit. Schroeder was an able artist. One of his paintings of early Corning hangs in the Corning Library today. Cit. Schroeder did the painting and decorating of the new refectory. His three sons were also artists and they helped him. They spent many months frescoing the walls with lovely designs. He even painted scenes on the bottom section of the big divided window shades.[19] After he completed the decoration of the new building, the scenery for

[18] Edith Stevenson, "Icarian Colony," unpublished.
[19] Ross, *op. cit.*, p. 38.

the dramatic presentations had to be remodeled somewhat to fit the new quarters.

The homemade candles which were first used for light had now been replaced by new glass kerosene lamps in each home. The new building had large lamps which held about a quart of oil. There were four of these on hanging brackets at each end of the hall and one with a reflector between each of the windows.[20]

Christmas and New Years were festive holidays for the Icarians. Marie Marchand Ross told of one of the early Christmases. There were no evergreen trees in the Iowa forests; so Cit. Schroeder planned a surprise for the children. He and his sons constructed a Christmas tree from small strips of wood which were covered with colored, fringed tissue paper. This was covered with painted ornaments, gilded nuts, red apples and strings of popcorn. It was lighted with candles. This was the first time the children had heard of Santa Claus, and this was their first Christmas tree. The children were sent to the second floor until the tree could be placed in the main dining room. Gifts for each child were placed in a little pile with a card containing the child's name. The children marched around the tree several times; then they were told to find their own places. The presents included toys, candy, apples, nuts and popcorn; but perhaps the most wonderful gift of all was the oranges, for the young Icarians had never tasted them before.

The Icarians contributed much to the culture of the people of Corning and of Adams county in general. In the days before radio and movies or television sets, the operas and theatricals given at Icaria were well-attended. They were always given in French but everyone seemed to enjoy them. The people of the French Colony were well-educated. Many of the people of Corning studied French with Cit. Marchand or German with Cit. Gauvin. For a time Cit. Peron taught classes in electricity. Many took lessons on the organ and other instruments and others studied art with Cit. Schroeder while he was with the Colony.

Cit. Schroeder's three older sons were nearly grown, and as they did not care for farming, he decided to go elsewhere

[20] *Ibid.*

so that Hugo, Adelmo and Fremont could find other work. The young people of Icaria hated to see them go. The three boys had been instrumental in getting the Assembly to install gymnasium equipment, and they taught the other boys how to use it. They had brought steel skates with them and introduced ice skating. They also helped to build a billiard table and taught the men and boys how to play. After leaving the Colony they first went to Creston and were near enough for occasional visits. Later they moved to San Francisco.

Perhaps the favorite summer amusement for the Icarians was what they called fishing parties. A large group would pack a picnic lunch and start out. They first would select a nice shady spot by the river for their camp. Those who wanted to fish were then provided with the necessary equipment and went to select their own places along the river bank. Some went alone while others went in groups of two or three. Those who did not fish put up rope swings and cleared a place for playing games. They then would arrange fireplaces and cook the dinner. They had fresh, fried fish if some were caught in time to fry them. When the meal was ready the horn was blown to call everyone to camp. After the meal, games were played; and when it began to get late the horn was again sounded, and all who had wandered away returned to camp for the homeward trip.

All was not in harmony with the Icarians, however. Two factions developed. The minority, composed mostly of the younger people, said the majority were old men, set in their ways and opposed to progress. These older men had gone through many hardships in the founding of Icaria and had had many disillusionments; therefore they were very cautious in spending the money and admitting new members. They feared that these new members, being admitted at a comparatively easy time, would not be dependable if hardships should fall again. New members were admitted on probation for a term of six months, after which the Assembly would vote on their proposed membership. There were a few unfortunate incidents with new people who were still on probation.

A group of French families in New York heard of the troubles and asked to be allowed to send families to act as peacemakers. The Assembly finally agreed to accept five families as outright members. It seemed as if the new blood would bring renewed harmony into the French Colony. The new families brought new trades. Cit. Suava was a tailor, Cit. and Cite. Levy were hairdressers, Cit. Doreur was a shoemaker, Cit. Peron a machinist and Cit. Tanguy had been a sailor. Cit. Suava started the programs for each Sunday afternoon which consisted of songs, recitations and readings from Cabet's writings or other articles of interest. The amusements which had been almost discontinued were revived. Doreur was also a musician; so he reorganized their orchestra and began teaching the young children music again. Another new member admitted at this time was William Moore, who had been brought up in a Shaker Community. He was interested in horticulture and was very well-educated.

At the suggestion of Moore, fruit trees were bought and planted. He also set out a large strawberry patch with the help of the women. The men helped to plant blackberries and raspberries as well as the orchards of pears, apples and peaches. Cit. Moore also taught the women to can the surplus fruit. They planted numerous lilac bushes. Many of these lilacs can still be seen along the railroad right-of-way on what was then Icarian land.

Troubles began again. The new members wrote back to New York to their friends, each giving one side of the quarrel. Their friends in New York began to take sides too. The older members did not want to force the issue and believed that the younger group would soon see their error; therefore they let the minority do much as they wished. One of the things the minority did was to send open letters to friends in many cities which were very damaging.

When Jules Leroux and his wife came to Icaria to join their two sons, Paul and Pierre, Jules brought with him all of his printing equipment. He had printed a paper in Kansas called *Etoile du Kansas*. Here he continued the paper with the name, *Etoile du Kansas et de l'Iowa*.[21] As Cit Leroux sided with the separationists (minority), he allowed them to use his paper as they pleased.

It was decided that the majority must do something to coun-

---

[21] *Ibid.*, p. 91.

teract the damage which was being done by their paper. Suava, Levy, Gentry, Marchland and others of the majority wrote articles, and in the evenings volunteers made copies by hand. After a time an old, abandoned lithographic press was brought into use.

The minority or the "Branche" as they called themselves were admitting new members. These new members, hearing only the side of the minority, were even stronger in the advocation of a separation than the original agitators.

In 1876 one of the many visitors to the community was a Mr. John W. Dye. He had been visiting the Amanites, the Oneida Community and the Shakers. Mr. Dye talked with both parties and could not sympathize with the separationists at all. He did not stay long with the colony, but he returned the following year and asked to become a member.

He was accepted and began to publish the paper, *La Revue Icarienne*. At first he arranged to have it printed in Corning, but later it was printed in the Colony. Marie Marchand did most of the typesetting, although she was only a child at the time. Soon after the paper was going well, Mr. Dye left; and Marie and her father continued the paper, which was sent all over the United States.

A few years later the war, as it was sometimes called, ended in a separation.

> The minority had finally gone to court to secure the separation, and the verdict being against them, they had taken it to a higher court and secured the best lawyers and finally, through a technical trick, succeeded in having the community dissolved.[22]

The community had been incorporated for farming only, but they had been operating the flour mill for the neighboring farmers as well as for themselves.

Three arbitrators were selected from the neighbors to settle the affairs. The separationists (younger people) were the first to reorganize; so they took the name of Icaria and the old site for which they paid $1500 to the majority group.

The majority group of older people then reorganized and took the name of New Icaria. They moved their houses to a new location about one mile southeast of the old site. They had a housemoving concern move the eight houses to the

---

[22] *Ibid.*, p. 99.

The "New" Icarian Community — Established in 1877. Boy in foreground is the late Jules Gentry of Corning, Iowa, born in 1872.

plateau upon which they had built a new communal building. This new refectory was much smaller than the one at the old place. The first floor was used as the kitchen and dining hall. The upper floor was divided into rooms for the single men and an apartment for the Claudy family. Under the entire building was a cellar to keep provisions.

Mr. Jules Gentry told of the housemoving. It was in the dead of winter. There happened to be a mid-winter thaw and the Gentry house was mired in the mud about halfway between. Then it turned exceptionally cold. Mr. Gentry, who was only a child at the time, remembered how awfully cold the house was.

Some of these eight houses remain and are used as tool sheds and various outbuildings today. The refectory has been remodeled into a home. The kitchen is now used as a kitchen and dining room. The dining hall has also been divided into rooms. The Howard Townsend family lives there at the present. A small enclosed porch has been added to the east end. Between that wall and the door seen on the front proch was the original kitchen. Directly inside the door is the upstairs stairway. The outside cellar entrance is near the center of the front of the house. The rest of the lower floor was the dining hall.

New Icarian refectory has been remodeled and is now the home of the Howard Townsend family. Photo by Norma Brooks

The Story of Icaria

Icarian schoolhouse before restoration.

After the houses had been moved, the schoolhouse was moved to a place about halfway between the two settlements. This was used for many years as an Adams County country school after the close of the Icarian Colony. [For years the schoolhouse stood in a state of disrepair until it was moved to Corning and restored by the Centurama Historical Society of Adams County.]

The Historical Society of Corning holds its meetings in the schoolhouse today.
Photo by Norma Brooks

The Elmer Olive home near Corning.   Photo by Norma Brooks

Among the buildings still standing are two of the houses of the original colony. They have been moved together, and with the addition of a porch they are now the home of Mr. and Mrs. Elmer Olive.

The younger group did not last very long after the separation. They moved to California where they only stayed for a year or two before they broke up.

The majority now in New Icaria lasted until 1895. They had many difficulties. By their way of life it was necessary that they farm for their food. There were not enough young men left to do all the farming; the older men were not able to do the heavy work. It was necessary to hire many men from outside to help with the farming. There also was much dissatisfaction among the young men of the Colony. Although they were required to work along with the hired men, they received no remuneration. They were typical young Americans — they had ambitions to rise above their surroundings and many wanted to pursue a vocation of their choice. In Icaria there was no choice; the older men could do the other work so the young men must farm.

Also the younger people had more and more friends outside the colony. They naturally wanted to be like them. They felt awkward in their clothes which were all made alike of blue jean material. Their wooden shoes also added to their self-consciousness.

Mr. Gentry said that in 1893 he applied to the Assembly for a furlough. This was granted and he went to work on a farm some miles distant. His salary was twenty dollars a month. After the first month he brought his money and came to Icaria on a borrowed mule. He got his father and together they went into Corning to buy some "store" clothes and shoes. He was delighted with them. He said he wanted to look like an American. He went back to work and stayed for several weeks. When he did return, his mother told him how badly his father, who was in ill health, felt about his being away. After this he soon decided to return to New Icaria.

At the next election, February 3, after his return, he was elected Director of Agriculture. Although he was just twenty-one at the time, he was in charge of all the farming operations over all the older men who were still able to farm. They had been farming before he was born and it was hard for them

Built by the Icarians, this wooden silo was the first in Adams County and perhaps the earliest in Iowa.

THE LAST GROUP OF ICARIANS, ABOUT 1885

Standing, from left: Marie Marchand, Jules Gentry, Jr., Claire Gentry, Bert Rouser, Alice Sauger, Cite. Gentry, Eva Bettannier, Jules Gentry, Sr., Leon Bettannier, Lucian Rouser, Cite. Rouser, Cit. Rouser. *Seated, from left*: Cit. and Cite. Marchand, Mignot, Elsie Sauger, Maillon, Richard, Caille, Eugene Bettannier and wife. *Children, from left*: Edward Gentry, Bertha Bettannier, Eugene Bettennier, Jr., Bob Rouser and Lucie Bettannier. One girl standing unidentified.

to take orders from Jules, who seemed to them only a child.

The younger generation desired to have things of their own like their friends outside New Icaria and to do the work of their choice. These natural desires caused many to leave the French Colony. Many of the girls married and left.

At the next election it seemed impossible to get anyone to be a candidate for president of New Icaria. Cit. Marchand was excused because of his age and long years of service. Cit. Eugene Bettannier had just served ten consecutive years. The elder Cit. Gentry was then in failing health. After long deliberation, Cit. Marchand proposed that the community be dissolved. The few remaining members agreed to the dissolution on February 16, 1895.

The estate was divided among the remaining members according to the number of years of service. Cit. Eugene Bettannier, as the last president, was appointed to receive the estate. Some of the members took part of the land. Cit. Marchand chose cash, for he was planning to go to the home of his married daughter. His payment was about $3000.

This house, no longer standing, was once the home of the Bettannier family.

Icaria, as an experiment in true communal living, showed that such a life could not possibly work in America. The young people of America seem to have too much ambition and a desire to stand on their own feet to put their lot in with an entire community. For people with little ambition it would be fine, but then a community populated entirely with people who lacked ambition could not possibly succeed very long either. People with initiative could see that they would have a better chance away from those who were the free riders. Mr. Gentry said he had a lot more later on than he ever would have

had in Icaria. He said he never even considered that type of life again. Many of the descendents of the Icarian people have gone on to important positions all over the United States.

Although Icaria failed as a communal colony, it gave much to the development of the culture of Adams County and Corning. This was accomplished by their theatrical performances and through the private teaching that was done. In addition to this there were many plants that were first introduced into this section of the state in the Icarian Colony.

A Doctor's Wife in the Nineties
CORA FREAR HAWKINS

THE FOLLOWING SELECTION is a delightful and lucid account of family life in northwestern Iowa in the 1890s. While most accounts of Iowa pioneering deal with the decades between 1830 and 1860 and center on farm living, this material describes a town family in Iowa's last frontier area, the Northwest. Excerpted from the book, *Buggies, Blizzards, and Babies,* the chapter centers on Sue Frear, wife of a pioneer doctor in Sloan, Iowa. Wife, mother, medical assistant, receptionist, and comforter of the sick were a few of the duties of Mrs. Frear.

Accounts that describe the role and behavior of American women are far too limited. Histories of early pioneers generally center around male-dominated roles; accounts of early male physicians, newspaper editors, farmers and schoolteachers are frequently encountered while the role of women is often ignored. The possible exception was the wife whose husband was a famous personality or the woman who had earned distinction through some type of reform work such as the suffrage movement. The lives of ordinary people—their common, everyday practices and work habits—have all too often been passed over as insignificant. It is encouraging to note that more and more historians are beginning to realize the importance of what the majority of people were doing as opposed to the activities of a select few.

As well as offering information on the Frear family, the selection gives us a brief look at town living in nineteenth century Iowa and a glimpse of pioneer medical practices.

From Cora Frear Hawkins,
Buggies, Blizzards, and Babies
(Ames: Iowa State University Press;
© 1971 by The Iowa State University Press),
pp. 31–48.

Her dedication as a doctor's wife was Sue Frear's ruling passion. But she also had an ear for music and a love of learning.

Chapter 5

A DOCTOR'S WIFE IN THE NINETIES

A CALL had come for the doctor about four thirty. Slipping a robe over her nightgown, Mother had started a fire while the doctor dressed, and by the time he had hitched up, she had a hearty breakfast ready for him, for this was to be a long, hard trip.

Now it was too late to go back to sleep, so Mother had a long day ahead of her. She could catch up on the housework she had neglected while doing her fall housecleaning, particularly the ironing. She sprinkled down her clothes, then turned to her baking.

The evening before she had made up sponge from her starter yeast. Now she made it up stiff, pounded and kneaded it, and set it aside to rise, then scrubbed the rough, unpainted kitchen floor.

Her next task was a disagreeable one, made so by an annoying habit of the doctor's. Often when making a call he would go directly to the patient's room and lay his coat across the bed while making the examination. Coming home later with but one thought in mind—to get some sleep—he again threw his coat across the bed, theirs. Mother had learned from experience what that could mean for her—and probably for others where he and his coat went.

In vain she pleaded with him, and scolded. "The bed isn't the only place to put a coat. There's always a kitchen chair somewhere. Think of all the work it makes for me."

"All right, all right. I'll remember," he'd promise, really meaning to, but he'd forget. Just the thought of bedbugs made her flesh creep, but as a country doctor's wife she had to face the problem, and a daily inspection had become routine.

That done, she stirred the straw tick, made up the bed, and covered it with a spread made by a patient in payment of her bill. Her pillow shams showed cherubs outlined in red, floating on rededged clouds. They gave a sense of security to the room with the legends:

Angels sing thee to thy rest.
Angels wake thee—thou art blest.

Now to tidy herself for the day. She twisted her brown hair in a knot high on her head. The short ends that for some women became unsightly scolding locks, curled about her face and neck.

Her gray calico wrapper, the only type of ready-made dress available in Sloan at the time, was floor length, with long, straight sleeves and a high neck; fitted at the waist, it enhanced the figure nature had given her. Many a young woman of the nineties tied her corset laces to the bedpost, then walked away in order to pull herself in to the nineteen-inch waist and hourglass lines so popular at the time. The doctor could, and did at every opportunity, recite a list of horrible things such lacing would do to a woman's health. So it was good that his wife, conceding an inch or two at the waist, found such procedure unnecessary. Too, her cheeks had a rosy glow without being pinched.

Now she dabbed at the shine on her nose with a cornstarch puff, pinned a bit of lace at her throat, took a last look in the mirror, then went to call the children.

We three, Edna, Charley, and I, slept in the room above the kitchen, at the top of the closed-in stairway. We were talking and laughing, and we jumped out of bed when she called. We were always wide awake in the morning, for our health-minded father insisted on a seven thirty bedtime for all three.

We finished dressing by the kitchen stove while she put breakfast on the table. She made up her loaves; at the same time she checked to see that we ate our oatmeal and drank plenty of milk. Soon all were fed, buttoned, and combed. From the sitting room window she watched all three of us in homemade jackets as we left for school; the girls' stubby braids showed below brown velvet hoods; little Charley had his collar turned up, his cap pulled down over his ears, and his hands in his pockets as he braced himself against the wind. We started on a run, but Charley turned and waved at her.

She saw that it had clouded over and a light drizzle was falling—not a pleasant day for the doctor's long trip. By contrast, the sitting room was cheerful and comfortable. She had washed the rag carpet by hand in wooden tubs, one strip at a time, then had sewed them together again while the children carried in straw to cover the floor. They had stretched the carpet while she tacked the edges; then they had skipped and rolled on the puffed-up carpeting while the straw snapped and crackled under their feet. The straw would add warmth to the floor and wear to the carpet.

The wood heater with its isinglass windows had been set up for the winter. Outside, a bank of earth and straw held in place by boards had been thrown up around the base of the house, the better to keep out the cold winds. The house had been made as warm as possible, and as comfortable.

Against the wall stood the red plush sofa; across the room, the spring rocker, with its crazy-patch velvet antimacassar. The melodeon had a bouquet of red paper roses on the round shelf at the right of the keyboard; an oil lamp with a bit of red flannel in the oil for color stood on the left.

The muslin curtains hung crisp and straight. She hoped to get lace curtains and maybe ingrain carpet next year if collections were good—cash collections, that is; to be sure there would be plenty of produce brought in. The farmers shared with the doctor the best their farms had to offer when money was scarce.

There might be a quarter of beef or half a hog at butchering time; after cornhusking there would be plenty of cobs, maybe even corn on the cob, to burn. But you couldn't trade them, or runty pigs, or old hens, or hubbard squash, for luxuries for the home.

She straightened the chenille cover on the walnut center table and raised the hanging lamp; the glass prisms swinging from the shade tinkled musically and scattered bits of dancing color on the wall.

Remembering the time, she went to call the remaining member of the family, the doctor's younger brother, who had come west with them from Pennsylvania. At that time he had been a good looking youth of eighteen, spoiled by his father and older sister, Carrie, who had raised him since his mother's death when he was five. They had planned the trip for him, hoping that the great west and his older brother would make a man of him. As yet, nearly four years later, there had been no miracle of transformation; still he had presented no really serious problems, although the doctor worried constantly because he didn't settle down.

His name was also Charles, but Mother, after slight acquaintance, had called him "the old Nick himself," and the name Nick had stuck.

There was no answer when she called him. "Goodness knows, he could use some sleep," she said half aloud, "and for all he'll do when he gets up, it's hardly worthwhile." Had she cared to, she could have gotten him up very quickly. At one time her nephew, Ernest Smith, had roomed with Nick, and getting the two of them up had proved a problem. But my resourceful mother had worked out an effective alarm system.

Beside Nick's bed was an open drum to let the heat come up from the sitting room below. In the barn Father had two tame ferrets whose job was to keep the grain bin free of rats. One morning Mother placed one of them, Jerry, on a long forked stick, with which she pushed him up through the drum, then under the edge of the bed covers; Jerry headed for a cozy nest beneath them. In seconds he had the bed all to himself. After that she had only to mention Jerry to get the boys wide awake. She held the trick in reserve, but today she would let Nick sleep.

She closed the stair door and filled the stove with wood she had saved for the baking. While the oven was getting hot, then while the loaves took on their golden brown color, she sat humming softly to herself and mended stockings. They were all black:

coarse ribbed ones for Charley; finer ribbed ones for the girls; ribless gauze for herself; wool knit socks for the doctor.

The mending done and the bread baked, she laid the ironing board from the table to the back of the chair. She lifted one of the old-fashioned sadirons with a quilted holder, and started with the hardest part of the ironing, the doctor's shirts. He wore the popular (well, not so popular on ironing day) white shirts with stiff bosoms; also the stiff white wing collars. The fashionable celluloid collars were too high for his short neck, unfortunately, for they would have saved ironing seven or more collars every week.

But the shirts were her real problem. She had the first one half-ironed when there was a loud knock at the door. She set the iron on the stove and went to answer. As soon as she turned the knob, a wet wind blew the door wide open. There stood a stocky, ruddy-faced man, warmly dressed from ear-tabbed cap to felt boots. "Good morning, Mr. Johnson. Come on in!" she said, but he declined.

"No, I guess not. I just wanted to see the doctor. He ain't in the office."

"No, he won't be back until noon. Please come inside."

"No, thanks, my feet's dirty, You tell Doc——"

She tried once more. "Don't worry about the mud. If you'll just step inside—it's so cold."

"Oh, I ain't cold." (Naturally not, in his sheepskin-lined coat. She shivered in her cotton dress while he kept on talking.) "Anyhow, I ain't got but a minute. You tell Doc the old woman ain't so good. That pain in her stummick—" and so on, and on, for fifteen minutes. When he finally left and she could close the door she found the fire was out; the house was cold and so were the irons; the half-ironed shirt was dry and had to be dampened so she could start over. But what concerned her most were her aching head and shoulders. She built up the fire and sat with her feet in the oven, her gray shawl pulled close about her, and wondered. Why must people be so inconsiderate? And it would happen again and again all winter—of that she could be sure—while the catarrh she had suffered from since childhood would grow steadily worse.

Presently she got up to finish the ironing. When Nick came down yawning and dragging his feet, she pushed the irons to one side and pulled the coffeepot and heavy skillet to the front of the stove. She glanced at the clock and said, "I suppose you call this breakfast. I'll fry you some eggs." He looked hungrily at the fresh bread, but she laughed and said, "I'm not cutting my warm bread for anybody. Get some bread and the butter from the pantry and bring me your plate."

She served the eggs, then started to iron a pillowcase. "Doctor heard you come in last night, or rather this morning," she said, pausing to look at him.

Nick laughed as he attacked his breakfast. "Did he blow up?"

"No, he turned over and went to sleep. He'd been tossing and listening for you most of the night. Then he was called out at four thirty. He had less than two hours' sleep. This worry is getting him down, Nick. He needs his sleep."

"I'm sorry, Sue, but why in hell should he worry about me?" He got up for more coffee. "Now last night, for instance, a bunch of us got together for"—he hesitated just a second; "for a taffy pull. Certainly no harm in that."

She laughed. "You must have been pretty full of taffy by two o'clock in the morning."

He grinned. "Yep! That's why I left the party so early." He finished his coffee and sat thoughtfully twisting the ends of his mustache. "Well, I'll try to get in early tonight." He looked at the clock. "Gosh! I'm due at the printing office. *The Star* comes out today." He pulled a cigar from his pocket, struck a match on the stove to light it, and hurried out.

She ironed a petticoat with quick, irritated strokes as she thought of Nick. Evidently all he cared about was having a good time, working just enough to keep in spending money; he worked only part time at the printing office.

Fortunately, there was no saloon in town. There had been one a few years earlier; then some of the women, Mother included, decided they didn't want a saloon in Sloan. There was no big campaign with temperance rallies and bottle smashing. The women simply went by twos, took their sewing or knitting, and sat by the hour in the saloon. A few men sneaked to the back door to get their drinks, but there was no meeting with good fellows around the bar, hence less drinking. The saloon keeper found himself unable to cope with the situation, so closed shop.

Naturally, some liquor was brought in from nearby towns, but drinking as a pastime became less popular, so it was easier for young people to gather in homes, where music and clean fun were the rule. Nick with his ready wit, his good voice, and his guitar was always one of the crowd. In a way, his popularity was a blessing, Mother said to herself as she put the ironing board away and started lunch for the children.

At that time she had never heard of peanut butter, canned soups, or prepared cereals, but she had plenty of good bread and butter and wild plum butter—she had put up ten gallons that summer; she fried some potatoes, set out applesauce and a pitcher of milk, and lunch was ready when her two youngest burst in. Edna followed with a schoolmate, Alice Lee. The two girls had been inseparable since they had discovered each other in the first grade. Alice, a pretty child with hazel eyes and dark curls, lived a short distance out of town; she always came home with Edna for lunch. Mother enjoyed their chatter, and laughed with them, but she watched Charley closely. Only five and not a robust boy, he attended the kindergarten that had just been started.

Before she cleared the table, Mother started vegetables for the doctor's dinner. He came home and fell asleep before she had it on the table. He slept for an hour. While he ate, she finished the ironing, then carried the children's clothes upstairs. When she came down he was mixing and heating something in a pan on the stove. "What are you doing with my new saucepan?" she demanded.

"Now, I'm not hurting a thing," he said. "You go on with your work."

"But you're making such a mess! What *are* you doing?"

"Well, I'm trying to make some calomel salve, but it's too runny."

"And you're using lard? No wonder!" She handed him a jar of mutton tallow that she had rendered out to rub on croupy chests. "Try adding a little of this." After a little experimenting, the mixture had just the right consistency. "Now will you admit a woman knows a thing or two, even about a man's work?" she teased.

"Well, I was about to try tallow, but I wanted to give you a chance to show off." He picked up his jar of calomel salve and left.

Soon he was back, with an embarrassed young woman whom he introduced, then he whispered that he wanted a "specimen." She waited on the patient with a cheerful casualness that put her at ease. Since that time urinalysis has become increasingly important in the diagnosis of disease but has ceased to be the concern of the physician's wife.

Just as rare today is the type of patient who next accepted Mother's hospitality. No dentist being available, the doctor had pulled her abscessed tooth. She was made comfortable beside Mother's kitchen stove in a tilted rocker, and when her sore mouth would permit it, given hot coffee to drink. Her husband called for her later, and they left for a long, cold ride in a lumber wagon.

For the remainder of the afternoon, the doctor's work kept him in the office. At four o'clock school was out, and there were a skinned knee for Mother to dress, a torn coat to mend so it could be worn the next day, and a spelling lesson that needed a workout. Then both the doctor and Nick came home at six, and they all had supper together. Mother had prepared only six meals that day. Sometimes it was more. The supper dishes done, she sat down in the spring rocker to read, but she soon fell asleep. The doctor's wife had had a full day.

The unexpected guest was a common occurrence in our home. If a patient was in the office at mealtime, Father brought him home. Mother, working by the kitchen window, would see them coming across the vacant lot; she could add bread to the fried potatoes, or dumplings to the stew, cut the pie in smaller pieces, or open a jar of fruit; there were always plenty of vegetables.

But sometimes, maybe on washday when the boiler filled with sudsy clothes took up most of the stove, and she had had a hard morning, she would send a child to the office with definite instructions: "Go see if there is anyone in the office with Papa. If he's alone, tell him to come to dinner."

I remember well one unexpected guest. That was the day Papa sued a man for a doctor bill. The case had not come up when the court adjourned for noon recess, and Papa brought the man home with him for dinner. Unknown to our parents, that morning Edna had heard Papa say: "His sisters say he's got the money, but he's boasted he won't pay a cent, so they've urged me to sue. If the judge orders him to pay, he'll be afraid of going to jail for contempt of court and pay up."

Edna had repeated the conversation to Charley and me, adding her own embellishments, and we three had interpreted it in our own way. To us, the man was a criminal, no less. It was our first meeting with a criminal, and we must watch his every word and act. We sat opposite him at the table and stared at him. We whispered behind our hands—and stared. Mother—always the disciplinarian—nudged us under the table, but we failed to understand; we ignored her signal. We still whispered—and stared! It must have been a relief to the defendant to get away from us and have only the court to face.

It was probably the only time Father ever sued for a bill. As I remember it, he got seventy-five dollars, and my Scotch-Irish mother was just the one to spend it so as to get the best possible value.

It was an asset to be Scottish in those early days in Iowa, but the love and laughter of the Irish provided the answer to many a problem. Mother laughed at her troubles, her worries, her shortcomings; when she could without sacrificing discipline, she laughed at her children's pranks. She usually had just the right answer to turn away a personal or annoying question.

I remember when Nannie Williams, a maiden lady in her thirties whose flashing black eyes made one wonder about her demure manner, stayed at our house for a time to be near the office and take treatments.

Little was said about her ailment—it probably wasn't very interesting anyway—but the neighborhood busybody couldn't stand the suspense. One day as I stood in the doorway watching Mother put up strings for her sweet peas, I saw this woman stride into our yard, head thrust forward, long arms swinging. I was reminded of a rodent by her pointed face with her thin lips drawn back from crooked, brown teeth.

She stomped up to Mother without any preliminary remarks, and, accenting each word, she said, "Mrs. Frear! I want to know what ails Nannie Williams!" There was no parrying such a demand. It called for an answer, and Mother was ready with one.

Imitating the woman's tone and inflection perfectly, Mother looked her straight in the eye and said, "Mrs. Bunce! I do not know what ails Nannie Williams!"

Completely taken aback, the woman stared at Mother, snorted her disbelief, and stalked angrily away. Mother just grinned at me and went on with her work. She had told the truth. Of course, she could have told some things about the case, and, adding some details of her own, Mrs. Bunce would have spread it over the neighborhood. But even if Mother had known a big-sounding name and all the symptoms for Nannie's ailment, neither a gossiping neighbor or her own best friend could have pried the information out of her. She knew that, by indulging in gossip, many a doctor's wife had brought professional criticism on her husband and sometimes caused unnecessary suffering for a patient or his family.

Just as disastrous, then as now, was jealousy. Certainly there was opportunity for a young woman to misinterpret the contacts her doctor-husband had with his women patients, especially since some of them were careless or even deliberate in creating wrong impressions. But Mother laughed off many an incident that might have brought on a crisis between people of less sympathetic understanding.

For a time one of Father's patients was a young and attractive divorcee, Molly Burns. Her only source of income was from a farm that she had tried to run by herself after her husband left her. It was hard work for a frail woman, and her health suffered. Unable to get away in the daytime, she always waited until evening, when she could no longer see to work, then came to the office for consultation and treatment.

In our community in the early days, divorced persons were rare and the gossips were obliged to concentrate on poor Molly. So one morning a thin-lipped sister, leaning backward the better to carry her own impeccably righteous load, called on Mother and said, "Mrs. Frear, there is something that your friends all think it's best for you to know. I've come to tell you that Molly Burns comes to town and meets Dr. Frear in his office every night after dark."

Mother had trouble to keep from laughing. "Oh, I've known that all along," she said. "It's all right with me."

Her caller looked horrified and started to speak, but Mother went on: "Last night Molly paid her bill, and I've got the money." She pulled a handful of bills and silver from her apron pocket. "And I'm going downtown and spend it this very day."

The woman left hurriedly, plainly disappointed that her call had ended on such a happy note.

Besides having a sense of humor, Mother enjoyed poetry and music and sang as she went about her work, sometimes softly, sometimes with abandon, depending on her mood.

There was one day in early summer when for the first time we could open all the doors. Outside, birds sang and contented hens visited in the dooryard. Father was setting out tomato plants and a light breeze carried in the fragrance of freshly turned soil. Sunlight streamed across the kitchen floor, and Mother burst into the old song, "There Is Sunshine in My Soul Today!"

Presently a lady from our church came to the door. Without waiting for Mother's greeting, she said, "Mrs. Frear, I'm here to tell you it's your Christian duty to sing in our choir. I've been listening to you all the way from town, and I'm telling you, it was beautiful! We haven't another voice in the church half as good."

Mother's response to that announcement was a hearty laugh. Then she said, "I'm so glad you told me. I'll try not to make so much noise after this so as not to disturb the town. But you know very well that I seldom can get to church, let alone go to choir practice."

Mother attended church whenever possible, but she could never count on going. Many farmers who would not think of working in the fields on Sunday failed to consider the doctor's need of rest; since the team was not being used in the fields, they would drive in to see the doctor and have him look at Johnny's wart, or dress a bad burn that hadn't healed, or give the wife something for that awful cough.

Mother felt she must be home to take messages or talk with patients who came. And if the doctor had had a hard night she might try to devise some way to avoid or postpone a consultation so the doctor could sleep. And on Sunday as well as on a weekday, a compress or an arm sling might be needed; the obstetrical instruments might have to be cleaned and boiled after a delivery; the doctor might need hot water, and sometimes this alone posed a problem. Wood was scarce in that part of Iowa, and the soft coal brought in was limited in supply and high priced.

Possibly my memory is distorted by the feel of the old bushel basket that bumped against my knees as I carried it, overflowing, from corncrib to kitchen; but we seemed to burn corncobs most of the time. I remember too that we sometimes twisted hay into ropes, then tied them in knots for fuel. There were special stoves —hay burners—for utilizing the prairie grasses, and one still heard of burning buffalo chips, but my childhood was spent, one might say, in the corncob era.

Regardless of the fuel problem or the heat of summer, Mother was seldom caught without hot water when it was needed. However, it was working beside her husband in an emergency that gave her the most satisfaction. She knew instinctively how to ease a patient's position, massage a back, or stimulate circulation in a bed-weary limb. Many a newborn baby was placed in her arms, and the first sound to meet his pink ears would be Mother's voice whispering sweet nothings as she dressed him to meet his world.

At times situations called for a special kind of courage, when so little could be done and she must forget the tremendous need that could not be met. One early summer morning Father returned from a call on a young woman who lay dying of abdominal cancer in a two-room cabin near the railroad track. As usual, he called as he came in, "Sue? Oh, Sue! Where are you?"

She came in from the entry where she was straining the morning milk. Seeing that he was distressed, she asked, "What's wrong? Is she gone?"

"No. Not yet, poor soul," he said. "But it can't be long now, twenty-four hours at the most."

"Who is with her?" she asked, sensing a need.

"Only her husband. Her sister is coming this afternoon. The two children are with neighbors. They came in to help at first, but one after another they've given up. You can't really blame them." He poured a cup of coffee, but set it down and walked back and forth across the floor. "Lord, it's awful, Sue. The stench—flies swarming all over her—and she cries and moans when she is conscious—which isn't often now, thank God. I've given her all the morphine I dare. I don't know what more I can do."

Mother washed the strainer cloth while he talked. "Her husband isn't much help. Just sits with his head in his hands. I roused him up to keep the flies away from her when I left." He sat down to drink his coffee.

Mother opened the trap door in the kitchen floor and carried the crock of milk down the steps to cool on the cellar bottom. Returning, she scribbled on a piece of paper. "I'll leave a note for Edna. She and Alice can put the lunch on," she said.

Father spoke quickly. "I can't ask you to go over there, Sue."

She said, "You haven't. But she needs someone with her." She tied on a clean apron and reached for her sunbonnet. "Come on. I'm ready."

She found conditions even worse than she had expected. She had all she could do to keep patient and bed clean, shoo flies (with strips of paper tied to the end of a stick), wipe the poor drooling mouth, and pray—for what, she hardly knew. In late afternoon relatives came by train, and she went home, depressed by a sense that she had failed.

They came for Father before daybreak next morning. When he returned later, quiet and tense, she knew without asking that the end had come. She knew too what was in his mind. She said, "You did everything possible for her, all anyone could do."

"I know, but it wasn't enough," he said sadly. "Someday they'll find a cure for cancer. I hope it won't be long." He looked out the window, then said, "I think I'll go out and hoe the potatoes while you get breakfast on." Her eyes followed him; she smiled at the energy he put into his work. There his tension would disappear and his spirit be renewed for another day's work.

She heard the bell on the Methodist church toll to announce the death, its muffled tones marking the age of the deceased. Mother counted them as she fried golden slices of cornmeal mush. Only thirty years old! Long folds of black crepe would fall from the doorknob of the deceased's home. Her husband might wear a band of crepe on his sleeve—it wasn't always done although a widow would certainly wear a black dress and long crepe weeds. (Father deplored them as a hindrance to a woman's health and to her mental and spiritual adjustment.)

The funeral would be in the church, of course. There would be few flowers, possibly some from neighbors' gardens. Mother decided to pick all her sweet alyssum and make a wreath for the altar. Right now she must call the doctor to breakfast and start another day, with its many possibilities.

Mother's interest in his patients was a source of great pride for Father; for her, the sympathy and understanding toward his work gained from her relations with them added much to the richness of her life.

Sometimes mothers would leave their children with her while they consulted the doctor, then did a little shopping. A baby might be left to lie on her clean bedspread (with plastic panties unknown) for an hour—or half a day. She welcomed them all for she loved children, especially babies.

But occasionally the older children overplayed their welcome. One young mother of three, who lived in town while a patient of Father's, had found the brief interlude without her children so enjoyable that she started dropping them off at our house whenever they became a nuisance, and this happened increasingly often.

One day the five-year-old boy set a kitten on the hot stove "to see him dance." Later, Mother, investigating meows and cries, rescued a half-suffocated kitten from the oven. On her return the mother found her son securely strapped in a chair and was informed that, for her offspring, the door would remain definitely and permanently closed. Mother loved animals, and to abuse them was not to be tolerated.

Father, too, loved animals. On one occasion his fondness for cats could have gotten him in serious trouble. It was cold, and a heavy snow had fallen, when he took the sleigh for a five-mile drive north of town. He returned about noon and took an unusually long time to stomp his boots and shake the snow from his fur coat before coming in. He tossed his coat on a chair and asked, "Have you got some hot coffee?" Mother set the coffeepot on the stove.

He stood there warming his hands. Soon there was a meowing and scratching at the back door. Father was there so soon one might suspect he was waiting for the summons. "Well, well! Look here, Sue!" he said. " 'The wicked wandereth abroad for food.' Have you got any food for the wicked?" He set a scrawny, mangy black kitten on the floor.

Mother looked suspiciously from him to the emaciated animal, but she produced a saucer of table scraps. "All right, Wicked, eat, then please go home." She picked up Father's coat and started to spread it out to dry.

Father took it from her. "Never mind that coat. How about the coffee?"

But Mother had noticed something. She pointed to a jagged tear in the back of the coat. "How in the world did you do that?"

"Oh, that? I must have snagged it a little."

"Snagged it a little? Doctor, that tear is over a foot long! I want to know what happened," she demanded.

"Sue, don't nag me. I just got home from a long, cold trip. What I need is a cup of hot coffee." He sounded almost pathetic.

She filled a cup, stirred in sugar and cream, and handed it to him. "There's your coffee. Now! Where did that cat come from?"

He dodged the question. "Don't you ever read Job? 'The wicked wandereth abroad——' "

"Humph!" she interrupted. "Job had nothing to do with this. You picked this cat up someplace." She half-suspected the truth, even before she wormed it out of him next day.

About three miles out of town he had heard pitiful cries and thought it might be the voice of a lost child. He stopped to listen, then discovered this kitten, caught in the crotch of a tree, about ten feet above the ground, on the other side of a barbed wire fence. He tried to go on and leave it, but couldn't.

It was too cold to remove his coat and felt boots; it would be hard to get through the fence with them on, then climb the tree far enough to reach the kitten—but that's what he had done. Then, holding the clawing kitten, he had had trouble getting back through the fence, and his coat had caught on the wire.

"You've no right to take such a risk at your age," she scolded.

"Sue, I couldn't have slept a wink with that cat on my conscience," he said earnestly.

"And if you'd fallen from the tree and broken your leg, I suppose you'd have slept just dandy, lying there on the ground until someone found you, a day or so later." Mother's patience was exhausted. "Well, we don't need any more cats. You can just find a home for him."

But no one wanted Wicked. Moreover, he seemed to like it with us, which wasn't too bad, until he started taking the best chairs for his naps, stealing the kittens' food or jumping on the dining table for snacks, and using the far corner of the bedroom closet for his private sandpile.

Father would make excuses for him when reminded that Wicked was his cat, until he started biting and scratching patients who came to the door; now there was no alternative—Wicked had to go.

Father said, "Chloroforming will be the most humane method; I'll take care of it." But he dreaded it and procrastinated. until Mother set three o'clock on a certain day as a deadline.

At the appointed hour, she said, "We are all ready. Wicked is down cellar in a washtub covered with boards weighted down with bricks."

Father went to the office for chloroform. Returning, he handed her a large wad of cotton and a bottle that he said contained enough chloroform to kill three cats; he added sheepishly, "Sue, I'm really sorry I can't stay and do this, but Bert Owen was in the office waiting for me, and I've got to go over there. I'll be back by five, if you'll just wait——"

"I've done all the waiting I'm going to," she snapped. "I'll do it by myself."

She saw the expression of mixed guilt and relief as she turned away, but she was so angry that nothing could stop her now. With the cotton tied around a slender stick, she soaked it well with chloroform and pushed it between the boards in front of the feline nose, only to find the nose was somewhere else. She probed, he jumped. Wicked was neither ready nor willing to meet his Creator, and since the crack was straight and narrow, and the tub was round and wide, he had the advantage as he tore madly about his small prison and yowled, spit, and scratched.

When he raised the boards a few inches, she tried to hold them down with her hands, and the bottle fell and rolled across the floor, spilling most of the contents. She sat on the cover and looked around for something to use as a weight, but nothing was within reach; she sat still trying to figure out a way of escape. No one would hear if she called for help. There were the cellar steps and the door at the top, but, with old Wicked shoving and clawing frantically, if she took her weight off the boards for an instant he would jump out and tear into her. For the present she must stay right where she was.

She was cold, and the musty odor from the bins of stored vegetables was oppressing; but above all she was nauseated and drowsy from the fumes of the chloroform. She must stay awake at all costs; maybe Wicked's yowling would help there.

After an hour she heard the sound of running feet—school was out. She called to us, and there we found her, weeping, pale, and weak from nausea and nervous exhaustion. Charley cried from sympathy, first for her, then for the cat, while Edna and I offered to help finish the task, but she said, "No, thanks! That pleasure belongs entirely to your father." Together we lifted a sack of potatoes onto the cover of the tub and left Wicked there.

Mother went to bed and lay with her face to the wall. No one spoke when Papa opened the door and called, "Sue? Oh, Sue! Where are you?" He looked at our long faces as we stepped from the bedroom. He hurried to her calling, "Sue! For God's sake, what's wrong?" She neither moved nor spoke, but she let him feel her pulse.

He appealed to us children, but we only kept quiet until

Edna suggested, "You might look in the cellar."

Wicked started a wild fight, but Father dealt a blow to his head which quieted him until the lethal dose could be administered. The end was total. Poor Wicked did not even live on in the affection of his family.

Mother was humiliated by her failure. Later, when she could talk about it, she said a doctor's wife should know how to chloroform a cat, or have sense enough not to try.

Mother's dedication as a doctor's wife was her ruling passion, and its major expression was in sharing the doctor's hopes and plans for their children. They must have a happy home life, with both affection and discipline, and strong, healthy bodies. They must have the education she had missed and for which he had struggled so hard. She carried a full share of this responsibility.

She taught us girls to do housework and sewing and expected us to do our share, but if there was something to do for church or school, that came first. She did the work gladly while we studied, went to church, rehearsed for a program, or even went to one of the few parties held in our town. She helped us to memorize poems and songs, and if we took part in a program, she always managed to attend.

She shared with us her joy in creating things both lovely and practical. We made countless dresses for our dolls, so slipped easily into sewing for ourselves, even to the lined and fitted skirts of seven gores worn when we were fourteen and sixteen years old. Mother herself revelled in making pieced quilts, as well as feather-stitched crazy-quilts and antimacassars. In her hands, seven tomato cans covered with heavy woollen material—probably a discarded pair of trousers—were joined together to become an attractive hassock, padded on top and brightly embroidered.

I'll never know how Mother found the time for handicrafts and needlework, with all the housework she had to do, besides helping Father when he needed her. And still there were times in the winter when, with the supper work done, the children in bed, and Father out on a call, she had an evening alone to spend as she pleased. At such times she often sat down at the organ and played and sang the old songs she loved.

I remember one night when I lay awake listening to the plaintive strains of "Sunset Reverie." I slipped out of bed and went into Nick's room—he was out for the evening—to lie on the floor beside the open drum so that I could hear better.

Presently she played "The Bridge" and began to sing, softly at first; then as she yielded to the sweetness of the hour, my mother's voice floated up to me in full, rich tones. "Juanita" followed, then "Ben Bolt."

But the song that brought tears to my eyes was "I'll Take You Home Again, Kathleen." In childish imagination, I pictured my mother as the bonnie bride. I wondered about the place "where your heart has ever been," and whether Papa would take her back again "across the ocean wild and wide." Could it be that Mamma wasn't happy with us? And was it because we children were so bad?

Lying there with my feet curled up in my nightgown, I thought of how hard Mamma worked to take care of us, and I remembered many times when I had been naughty. I'm sure I wasn't a really bad child, but little acts of disobedience stood out pretty big as I listened to my mother's voice. I buried my face in my arms and cried.

When I heard her close the organ and sit down in the squeaky rocker, I slipped down the cold, dark stairway, and across the bare kitchen floor to the sitting room. She held out her arms to me and wrapped me in her gray shawl. With my arms around her neck, I sobbed, "Mamma, will you forgive me for being such a naughty girl? Please, Mamma, I'll be good. I promise. I want you to be happy so you'll stay with us." She must have been puzzled by that last statement, but I was promptly forgiven, and warmly loved. And I was reassured by her tenderness as she took me upstairs and tucked me in bed.

I promised to go right to sleep if she'd sing one more song—"I Think When I Hear That Sweet Story." As her voice drifted up to me, I thought that my mother's singing must be the most beautiful music in the world. As I grow older, I am inclined to think that I was right.

1872-1920—Carrie Chapman Catt
LOUISE R. NOUN

IN 1920 after many long and arduous battles, American women won the right to vote. Prior to this, however, feminists from all over the country had participated in many campaigns to win state-by-state approval of woman suffrage; among them was a highly gifted Iowan—Carrie Chapman Catt.

The following selection, excerpted from the book *Strong-Minded Women* by Louise R. Noun, presents an excellent account of Mrs. Catt—the person—as well as the cause for which she labored so long. Born and reared in Wisconsin, Carrie Lane was described as a "strong-minded girl." Following her graduation from Iowa State Agricultural College (now Iowa State University) in Ames, she accepted a position as school principal in Mason City where she first became active in the women's rights crusade. From this moment her life and the suffrage movement were closely intertwined. An extremely energetic, capable woman, a gifted organizer, and an excellent public speaker, Mrs. Catt made an indelible mark on the woman suffrage movement, not only in Iowa, but throughout the entire nation.

The selection is also pertinent because it places the Iowa suffrage movement in the context of the national movement; it is then possible to see the total scope of the campaign for women's rights as well as its effect on Iowans.

From Louise R. Noun, *Strong-Minded Women*
(Ames: Iowa State University Press;
© 1969 by The Iowa State University Press),
pp. 224–61.

10

1872-1920

Carrie Chapman Catt

W<small>HEN</small> S<small>USAN</small> B. A<small>NTHONY</small> retired at the age of 80 as president of the National Woman Suffrage Association in February 1900, she took deep satisfaction in knowing that her successor, forty-one-year-old Carrie Chapman Catt, was ideally suited to take the helm of her beloved suffrage craft. Mrs. Catt, reared and educated in Iowa, began her suffrage work with the pioneer Iowa suffragists Mary Jane Coggeshall and Martha Callanan as her mentors. She was destined to lead the woman-suffrage forces of the United States to final victory in 1920 with the ratification of the Nineteenth Amendment to the federal Constitution.

AN IDEAL LEADER

B<small>ECAUSE</small> M<small>RS</small>. C<small>ATT</small> was a former Mason City resident, the convention in Washington, D.C., at which she was elected president of the National Association was of particular interest to the citizens of this community. One of them (probably a delegate to the convention) who served as a special correspondent for the *Mason City Republican* observed that "no person could see the remarkable interest that has been taken in this convention, the immense crowds that have thronged the doors of the church where the meetings were held, and could hear the brainy speeches from their platform and read the account of the ovation that was given their leader, Miss Susan B. Anthony, at the close of fifty years she has given the cause . . . without realizing that the woman's suffrage movement has 'come to stay.'"

This writer goes on to quote the *Washington Star*'s description of the dramatic scene when Miss Anthony presented their new president to the delegates: "The women went wild as Miss Anthony, erect and alert, with her snow white hair walked to the front of the platform, holding the hand of her young co-worker of whom she expects great things. Miss Anthony's eyes were tear-dimmed and her tones were uneven, as she presented to the convention its choice of a leader and paid her tribute of praise to the woman who had been her 'right-hand man' for so many years. It was such a tribute as most people get only after the sun of another world dawns on them. It was a tribute freighted with love and tender solicitude and rich with reminiscences of the past and full of hope for the future of Mrs. Catt and her work."

"In Mrs. Catt you have my ideal leader. I present you my successor," Miss Anthony concluded. By this time, reported the *Star*, "half the women were using their handkerchiefs on their eyes and the other half were waving handkerchiefs in the air. Mrs. Catt said quickly, 'Your president if you please, but Miss Anthony's successor, never! There is but one Miss Anthony and she could have no successor.'"

A handsome, vigorous, dynamic woman with a quick sense of humor, Mrs. Catt was highly skilled both as a presiding officer and a public speaker. For the preceding five years she had done outstanding work as chairman of the organization committee of the National Association.

Of medium height, Mrs. Catt had a dignified and erect bearing, a fair complexion, deep blue eyes, resolute chin, and light brown hair streaked with gray. She dressed tastefully but elegantly, usually in a shade of blue which accented the color of her eyes. "Mrs. Catt is fortune favored," the *Mason City Globe* had commented the previous October. "She possesses both physical charms and intellectual endowments. Always regarded as a handsome woman, she is more charming than ever."

A STRONG-MINDED GIRL

CARRIE LANE WAS BORN in Wisconsin in 1859 and came with her parents to Iowa in 1866, where they settled on a farm near Charles City. As a thirteen-year-old farm girl in 1872—the year that a woman-suffrage amendment met its first defeat in the Iowa legislature—Carrie Lane began her career as an outspoken feminist.

One afternoon during this summer her mother overheard a heated argument between Carrie and a male contemporary, as their words drifted into the house from the orchard where the young people were arguing. "Women can't fight, why should they vote?" the boy asked. Carrie countered by naming all the physically defective men in the neighborhood who were permitted to vote but were not able to fight. "If they can vote, why shouldn't women have the same privilege?" she asked.

"Where does that girl get her outlandish notions?" asked Mr. Lane when his wife told him about their daughter's encounter. "She'll never get married, I'm afraid!"

As the year 1872 progressed, Carrie followed with great interest the election campaign in which Horace Greeley, editor of the *New York Tribune,* headed an insurgent liberal Republican ticket in an effort to defeat Ulysses S. Grant for a second presidential term. Carrie's parents were Greeley supporters, and she was dismayed on election day when her father and the hired man went off to vote leaving her mother behind. Upon her father's return she challenged him about this. Mr. Lane explained that he owned the farm and therefore should have the responsibility of voting. Carrie countered that her mother through her labor had helped pay for the property. Her father then said that men know more than women. Carrie retorted that the hired man didn't know half as much as her mother. In recalling this incident in 1916, when campaigning for woman suffrage in Iowa, Carrie Chapman Catt told her audiences that she became a suffragist then and there. She also made a suffragist of her father.

After graduation from Charles City High School, Carrie went to the State Agricultural College at Ames, where in 1880 she graduated with top honors—the only girl among the seventeen members of her class. The following year she settled in Mason City, a community of 3,500, where she had been appointed principal of the high school. She subsequently was promoted to superintendent of schools. On February 12, 1885, Carrie, who had given up her school position the previous fall, married Leo Chapman, twenty-eight-year-old editor of the *Mason City Republican*, a weekly paper which he had purchased in 1883 after serving four years' apprenticeship with the *Des Moines Register*. Chapman, a native of Indiana who had come with his parents to Marshalltown, Iowa, in 1870, was an ardent, reform-minded young man who promptly made his wife a coeditor of the paper, carrying her name on the masthead along with his.

"WOMAN'S WORLD"

ON MARCH 19, 1885—four weeks after their marriage—a new feature entitled "Woman's World"[1] was added to the *Republican*, and its editor, Carrie Chapman, announced it would be "devoted to the discussion of such questions as purport to the welfare, the social, the political and intellectual position of women." Correspondence would be welcomed.

The following week a welcoming letter from a "Mrs. S. E." was published in the "Woman's World" which noted that "there are plenty of suffragists in this county but the absence of any organization deprives them of influence." She hoped the column would promote the cause. On April 9 a second letter, signed "Philes," endorsed the idea of a local suffrage society. "Nearly all other counties and towns have them," this writer asserted. "There is also a State Association. . . ." However, the time did not seem ripe for a suffrage society in Mason City. At least the "Woman's World" made no further mention of a local suffrage organization, nor did it carry any more correspondence from its readers on this or any other subject.

Carrie Chapman, nonetheless, was not to be easily discouraged in her woman's rights crusade. A firm believer in the theory of social evolution, she regarded any setback to the woman-suffrage cause as only a temporary rebuff. Commenting on the veto of a woman-suffrage bill by the governor of the Dakota Territory, she wrote on April 9, "Reforms of all kinds have grown sluggishly and public sentiment is slowly educated. No step of progress was ever made but its advocates fought dearly for victory. Such a

---

1. This column was modeled after a column titled "Woman's Kingdom" which Elizabeth Boynton Harbert edited for the *Chicago Interocean* during 1877–1884. The Lanes were subscribers, and Carrie was deeply impressed with Mrs. Harbert's woman's rights views.

reform as this . . . was never accomplished in a single generation. That women will have a voice in governmental affairs is inevitable."

On May 28 the "Woman's World" carried a long excerpt from a speech delivered by Mary Jane Coggeshall at the annual meeting of the Polk County Woman Suffrage Society. During the summer other columns defended women's right to strike for better pay and working conditions; deplored the "pernicious habit of calling a girl who remains unmarried until 25 an 'old maid'"; attacked the usual columns "devoted to women" which "are composed of quibs upon ridiculous subjects that ordinary people would not consider worth reading. Poodle dogs, hair pins, ice cream eaters and 'mashes' being specimens of the subjects treated." A series of columns was devoted to answering arguments against woman suffrage. "It is the duty of all women to inform themselves about suffrage," Carrie Chapman declared. "For a woman to say she does not know the results to be obtained from suffrage is to acquire knowledge that she has no interest in the welfare of women."

In the October 15 "Woman's World" Carrie Chapman gave an enthusiastic report about her visit the previous week to Des Moines, where she attended the Woman's Congress—a three-day convention sponsored by the Association for the Advancement of Women, an organization founded in 1873 for their cultural, social, economic, and political advancement.[2] This meeting was chaired by the association's illustrious president, Julia Ward Howe of Boston—author of "Battle Hymn of the Republic" and first president of the New England Woman Suffrage Association. Other notable women who attended this meeting were Mary Livermore, leader of the Northwest Sanitary Commission during the Civil War and former editor of the *Woman's Journal;* Frances Willard, president of the WCTU; Reverend Antoinette Blackwell, pioneer woman minister in the United States; and Elizabeth Boynton Harbert, former Des Moines resident living in Evanston, Illinois, who was well known in the Middle West for her writing on woman's rights. Among the Iowa women attending the meeting were a number of prominent suffrage advocates, including Amelia Bloomer, Mary Newbury Adams, Mattie Griffiths Davenport, Martha Callanan, and Mary Jane Coggeshall.

2. The Association for the Advancement of Women was an outgrowth of Sorosis, pioneer New York woman's club established in 1868. The Des Moines congress sparked the organization of the Des Moines Woman's Club, organized October 14, 1885, by twenty-two women meeting at the home of its first president, Dr. Margaret Cleaves, an 1873 graduate of the University of Iowa Medical School.

"It was not a convention of mannish women or men-haters, who met to bewail their fate in common, as many Iowa people seemed to suppose, but an Association the superior of which in point of intellectual quality and praiseworthy achievements does not exist," reported Carrie Chapman. "No woman could listen to the masterly papers and able discussion without forming a higher ideal of life and receiving a strength to help her realize it. . . . As the advancement of women is complicated with many theories and principles of political and social economy," Mrs. Chapman explained, "its object is more properly the solution of any political, social, moral, sociological, or psychological problem which may come before it. . . ." Despite this enthusiastic report, Carrie Chapman in later years confessed that she had felt a sense of frustration about this meeting. Here were too many fields to explore, no well-defined focus.

FIRST SUFFRAGE WORK

ON NOVEMBER 9 Carrie Chapman reported in the "Woman's World" about her first woman-suffrage meeting—the annual convention of the Iowa association at Cedar Rapids, which she had attended on October 20 and 21. About sixty-five delegates from different parts of the state were in attendance along with two out-of-state visitors—the sixty-seven-year-old suffrage pioneer Lucy Stone and her husband Henry Blackwell, who was the only man present. Lucy Stone, who "made one of her matchless addresses," was described by Mrs. Chapman as "a quaint appearing little old woman with round face wreathed in smiles and a demeanor so motherly and attractive as to win the hearts of all at a glance."

The plan adopted by the Iowa association for the coming year, Carrie Chapman told her readers, was the circulation of three petitions to be presented to the 1886 General Assembly: "One asking for a statute giving women municipal suffrage, one for a statute giving presidential suffrage to women, and one for an amendment removing all political disabilities from women."

The petitions asking for statutes giving presidential and municipal suffrage to women reflected the increasing discouragement among the suffragists of Iowa over their failure to persuade the Iowa legislature to submit a constitutional amendment, a process which required approval by two successive sessions. Only twice since the General Assembly first approved a woman-suffrage amendment in 1870 had the legislature again approved such an amendment, and in intervening years the measure had been killed in the House or the Senate, always by one or two unexpected votes.

Looking for a quicker and easier method of enfranchisement, suffragists in 1880 began a campaign for a law giving women the right to vote in municipal and school elections. This effort (which paralleled similar efforts by women in other states) met with very limited success in Iowa in 1894 when the General Assembly granted women the privilege of voting in elections involving the issuing of bonds, borrowing money, or increasing the tax levy.

Meanwhile, in 1886 during the session following the Cedar Rapids convention,[3] when Carrie Chapman learned that a municipal-suffrage bill had been introduced in the legislature, she organized a house-to-house canvass through which she succeeded in securing the signatures of all but ten Mason City women on a petition asking for favorable action on this bill. For the rest of her suffrage career this successful canvass was to be Carrie's stock answer to those who claimed that women did not want to vote.

A FUNEREAL DEPARTURE

DARK CLOUDS were looming on the horizon for Carrie and Leo Chapman, who were too ardent in their reform activities to suit the taste of some of their fellow citizens in Mason City. During the election campaign of 1885 Leo Chapman had antagonized the local Republican hierarchy by opposing for reelection the party's nominee for county auditor whom he charged with feathering his nest with the proceeds of office. Chapman's choice for the office was an independent candidate who was also endorsed by the Democrats. Despite Chapman's vigorous campaign against the regular party nominee (some said because of it) he was returned to office by a small majority. The auditor and his friends subsequently secured an indictment for crim-

---

3. Mrs. Catt in later years recalled that this petition was circulated prior to attending her first woman-suffrage convention. If this were so, it would mean that the petition was circulated during the 1884 General Assembly while Mrs. Catt was superintendent of schools in Mason City. In 1939, when eighty years old, Mrs. Catt wrote to Mary Hunter: "I did not know any suffragists anywhere when I read in the paper that a certain representative had introduced a bill granting municipal suffrage to women. This must have been in 1885 or 1886. So I organized a committee and we surveyed the town, asking women only to sign our petition for the passage of this measure. We did not approve municipal suffrage, but that was the bill. We got every woman in the town to sign that petition except ten and the story of these ten was amusing, so I wrote a letter telling about the ten who did not sign, and sent the petition to the man who had introduced the bill. He showed that letter to some of the suffragists who were working in the Capitol. . . ."

inal libel against Leo Chapman. Judging from future events, it seems evident that their intention was to run him out of town.

At first Chapman was jaunty about the affair; but when the matter came before the court in the spring of 1886 and the judge upheld the indictment over Chapman's demurrer, it was announced a few days later that Chapman had severed his connection with the *Mason City Republican* because of "failing health." The *Mason City Times,* a Democratic weekly, warned the new owner of the *Republican* "lest he too stumble into the pitfall that so completely engulfed his predecessors that their trumpeted coming was only equalled by their funereal departure. They flashed as the rocket," the *Times* said, "and fell as the stick." The *Times* suggested that Chapman's successor leave the shaping of the city and its destiny to "the good old pioneers and their sons." This debacle was so traumatic for Carrie Chapman that she never mentioned it in any of her biographical reminiscences, and it would have remained buried in history were it not for old newspaper files and court records.

After disposing of the *Mason City Republican,* Leo Chapman went to San Francisco, intending to buy a paper in that area. However, in August 1886 he was stricken with typhoid fever and died before Carrie, who was spending the summer with her parents on their farm near Charles City, could reach his bedside. The next year was a despondent one for Carrie Chapman. Reaching San Francisco after Leo's death, she stayed on to work as a newspaper reporter but felt that her life was without purpose or meaning. By the fall of 1877 she had determined to devote her life to the enfranchisement of women and with this in mind returned to Iowa, where she had family and friends. To earn a living, she began a career as a professional lecturer.

STATE ORGANIZER

CARRIE CHAPMAN's full involvement with the woman-suffrage movement began in October 1889 when she attended the annual meeting of the Iowa Woman Suffrage Association in Oskaloosa. Here she delivered an address which the *Woman's Standard* (an Iowa woman-suffrage paper established by Martha Callanan of Des Moines in 1886) described as "scholarly, witty, and convincing." Mrs. Chapman, the *Woman's Standard* said, "gave the fullest evidence of being a thorough student of the question and a woman who will make her individual force felt among the people of Iowa."

Iowa Woman Suffrage Association convention, Oskaloosa, 1889. Carrie Chapman Catt is in the first row center, wearing cape. The man in the second row is Henry Blackwell, and the woman to his left is his wife Lucy Stone. Martha Callanan is seated on Blackwell's right, and Mary Jane Coggeshall is seated second from the left in this row. It was at this convention that Mrs. Catt was persuaded to become an organizer for the Iowa Association.

Carrie Chapman was elected to the office of secretary of the Iowa association for the coming year and was also persuaded to try her hand at organizing. She lost no time in getting to work, starting at Sioux City on November 19, where she organized a Political Equality Club. From there, according to the *Woman's Standard,* she was scheduled to go to Cherokee, Aurelia, Alta, Fonda, Fort Dodge, Humboldt, Webster City, Williamson, Allen, Iowa Falls, Ackley, Waterloo, and Manchester. She also visited Independence, where she organized a Political Equality Club to replace Iowa's first Equal Suffrage Society which John L. Loomis had organized in 1867 and which had died in the wake of the free-love furor of 1872.

In February 1890, three months after the Oskaloosa meeting, Mrs. Chapman traveled to Washington, D.C., with Martha Callanan and other Iowa delegates to the national woman-suffrage convention. Here she delivered a speech which the *Woman's Standard* reported "did our state credit." However, the appearance of this new worker on the national platform was of minor importance to the delegates at this meeting whose interest was centered on the ceremonies marking the unification, after more than twenty years separation, of the two factions in the suffrage movement—one led by Lucy Stone under the banner of the American Woman Suffrage Association and the other by Elizabeth Cady Stanton and Susan B. Anthony under the banner of the National Woman Suffrage Association. A merger of the two organizations, under the name of National-American Woman Suffrage Association,[4] was headed by seventy-five-year-old Elizabeth Cady Stanton, who attended the convention only long enough to make a witty and eloquent speech and then left for England with her daughter Harriet Stanton Blatch. Susan B. Anthony, seventy-year-old vice-president of the new association, continued to carry the work load; and upon Mrs. Stanton's retirement as president in 1892 she was elected to that office. Seventy-two-year-old Lucy Stone was ill and did not attend the 1890 convention but was elected chairman of the executive committee, a purely honorary position as her days of active work were nearing an end. She died in 1893.

"SHE WENT OFF AND GOT MARRIED"

AFTER HER RETURN from the national convention, Carrie Chapman made another organization trip sponsored by the Iowa Woman Suf-

---

4. Although the official name of the national association after 1900 was National-American Woman Suffrage Association, it was usually referred to as the National Association. For the sake of brevity, it will be referred to in this chapter as the National Association.

frage Association. In June, however, she gave up her Iowa residence when she married George Catt of Seattle, Washington, a native Iowan who had graduated from the State Agricultural College at Ames in 1882 and was a successful engineer with a widespread business on the West Coast. In accordance with the terms of a written prenuptial agreement Carrie was to continue to use the name Carrie Lane Chapman, but after a few years she found it more convenient to use her husband's name and became known to the world as Carrie Chapman Catt. More important, the agreement also stipulated that she was free to devote at least two months each spring and each fall to suffrage work. As a matter of fact, she continued to devote more time than this to the cause. In the fall of 1891 Carrie and George Catt moved from Seattle to Boston; and the following spring they settled in the New York City area, where Carrie continued to reside after her husband's death in 1905. Since George Catt was a man of means, this marriage enabled Carrie to continue her suffrage work without financial worries; and at his death she was left an independently wealthy woman, able to support the suffrage cause with liberality.

Carrie Chapman's marriage to George Catt was distressing to the suffragists in Iowa. "I went around town with Mrs. Ankeny and begged money to keep Mrs. Chapman working, and then she went off and got married," Margaret Campbell,[5] president of the Iowa association, complained to Lucy Stone in a letter written July 30, 1890. "She promised to come back and work in September for us, but Miss Anthony has secured her for the South Dakota campaign. She still thinks she can come to Iowa for six or seven weeks before Christmas so the money is kept in reserve for her work. We are in a rather hard place here now," Mrs. Campbell lamented, "the loss of Mrs. Chapman after I had taken so much pains to secure her help for the State is very discouraging."

The South Dakota campaign referred to by Mrs. Campbell was Carrie Chapman's first campaign experience. Here, where a woman-suffrage amendment was submitted to a referendum at the November 5 elections, Carrie worked for two months, traveling under the most difficult conditions in this new, sparsely settled, and poverty-stricken state. The campaign had begun with high hopes for success, but Carrie soon saw that the women were fighting a hopeless battle. On election day they were beaten by a vote of two to one.

---

5. Margaret Campbell, fifty-nine-year-old native of Maine who had lived for a number of years in Massachusetts, was a close friend of Lucy Stone's and other New England suffrage leaders. She and her husband John canvassed Colorado during a campaign for a constitutional amendment for woman suffrage in 1877. In 1879 they settled in Des Moines, where Mrs. Campbell was active in Iowa suffrage work until 1901 when she and her husband moved to Joliet, Illinois.

A CLEAR-HEADED YOUNG WOMAN

WEARY AS SHE WAS after her South Dakota experience, Carrie Chapman made good her promise to the Iowa suffragists and returned to carry on her organizing work for the Iowa Woman Suffrage Association. At the annual convention of the Iowa association held in Des Moines on December 5, Mrs. Chapman, who was described by the *Des Moines Register* as a "clear-headed young woman with a business-like manner and energetic ways," outlined a plan for holding a convention in each of the state's ninety-nine counties, using these meetings as springboards for organizing local societies.

"There was a lively discussion over the plan of work," the *Register* reported. "The principle difference of opinion being over the formation of societies. Some weak sisters thought it was indecent to put forward the name of suffragists too much. . . ." These women preferred to work quietly in their churches until there was more sentiment in favor of the cause. But Mrs. Chapman in "a ringing speech frequently interrupted with applause contended there was no use to wait for more sentiment. The sentiment was here in every county in Iowa and she herself felt sure she could organize a convention in each of them. What was needed was the organization and crystallization of this sentiment so that when the Legislature met, the member would know that some of his constituents wanted him to vote for woman suffrage and that if he didn't he would be defeated. That was the only way to get anything done." Carrie Chapman's motion that the Iowa association arrange for a convention in every Iowa county was carried, and Mrs. Chapman was engaged to come back and work in the state during the coming April and May. The convention closed with the adoption of the following resolution: "That we are greatly pleased by the good work done by our lecturer and organizer, Carrie Lane Chapman, and regret her departure from our State, and our love and good wishes go with her to her new home."

"SHE HAS DONE US PROUD"

MRS. CHAPMAN, as agreed, returned to Iowa in the spring of 1891 and again in the fall of that year. She also worked in the state during the summer of 1892, taking the lead in organizing a four-day Mississippi Valley conference held in Des Moines in late September in conjunction with the annual convention of the Iowa Woman Suffrage Association. The convention met in the auditorium of the YMCA on 4th and High streets. Flying from the east window of the convention hall and extending out over 4th Street was a suffrage flag—a replica of the red, white, and blue flag of the United States except that it carried a single white star on the field of blue. This lone star represented Wyoming, which had been admitted to statehood in 1890 and was the one state in the Union where women had equal suffrage rights with men.

Delegates from fourteen states attended the Mississippi Valley conference—Iowa, Minnesota, Missouri, Wisconsin, South Dakota, Kentucky, Illinois, Indiana, Kansas, Nebraska, Florida, Mississippi, New York, and Massachusetts. In fact, the meeting had been so carefully planned and widely publicized that the officers of the National Association feared that Mrs. Chapman and her Iowa associates were trying to organize a rival society. "They put the chief blame on me," Mrs. Catt recalled in later years, but all the Iowa officers came in for a little distress. . . . I was very much disturbed about it for of course, such a motive did not exist."

The first program of the meeting was devoted to a panel discussion on the following question: "The growth of the work demands more money. How shall we raise it?" Mrs. Chapman, a member of the panel, told about methods of raising money which she had used successfully in Iowa. Miss Anthony, who had come to Des Moines to protect the interests of the National Association, was so delighted with Mrs. Chapman's interest and ability to raise money that she appointed her finance chairman of the National Association.

Another session of the Mississippi Valley conference was devoted to outlining a work plan which Carrie Chapman had used as state organizer in Iowa. This plan, which revealed to the delegates that a dynamo was at work in the suffrage ranks, included the following:

1. Groups to be organized by voting districts.
2. Work to indoctrinate all community leaders.
3. Suffrage lectures to be given before each teacher's institute.
4. Working women to promote suffrage for their own protection.
5. Suffrage cause to be presented at various meetings and conventions.
6. Itemized blanks to be furnished each society for the purpose of uniform reporting at annual conventions.
7. County woman-suffrage conventions to be organized at the same time as county fairs.
8. Each society to open an enrollment book and to make a systematic annual canvass of each district.
9. Cooperation to be invited from the WCTU, Women's Relief Corps of the GAR, and all other women's organizations.

A dinner for the delegates at the Kirkwood (former Savery) Hotel on the second day of the convention was, according to the *Register*, "perhaps the most elegant banquet ever given in Des Moines." The decorations which were "the finest ever seen on a Des Moines banquet board" consisted of "nasturtiums, goldenrod, wild sunflower, turned leaves of sumac." The programs were handsomely designed and beautifully printed in yellow. And climaxing all, were the after-dinner speakers "seldom equalled for brilliance." Carrie Chapman who served as toastmaster for the occasion, rushed off after the banquet (which ended at 1:00 A.M.) to speak at the Mills County Fair the following day, returning to Des Moines in time for the last day of the meeting. At the conclusion of the conference, the *Register* paid tribute to Carrie Lane Chapman's "queenly grace and charming voice, her eloquence and logic. . . . We may claim her as our very own," this paper said. "She has done us proud."

Two Heads in the Country, Two upon the Hearth, Two in the Tangled Business of the World.

Programme.

Toast Master	Carrie Lane Chapman
Happy a woman's voice may do some good—here's a woman will speak	Catherine Waugh McCulloch
Individual Rights	John J. Hamilton
The Dangers of an Irresponsible Educated Class	Alice Stone Blackwell
The Ideal Woman—"Let your ideal run before you, and do you run after it"	Rev. Ida C. Hultin
Either Sex alone is but half itself	Hon. M. B. Castle
Is Housekeeping one of the Industries	Mrs. A L. Frisbie
The Stone which the Builders rejected the same has become the head of the corner	Rev. H. O. Breeden
Our Wage-Working Women	Susan B Anthony
Attend to the Women	Pres't. B. O. Aylesworth
Are Men Responsible for the Present Situation	Henry B. Blackwell
Good-will to Men	Emma Smith DeVoe
Woman's Sphere is Bounded alone by Woman's Duty	Hon. J. S. Polk
More Father in the Family, More Mother in the Councils of the Nation	Rev. Olympia Brown

Menu

BLUE POINTS, ON HALF SHELL
CELERY

CONSOMME ROYALE, EN TASSE

OLIVES   PICKLED LIMES

SWEET BREAD PATTIES, A LA REINE

SUPREME OF CHICKEN, A LA PRINCESSE

GREEN PEAS   POTATO CROQUETTES

ORANGE SHERBET

COLD HAM   COLD TONGUE

TOMATOES, MAYONNAISE

ANGEL CAKE   MERINGUES   MACAROONS

ICE CREAM, AUX FRUITS

PEARS   GRAPES   PEACHES

NUTS   RAISINS

COFFEE

Program and menu for the Mississippi Valley woman-suffrage conference $1.00-a-plate banquet held in the Kirkwood Hotel in Des Moines in 1892.

CAMPAIGNS IN THE WEST

AFTER 1892 Mrs. Chapman no longer served as organizer for the Iowa association. Her interest in the state, however, did not wane despite her increasing involvement with suffrage work elsewhere. Coming directly to Iowa from Colorado on November 10, 1893, Mrs. Chapman was able to report to the delegates at the state convention in Webster City about the Colorado campaign, where woman suffrage had been endorsed by the voters just three days previously. This was the first referendum victory in the history of woman suffrage; and Carrie Chapman, who had stumped the state for two months prior to the election, was the heroine of the Colorado campaign. The principle reasons why the cause was successful in Colorado, Mrs. Chapman told the Iowa convention, was "because it had been recognized by all political parties; then too the inhabitants were mostly miners who had emigrated to the West at the time eastern capitalists had imported foreign labor, and these men formed labor unions which universally advocate equal wages for men and women." In addition the fact that Wyoming, a woman-suffrage state, was adjacent to Colorado was also a favorable influence on the Colorado electors.

Mrs. Chapman's success in Colorado marked her as an outstanding worker among the suffragists of the country and brought urgent requests for her help wherever there was a campaign in progress. During 1894 she participated in two major campaigns, New York and Kansas. Both resulted in disappointing defeats for the women.

In August 1896 Carrie Chapman Catt (by 1895 she was using this name) helped organize a campaign in Idaho, where she persuaded four political parties—Gold Republican, Silver Republican, Democratic, and Populist—to endorse a woman-suffrage amendment which was to be submitted at the November elections. The referendum resulted in a victory for the women, and Idaho became the third suffrage state in the country. (Utah, where women had voted from 1870 to 1887, had become the second suffrage state when it was admitted to the Union the previous January.)

From Idaho Mrs. Catt went to California, where a suffrage amendment was also to be voted on in November. Here she worked for two months in one of the best organized campaigns in woman-suffrage history. Nonetheless, the women met defeat in the election, adverse majorities in San Francisco and Oakland overcoming favorable majorities in the rest of the state. The California defeat was a heart-

This photograph of Carrie Chapman Catt was taken in Los Angeles in 1896 during the California referendum campaign and gives a good idea of the elegance of dress for which she was noted.

breaking experience and left the state suffrage organization exhausted and in debt. Many years passed before it recovered to fight again.

But Mrs. Catt never wasted a moment bemoaning a defeat; she headed east with Miss Anthony after the California election, stopping en route to visit several state conventions. She returned to New York shortly before Christmas to entertain the board of the National Association whom she had invited to her spacious home at Bensonhurst, Long Island. At this meeting she outlined the ensuing year's plans for the organization committee of which she was chairman.

A WOMAN OF SUPREME ABILITY

THIS COMMITTEE, she told the board, planned to launch intensive campaigns in several states, one of them Iowa, where it was hoped enough sentiment could be created to force the legislature to submit a suffrage amendment to the voters of the state. Two-day conventions, presided over by workers from the National Association, were being scheduled in each of the state's ninety-nine counties—two adjoining counties to hold simultaneous meetings so that speakers could be exchanged. The northern half of the state would be covered in the spring and the southern half in the fall, ending with a state convention in Des Moines where headquarters would be opened prior to the 1898 session of the General Assembly.

The Iowa campaign which Mrs. Catt outlined to the board was launched in late January 1897 when the National Association held its annual convention in Des Moines. This was the first convention of the National Association held west of the Mississippi and only the second held outside the city of Washington. The Central Christian Church, where the delegates met, was decorated with green palms and the suffrage flag which now displayed four stars, representing, in addition to Wyoming, the new suffrage states of Colorado, Idaho, and Utah. Susan B. Anthony, the association's revered and stalwart seventy-six-year-old president, presided over the convention; and Carrie Chapman Catt took a prominent part in the proceedings. "Iowa has done more for the National Association and suffrage work throughout the country than any other state," Alice Stone Blackwell, Lucy Stone's daughter, told the delegates. "She has made the most valuable present of twenty years or more to the Association when she gave it Carrie Lane Chapman Catt."

"Some people feel that progress is slow, and some of our enemies feel that our progress is so slow that they can take courage. But it is not slow, for the evolution of society is ever gradual," Carrie Chap-

The woman-suffrage flag with four stars representing Wyoming, Utah, Colorado, and Idaho—the first four states to give woman the vote—was used from 1896 to 1910, when a fifth star was added representing the state of Washington.

man Catt told the convention. "Our movement is not so far behind as may be supposed. In fifty years thirty states have granted partial suffrage to women," she pointed out. She was ashamed that Iowa (where women had tax and bond suffrage only) had granted the most limited privilege of any of these states.

Miss Anthony, who told the delegates that the Iowa legislature had played with the woman-suffrage question "like a cat plays with a mouse," urged the suffragists of the state to have suffrage planks inserted in the platforms of the political parties and "from that it will be an easy step to submission by the Legislature. . . . To the four states in our banner today," she said, "we expect to add in 1898 California, Nevada, Oregon, Washington, and Montana." By 1900 she expected a tenth star to be added to the flag representing Iowa.[6]

The Iowa legislature was meeting in special session at the time of the national convention in Des Moines in 1897, and an invitation was extended to the delegates to appear before the Senate. (The House refused to invite the women.) Miss Anthony acted as master of ceremonies for the occasion and presented speakers representing each of the four suffrage states as well as Mrs. Catt, who told the legislators that even though not a single member favored woman suffrage it was the duty of the General Assembly to submit the question to the voters of the state. She pointed out that even in a referendum only men could vote.

Following the national convention Mrs. Catt proceeded to put her plan for Iowa into action. The *Woman's Standard* in April 1897 listed fifty-eight county conventions which were scheduled between March 29 and June 18. Two national workers were in the state to help with this program. Mrs. Catt herself conducted the Cerro Gordo County convention which met in Mason City on May 20. Here the *Republican,* which she and Leo Chapman had once owned, paid glowing tribute to this woman of "supreme ability" and devoted nine full columns to reporting the convention.

Mrs. Catt returned to Iowa again in October to attend the annual convention of the Iowa Woman Suffrage Association in Des Moines, after which she chaired several county conventions. An ecstatic reporter for the *Woman's Standard* called Mrs. Catt's speech at the state convention "one of the most beauiful addresses we have ever heard. This beautiful woman in her elegant attire as she stood before that interested audience made a picture never to be forgotten."

At the Linn County convention in Cedar Rapids on October 23 Mrs. Catt reported that "we have succeeded admirably in our work in Iowa, and before the end of the year we hope to have every county in the state organized." At that time there were in existence eighty-five county societies and 150 local clubs all "in flourishing condition." This plan, she said, "gives us strength in every locality in Iowa and

---

6. There were no new suffrage states from 1896 when Idaho women were enfranchised to 1910 when a woman-suffrage amendment was adopted in the state of Washington. In 1969 the Iowa constitution still carries the word "male" as a qualification for voting. However, the 63rd General Assembly has given second approval to a constitutional amendment providing for changes in residence requirements for voters. This amendment, which will be submitted at the general election in 1970, brings the amendment in line with federal law by deleting the word "male" as a qualification for voters.

places us in a position to influence members of the Legislature directly. . . . We expect to be able to submit a suffrage amendment to the people of Iowa in 1900. . . . Once we get the measure before the people we have not much doubt as to what the result will be."

In accordance with Mrs. Catt's plan a state office was opened in Des Moines prior to the 1898 General Assembly, and on February 3 the women were granted a hearing before the House and Senate committees on constitutional amendments. Mrs. Coggeshall, president of the Des Moines Equal Suffrage Club; Mrs. Belden of Sioux City, the vivacious and witty president of the Iowa association, and other suffragists spoke. For the first time the antisuffragists were also represented at this hearing by several prominent women who protested that they were appearing only out of a deep sense of duty, as they preferred to remain quietly at home. All during this session, petitions for woman suffrage poured into the legislature, with as many as fifty being presented in a single day.

The legislature's response to all this activity was a refusal by either house to approve the woman-suffrage amendment. The amendment also met the same fate in the 1900 General Assembly, despite a deluge of petitions carrying more than 100,000 signatures. These defeats after so much work left the Iowa woman-suffrage movement exhausted and despairing for a number of years. But Mrs. Catt, with her firm faith in the evolution of society toward greater perfection, regarded these defeats as only temporary setbacks and kept on working at the same driving pace.

PRESIDENT OF THE NATIONAL ASSOCIATION

WHEN INSTALLED as president of the National Woman Suffrage Association in February 1900, Carrie Chapman Catt was universally considered to be the ideal successor to Susan B. Anthony. "Mrs. Catt plans for the object she has in view and her plans are deep and broad," said the *Boston Transcript* in a story reprinted in the *Des Moines Leader* shortly after she took office. "Abounding health, her cheerful visage, and elastic step suggest a reserve fund of energy stored up in youth on a western farm. Mrs. Catt has acquired the art of wise conservation of time and energy," said the *Transcript,* "and is never hurried or disturbed in spirit by small annoyances. . . . She is able, as few people can, to plan campaigns on long lines, forming strong combinations and bringing her force to bear on strategic points with a minimum expenditure of time and effort. She is an exceedingly

ONCE MORE THE CASTLE IS BEING STORMED.

This cartoon by J. N. Darling appeared in the Des Moines Register *February 20, 1909, while the Iowa General Assembly was in session.*

❃ *Two English militants attending the annual Iowa woman-suffrage convention in Boone, Iowa, in 1908 instigated this early woman-suffrage parade.*

practical woman and believes that nothing can be accomplished without organization."

Despite her organizational genius, not a single suffrage campaign was won while Mrs. Catt was president of the National Association, a position which she held from 1900 to 1904. The successful referenda in Colorado in 1892 and in Idaho in 1896 had stiffened the opponents of woman suffrage and they were able to hold off another suffrage victory until 1910. Mrs. Catt, saw three factors—ignorance (especially in the foreign-born voter), indifference, and fraud—as the greatest enemies of woman suffrage. In her farewell address as president of the National Association she proposed the formation of a nation-wide good-government committee to consider the following methods of improving democracy:

1. Establishing an educational qualification for the ballot.
2. Lengthening the five-year residency requirement for citizenship for the more ignorant classes of immigrants.
3. Amending existing naturalization laws which make possible the

forging of citizenship certificates and the addition of noncitizens to the voting lists.
4. Increasing the period of residence required where the system exists of importation of voters just before the election with the intention of adding their names to the corrupt voting lists.
5. Establishing a slight property qualification for the ballot.
6. Disfranchising both the bribed and the briber in voting frauds.
7. Disfranchising eligible voters who fail to vote.

"Yet with the curtailment of the irresponsible vote at the bottom and the indifferent or dishonest vote at the top, we would not have completed our task," Mrs. Catt warned the convention. "An education of public sentiment must be conducted through every school and college and church, through the press, the pulpit, and the platform, until a healthy, wholesome hatred has been created for the selling and buying of votes at the polls, the graft of municipalities, and the corrupt control of Legislatures. . . . We must galvanize the whole electorate with the spirit of public service, and bring back the old enthusiasm for democracy."

Anna Howard Shaw, president of the National Woman Suffrage Association spoke at 8th and Story streets in Boone after the 1908 parade. Street parades and meetings were a new and daring technique for propaganda at this time.

CUTS TIE WITH THE NATIONAL ASSOCIATION

IN 1905 Mrs. Catt attended the national convention in Portland, Oregon, where the suffragists hoped to get a woman-suffrage referendum on the Oregon ballot in the fall. Delegates to the Portland meeting traveled west in three special cars. Mrs. Catt, who had been visiting her mother in Charles City, joined the train at Boone. Here members of the Boone Political Equality Club met the train with bouquets which they presented to Mrs. Catt, now a vice-president of the National Association; Anna Howard Shaw, president; and Susan B. Anthony, honorary president, who at the age of eighty-five was also making the trip. All three women delivered short speeches from the back platform of the train.

Among the Iowa delegates at the Portland meeting was sixty-seven-year-old Mary Jane Coggeshall, pioneer Iowa suffragist and long-time friend of Carrie Chapman Catt. "When I get discouraged I think of Mrs. Coggeshall," Mrs. Catt told the convention. "She has been one of my strongest inspirations."

Unable to get along with her successor Miss Shaw, who was a brilliant speaker but lacked organizational ability, Mrs. Catt cut her ties with the National Association after 1905. She did this so quietly that even her friends were puzzled. "Mrs. Coggeshall spent two days with me on her return from the national convention," Margaret Campbell, former president of the Iowa Woman Suffrage Association, wrote to Alice Stone Blackwell on February 25, 1907. "We wondered why Mrs. Catt was not at the convention and feel sure that something has gone wrong between her and the powers that be." Mrs. Campbell reported that she had read in the *Interocean* that Mrs. Catt had opened an office in New York City where she would work for woman suffrage, believing that the time had passed when great conventions would do much good.

As this letter indicates, Mrs. Catt never publicly quarreled with Miss Shaw; but beginning in 1907 she began to build a Woman Suffrage Party in New York State, an organization which succeeded in 1917 in winning the first and most important referendum victory east of the Mississippi.

In addition to her work in New York State, Mrs. Catt was busy, from 1904 to the outbreak of World War I in 1914, building up the International Woman Suffrage Alliance of which she was president. She traveled to Europe a number of times in the course of her work for this organization; and following a serious illness in 1911–1912, she made a tour around the world, visiting with woman-suffrage leaders wherever she went.

RESURGENCE OF THE WOMAN-SUFFRAGE MOVEMENT

MEANWHILE, despite the fact that the National Association was relatively ineffective under Miss Shaw's presidency—a position which she held from 1904 to 1915—there was a resurgence in the woman-suffrage movement during these years brought about by several factors: the upsurge of Progressivism, the rise of new leaders in many of the state organizations, and the emergence of a militant wing of the suffrage movement whose members were known as suffragettes.

Miss Flora Dunlap, forty-one-year-old social worker and close friend of Jane Addams, represented the new leadership in Iowa. A native of Ohio, she came to Des Moines in 1904 to head Roadside

Flora Dunlap was president of the Iowa Equal Suffrage Association during the referendum campaign of 1916 and the first president of the Iowa League of Women Voters in 1919.

Settlement House. On October 10, 1913, she was elected president of the Iowa Equal Suffrage Association (successor to the Iowa Woman Suffrage Association) by a vote of 49 to 35 at a stormy annual convention at Boone. According to the *Des Moines Register,* "So tense was the situation that when the ballots were being prepared for counting Mrs. Ida Wise Smith pleaded from the convention floor for the women to forget petty ambitions and personal bitterness of feeling and receive the announcement of the vote in silence. When Miss Dunlap was declared the presiding officer, the delegates in one accord rose and sang the hymn, 'Blest Be the Tie that Binds.' Many of the women in the audience wept, but Miss Dunlap calm and self-possessed, sang."

"In naming Miss Dunlap the woman suffrage movement of the state has taken a very important first step towards realization of their hopes," said the *Register* in an editorial the following day. "The newly elected president combines with a tactful disposition and perfect poise and self control, a much more thorough knowledge of the practical phases of the woman problem than any woman could possibly have who had not been meeting the world on its practical side as Miss Dunlap has been meeting it."

The rise of militancy in the suffrage movement came with frustration over lack of success with traditional campaign methods. This movement, which began in England in 1906, soon spread to the United States; methods included street meetings, parades, picketing, and civil disobedience. Mrs. Catt, with her faith in education and organization, had no sympathy with these tactics. The *Woman's Standard* of July 1909 quotes Mrs. Catt as saying she was a "suffragist" not a "suffragette." She denied ever having advocated militant methods and took a firm stand against suffrage parades. "We do not have to win sympathy by parading ourselves like the street cleaning department or the police," she said. Although Mrs. Catt never condoned the extreme tactics of the militants (such as picketing the White House), she did eventually accept the parade as a valuable publicity tool for the suffrage movement. In October 1915 Mrs. Catt was one of 30,000 women who marched up Fifth Avenue in New York City in the largest suffrage parade ever organized in the United States. Two years later, draped from head to foot in a white broadcloth military cape, Mrs. Catt led another New York City parade.

By 1915 the suffrage flag was proudly displaying fifteen stars— the eleven added since 1896 representing Washington (1910); California (1911); Oregon, Kansas, and Arizona (1912); The Territory of Alaska (1913); and Montana and Nevada (1914). In addition to these full-suffrage areas the Illinois legislature granted presidential suffrage to women in 1913. This was the first break in the solid opposition to woman suffrage east of the Mississippi. In 1915 the Iowa General Assembly at long last gave second approval to a woman-suffrage amendment and provided for its submission to the voters of the state at the primary elections in June of the following year.

On the national level the federal amendment—the Susan B. Anthony amendment which had lain dormant since it was first voted on in the Senate in 1887—was also coming to life. It was brought to

Hooray for Mother

These drawings of a 1912 woman-suffrage parade in New York City were made by John Sloan to illustrate an article for Collier's Weekly.

(Courtesy of the University of Michigan Museum of Art)

Aw Susie, Be Them Dishes Washed?

Women Marching

a second vote in the Senate in March 1914, and the following January it came to a vote for the very first time in the House of Representatives.

RETURN TO THE HELM

VICTORY at last seemed in sight for the woman-suffrage forces of the United States, but a strong leader was needed for the final push. Carrie Chapman Catt, who at fifty-six considered herself too old for the position, was nonetheless persuaded to again assume the presidency of the National Association to replace Anna Howard Shaw, who had permitted the organization to disintegrate into numerous factions, each nursing its own petty jealousies. Mrs. Catt took office in December 1915 at the annual convention in Washington, D.C.

IOWA REFERENDUM

ONE OF THE IMMEDIATE TASKS facing Mrs. Catt was to help the Iowa suffragists prepare for the referendum set for the following June. "At a secret conference held Thursday in Washington, D.C.," the

A woman-suffrage parade in New York City in 1915 with 40,000 women dressed in white carrying 15,000 yellow banners was the largest in the history of the movement. The Iowa banner reads, "Iowa men will vote on a woman-suffrage amendment in 1916."

Iowa Equal Suffrage Association board of directors, 1915: From left to right: Mrs. H. W. Spaulding, Grinnell; Mrs. Jansen Haines, Des Moines; Mrs. A. J. McNeal, Des Moines; Rev. Effie McCollum Jones, Webster City; Mrs. Carrie Chapman Catt, New Rochelle, N.Y., president of the National Woman Suffrage Association; Miss Flora Dunlap, Des Moines, president of the Iowa Equal Suffrage Association; Mrs. James K. Devitt, Oskaloosa; Mrs. Harriet B. Evans, Corydon; Mrs. Ella Caldwell, Adel.

Mason City Globe-Gazette reported on December 21, 1915, immediately after the national convention, "the suffrage situation in Iowa was canvassed. At this conference were Miss Dunlap and Mrs. Catt. Since Iowa is one of three suffrage campaign states next year it is understood the national board will vote a large campaign fund and send national workers to the State." The *Globe-Gazette* also reported that as evidence of her loyalty to Iowa Mrs. Catt was sending, at her own expense, a national suffrage worker who would spend five months in campaign work in the state.

Mrs. Catt devoted a great deal of her time and attention to the Iowa campaign in 1916, including three short visits to the state to consult with suffrage workers and a month devoted to intensive campaigning. On Sunday afternoon February 6, while in Des Moines to meet with the board of the Iowa Equal Suffrage Association, she addressed a public meeting at the University Christian Church, where old friends and acquaintances as well as suffrage supporters flocked to hear her. "It was an impressive homecoming back to Iowa where she grew up . . . when Mrs. Carrie Chapman Catt, international suffrage leader, walked to the platform yesterday, . . ." said the *Des Moines Register* of this occasion. "Mrs. Catt who has addressed thousands of persons in this and other lands . . . was moved almost to tears as she faced the men and women, many of whom had been her school and college companions. . . . There were before her gray-haired men and women who were her classmates thirty-five years ago at the Iowa State College at Ames; middle-aged men and women who were her pupils in Mason City thirty-two years ago; a few of the small band of women who invited Mrs. Catt to give her maiden speech here twenty-five years ago; pioneers of Iowa who remembered her as a slip of a girl on a farm near Charles City. These together with leaders in the suffrage movement in the State and enthusiastic suffrage supporters gave her welcome."

Mrs. Catt told the audience, the *Register* continued, that "a bunch of violets in her room at the hotel that morning had brought back old memories. . . . She could see herself a child of eight again standing for the first time in front of their new frontier home and looking over the unbroken and violet carpeted prairie. . . . She told of the hardships experienced by the early pioneers in Iowa . . . and of her first suffrage work which was a house to house canvass in Mason City." After reviewing the development of suffrage in the United States, Mrs. Catt outlined the plan of attack of the organized opposition, paying special "respects to the anti-suffragists at work in Iowa in a tone that was cool and controlled but the words were caustic." This opposition, she said, was allied with the liquor interests and the unscrupulous railways of the country.

From the middle of April to the middle of May Mrs. Catt worked in Iowa, conducting training sessions for workers and lecturing in all the major cities. In Council Bluffs, where she spoke on April 16, the auditorium was completely filled. "It was the biggest affair of the kind ever staged in southwest Iowa," the *Council Bluffs Nonpareil* reported. "When all is said and done, there is really just one argument in favor of woman suffrage," Mrs. Catt told her audience, "that

Carrie Chapman Catt

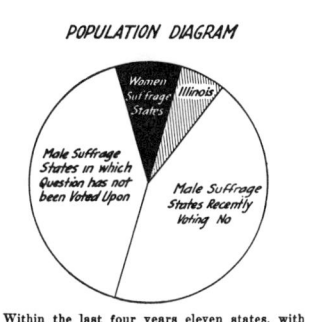

Propaganda for woman suffrage included a blotter (below) put out by the Iowa Woman Suffrage Association in 1910 and a postcard (upper right) circulated by the WCTU of Iowa, date unknown. "Population Diagram" (upper left) is a postcard circulated in 1916 by the Dubuque Association Opposed to Woman Suffrage.

is that we are part of the nation; we obey its laws and we pay our taxes; and we are entitled to a part in making the laws that regulate our welfare."

In Waterloo, where Mrs. Catt spoke to a crowd of 1,400 on May 4, she told her audience, "Some dead men vote as do some who have never been born and yet the women are not let in. They are allowed to go to schools and universities with the boys and yet when they want to have free speech they can only have it 100 feet from the polls on election day."

In Dubuque, where Mrs. Catt spoke at the Grand Opera House on May 21, "the audience filled the seats, boxes, packed the aisles and left men and women standing at the doors. . . . Twenty-five years from now woman suffrage will be a forgotten issue," she said. "Suffrage is coming from every direction. You can't stop it."

Touring the state at the same time as Mrs. Catt was another former Iowan, John Irish of California, champion of woman suffrage in the 1870 Iowa General Assembly. A professional antisuffrage campaigner since 1911, Irish drew only small audiences wherever he went in the state. His sponsorship was never announced, although it was generally assumed to be the liquor interests. Irish had alarming tales to tell about the dire effects of the woman-suffrage "experiment" in his home state of California, where women had voted since 1911. Not only had woman suffrage resulted in increased taxation but it had caused increased delinquency among women and children and given rise to the corrupt woman politician. If this were not enough to convince his audiences, Irish also warned that suffrage had put lines in women's faces and that men no longer took off their hats in elevators.

"It is really too bad that so many estimable people begin to see everything going wrong at about the time their own blood begins to cool," said the *Des Moines Register* of the seventy-three-year-old Irish. The *Register,* now a firm friend of woman suffrage under the editorship of Harvey Ingham—son of Algona's pioneer advocate Caroline Ingham—favored "youthful minds in old bodies. Every extension of liberty has vindicated itself," the *Register* declared. "The more rights the people have the more responsibilities they assume. No nation ever went upon the rocks because of liberty."

Despite a well-organized and well-financed campaign supported by a majority of the papers in Iowa, the woman-suffrage amendment was defeated on June 5 by a total of 10,341 votes, the four "wet" counties on the eastern border of the state—Scott, Clinton, Dubuque, and Des Moines—returning a large adverse vote which overcame favorable majorities in the rest of the state. Most astonishing was the fact that there were 29,341 more votes cast on the equal-suffrage amendment than the total cast for all candidates for governor.

An investigation by the WCTU subsequently revealed that victory was literally stolen from the women in Iowa. Thousands of unregistered votes were cast on the amendment despite the fact that registration was required by law. No record was kept of ballots officially issued to each precinct, and in most cases no unused ballots were returned. In fifteen counties there were 8,067 more ballots on the amendment than voters checked as having voted. Suffragists were advised, however, that even if fraud could be proved there was no way the election could be declared invalid.

THE PROMISED LAND

THE IOWA SITUATION, coupled with similar experiences in other states, convinced Mrs. Catt that women faced insurmountable odds in most state referenda and that the time had come to concentrate on an amendment to the federal Constitution. At a meeting of the executive committee of the national board, prior to a special "emergency" convention of the National Association held in Atlantic City in September 1916, Mrs. Catt laid out what came to be known as her winning plan. The state auxiliaries were to be divided into four groups, with each assigned to a particular task.

1. The twelve states where women could vote for presidential electors were to secure from the next sessions of their legislatures resolutions asking Congress to submit a woman-suffrage amendment.
2. The few states where there was a chance of carrying a state constitutional amendment were to try for that.
3. The largest group of states was to work for presidential suffrage.
4. Southern states, where the primary virtually determined the election, were to try for primary suffrage.

"When we filed out of the room at the close of that meeting, I thought I understood how Moses felt on the mountain top after he was shown the Promised Land," Maude Wood Park, congressional leader of the woman-suffrage forces, later recalled. "For the first time our goal looked possible of attainment in the near future."

The state organizations did their work so well that by May 1919 four new stars representing New York, Michigan, South Dakota, and Oklahoma had been added to the suffrage flag. Thirteen legislatures,

TO THE IOWA FARMER!--REMEMBER!
WOMAN SUFFRAGE MEANS HIGH TAXES

TAX RATE IS BOUND TO INCREASE

The History of Equal Suffrage States is the Story of Taxpayers' Money Wasted---Money Thrown Away in Hysterical Legislation, Useless Commissions, Uncalled for Bond Issues, Increased Election Costs---Taxes are Squandered Because of a Catering of Legislative Interests to the Irresponsible Elements Among Voters. Compare this Government Report:

Non-Suffrage States	Tax per $1,000	Equal Suffrage States	Tax per $1,000
Wisconsin	$11.80	Washington	$31.00
New Hampshire	16.00	Colorado	40.10
Vermont	18.83	Utah	32.60
Missouri	19.00	Wyoming	32.40
Massachusetts	17.30	California	21.50
IOWA	12.04	Idaho	41.50

(*Vol. I, p. 761—Taxation Statistics Census Report.*)

TAX RIDDEN CALIFORNIA

During the first four years of Woman Suffrage in California, 1911 to 1915, state taxes were increased from 18 to 36 millions, or 100 per-cent increase. The cost of county government is the highest of any state in the Union. Los Angeles alone cost the taxpayers 42 millions. Los Angeles Times says: "10 millions is political plunder."

DO YOU WANT THIS IN IOWA?

COLORADO'S EXPERIENCE

Denver has the highest tax rate of any city of its size in the world—$26.00 for every man, woman and child in the city. Colorado has the highest state tax in the Union. The Denver Post protests that "Public funds are notoriously wasted through useless commissions, and loose political methods."

DO YOU WANT THIS IN IOWA?

TAX CRISIS IN IOWA

Taxpayers of Iowa today are entering a Protest against the Squandering of Public Funds. The Cost of running the State of Iowa has been for the Biennial Periods: Ending June 30, 1895, **$3,624,000.** Ending June 30, 1914, **$11,996,000.** Note this Enormous Increase in Taxes with no Increase in Population.

Facing this Critical Situation It Is No Time to Increase State Expenses by adopting Woman Suffrage and assuming Additional Election Expenses of a Million Dollars.

VOTE "NO" ON JUNE 5

The Farmers of Iowa should remember that the granting of Woman Suffrage means the doubling of the city vote in Iowa which has no thought of their interests and does not materially increase the farm vote. "It is not your wife and daughter who will vote, but the women of towns and cities who have easy access to the polls and axes to grind."

YOU, MR. FARMER, MUST PAY THE BILL. CAN YOU AFFORD THIS EXPERIMENT AT THIS TIME?

IOWA ASSOCIATION OPPOSED TO WOMAN SUFFRAGE   **DES MOINES, IOWA**

THIS ADVERTISEMENT PAID FOR BY POPULAR SUBSCRIPTION AMONG PATRIOTIC IOWANS

Full-page advertisement in the Iowa Homestead, *May 25, 1916. According to Carrie Chapman Catt, when James M. Pierce woman-suffrage advocate and editor of the* Homestead, *was chided for his act to perfidy in publishing this ad, he meekly replied, "I got $600 for it."*

including Iowa, had granted presidential suffrage to women, and two had given primary suffrage. In less than three years the number of presidential electors for whom women could vote had jumped from 91 to 339. The suffragists had at last achieved enough political power to get favorable action in Congress.

The presidential suffrage bill which passed the Iowa Senate on April 4, 1919, passed the House on April 19 in the closing hours of the session. This session of the General Assembly had previously defeated a primary suffrage bill. The *Des Moines Capital* on Sunday, April 6, 1919, carried the following story:

> Iowa, one of the first states to consider equal suffrage, and now certain to be one of the last states to adopt it. That's a new Iowa record, set up when the Senate a few days ago defeated a measure proposing equal suffrage at primary elections and substituted for it a State constitutional amendment to drag itself wearily through a succeeding General Assembly and a statewide balloting.
>
> To the suffragists it represents fifty-one years of unceasing effort come to naught, and their movement done to death, at that, by those who seemed to be its best friends. The suffrage bill [amendment] passed the House again in 1917 but failure of the office of Secretary of State to publish the notice within the stipulated time nullified the Legislature's action. In order to avoid delay, the women substituted a bill providing for suffrage in primaries. It was this bill that was recently lost in the Senate.
>
> "On what ground do the legislators oppose the bill?" Miss Dunlap [president of the Iowa Equal Suffrage Association] was asked.
>
> "Because it would be such a shame for woman, sacred woman, to have her soil her fair hands with the sordid machinery of politics."
>
> "And the real reason?"
>
> "Politics. They are afraid it will mean trouble for the Republican party if the women get the vote. But it's only occasionally that they will admit it. Woman suffrage became a political issue in 1912 when Roosevelt put it in the platform of the Progressive party, and it has bulked large in the minds of politicians ever since. Of course they keep on spouting the old pedestal idea, while they beat their wives at home, I suppose."

On May 21, 1919, three days after the Sixty-sixth Congress convened, the woman-suffrage amendment was brought up in the House (where it had been defeated three times in the past four years) and was approved by a comfortable majority. On June 4 the amendment was brought up in the Senate (where it had been defeated four times in the past five years) and was passed by a narrow margin—five senators who had previously voted "no" changing to the winning side because of suffrage gains in their states. After the Senate vote Vice President Marshall, the presiding officer and an opponent of woman suffrage, gave the chair to ardent proponent Senator Albert Cummins of Iowa, so that he could make the victory announcement. Senator Cummins' voice trembled, Maude Wood Park recalled, as he declared the joint resolution for the Nineteenth Amendment to have received the affirmative vote of more than two-thirds of the senators present and voting. This amendment reads: "The right of the citizens of the United States to vote shall not be denied or abridged by the United States or by any State on account of sex."

Within an hour after the Nineteenth Amendment had been approved by the Senate, Mrs. Catt, waiting in New York where the suffrage headquarters were located, had sent telegrams to the governors of all states asking them to take immediate steps to secure ratification of the amendment. On July 2 Iowa became the tenth state to ratify when the legislature approved the amendment in a special session lasting just one hour and forty minutes, the shortest session in Iowa history.

"It was a short-sleeved, perspiring Legislature, closely flanked by a solid bank of georgette-clad femininity, which wore the smile of triumph earned by long and persistent effort," said the *Des Moines Capital* of this occasion. "The legislators took their dose without a grimace. Of course, it was not unpleasant to a large proportion of them, but there were some, notably in the Senate who were traditionally opposed to suffrage, who nevertheless voted 'yes' with smiling faces. It was entirely apparent that none of the politically ambitious was overlooking the fact that probably at the next election a body of voters will be added to the Iowa electorate fully two-thirds as large as the present voting strength."

"It was a wonderful moment," wrote Lillian Crawley (corresponding secretary of the Iowa Equal Suffrage Association) to the *Woman Citizen*. "The joyous expressions of these men who had taken hot and dusty rides on day trains, from their farms and stores in the scorching July weather that is Iowa's best corn grower, to come and cast their votes for ratification assured us of victory. So the work begun in 1868 by the women of Iowa is finished in 1919," Mrs. Crawley said. "It may have been a good thing that we have had this long, hard struggle, for we have learned many things in getting an insight into politics."

On August 26, 1920—following ratification by Tennessee,[7] the thirty-sixth state to fall into line—the Secretary of State of the United States proclaimed the Nineteenth Amendment the law of the land. On August 27 Mrs. Jens Thuesen of Grundy County, Iowa, became the first woman in the state to vote under the Nineteenth Amendment (and perhaps the first in the United States) when she cast her ballot in an election to establish a consolidated school district carved out of Black Hawk and Grundy counties. A total of seventy-seven women cast their ballots in this election.

"That vote of yours has cost millions of dollars and the lives of thousands of women," Mrs. Catt reminded the women of America in a message in the *Woman Citizen*. "The vote has been costly," Mrs. Catt declared. "Prize it. . . . Understand what it means and what it can do for your country. No soldier in the great suffrage army has labored and suffered to get a *place* for you. Their motive has always been the hope that women would aim higher than their own selfish ambitions; that they would *serve* the common good."

"The vote is won. Seventy-two years the battle for this privilege has waged, but human affairs with their eternal change move on without pause.

"Progress is calling on you to make no pause. Act."

---

7. On August 31, 1920, John Irish wrote to George Parker, an Iowa friend: "I think the perjury of the Tennessee Legislature has finished the destruction of States Rights and slaughtered the element of personal honor. What a pity that the great dust of Andrew Johnson [a native of Tennessee] has to rest under the sod of a state so craven."

The University as Head of the Iowa School System
VERNON CARSTENSEN

AMONG THE MOST pressing concerns of settlers who moved into a newly opened territory was the matter of establishing schools. Pioneer mothers usually made the first attempt to teach children the three Rs, but very soon neighbors were pooling resources to establish a community school and hire a teacher. As settlement increased and statehood was achieved, the task of establishing public educational facilities rested with the state legislature. At first elementary schools (or common schools) were sufficient but as population increased, high schools were established as well as a state university, necessitating some unification between the three levels.

In this article Vernon Carstensen traces the development of Iowa's unified public school system. Although he focuses on the establishment of the proper relationship between high schools and the state university, he also describes the development of the three levels involved. The problems confronted in developing a correlated system were many and varied. Money was scarce and legislators were reluctant to commit even modest sums for educational purposes; constant disagreements and misunderstandings between university officials, legislators, and regents plagued attempts to relate programs and facilities; personality conflicts between university personnel and other state officials also restricted educational development.

Even though the problems of bridging the gap between elementary schools and the state university would not be solved until the twentieth century, at least by the 1870s the outline for a unified system was clearly defined and the building process underway.

From *Iowa Journal of History,*
Vol. 53, No. 3, July 1955,
pp. 213–46.

THE UNIVERSITY AS HEAD OF THE IOWA SCHOOL SYSTEM

By Vernon Carstensen*

The State University of Iowa today stands at the head of the public school system of the state. Such is the organization of the system that each unit — the elementary school, the junior high school, the high school, and even the junior college — articulates with the one above. Complete from base to apex the educational pyramid stands as a massive symbol to attest the abundant faith of democratic people in education. This vast system is the result of years of slow educational evolution, but it does not represent the upward thrust of the elementary schools. It is one of the most striking features of American educational history that provision was first made for elementary schools and colleges. When Harvard College was founded in the seventeenth century, no general provision was made for the middle schools. Almost the same condition obtained when the University of Iowa was established a little over two centuries later. Only after a long struggle was the gap between the elementary schools and the university effectively bridged and there emerged that peculiarly American institution, the unified system of education.

It is not within the scope of the present study to treat the whole process of unifying the educational system of Iowa, but in order to view in proper perspective the movement which resulted in placing the University at the head of the public school system, it will be necessary to sketch in some detail certain aspects of the movement toward unification. It is the purpose of this article to describe certain phases of the process of articulating the high schools and the University in Iowa. In doing this it will be necessary to suggest the origin of the unified system of education and the circumstances which gave the movement support in America; to show how the idea was adopted in Iowa and found expression in law; and how the system became effective through the establishment of high schools, the articulation of the University and these high schools, and the abolition of the preparatory department of the University in 1878.

*Vernon Carstensen is professor of history at the University of Wisconsin.

The idea of a unified system of education is clearly linked, in its origin, with the spirit of nationalism. Nineteenth century leaders saw in education a powerful instrument which could be used to advance nationalistic ends. This idea found expression in the reports of Condorcet early in the French Revolution. By means of education, widely diffused among the people, the idealists of the Revolution thought to perpetuate the new order that they were in the process of creating. But their bright hopes faded before they found embodiment, and it remained for a Prussian king, Frederick William III, to create a centralized and unified system of education. In America, the Jacksonian era, with its multitude of humanitarian reforms, its vigorous avowal of democracy, its intense nationalism, brought renewed and active interest in education. In the movement which sought to extend and increase the opportunities of education the imperative need for some centralized control was clearly perceived. Because of the peculiar historical development of the United States, the states rather than the central government became the units of educational organization. In the movement which sought both the extension and central control of schools, the example of the Prussian system was not lost upon American educators. At the time when the state systems were beginning to take form, such men as Horace Mann and Henry Barnard were publishing descriptions of the Prussian system, ardently advocating parts of it to their countrymen, and in every way making possible the adaptation of the Prussian system to the American situation. The English translation of Victor Cousin's famous report on the Prussian system of education appeared in America early enough (1835) to have considerable effect. It was the effective state-wide organization which the Prussian system entailed that served as an example for progressive American educators.[1]

The Prussian system afforded an example of what efficient centralized education could be, but the undemocratic philosophy on which it rested found little support in the United States. There were forces at work which were to alter considerably the Old World concept of education. It must be remembered that the educational revival in the United States was part of the humanitarian movement as well as of the movement toward nationalism. Not only was education conceived to be the instrument by which demo-

[1] See Edward H. Riesner, *Nationalism and Education* (New York, 1922), 351-81; Ellwood P. Cubberly, *Public Education in the United States* (New York, 1919), 270-78; I. F. A. Pyre, *Wisconsin* (New York, 1920), 42-3.

cratic government would be transmitted, untarnished, to succeeding generations, but it was also looked upon as an instrument which would inevitably enable a person to improve his economic and social position. "Education" was often recommended and supported as the universal solvent of social ills: it would prevent crime, pauperism, and the like. The absence of a class system in America, the intense democratic sentiments of the time, the idealistic objectives of education — these factors gave to the American schools a democratic character distinctly unlike any European system. Moreover, there seems to have been, even at the beginning of the educational revival, a philosophy of education, never fully stated yet implicit in the very nature of the system, which is profoundly significant. Intelligence was conceived to be the natural possession of all men, and education was accepted as the instrument which would release this intelligence. Hence the constant and repeated use, even at the present time, of the terms literacy and intelligence, as if they were synonymous. Humanitarians, nationalists, democrats — all had just cause for desiring a unified system of schools.

Lying directly in the path of the westward movement of population, organized as a territory in 1838 and as a state in 1846, Iowa was to feel the full impact of the educational revival. Iowa, like other new states, had to build and adapt an educational system while settlement was taking place rapidly, while the settlers were in the very act of building a material civilization on the frontier.

The process of unifying the educational system did not begin at the outset of the political history of the territory, but numerous attempts were made to provide a basis for uniform organization of the schools. Early in his first message to the territorial legislature, Governor Robert Lucas pointedly called attention to the necessity of adequately providing for educational facilities in the territory. "There is no subject," he declared, "to which I wish to call your attention more emphatically than the subject of establishing, at the commencement of our political existence, a well digested system of common schools; and as a preparatory step towards effecting that important object . . . I urge upon your consideration the necessity of providing by law for the organization of townships."[2]

Although Lucas was not successful in getting the legislature to adopt laws providing for a uniform organization of the school districts of the

[2] Iowa, *Journal of the Council of the First Legislative Assembly*, 1838, 6.

state, his was not the only attempt to secure such legislation. The two territorial governors who followed him, John Chambers and James Clarke, repeatedly urged the legislature to enact laws which would make possible a complete and effective organization of elementary education, and would protect school lands from intruders.[3] Although the territorial legislature adopted many laws dealing with education, the only act which can be said to have in it the suggestion of state supervision of schools was one which provided for the establishment of the office of a territorial Superintendent of Public Instruction. This officer was empowered to organize the educational system of the territory and required to report to the legislature. Dr. William Reynolds was elected to this office, served for one year, made a report to the territorial legislature, and then the office was abolished.[4]

When Iowa became a state, at least one notable provision was made for the eventual unification of the schools. The constitution provided for a Superintendent of Public Instruction. It is true that during the first few years his duties were principally fiscal, but the act gave centrality to the educational program, and it created a responsible officer who, in the future, would assume a measure of supervision over the schools of the state. Furthermore, the first General Assembly, in providing for the establishment of of the State University, made the Superintendent of Public Instruction president of the Board of Trustees and declared that there should be established in the University a professorship for the training of teachers.

Little of real importance was done to unify or completely organize the school system during the early years of statehood. Provision was made for the establishment of elementary schools throughout the state, and in 1849, in answer to the request of the Superintendent of Public Instruction, the legislature passed a law permitting communities to organize "union schools" to carry education beyond the elementary grades. In the years between 1846 and 1857, when a new constitution was adopted, the Superintendents of Public Instruction asked for better school laws, and the governors repeatedly called the attention of the legislatures to the need for more adequate provision for education, while the educators deplored the inactivity of the legislature and the lethargy of the communities. The legislature, not

[3] Benjamin F. Shambaugh (ed.), *Messages and Proclamations of the Governors of Iowa* (7 vols., Iowa City, 1903-1905), 1:257, 266, 341-2.

[4] *Laws of Iowa, 1841*, Chap. 46; *Iowa Council Journal, 1841-1842*, 278-88; *Laws of Iowa, 1841-1842*, Chap. 108.

to be outdone, passed more and more laws in a futile attempt to patch up an ill-digested educational system.

In his second biennial message, submitted as he retired from office, Governor Stephen Hempstead spoke of the immediate and urgent need of revising the school laws which provided for education. "Experience has taught us," he said, "that these laws are too complicated and by frequent amendment have become difficult to understand, or carry [sic] them into force without the commission of errors, which not unfrequently leads to protracted and burdensome litigation."[5] On the day that Hempstead delivered this message, there came to the office as governor a man who was to give impetus to the movement. James W. Grimes, himself an Easterner and a college trained man, brought to the governorship a broad conception of the function of government as an instrument for social improvement. In his inaugural address Grimes presented what he considered to be an analysis of the function of government. He realized the difficulty of making equitable and necessary laws for a state still in the throes of rapid settlement, but he contended that the time had come for the lawmakers to relinquish their local interests and to view the problems of the state as a whole. In words which strongly remind us of Horace Mann, he explained the function of government and the object of education.

> Government is established for the protection of the governed. But that protection does not consist merely in the enforcement of laws against injury to the person and property. Men do not make a voluntary abnegation of their natural rights simply that those rights may be protected by the body politic. It reaches more vital interests than those of property. Its greatest object is to elevate and ennoble the citizen. It would fall far short of its design if it did not disseminate intelligence, and build up the moral energies of the people. It is organized "to establish justice, promote the public welfare, and secure the blessings of liberty." It is designed to foster the instincts of truth, justice and philanthropy, that are implanted in our very natures, and from which all constitutions and all laws derive their validity and value. It should afford moral as well as physical protection, by educating the rising generation; by encouraging industry and sobriety; by steadfasting adhering to the right, and by being ever true to the instincts of freedom and humanity. To accomplish these high aims of government, the first re-

[5] "Biennial Message of the Governor of Iowa . . . December 9, 1854," *Iowa Senate Documents, 1854-1855,* 5.

quisite is ample provision for the education of the youth of the State. . . . The State should see to it that the elements of education, like the elements of universal nature, are above, around, and beneath all.

It is agreed that the safety and perpetuity of our republican institutions depends upon the diffusion of intelligence among the masses of the people. The statistics of the penitentiaries and almshouses throughout the country, abundantly show, that education is the best preventive of pauperism and crime. They show, also, that the prevention of these evils is much less expensive than the punishment of the one, and the relief of the other. Education, too, is the great equalizer of human conditions. It places the poor on an equality with the rich. It subjects the appetites and passions of the rich to the restraints of reason and conscience, and thus prepares each for a career of usefulness and honor. Every consideration, therefore, of duty and policy, impels us to sustain the common schools of the State in the highest possible efficiency.

Education, he contended, should be supported by a general property tax, for "Property is the only legitimate subject of taxation. It has its duties, as well as its rights. It needs the conservative influences of education, and should be made to pay for its own protection."[6]

Nothing constructive was done by the General Assembly during the first session under the governorship of Grimes, but at a special session in the summer of 1856 a measure was approved which empowered the governor to appoint a commission of three to revise the school laws of Iowa.[7] To do this work, Grimes appointed Horace Mann, Amos Dean, then chancellor of the University, and Frederick Bissell, an Iowa teacher.[8] Bissell, much to the regret of the other two commissioners, was unable to assist in the work, but Amos Dean and Horace Mann drew up plans for the revision of the educational system and submitted them to the Sixth General Assembly.[9]

Although the revision proposed was not adopted at that time, the report

[6] "Inaugural Message of James W. Grimes . . . December 9th, 1854," ibid., 4-5.

[7] *Laws of Iowa, 1856*, 78.

[8] Leonard Fletcher Parker, who was in a position to know the facts of the case, explains the appointment of Dean and Mann thus: ". . . they were appointed . . . by Governor Grimes because of their well-known opinions as well as for their ability. He understood what kind of a law they would report, and appointed them for the sake of that report." Leonard F. Parker, *Higher Education in Iowa* (Washington, 1893), 29.

[9] *Iowa Legislative Documents, 1856*, 191-200.

of the commissioners revealed plans for a unified system of education extending from the elementary schools to the University. Among other things the commissioners recommended that provision be made for the establishment of "high academies" or "polytechnic" schools in counties having a population of 20,000 or over. They insisted that the University should be "the head and also the aim of Iowa education," and they desired "to send into every family of Iowa now, and through all future time, a spirit stirring impulse, an animating principle, which shall penetrate the depths of every young heart, and arouse the latent energies of every young spirit, and thus carry forward the common school system into the fullest and completest realization of its glorious mission."[10]

That the suggestions of the commissioners were not adopted and written into the laws of the state does not mean that a state-wide and unified sysem of education was in disfavor among the leaders in Iowa.[11] On the contrary, all indications suggest that the movement toward unification had set in strong and sure. In August of 1856 the people of Iowa, by an overwhelming majority, had voted to call a constitutional convention. In December the delegates to the convention were chosen. Of the thirty-six members of that convention, twenty-one had been elected by the newly organized Republican party.[12]

Education was the subject of much spirited if not always lucid debate in the convention. A Committee on Education and School Lands was appointed on the second day. Four days later Edward Johnson of Lee County offered a resolution recommending that this committee be requested to inquire into the expediency of so amending the constitution as to create a board of education. The board was to be made up of ten or twelve mem-

[10] *Ibid.*, 199-200. The Sixth General Assembly passed an appropriation bill allowing fifty dollars to Horace Mann and Amos Dean "for services as commissioners to revise the school laws." The measure which had created the commission provided that the commissioners were to receive four dollars a day. *Laws of Iowa, 1856-1857*, 446.

[11] George W. Ells, delegate to the constitutional convention, resident of Scott County, charged in debate on the convention floor that the reason for the failure of the educational reform bill to pass was that the General Assembly split over the question of admitting Negroes to the schools. *The Debates of the Constitutional Convention* (2 vols., Davenport, Iowa, 1857), 2:728-9.

[12] Benjamin Gue, *History of Iowa* (4 vols., New York, 1903), 1:284. The convention assembled at Iowa City, Jan. 19, 1857, and remained in session until March 5. The constitution drawn up was adopted by the people of the state in August of the same year.

bers, it was to govern the University and have "general charge of the common and other public schools of the state." After a short flurry of debate on the floor, the convention approved the resolution.[13]

On January 28 the Committee on Schools submitted a majority and a minority report. Both reports contemplated the creation of a board which would control the educational system of the state. The reports differed chiefly in that the majority one would assign definite powers and duties to the board and have these powers written into the constitution; the minority report sought to write into the constitution only the provisions which would create the board and declare its general function. The details of organization and duties were to be left to the legislature.[14] That there would be a board of education created to control the public system of the state seemed to be generally agreed upon. Why it should be created, and what it should do was best explained by James Hall, delegate from Des Moines County, in his defense of the majority report.

> By this majority report, you separate this subject, you divorce it, from all this variety of topics, subjects claiming the attention of the legislature. You take it from the legislature, to which men are elected upon other and different grounds from those which should be taken into consideration here, and whose minds are absorbed in the consideration of other topics. This report keeps the subject of education by itself, and places it in the hands of those elected solely in reference to that subject. . . . The leading feature of this majority report is to divorce and separate the cause of education from the wild and hurried scramble of the political arena, and consign it untrammelled and unfettered to the care of those who are best qualified by experience and education to promote its interests and mature it into healthful growth. . . . It must be acknowledged that the General Assembly is not the fit body to manage and have jurisdiction of the system of education.[15]

In a later debate on the same subject, he stated:

> I ask the convention to consider most thoroughly all the principles contained in this report, which is to give independence to the school district, which is to sever and divorce it from that great political cauldron which forever boils and bubbles throughout the State. Let it have a chance to breathe, where it may not inhale

[13] *Debates of the Constitutional Convention*, 1:21, 39-40.
[14] *Ibid.*, 1:78-9.
[15] *Ibid.*, 2:526-7.

the festering atmosphere of political excitement. Give it a chance to rise, without being clogged by inattention, as it has been heretofore.[16]

The board was objected to by some of the delegates because it would create a second legislative assembly in the state and thereby violate that American tradition of having only three departments of government. Moreover, since no one was willing that the board should have the power to levy taxes for the support of the schools, the power to legislate on school matters would be divided between the General Assembly and the Board of Education.[17]

It is not necessary here, in tracing the development of unification of education in Iowa, to follow in detail the debates over the establishment of the board. The board was created without any great objection to the two important ideas on which it was based: that education should be placed beyond the reach of the ordinary legislature; and that the whole system should be organized under one body. It is apparent that Amos Dean and Horace Mann had not attempted to impose upon an unwilling state a system of education alien to the demands of the state.

In the last report of the Superintendent of Public Instruction under the constitution of 1846, Maturin L. Fisher emphasized the need for a complete organization from the elementary schools to the University, and he asked for a system of scholarships to support superior students in the "High Schools" and the University.

> A scheme of public instruction would be incomplete without some provision for a higher degree of mental culture, without an institution to facilitate the cultivation of philosophy in all its branches, and the pursuit of the sciences in all their ramifications. We have such an institution in the State University already organized and handsomely endowed. In the high schools young men should be prepared to enter the University, and in the University young men should be educated without charge for tuition, to become professors in the high schools. The proposed system, then, is thus constituted: 1st, the Common School; 2nd, the High School; 3rd, the State University — each in its order, preparatory to the other.[18]

[16] Ibid., 2:753.
[17] Ibid., 2:744ff., 748-9.
[18] "Report of the Superintendent of Public Instruction," *Legislative Documents,* 1857, 15ff., 18-19.

Although the constitution of 1857 created a Board of Education and expressly provided that "the board of education shall have full power to legislate and make all needful rules and regulations in relation to Common Schools, and other educational institutions, that are instituted, to receive aid from the school or University fund of this state . . .,"[19] the first General Assembly to meet under the constitution passed a general school law. The law then enacted was based largely upon the unadopted report of the school commissioners of two years before.[20] Approved by the governor on March 12, 1858, this law provided for free elementary schools, for the establishment of county high schools, and the government of the University. It provided a number of scholarships to both the "High Schools" and the University for those who sought to become teachers. A plain violation of the constitution, the law was held unconstitutional by the supreme court of the state the same year on the grounds that the legislature had exceeded its authority. The Board of Education, meeting in Des Moines in December of 1858, was then faced with the necessity of either drawing up a whole school law or enacting the one which had been declared unconstitutional. It re-enacted what was substantially the old law, save for the provision for scholarships. Since the Board of Education had no power under the constitution to levy taxes and no source of income, the only scholarships which it could provide were free tuition scholarships to the University.[21]

The idea of a unified system of education was accepted by the end of the fifties, but the educational development of the state was not such that unification could be reckoned as more than an abstract principle. Moreover, no attempt had yet been made to define the exact relationship between the several units of the school system. It was not until 1870 that the legislature attempted a tenuous definition by declaring that "The University, so far as practicable shall begin the course of study . . . at the point where the same [is] completed in the High Schools."[22] Eight years later the legislature attempted further to define the function of the University by prohibiting the University from using any part of its funds for the support of any department which did not properly belong to the University. This law, which was passed for the purpose of abolishing the preparatory department

[19] *Constitution of Iowa*, Article IX, Sec. 8.
[20] Parker, *Higher Education in Iowa*, 29.
[21] *Acts . . . Board of Education . . . Des Moines, 1858* (Des Moines, 1858).
[22] *Laws of Iowa, 1870*, Chap. 87.

of the University, declared in effect that it was the function of the high schools, among other things, to prepare students for the University.

Thus, slowly and uncertainly was the idea of a unified system of education written into law. The last and final step in the process was taken when the State Board of Education, after the turn of the twentieth century, adopted a resolution which demanded that the three state institutions — the University, the Agricultural College, and the State Teachers College — accept all high school graduates who possessed the proper certificates from the high schools.

But the story is not told simply in a review of the legal steps taken to insure unification of education in the state. In 1856, when the idea of a unified system of education first found expression in Iowa, the population of the state did not exceed 500,000. At the time the preparatory department of the University was abolished, the population exceeded 1,500,000. Hence such unification as was achieved during the years under study was accomplished while immigration was at flood tide. The whole movement must be studied against the chaotic background which such a vast migration and increase of population implies and in terms of a fluid society, frontier conditions, rapid and materialistic building, and of all other concomitants to the rapid settlement of a new country. It was only with difficulty in this situation that anything resembling an organized and effectively executed system of unified education could be begun. Since it is as impossible as it is inappropriate in this study to consider the whole evolution of the middle schools during the period under discussion, the process of articulating the University to the high schools will be approached chiefly from the standpoint of what the University, as represented by the action of the governing board, the faculty, and the friends of the institution, did in working out the details of the unification.

Established at Iowa City, Johnson County, in 1847, the University did not open until the spring of 1855. After that haphazard session, the Board of Trustees made provision for the establishment and maintenance of a preparatory school in connection with the University. This was necessary, since at the time there was no place in the public school system where a student might prepare himself to enter the University. The preparatory department attracted a great many more students than did the collegiate department of the University. The great majority of these students came from Iowa City and Johnson County. Of the 125 students listed on the rolls in 1857, over 100 were either in the normal department or the preparatory department — over 60 were in the preparatory department alone. Small wonder that the University, in the first years of its existence, was sometimes called the "Johnson County High School."

When the General Assembly first convened under the constitution of 1857, it adopted a new school law for the state. As has been noted above, this law made provision for a public school system extending from elementary schools to the University. With reference to the University, it provided a new governing board and a new act under which the University was to be governed. The Board held its first session in April, 1858.

During its three-day session the Board of Trustees adopted a new plan of organization for the University, abolished the preparatory department, and decided to close the University until more funds had accumulated and the high schools had prepared students for the University.[23]

Anson Hart, Secretary of the Board, in a public statement explained the action of the Board by saying that under the new law the Board assumed that it had no authority to continue the preparatory department. Because the Board desired to raise the standards of the University, because it could not legally maintain a preparatory department, and because the high schools had not yet become sufficiently numerous or effective to prepare students for the reorganized University, the institution was to be closed for a while. The Board had acted with reluctance. Hart asserted that "all western colleges and Universities have this department, which is used as a feeder to supply the institution with which it is connected." To continue the University without a preparatory department would be disastrous. Without this department, Hart proclaimed, "the University could at best amount to little more than a High School as it has hitherto been, for the benefit of Iowa City."[24]

Thus early in the history of the University the problem of the relationship between the University and the state school system vexed and perplexed the governors of the University, the faculty, and many a public man. It was assumed that the University was to be the head of the public school system of the state, but mere assumption did not make the Univer-

[23] Minutes of the Board of Trustees, Book A (1847-1876), April 27, 1858, p. 92 (University Archives). Unless otherwise noted, manuscript materials noted are in the University Archives at Iowa City.

[24] Iowa City *Weekly Republican*, May 5, 1858.

sity in actuality what it was conceived to be in theory. The years that followed this first attempt to abolish the preparatory department reveal the slow process by which the theory of a unified school system found practical expression in the abolition of the preparatory department and in the articulation of the high schools and the University.

The Board of Trustees created under the School Law of 1858 held only two sessions. When the law under which it had been created was declared unconstitutional, it was succeeded by a Board of Trustees appointed by the Board of Education. Attempts on the part of the new Board to reopen the University in 1859 failed. Not until 1860 did the collegiate department of the University, under a new faculty, resume work.

Hardly had instruction begun before the faculty was clamoring for the establishment of a preparatory department. Few of the students who came to the University were qualified for college work, and all were unequally prepared.[25] After discussing the situation informally, the faculty called a meeting "to discuss the propriety of organizing a preparatory department at the opening of the next term." What arguments were advanced we do not know, but the conclusion of the faculty is unmistakable: "It was unanimously agreed to establish, with the concurrence of the Board, a preparatory department under the supervision of the faculty and Professor Spencer was appointed a Committee of one to have a conference with Professor Guffin with reference to his taking charge of said department."[26] The faculty then addressed a circular letter to members of the Board, asking permission to open this department.[27] By the end of January a majority of the Board had assented to the request, and on January 31 the faculty adopted a resolution to organize a preparatory department "under the supervision of the several professors." A fee of six dollars a session was charged, and the fee was to be reduced by one third for each class which a student had in the University.[28] The department was opened at the beginning of the second semester.[29]

[25] Nathan R. Leonard, "The State University of Iowa in 1860-1," *Iowa Alumnus*, 4:227-30 (1907).
[26] Minutes of the Faculty, Book A (1860-1881), Dec. 6, 1860, pp. 8-9 (MSS, University Archives, Iowa City).
[27] Report of President Totten to the Board of Trustees, June 27, 1861 (MSS, University Archives).
[28] Minutes of the Faculty, Book A, Jan. 31, 1861, p. 10.
[29] Report of President Totten . . ., June 27, 1861.

In his report to the Board of Trustees in June, 1861, President Silas Totten asked that the preparatory department be given permanent organization. "It is the opinion of the Faculty," he wrote, "that such a department is essential to the success of the University in the present condition of Classical Education in the State. They hope, therefore, that provision will be made for its permanent organization. In order to do this properly, it will be necessary to furnish a study room in the University building, and employ a teacher, whose business it will be to maintain order in the room, and give instructions in the lower branches. This teacher need not be one of high attainments as the Professors will have time to instruct in all the higher studies of the department."[30] The Board of Trustees complied with the request the next day, prescribed the requisites for admission,[31] and provided that the course should be two years in length. Thus the preparatory department again became a part of the University, not because it was wanted but simply because there was no way to avoid having it.

The importance of the department in the 1860's is suggested by the enrollment figures. Of a total of 254 students at the University during the academic year 1861-1862, 104 attended classes in the preparatory department, 129 in the normal department. Five years later, 79 students were registered in the collegiate department, 62 in the normal, and 241 in the preparatory; 248 were classified as irregular.[32]

In 1865, in order to effect greater uniformity in the University and offer better facilities for preparation, the preparatory course was lengthened to three years.[33] The condition which made the University unwillingly responsible for the preparation of its students was inescapable. In 1865 the term "high school" still had very little meaning in practice. In fact there were only eighteen public high schools in Iowa, and these were vague and indefinite, often embracing no more than a year's work beyond the elemen-

[30] *Idem.*

[31] Minutes of the Board, June 28, 1861, pp. 185-6.

[32] *Catalogue of the University of Iowa, 1861-62* (Iowa City, 1862). (Hereafter, the catalogues will be referred to as *University Catalogue.*) These statistics are not exactly accurate since it often happened that a student attended classes in both the preparatory department and the collegiate department, but even though they may not show precisely what the enrollment was, they indicate the great popularity and the necessity of the preparatory department. *University Catalogue, 1866-1867.*

[33] Report of Nathan R. Leonard (president pro tem) to the Board of Trustees, June, 1867 (MSS, Univ rsity Archives). See *niversity Catalogue, 1865-66,* 21, for report of additional year.

tary schools.[34] None was adequate or willing to prepare students for the University. The Superintendent of Public Instruction might write in glowing terms of the high school, might insist that it "prepares its pupils for business life or for the University," and publish a high school graded course;[35] but this part of the unified system of education was still far from reality.

The fact that the middle schools were not yet ready to do their work did not save the University from criticism because of its preparatory department. As the first faculty of the University had observed, the preparatory department served the students from Iowa City and Johnson County principally. Hence the University came to be regarded as a local institution. Even though the middle schools had not yet been created, there were critics who insisted that in maintaining the preparatory department the University was pre-empting ground which should be the province of the high schools. Both the University faculty and the governing Board recognized the cause of the unpopularity of the preparatory department, and they did what they could to improve the situation.

In May, 1867, a faculty committee was appointed to "present to the Board a plan on the contraction of the course of studies in the preparatory department."[36] The committee report was presented to the Board at its June meeting, together with the report of the president pro tem of the University, Nathan R. Leonard. In his report, Leonard called the attention of the Board to the necessity of reducing the time for the preparatory course from three to two years. He explained that the preparatory department had been organized in the beginning because "it was thought necessary to meet a pressing demand in the then condition of the State for preparatory instruction, and also as affording the only means of drawing students to the university." In order to serve this purpose better, the course had been lengthened to three years. "It is believed that the condition of the public and high schools of the state is now such that we may by the modifications suggested reduce the number of years in this department from three to two . . . with advantage to the University and without detriment to the interests of the State."[37] The recommendations of the faculty committee and

[34] Parker, *Higher Education in Iowa*, map opposite p. 44.
[35] "Biennial Report of the Superintendent of Public Instruction," *Legislative Documents, 1866*, Vol. I, 23, 25-6.
[36] Minutes of the Faculty, Book A, May 8, 1867, p. 226.
[37] Report of Nathan R. Leonard . . ., June, 1867.

the president were made the order of the day for June 23; after discussing the matter, the Board adopted the following resolution:

> Resolved that the preparatory department be raised to two years instead of three, that the rule heretofore established for admission in the preparatory department be strictly enforced, and that when there are children in the preparatory department who are inpacitated [sic. incapacitated] from any cause to make such advancement in education as to give hope of their ever entering the collegiate department they be dismissed from the preparatory department as that department is not intended to take the place of common school but to prepare children for the University.[38]

In accordance with this resolution the first year of the preparatory department was dropped, and the result was immediately to be seen in the enrollment. During the academic year 1867-1868, the collegiate department showed an aggregate of 100 students, the normal 103, and the preparatory 232, with only 14 irregular students listed.[39]

This act, however, did not quiet complaints about the preparatory department. In March, 1868, the University became the subject for severe criticism from the Davenport *Gazette*. In answer, C. A. Eggert published a long letter pointing out that it was only the preparatory department the *Gazette* was attacking and that this department would be abolished as soon as the high schools could take over the work.[40] At the meeting of the trustees the following June, the member of the Board of Trustees from Iowa City moved that the department be abolished, but the motion failed to carry.[41]

If the preparatory department could not be abolished, there were other ways the governors of the University might try to deal with the opposition it aroused. In September, 1868, James Black assumed the presidency of the University. Like Amos Dean, Silas Totten, and Nathan Leonard, he might object to the preparatory department, he might recognize that it mitigated against the welfare of the University, but he, too, found that it could not be dispensed with. But he did contrive to abolish the name. On June 29, 1869, the Board of Trustees adopted the new course of study by President

[38] Minutes of the Board, June 23, 1867, p. 270.
[39] *University Catalogue, 1867-68.*
[40] Iowa City *Republican*, Apr. 8, 1868.
[41] Minutes of the Board, June 23, 1868, p. 302.

Black. Although no mention is made in the minutes of the changes proposed, it is clearly shown that the Board understood that the preparatory department was to be altered. A few days after adopting this course of study the Board agreed to a resolution stating that since Professor Ebersole had been deprived of his position as assistant instructor of ancient language, he was to be reappointed to teach "introductory classes."[42]

Just what this new course of study involved is revealed in the catalog printed shortly after this Board meeting. "At a late meeting, the Board of Trustees ordered the discontinuance of the Preparatory Department as such, but provided for instruction in its more advanced studies by placing an additional year to the Collegiate Course. To meet the wants of those students who may not have in the public schools the means of preparing for admission to the Collegiate Department, as now arranged, Introductory classes will be formed for instruction in the more important of the remaining studies of the former Preparatory Course."[43] Thus, by making the collegiate course five years in length and by adding what the president chose to call an "Introductory class," the old preparatory department was discontinued in name. Thenceforth, although the "Introductory classes" were popularly referred to as the preparatory department, the actual words were never again to profane the University catalog.

A few weeks after this ostensible abolition of the preparatory department of the University, the Iowa City School Board voted to discontinue the "high school" which had been established a few years before. The Board justified its action on the grounds that the high school cost too much and that all the work which it offered could be secured either in the Iowa City Academy (a private school) or the preparatory department of the University.[44] Even before the Board's letter of explanation had appeared in the Iowa City Republican, the editor of the State Press had raised an indignant protest. He insisted that Iowa City should have a high school, that the abolition of the preparatory department of the University made it necessary. The high school should, he declared, prepare students for the University. "It can be easily arranged," he asserted, " so soon as the University course shall be permanently adjusted that this Academic curriculum shall terminate the work of education at that point where the University begins. Each can

[42] Ibid., June 29, 1869, p. 334; July 1, 1869, p. 341.
[43] University Catalogue, 1868, 43.
[44] Iowa City Republican, Aug. 11, 1869.

thus be complete in itself and the Diploma of the City Academy can carry its possessor into the first classes of the University."[45]

The abolition of the Iowa City high school also provoked a spirited letter from Gustavus Hinrichs of the University faculty. Hinrichs stated that the preparatory department was simply a temporary arrangement, that it had already been reduced to one year, and that the introductory classes were provided only for students who came from the newer parts of the state. He contended that the high school should serve as a connecting link between the elementary schools and the University. Because Johnson County insisted on using the preparatory department of the University as a high school, the legislature was exceedingly reluctant to provide the University with adequate financial support. The suspension of the Iowa City high school was a serious menace to the rapid development of the University, for it would lengthen the life of the preparatory department. "If the University, freed from this terrible encumbrance, can devote its very limited funds to the legitimate object of High Collegiate and Professional training, students will flock hither from all parts of this and adjacent states, and Iowa would soon become a rival of Michigan." Three days after Hinrich's letter appeared, the Iowa City School Board by a special vote rescinded the motion to abolish the high school.[46]

The attempts to shorten the preparatory course and to maintain the high school in Iowa City are not the only indications that there were many influential people who looked forward to a more clearly defined system of education in the state, a system which would reveal the relationship of the University and the other public schools. When the Board of Trustees met in Des Moines in December of 1869, it resolved that "in the report of the Board to the legislature Dr. Black be instructed to incorporate in said report a suggestion pertaining to the status of the University toward the Public School system of the state that may extend the usefulness of the instruction and more efficiently result in the educational advantages of the whole people of the state."[47] This President Black did. In the "Report of the Trustees" he stated that the lower class of the preparatory department had been dropped because the subjects taught there belonged properly to the high

[45] Iowa City *Press*, July 14, 1869.

[46] *Ibid.*, Aug. 11, 1869. The letter was dated Aug. 9. Iowa City *Republican*, Aug. 18, 1869.

[47] Minutes of the Board, Dec. 22, 1869, p. 345.

schools, and the upper class had been attached to the collegiate department. Black insisted that in making the changes the Trustees had kept in mind "the place of the University in the system of State Education of which it is a part. . . ." Furthermore, in discussing the needs of the University, Black insisted that the University crowned the educational system of the state and that it should be so recognized.[48]

In his report for the same year, A. S. Kissell, Superintendent of Public Instruction, devoted considerable space to describing the attempts to secure a unification between the high schools and the colleges in Illinois under the leadership of Newton Bateman. He then called attention to the relationship between the high schools and colleges in Iowa. Each unit, he pointed out, must do its own particular work without encroaching upon the sphere of the other. The educational system in Iowa was far from realizing this aim, for "many of the graded schools and High Schools adopt courses of study which in no way harmonize with the curriculums of these higher schools." Kissell complained that all too often the teachers in these high schools did not encourage the pupils to go further than such schools allowed, and he sounded the note, now grown so familiar: "Every teacher in a high school should encourage his pupils to higher and more diligent efforts in the pursuit of knowledge, and the university and colleges should be stimulants to pupils in lower schools, and awaken within them aspirations for higher culture."[49]

This agitation was not without some effect, for the Thirteenth General Assembly in 1870 drew up and adopted a new law for the government of the University and for the first time essayed definitely to fix the relationship of the University to the high schools of the state. "The University, so far as practicable, shall begin the courses of study, in its collegiate and scientific departments, at the point where the same are completed in the high schools; and no students shall be admitted who have not previously completed the elementary studies in such branches as are taught in the common schools throughout the State."[50] In adopting this law, the legislature gave definite legal sanction to the belief which had so long been held that the Unversity was the head of the public school system.

[48] "Report of the Board of Trustees," *Legislative Documents, 1870*, Vol. I, 24ff.

[49] "Biennial Report of the Superintendent of Public Instruction," *Legislative Documents, 1870*, Vol. I, 27, 28.

[50] *Laws of Iowa, 1870*, Chap. 87. See appendix.

When the law of 1870 was adopted, it was in many ways an act of sheer optimism to insist that the University should begin its work where the high schools left off. There were only forty-one high schools in the state in 1871, and of these only twenty-three had well-defined courses of study; no high school course of study was devised primarily for the purpose of preparing students for the University.[51] Hence the problem of connecting the University and the high schools even after 1870 involved a great many compromises on the part of both institutions. Articulation, such as it was, was brought about by the leaders in secondary education in the state, working through the Iowa State Teachers Association, the Board of Regents of the University, the faculty of the University, and the newspaper editors of the state. No one group can be given all credit for the work. It was the result of cooperation and compromise, and it was done in the face of great material difficulties.

The impulse toward standardizing the secondary schools found its first expression in the Iowa State Teachers Association. In 1871 a committee of that organization, made up of representatives of the high schools, the academies, the colleges, and the State University, arranged a course of study for secondary schools in the graded systems. The work of this committee was entirely without legal standing, but it focused attention upon the problem of standardizing the high schools so that they might prepare students for college. It meant that the high schools had begun to incorporate a function which had formerly belonged to the academies. At the June, 1872, session of the Board of Regents, the problem of the relationship between the high schools and the University was discussed. In order to effect a working basis of articulation between the two, the Board adopted the following resolution: "The academical faculty may admit to the various classes without examination students from such schools or academies as in their judgment offer sufficient facilities for preparation, but this privilege shall be withdrawn from any school found to be deficient in this respect."[52] Thus the Board placed in the hands of the faculty the power necessary for them to begin seriously to cooperate with the Iowa State Teachers Association and

[51] Clarence R. Aurner, *History of Education in Iowa* (5 vols., Iowa City, 1915), 3:223. See also Parker, *Higher Education in Iowa*, 39, 105. Parker asserts that before 1870 the word "high school" had no definite meaning in the state.

[52] Minutes of the Board, June 21, 1872, p. 406; Aurner, *History of Education in Iowa*, 3:225. On pp. 305ff, he presents the courses which this committee devised for two, three, and four-year high schools.

the high school officials of the state in the work of connecting high schools and the University.[53]

At the annual meeting of the Iowa State Teachers Association, held late in the summer of 1872, Professor Fellows, who had been elected president of the organization, devoted his inaugural address to a consideration of the relations between the schools of the state. The address was referred to a committee of which Professor Parker, also of the University, was a member. The committee reported in part, "That the munificence of the Federal and State Governments in the creation and support of State Universities has been timely and wise, that the growth and influence of these institutions have been gratifying, and that we welcome them as the crown and glory of our public school system."[54] The adoption of this report by the convention placed the Association on record as definitely espousing the plan of the unified system of education — a matter which was greeted with joy in University circles. President Thacher, in a letter to the *Iowa School Journal*, announced with delight the recent ruling of the Board with reference to the admission of properly certified high school graduates, pointed with pride to the fact that this arrangement was in entire agreement with the action of the State Teachers Association in recognizing the University as head of the public school system of the state, and invited the superintendents and principals of the high schools to investigate the proposition at once.[55]

The actual articulation of the high schools and the University was not a thing accomplished by passing resolutions and adopting reports, however. It required a great deal of work on the part of the faculty of the University, and on the part of the secondary teachers. It also required vast improve-

[53] In March, 1873, Dr. Thacher presented the following motion which changed slightly the rule of the preceding June: "Resolved that the action of this board in June, 1872, in reference to this admission of students from the Schools and Academies of the state is hereby repealed and that the following rule be adopted. The Academical faculty may admit to the academical department students from such schools and academies in Iowa as in their judgment offer sufficient facilities for preparation on condition that the applicants for admission present certificates of qualification from the principal of their respective schools but this privilege shall be withdrawn from any school or academy found deficient in the facilities named above." Minutes of the Board, March 5, 1873, pp. 426-7.

[54] *University Reporter* (Iowa City), 5:4 (October, 1872).

[55] *Iowa School Journal*, 14:94-5 (October, 1872). The Iowa City *Republican* in an editorial comment had given a favorable reception to this action of the Board even before the state teachers had adopted their resolution. Iowa City *Republican*, Aug. 21, 1872.

ments in the educational facilities of the state. Early in 1873 a high school committee of the University faculty was "instructed to ascertain what arrangements can be made for visiting the various schools." Two weeks later the committee returned the melancholy report that since no funds had been provided for this work, and since none was available, the matter had best be dropped. But if faculty members did not possess funds sufficient to enable them to travel about the state investigating high schools, they were nevertheless active during the next few years. In May of 1873, "upon favorable reference to our city High School by members of the faculty, Professor Currier was appointed a committee to visit the school to examine its status with a view to allowing the high school the same privileges of preparing for our Freshman Classes as is granted to the City Academy." One week later, upon receiving a "favorable report" from Currier, the faculty voted to admit students from the Iowa City high school to the sub-freshman class of the University provided they presented certificates from the principal of the high school. In June of the same year the faculty resolved "that students bearing certificates from Professor E. C. Ebersole of Cedar Rapids of having completed any of our preparatory studies shall be credited for the same here without examination, except as regards the last term of preparatory German."[56]

The practice of taking the case of each school under advisement and then rendering a decision on it was not entirely satisfactory. In May of 1874 the faculty, thinking to systematize the process, adopted a resolution providing that "admission to the Freshman Class shall be granted to all applicants bringing certificates of qualification from those high schools and academies whose course of study embraces the required branches and the quality of whose instruction shall be approved by the faculty." The faculty then appointed a committee, made up of Professors Leonard, Currier, and Eggert, to prepare a plan for carrying out the resolution.[57] Nevertheless, during the ensuing years the faculty continued to recognize individual schools as qualified to prepare students for the University.[58]

[56] Minutes of the Faculty, Book A, 336; Apr. 25, 1873, p. 337; May 23, 1873, p. 337; May 30, 1873, p. 338; June 13, 1873, p. 339.

[57] Ibid., May 29, 1874, p. 358.

[58] The Faculty Minutes reveal that the faculty accepted the following schools as qualified to prepare students for the University: Washington Academy for sub-freshman class, May 7, 1875; Springdale High School "for work done preparatory to our sub-freshman year," June 2, 1876; Hampton (Franklin County) for proficiency in any

The faculty of the University was not compelled to work alone in the project of articulating high schools and University. A number of the University professors, notably Currier, Parker, and Fellows, had long been active in the Iowa State Teachers Association. The faculty regarded this Association as best fitted to bring about the practical unification of the educational system. In 1874 the subject was once more brought up in the state convention, and, after discussion, the convention adopted a resolution acknowledging the importance of the work which the University was doing in unifying the educational system.

> Whereas public high schools have been established and are vigorously maintained in the principal cities and towns of the State as a natural local head of the free school system and constitute an essential link in it, therefore,
> Resolved, That high schools should be encouraged to take the rank of academies and seminaries in the preparation of students for the ordinary duties of life and in fitting them for the University;
> Resolved, That we recognize the recent action of the officers of the University as an important movement in this direction.

The Association then went on to appoint a committee "to devise and recommend the best means for the speedy and complete unification of our school system and to report at our next annual meeting."[59]

The committee faced a difficult situation. President George Thacher pointed out in September, 1875, that there were only forty-one high schools in the state, and of these only fifteen were able to prepare students for the freshman class of the University. Students who came from these favored districts could enter the freshman class of the University, but most of the students in the University entered the collegiate department from the preparatory department. Of the eighty-six freshmen of the preceding year, sixty-nine had entered the collegiate department through the preparatory department, and each of the other seventeen was obliged to pursue some sub-freshman subjects in order to make up previous deficiencies.[60]

---

sub-freshman study, June 9, 1876; the Iowa City Academy as preparatory to the Freshman Class of the University, and the Mitchellville Academy, June 7, 1878; the Decorah Institute, Aug. 1878; and Council Bluffs Academy, Sept. 13, 1879. There is no reason to believe that this constitutes a complete list of the schools so accredited.

[59] *Common School*, 2:4 (1875).

[60] "Report of President Thacher to the Regents," *Legislative Documents, 1875*, Vol. I, No. 7, pp. 6-8.

The discouraging picture of secondary education was abundantly verified by the committee of the Association when it reported in 1875. The committee report, the work of a group of educators representing the entire state, asserted that it found scarcely a trace of anything worthy of being called a system. The schools had no uniform courses of study and no two of them were alike. Moreover they bore out Thacher's declaration that only fifteen of the high schools in the state were qualified to prepare students for the University, that the University could not make Greek a prerequisite to the college because in many schools the language could not be taught. This condition derived from the school law which allowed the various communities to determine by vote whether certain subjects were to be taught. Furthermore, the committee found the same lamentable condition to obtain in 1875 which had caused Superintendent of Public Instruction Kissell such grave concern in 1870. The teachers in the high schools were not attempting to point their students to the University. In fact there seemed to be in many high schools a feeling "of indifference or of virtual opposition to colleges." In few of the high schools did they find enough students anxious to pursue college work to undertake preparation for it. This condition was either the result or the cause of the attitude in the high schools which the committee found so objectionable. The committee was profoundly discouraged with its findings, and declared that only time could remedy the situation, since the local communities could not be forced to provide an education for which no demand was made. In conclusion, the committee asserted that it was "compelled to conclude by affirming the impossibility of devising the means of a speedy and complete unification of our public schools."[61] This report illustrates clearly the wide gap between theory and practice in Iowa in the middle seventies. The high schools had not yet succeeded in assuming the work of the academies.

Another committee of the Iowa State Teachers Association, possessing a different personnel, was assigned to make a further report in 1876 on the prospects of unifying the system. This committee, made up of L. E. Parker of Iowa City, S. J. Buck of Grinnell, C. W. Von Coelln of Waterloo, J. H. Thompson of Des Moines, and J. E. McKee of Washington, submitted a report drawn up by three of its members. More optimistic than their predecessors, they recognized the failure of the high schools of the state to con-

[61] *Common School*, 3:29-30 (1876).

nect with anything above themselves, and the general lack of uniformity among the various systems, but, unlike the committee of the year before, had suggestions to offer and held out hope for the immediate future. Admitting that the condition was bad, they insisted that it could be worse, and urged that each public school officer do all that he could to bring about a practical uniformity between high schools and colleges whenever it could be done without violating local sensitivity. In summing up the movement toward unification between high schools and colleges, and between the high schools and the University, Professor Parker, who was himself exceedingly active in the work, wrote: "No high school courses were created primarily to connect the lower with the higher education, yet many were modified for the purpose. In some college towns they were affected by the preparatory course of the local college. College and university conditions were materially influenced by high school possibilities."[62]

While the Iowa State Teachers Association was showing an active interest in effecting articulation between the secondary schools and the universities and colleges of the state, the University officials were by no means inactive. In June of 1876 the general faculty voted to appoint a committee to prepare a circular concerning the relation of the high schools to the University. Their report was made and accepted by the faculty one week later, and it reached the Board of Regents the next day.[63] This report, together with the resolution offered two days later by Thacher, was referred to the Committee on Course of Study.[64] Two days after receiving Thacher's resolution, the chairman of the Committee submitted a report which was adopted by the Board.

> Your committee to whom was referred the resolution of President Thacher, and the communication of Professor Parker, relating to the admission to the University of students duly certified by teachers of High Schools, such teachers to be selected [approved] by the Faculty or Regents of the University, have considered the same and beg leave to report:

[62] Parker, *Higher Education in Iowa*, 105.

[63] Professors Hinrichs and Parker were appointed such a committee. Minutes of the Faculty, June 9, 1876, p. 414.

[64] Minutes of the Board of Regents, Book B, p. 6, June 19, 1876 (MSS, University Archives). The committee on Course of Study was made up of Regents Kirkwood, Ross, and the president of the University, George Thacher.

The University is properly a part of the school system of the state, and until its connection with that system shall have been defined and fixed, its stability will not be assured, nor will its capacity for usefulness be fully developed. As a means to both these very desirable ends, your committee recommend the passage of the following resolutions:

1. That the candidates will be admitted to the Freshman class without examination who shall present certificates from the principal of any High School organized under the School law of this State, showing that such candidates have studied in such High School the Sub Freshman or Preparatory studies, Classical, Philosophical, Scientific or Civil Engineering, prescribed for the Sub Freshman classes in the University Catalogue for 1875-6, and having attained the standard of scholarship in such studies therein prescribed.

That the Secretary be instructed to furnish each High School a copy of this preamble and resolution, and also five copies of the Catalogue for 1875-6, and that he also furnish to the press of the city for publication a copy of this preamble and resolution.[65]

The desire of the Board of Regents to effect a working arrangement with the high schools was further shown at the next meeting when the Superintendent of Public Instruction, C. W. Von Coelln, introduced a resolution requesting the faculty so to arrange the course of study that students could enter the freshman class without two years of preparatory German.[66] This admirable attempt to compromise one of the difficulties of articulating the high schools and the University was taken under consideration by the faculty, and made the special order of the day for the faculty meeting of April 13. After discussing it fully the faculty determined that the conditions which then obtained for admission "secured the end proposed by the re-

[65] Minutes of the Board of Regents, Book B, p. 17, June 21, 1876.

[66] The resolution introduced by Von Coelln is as follows: "Whereas the high schools of the state find it difficult to provide German instruction required by the present preparatory course for the University and whereas even other studies in mathematics and science are taught in many of the high schools of the state which are now a part of the college course of the University — Resolved: That the faculty of the Academical department be requested to consider the question whether German cannot be omitted from the first sub-freshman year and other studies substituted so as to include some of the freshman studies in the second year and continue German during the two terms of the Freshman year. Resolved: That the faculty be authorized to change the course in the next catalogue to conform to this suggestion, provided they find it advisable." Minutes of the Board of Regents, Book B, March 7, 1877, p. 28.

gents, and Professor Leonard was requested to prepare a note for the forthcoming catalogue clearly explaining this fact."[67]

At the same meeting in which Von Coelln proposed modifications in the entrance requirements to the University, Regent Parr proposed a resolution which slightly changed the general provisions dealing with the relations between the high schools and the University.[68]

In June, 1877, the Board of Regents called for and received the resignation of George Thacher. They then appointed Christian W. Slagle, a member of their own body, president until a suitable man could be found. Slagle had been a member of the governing board of the University from 1868 until he was selected to act as president. A lawyer by profession, he was a public-spirited man who, during the years of his membership on the Board, had constantly urged the need of closer relationship between high schools and the University. In the summer of 1877 he prepared a circular which was distributed at teachers' institutes. Writing to a friend, under date of August 1, he asserted that he wanted to get the subject of the University before the teachers of the state. "As a regent of the institution," he wrote, "one of my hopes has always been that some plan by which the public school system of our state and the University should be made to work together, and thus have a complete educational system worthy of Iowa." He asserted further that he should like the University to "get hold of the hearts of our people and do the work for the state as it is done in Michigan."[69] Thus Slagle, as president, continued the work which the Board now actively sponsored, demanding and securing the support of the faculty of the University and the Iowa State Teachers Association.

[67] The Minutes of the Faculty, Book A, Apr. 13, 1877, p. 434. It should be added that in the vote which was taken on this resolution of the Regents, Professor Eggert protested because he considered the proposal made by the Regents entirely feasible and was unable to perceive how the present arrangements for admission secured the end sought.

[68] The Parr Resolution, adopted without arguments on the part of the Board, is as follows: "That the candidates will be admitted to the Freshman Class without examination who shall present certificates from the principal and president of the Board of Directors of any high school recommended as such by the Faculty of this University, showing that such candidate has studied in such high school the sub-freshman or preparatory studies, classical, philosophical, or Civil Engineering prescribed for the Sub-Freshman classes in the University catalogue of 1875-6 and have attained that standard of scholarship therein prescribed." Minutes of the Board of Regents, Book B, March 7, 1877, p. 28.

[69] Letter to Professor E. Baker, Oskaloosa. Quoted by James F. Wilson, "Christian W. Slagle," *Iowa Historical Record*, 3:529-43 (October, 1887).

When a new president was employed at the end of the year, he was selected, according to the statement of the Board, as a man well fitted to complete the work of unifying the high schools and the University. Josiah Pickard, who had been active in the secondary school work in Illinois and Wisconsin, assumed his duties as president of the University in the summer of 1878. It is true that he did much to continue the work which had been begun, but it is not true, as has often been asserted, that he brought about a unification of the high schools and the University. The idea had been conceived and accepted before the fifties ran out, and the general pattern was established by the time Pickard arrived in Iowa City. Professor Nathan R. Leonard has very well summarized Pickard's contribution: "He doubtless contributed to such salutary changes as were made, but for the most part his contributions were in the nature of the adoption or the carrying out of plans of which he was not the originator. The historic development of the University was in progress and falling in with it his position was such that his was the usufruct of advancement that was made, so far as reputation was concerned."[70] Thus it was that during the seventies the foundations of the educational pyramid were laid and the plan was sketched. Time, prosperity, and social consciousness combined to carry the structure to completion.

During the period of the seventies, while the work of unifying the high schools and the University was going on, the preparatory department became more and more the object of severe and often unfair criticism. It will be remembered that it had been ostensibly abolished in 1869 by lengthening the collegiate course to five years and forming an introductory class. In his report to the Regents in 1871 President Thacher explained that the collegiate course required five years. This condition existed from necessity, not from any desire on the part of the faculty.

> The boys and girls have only very poor advantages in the public schools of the state for pursuing the studies preparatory for the Freshman year. They come to us earnestly desiring to enter the University. It would be in the last degree unwise to refuse them admission. The time has not come for that, and will not have come until the standard of instruction in the primary and high schools shall have been raised far above its present grade. The

[70] Autobiography of Nathan R. Leonard, MSS, p. 44; examined and used through the courtesy of his son, L. O. Leonard.

only remedy for the evil is to supply *in the university* the facilities which they cannot enjoy at home. Unless we would largely diminish our numbers and deplete our classes we must furnish in our own recitation rooms the preparatory instruction which ought to be provided in every large town, or, certainly, in every county of the State. The Sub Freshman is therefore, at present, a necessity from which there is no escape that would not involve serious detriment to the important educational interests for the state for which the University exists. As soon as the Academical course can be limited to *four* years without manifestly greater loss than gain, it should be promptly done.[71]

Thacher might point out the immediate and undeniable necessity of providing preparatory work in the University, but the department was often subjected to attacks by the sectarian schools and politicians. This almost constant criticism during the seventies explains in part the eager interest of the faculty and the Regents in establishing, as early as possible, a working relationship with the high schools. Meanwhile the faculty did what it could to keep the preparatory department out of the public eye.

In February, 1872, a member of the Iowa College (Grinnell) faculty bitterly denounced the University for preserving the preparatory department under another name, thereby living up to the letter of the law but not the spirit.[72] How fair the criticism was, and how seriously it was taken by the faculty, is shown by the fact that in the following December, Nathan R. Leonard submitted a paper to the Regents on the subject of the preparatory work. The first item which he discussed was the name by which this part of the University should be known.

> We have stricken from our catalogue the name of Preparatory department but have preserved the thing itself under the name of Sub Freshman Class. This action was taken merely to placate those who either from ignorance of the needs of the University or from motives of enmity to the institution chose to make the Department the object of unfriendly criticism. It is not right nor wise in my judgment because it was an act well calculated to deceive the unsophisticated public, leading them to believe that we have abolished a thing which we had retained, and we are charged with the intent to so mislead and deceive, and can make but poor

[71] "Report of the Board of Regents, Biennial Report of the Superintendent of Public Instruction," *Legislative Documents, 1872,* Vol. I, 58.

[72] Iowa City *Republican,* March 6, 1872, reprinted from Grinnell *Herald.*

defence. I will say further that the name Sub Freshman Class seems to me singularly inappropriate when its work is to extend over two years instead of one. I prefer therefore for the sake of honest appearances and for appropriateness the name Preparatory Department.

Leonard suggested separate organization for the department. Such organization should render it relatively independent of the University faculty, and should make it self-supporting. He concluded, "the effect of a separate organization of the Preparatory department would be to prevent much of that intermingling of the higher preparatory and lower collegiate work which constitutes the prolific source of much that is annoying in the practical operation of the class system."[73] This well-meant advice was received, but no action was taken. The sub-collegiate work continued to be referred to in the catalog as sub-freshman work, while the newspapers referred to it as the preparatory department.

In the summer of 1874 a series of criticisms of the University was printed in the Iowa City *Press*. Written by J. P. Sanxay and J. P. Irish, these criticisms were concerned at first with the University in general; by July the discussion was centering on the preparatory department. The *Press* insisted that the preparatory department was infringing upon the work of the high schools and that the first year at least should be dropped. Irish contended that he was not motivated by any feeling of bitterness toward the University, but that for the good of the institution he intended to continue the agitation against the preparatory department until that part of the University was abolished. He considered this the only method of getting the University to advance and the high schools and academies to assume the responsibility of providing students for the University.[74]

On the other hand the Iowa City *Republican*, in the interest of presenting the case fairly, pointed out that while the preparatory department was an unwelcome appendage to the University, it was, nevertheless, quite necessary to the institution. Most of the students entered the University classes through the sub-freshman classes. If they did not come that way, the *Republican* averred, they would not come at all. Furthermore, the

---

[73] N. R. Leonard, "Letter to the Board," Dec. 24, 1872 (MSS, University Archives).

[74] Irish, in order to give point to the assertion, insisted that Principals Rogers of Marengo Schools, Witter of Muscatine Schools, Saunderson of Burlington Schools, and Lytle of Oskaloosa Schools had admitted as much to him either orally or by letter. Iowa City *Press*, July 15, 1874. See also, *ibid.*, July 22, 1874.

Republican contended that the preparatory department was virtually self-sustaining and, unless it was maintained, students would go to other colleges which had such facilities.[75] The argument advanced by the *Republican* was borne out by the editor of the *Iowa School Journal*, who, while admitting along with all the others that the dignity of the University would be exalted without the sub-freshman course, pointed out that three-quarters of the counties of Iowa did not have high schools in which to train students for the University, and that of the denominational colleges in the state, sixteen had preparatory departments.[76]

The newspaper strife over the question of the preparatory department quieted down in the fall, but it did not die until the preparatory department was finally abolished by legislative action in 1878.[77] The first vigorous opposition to the preparatory department appeared just before the committee of 1874 was appointed. The discussion had begun in July; the Teachers Association appointed the Thacher Committee on High School and College Unification in August of the year. It is not correct, however, to say that the movement toward unification had its inception in these attacks. It is rather that the attacks show how general had become the idea of a unified system, and the Teachers Association was simply continuing a program which had been adumbrated years before. The University officials were keenly aware of the nature of the struggle concerning the preparatory department, and although George Thacher might have proudly boasted in 1870 that the University could no longer be styled the "Johnson County High School,"[78] in 1875 he felt called upon to present a rather lengthy

[75] Iowa City *Republican*, July 8, 15, 29, 1874.

[76] *Iowa School Journal*, 15:279-81 (October, 1874).

[77] In March, 1875, a letter was printed in the Iowa City *Press*, advocating that Iowa City build a high school to serve the town and the University as a preparatory department. Iowa City *Press*, March 18, 1875. In June the occasion of the publication of the University catalog gave rise to another attack on the preparatory department. Again insisting that the preparatory department was created as an expedient, John P. Irish argued that the need for it was gone, that it should be abolished. *Ibid.*, June 16, 1875. In November there appeared a letter signed "Citizen" in which the author came forward to praise as laudable the desire of the editor of the *Press* to secure a permanent endowment for the University. The author insisted, however, that the legislature was right in refusing that endowment so long as the University continued to support a work which belonged properly to the high schools. *Ibid.*, Nov. 17, 1875.

[78] "Report of the Regents of the University, Biennial Report of the Superintendent of Public Instruction," *Legislative Documents, 1872*, Vol. I, 41.

argument for the preservation of the preparatory department as a part of the University. President Thacher asserted that there were two leading arguments against the preparatory department: it cost too much, and it interfered with the public high schools. The first objection he disposed of by showing that the cost was almost negligible, since it amounted to no more than four mills per household in the state. As to the argument that it "entices from the high schools the promising students thereby exercising a discouraging and repressive influence on the schools of the state," he was more elaborate. He pointed out that there were not more than forty high schools in the state, hence at least sixty counties entirely escaped the "evil of the University." But only fifteen of these schools were prepared to train students for the University, and few students who came to the University from the districts so favored entered the preparatory department. It was from the counties having poor high schools or no high schools at all, he asserted, that the majority of the students of the preparatory department were drawn.[79]

Admitting that a preparatory department "is an undesirable appendage to a college or university and is endured or encouraged only as an unavoidable evil," Thacher urged that it be retained. To abolish it would save the state very little money, and it would increase tremendously the work of the professors of the collegiate department who would then have to tutor many students otherwise taken care of in the preparatory department. "Allow me," he wrote, "to inquire, gentlemen, whether there is any such stress of circumstances as to justify this ruinous policy and most respectfully to sugguest that this Board should set their faces with unfaltering purpose against every attempt to cripple this institution under the poor pretense of saving a little money."[80]

But the pleas of the president and the obvious usefulness of the preparatory department were to avail against public sentiment only a little while longer. The preparatory department became a political issue in one sense; in another it stood as a denial of the conception of the unified system of education. A little over two years after Thacher had presented his plea for the preparatory department, and in the face of the united opposition of the Board of Regents, the General Assembly, almost without dissent, passed a

[79] "Report of the Regents," *Legislative Documents, 1876,* Vol. I, No. 7, pp. 6-17.
[80] *Ibid.,* 10, 17.

bill abolishing the preparatory department of the University.[81] There was then nothing the Regents could do but adjust the University to the change. At their June meeting the subject was referred to a committee made up of Messrs. Duncombe, Ross, and Pickard.[82] After adopting a resolution providing that "irregular students are entitled to full privileges in their classes and that the professors and instructors shall not discriminate against them in recitations and practical work,"[83] the Board went on to consider the report of the committee on the sub-freshman course. After considerable difficulty it was finally decided to drop the first year of the preparatory department in 1878, the second year in 1879.[84]

[81] The bill which provided for the abolishment of the preparatory department was entitled, "An act to prevent the use of funds of the State University for support of the Preparatory Department after July 1, 1879." It provided, "That after the 1st day of July, 1879, no part of the funds belonging to or appropriated for the state university shall be used for the support of the preparatory or non-collegiate course of studies heretofore taught in said university." *Laws of Iowa, 1878*, Chap. 115. Approved, March 25, 1878. This bill, registered as S. F. 311, was introduced into the Senate on March 18, read twice, referred to the University Committee, reported out by that committee on March 20, voted on the next day, and passed, 42 to 2, with 2 not voting. It was adopted instead of an amendment to the appropriation bill restraining the Regents from using any of the appropriated money for a preparatory department. *Iowa Senate Journal, 1878*, 340, 371, 394. On March 22, S. F. 311 reached the House. It was taken up, read a first and second time, and on motion the rules were suspended and it was read a third time, and passed, 80 to 3, with 17 absent or not voting. *Iowa House Journal, 1878*, 543. Thus the bill passed without the sanction of the Board of Regents or the Faculty of the University. It passed because the legislators wanted the University to confine its activities to a specific field, and to cease offering so many advantages in secondary education to the citizens of Iowa City. Gustavus Hinrichs has left an interesting account of the attitude of the faculty toward this activity. Hinrichs had, since the beginning of his tenure as professor, been insistent on the abolition of the preparatory department. He asserted that he had urged its abolition long before the question came before the legislature, but that many of the faculty of the University were loath to see it abandoned. Hinrichs recorded that when the bill was up before the legislature, he was called to Des Moines to testify, and much against the wishes of President Slagle and some of the members of the faculty, he advocated the immediate abolition of the department. Gustavus Hinrichs, *False Statements Made by the Regents* (St. Louis, 1892), 20.

[82] Minutes of the Board of Regents, Book B, June 14, 1878, p. 84.

[83] *Ibid.*, June 17, 1878, p. 88. This motion seems obviously to have been adopted for the purpose of allowing students unqualified for the collegiate department and yet eager to come to the University the opportunity of attending.

[84] *Ibid.*, June 17, 1878, pp. 88-91. The secretary was obviously confused as to exactly what took place, since the records at this point reveal only that there was considerable dispute in the Board. Most of it seems to have centered in the question of whether the sub-freshman classes should be dropped one at a time, or whether both should be continued until July, 1879, and then dropped together. By a vote of six to three it was decided to drop the lower class that year, the next in 1879. *Ibid.*, p. 91.

Thus, one more step was taken toward the unification of the public school system of the state, an achievement which had been envisaged by Horace Mann thirty-three years before. The law of 1870 had described the relationship between the high school and the University in demanding that the University take the students as the high schools prepared them. The law of 1878 limited the sphere of University activity. Henceforth the students of the University would have to be prepared outside the institution. Many years were to pass before a unified system would be complete from base to capital, but the outline was fixed, and the general relationship of each part to the others was defined.[85]

[85] As late as 1893 about 40 per cent of the University freshmen were still obliged to make up some deficiency either by a local school in Iowa City or by tutoring. Parker, *Higher Education in Iowa*, 103n.

The Farm Strike
THEODORE SALOUTOS AND JOHN D. HICKS

ALTHOUGH IOWA traditionally has been characterized as one of the wealthiest and most productive farm states in the nation, it has not always been free from agricultural distress. As Myrtle Beinhauer noted in an earlier article, the Iowa Grange attracted widespread support in the 1870s because of agrarian discontent.

In the following selection historians Saloutos and Hicks explore a second period of strong agrarian unrest that developed in the 1920s and 1930s. At that time Iowa farmers, like farmers everywhere, felt the pinch brought on by rising costs and falling farm prices; in their attempt to find some relief they instigated a "farm strike" that began in 1931 and carried over into the following year. Milo Reno, the peppery leader of both the Iowa Farmers' Union and the Farm Holiday Association led the ill-fated movement. Under his guidance, Iowa farmers first attempted to block state veterinarians from testing their cattle for tuberculosis and secondly and more importantly they attempted to prevent members from shipping their goods to market. As the authors point out, the holding action had little effect on farm prices but the extreme discontent expressed by the participants did cause local and state officials to adopt a more lenient policy in such areas as tax collection and mortgage foreclosure, thus slightly easing the farmers' financial burdens.

In addition to presenting Iowa farm problems and actions in the early thirties, the selection gives us a brief view of similar farm problems in the neighboring Plains and Prairie states.

From Theodore Saloutos and John D. Hicks,
Agricultural Discontent in the Middle West, 1900–1939
(Madison: The University of Wisconsin Press;
© 1951 by the Regents of the University of Wisconsin),
pp. 435–51.

Chapter XV

THE FARM STRIKE

THE FARM STRIKE—short-lived, dramatic, and unsuccessful—was another episode in the expression of agricultural discontent. It began in Iowa, and its leader was Milo Reno, the militant president of both the Iowa Farmers' Union and the Farm Holiday Association and aggressive advocate of "cost of production" as the basis for the farmer's price. This opposition had two stages: first the farmers resisted the state veterinarians who tested cattle for tuberculosis; and then as conditions worsened they applied the principle of the "bank holiday" to agriculture, hoping that this would encompass the nation unless relief was forthcoming to them soon. The strikers sought to restrain their members from shipping goods to market—first by persuasion if possible, then if that failed, by using force. But in these and other efforts they were no more successful in alleviating the burdens of the farmers than the Federal Farm Board had been. If it accomplished anything, the strike helped dramatize the plight of the farmer as few events did.

This movement had its incubation in Iowa, one of the wealthiest farm states. The years 1929 to 1933 were among the most trying in its history. As elsewhere, prices were dropping and debt burdens were high; hence farmers who had purchased their land and equipment at inflated prices found themselves face to face with bankruptcy. What had made the situation especially acute was the fact that the Iowa farmers had been so prosperous.[1]

1. Staff of the Department of Economics at Iowa State College, *The Agricultural*

Milo Reno was hardly an untried hand in farm movements. He had been a leader in the McNary-Haugen campaign and later hurled anathemas at the Federal Farm Board in a manner that few farm leaders could duplicate. In dramatic and vituperative fashion, he had attacked the Coolidge, Hoover, and the Roosevelt administrations, and with equal vigor he denounced the federal and state governments, the agricultural colleges, the county agents, the professors, and all those affiliated with groups he believed were exploiting the farmers. He burst into the national limelight as head of the Farm Holiday Association.[2]

Despite his unorthodox views, Reno had affiliations and ties that were quite conformist. For instance, he served as president of the Iowa Farmers' Union life and automobile insurance companies and was a director of the fire insurance company—positions which, according to one source, had netted him a total salary of $9,600 a year. This sum, plus a $10 per diem expense allowance while in the field for the fire insurance company, was cited as evidence that farm organization work was hardly unprofitable to Reno at least, despite all that he had to say about the machinations of the capitalist system. He was also listed as a member of the Masons, the Odd Fellows, the Christian Church, and the Republican party, yet he did not adhere strictly to party lines. In 1928 he supported Al Smith, and in 1932 he endorsed Franklin Delano Roosevelt.[3]

His best-known activities before the farm strike were in connection with the McNary-Haugen campaign of the twenties. He was credited with having suggested the idea that led to the forming of the Corn Belt Committee in 1925. In 1928 he broke with Senator Smith W. Brookhart of Iowa because the latter defended Hoover, and then reunited with him in 1932 when both joined in an attack on Hoover. In 1930 Reno called Alexander Legge, the chairman of the Federal Farm Board, a liar and disagreed with Governor John Hamill of Iowa over the creation of a state-wide livestock-marketing organization. When the Corn Belt Committee broke up in 1931, he sided with the anti-Farm Board faction.

Reno's attacks on agricultural colleges and professors were amusing

Emergency in Iowa (Ames, 1933). This is an invaluable study by experts, dealing not only with the situation in Iowa, but also with farm relief in general.

2. *Des Moines Tribune*, May 5, 1936.

3. *Ibid.*, August 18, 1932; May 5, 1936. See also Roland A. White, *Milo Reno* (Iowa City, Iowa, 1941), pp. 17-19.

and interesting but reflective of the sentiments of the type of farmer that he led. He accused the colleges of distracting the attention of the farmer "from the real solution of his problems," and of preparing him to accept "the lowly position of the peasant."[4] His main charge was that the colleges were "controlled by exploiters." In bitter vein, he attacked Iowa State College at Ames, taking exception to a particular set of instructions which "advised the farmers' wives how to make undergarments for their children out of feed-sacks." To Reno, the works of the academic theorists were not "going to be worth a damn in the next two or three years in solving the practical problems that confront us." For the "brain trusters" of the New Deal and the other dispensers of "collegiate farm relief" he had this piece of advice: try to run a farm of your own. The central theme in many of his farm speeches was that agriculture was the only basic industry, because "ever since man appeared on this earth, the procuring of food for humans to eat has been the only basic industry whether it was done by bow and arrow or by our modern methods of agriculture."[5]

In 1931 Reno and his followers burst into the public eye when farmers in southeastern Iowa resisted the state veterinarians who had come into that part of the state to test cattle for tuberculosis. This was in line with the recommendations that the United States Bureau of Animal Husbandry had been making for some time. Medical associations also had been crying out that a substantial percentage of all tuberculosis in children was traceable to milk from infected cows. Unfortunately, this tuberculin test was undertaken at a time when the morale of the farmer had fallen to a low ebb.[6]

Testing began in Iowa in 1917, when the first accredited herds appeared in the state. In 1919 the legislature appropriated $100,000 annually, a sum to be spent for testing in cooperation with the federal government. Two years later this appropriation was raised to $250,000 annually. In 1923 the "area-plan law" went into effect which provided that when a certain percentage of farmers in a county requested the test, it must be adopted by the county. This meant that testing was compulsory in many places. About 1929 the test was made compulsory in the state, one of its

4. *Iowa Union Farmer* (Columbus Junction), January 11, 1933.
5. *Des Moines Register*, January 27, 1934.
6. Walter Davenport, "Get Away from those Cows," *Collier's*, LXXXIX (February 27, 1932), p. 11.

most ardent supporters being the Iowa Farm Bureau, which for some years had been the most powerful state farm bureau in the nation.[7]

The cow-testing program appeared to have been proceeding fairly well as late as 1930; there were sporadic complaints but no organized protests. In part this was because the farmers got something for their condemned cows. For every infected animal slaughtered, the federal government assumed one-third the loss, the state one-third, and the owner the remaining third. As time elapsed the farmers began to feel that they were getting less for their animals; many felt that due to the impact of the depression, the state was "paring down its evaluation scale." The packers also were said to be giving less for the salvageable parts of the condemned animals.

Because of the known opposition in the southeastern part of the state, the authorities seem to have postponed the testing of cows there with the hope "that time would make them less scornful of urban laws and more amenable to general government."[8] Many of these farmers belonged to the Farmers' Union and the Farmers' Protective Association, a body formed to oppose the test. Their objections were based on several grounds: the test was "wholly unreliable; it did not protect the public health; it permitted confiscation in the name of the law; it provided meat packers with millions of pounds of good meat at condemned prices; and it furnished salaries to an army of workers at the expense of tax payers." "We appeal to the people of Iowa," pleaded a group of Cedar County farmers, "to help us place upon our statute books a law which will not permit confiscation of our property and establish a test which will be reliable, not a mockery in the name of public health."

The Iowa authorities took exception to these protests. They said that the test protected human life and in the long run gave the farmers healthier cattle and better prices. The Iowa test was upheld as "the same test that has universal approval. When another test is brought forward, and wide use shows it to be an improvement, we shall adopt it in Iowa."[9]

Protesting farmers fought the compulsory test in two ways: one, by seeking legislation providing for an optional one in place of the com-

---

7. *Iowa Farm Bureau Messenger* (Waterloo), November, 1925; *Bureau Farmer* (Iowa Edition), May, 1931, p. 9; *Iowa Farm Bureau Messenger*, January-February, 1921; *ibid.*, April, 1922.
8. Davenport, in *Collier's*, LXXXIX (February 27, 1932), p. 11.
9. *Des Moines Register*, April 15, 1931.

pulsory measure; and two, by organizing committees to resist the state veterinarians when they attempted to apply it.

Typical of the methods employed in the latter instance were those used in Tipton, Iowa. On February 21 there were committees organized, one on every telephone line in the county, to notify farmers when the cow testers, or "cow squirters," as they were also called, started for the farm of anyone who objected to the test. Farmers who cared to chop wood, or pitch hay, were to go to the farm of the objector. State veterinarians, upon seeing these additional hands, would proceed with caution; either they would leave the farm peaceably or they would be subjected to force.[10]

In March farmers visited the state capitol in Des Moines to protest against the compulsory law; most of the farmers came from areas in which the test had been rejected by force and thus had brought about the jailing of some of their members. Reports that farmers would come to the capitol "armed with pitchforks" were disproved as the marchers moved through the downtown area. One placard read:

> Fake, Fake, Fake
> Vets condemn our cattle
> And to the packers take
> Fake, Fake, Fake
> We oppose compulsory T. B. Tests
> We demand justice.[11]

Reno used constitutional arguments in opposing the test, stating: "The real basis of the objection . . . lies in the fact that their property is no longer their own. Any little shyster who has come out of a certain college in the state can go on a farmer's property and conduct a test which is more apt to be wrong than right."[12] About that time a newspaper photographer and a veterinarian were forcibly ejected from the farm of one of the objectors in the Tipton area.[13] Shortly thereafter, word circulated that the state militia was being held in readiness.

These preliminary skirmishes resulted in a compromise between the

10. *Iowa Union Farmer*, February 18, 1931; *Des Moines Tribune*, March 10, 1931.
11. *Ibid*., March 19, 1931.
12. *Des Moines Register*, April 13, 1931.
13. *Des Moines Tribune*, April 15, 1931.

objectors and the state. According to the terms agreed upon, the farmers were to be permitted to choose an accredited veterinarian to test their cattle; assurances were made that the state officials would not be kept in the protesting areas if the farmers gave evidence that they were going to comply with the law; and finally, the state legislators, not the governor, were the ones who were empowered to bring the bill for the optional test out of the "sifting committee" for a vote. The attempt made to bring the bill out for a vote failed by a vote of 80 to 22, which was good evidence that public sentiment was not behind the objectors.[14]

While the governor restated his determination to enforce the testing law, farmers from Cedar County filed a petition seeking an injunction to restrain the state from acting. The Iowa supreme court upheld the law, however, when it reversed the decision of the lower court, and this time the appeal went to the United States Supreme Court. The office of the attorney general of Iowa called this appeal frivolous, because there was nothing in the state law that involved a federal issue; it did not deny due process of law because it was in the interest of public health and the general welfare. As predicted, the United States Supreme Court failed to pass on the case because there was no federal issue involved.[15]

A somewhat embarrassing situation was created in the spring and summer of 1931 when the daughter of one of the Iowa farmers who had had cows condemned was adjudged the healthiest girl in the United States. The recalcitrant farmers believed that here was a situation that was going to help their protests, because she attributed her health to drinking a quart of milk a day. Stories were circulating to the effect that all the cows of her father had been condemned, to which he replied that only eight of his twenty-seven animals had been condemned and that the objectors were doing too much "yapping" and spreading of "malicious propaganda." He further charged the objectors with opposing the laws of Iowa, President Hoover, Iowa State College, the Red Cross, the Farm Bureau, and other "worth-while organizations." He added that he was "mighty glad" that his cows had been tested.[16] By the once hopeful objectors, these utterances were taken with the greatest suspicion.

14. *Des Moines Register*, April 15, 1931.
15. *Ibid.*, April 19, 29, May 2, 26, 1931; *Des Moines Tribune*, September 22, 1931.
16. *Bureau Farmer* (Iowa Edition), May, 1931, p. 11; *Iowa Union Farmer*, July 1, 15, 1931.

In the fall of 1931 hostilities broke out again when "armed agents" met the resistance of about four hundred farmers in Tipton. Governor Dan Turner was advised of the situation while he was in Washington attending a conference. He immediately declared martial law and hurried back to the scene of the disturbances.[17] Violence broke out, accompanied by the exchange of heated words, mud, clubs, and tear gas. The law was enforced, but at an estimated cost of about $2,500 per day—a heavy item to an administration that had committed itself to economy. Threats of staging taxpayers' strikes and of boycotting unsympathetic merchants were heard, but the veterinarians proceeded with their work and the cows were tested.[18]

The bulk of the Iowa farmers were not in sympathy with the objectors, yet the outbreak was indicative of the temper of certain areas of the nation, both rural and urban, which had been floundering in the depths of depression with slight evidence of relief in sight. The "cow war" also demonstrated the hostility of certain farmers to the far-reaching hand of the government, colleges, and other centralized agencies, especially at a time of falling prices. In addition, this outbreak furnished a precedent for the farm strike that was to gain more attention and for which the "cow war" had served as more or less a proving ground.

A "farm strike" was nothing new. It had been attempted with limited success during the first decade of the twentieth century by the Equity and the Farmers' Union. In 1920 shortly after the withdrawal of government guarantees, wheat farmers were talking in terms of striking and holding their wheat until they got $3.00 a bushel for it. Milo Reno favored such action at that time.[19] As time elapsed farm-strike sentiment appears to have been gaining headway among certain Farmers' Union leaders.[20] In 1930 one Union leader suggested that "if the farmers of the nation would band together and for sixty days neither sell nor buy from industry, the farm problem would be solved any way farmers wanted it solved."[21]

17. *Des Moines Register*, September 22, 1931; *Des Moines Tribune*, September 22, 1931.
18. *Ibid.*, September 24, 1931.
19. *New Farmer*, October 30, November 27, 1920; *Oklahoma Union Farmer* (Oklahoma City), December, 1920, p. 323.
20. *Des Moines Tribune*, September 25, 1931; *Des Moines Register*, September 27, 1931.
21. *Ibid.*, September 19, 1930.

In March, 1931, Reno was reported sounding out the head of the Iowa Farm Bureau on the prospects of joint action in such a move, but there was very little encouragement extended.[22]

At the annual Iowa Farmers' Union convention in 1931, a resolution was passed asking for "a farmers' buying, selling and tax-paying strike" to be called unless the necessary remedial legislation was forthcoming. The convention instructed the president to name a committee of three to confer with a similar committee that was expected to be selected by John A. Simpson, president of the national Farmers' Union, to launch the movement. The Iowa convention described an acceptable farm program as one that included the following five points: inflation of the currency, increased graduated income taxes, higher inheritance and gift taxes, restrictions on federal borrowings, and the confiscation of wealth in times of war.[23]

By March, 1932, some progress was reported in getting the farm strike under way. Mass meetings had been scheduled for Grinnell, Webster City, Fort Dodge, Harcourt, and other places, and progress in organization was in evidence in Harrison, Cedar, Hamilton, and Marion counties. A farmers' convention held in Des Moines on May 3 voted to launch a strike beginning on July 4, the date selected apparently being to give a patriotic touch to the movement. The slogan for the campaign was "Stay at Home —Buy Nothing—Sell Nothing." The name "farm holiday" was adopted because the term "holiday" had been chosen by the banks which had closed and made it impossible for farmers to withdraw their money. If the bankers were entitled to a "holiday," so were the farmers.[24]

> Come, fellow farmers, one and all—
> We've fed the world throughout the years
> And haven't made our salt.
>
> We've paid our taxes right and left
> Without the least objection
> We've paid them to a government
> That gives us no protection.

22. *Iowa Union Farmer,* March 9, 1931.
23. *Des Moines Register,* September 9, 1931.
24. *Ibid.,* March 11, 1932; *Iowa Union Farmer* (Columbus Junction), May 4, 1932; *Farm Holiday News* (St. Paul), February 20, 1933.

> Let's call a "Farmers Holiday"
> A Holiday let's hold
> We'll eat our wheat and ham and eggs
> And let them eat their gold.[25]

When the movement was first considered in 1932, the purpose was simply to withhold products from market, especially if they sold below the cost of production. The movement was expected to last a month. By the fall of 1932, however, state units were in existence in Minnesota, South Dakota, North Dakota, Iowa, Montana, and other states; but at no time was it a cohesive, well-directed effort. From the start it appears to have been nothing more than a mob affair which first sought to keep farmers from marketing their products by peaceful means but next assumed the aspect of a group of angry, resentful men who wanted revenge against those of their kind who marketed their goods while they "picketed and struck."[26]

In August, 1932, when the strike officially began, farm prices were reported as follows: eggs, 22 cents; oats, 11 cents; butter, 18 cents—all of which were far below the cost-of-production levels named by the Farmers' Union. The farmers' cost of production, according to the Iowa group, had to take into account several items: 5 per cent on his real estate investment, 7 per cent on his personal property and equipment, and $100 per month for the farmers' own labor and management. The average farmer operating a 160-acre farm, in order to obtain these returns, had to receive 92 cents per bushel on corn, 49 cents per bushel on oats, $11.25 per hundred on hogs, 35 cents for eggs, and 62 cents for butterfat.[27]

The earliest attempt to launch the strike was made in the Sioux City area, where trouble resulted immediately. Roads were blockaded, fist fights broke out, arrests were made, and gun toting, exhortation, vituperation, picketing, storming of jails and capitol buildings, and stopping of trains and automobiles were among the other events that took place. In some places the old Populist cry of "Raise less corn and more hell" was heard; in others, Hoover was likened to Louis XIV, and the actions of

25. *Iowa Union Farmer*, March 9, 1932.
26. *Farm Holiday News*, February, 1933.
27. D. R. Murphy, "The Farmers Go on Strike," *New Republic*, LXXII (August 31, 1932), pp. 66–67.

the strikers were compared to those of the Boston Tea Party and William L. Garrison.[28] A patriotic tone was given when the Khaki Shirts of America, former members of the Bonus Expeditionary Force that had marched on to Washington, took the lead in blockading the Des Moines highways.[29]

Governors Bryan of Nebraska and Turner of Iowa both refused to call out the militia, thus leaving the matter of preserving peace to the local authorities. Businessmen, however, kept appealing to the governors for action. Finally, Governor Green of South Dakota announced that he had a plan for a conference of the fifteen chief executives of the agricultural states to promote an "orderly, practical, legal, and non-violent program for raising farm prices."

Criticisms against the strikers came from various sources. The liberal *Nation* referred to them as "rebels without ideas."[30] The Minnesota Farm Bureau, like other groups, conceded that the strike focused attention on the plight of the farmers, but charged that it failed to take into account factors that were of fundamental importance in determining prices, such as the tariff, purchasing power of the consumers, the monetary question, world competition, and the effects that the strike would have on the existing marketing machinery.[31]

What the strike achieved in the way of national publicity was offset by the lack of accomplishments; two victories scored by the milk producers in the Omaha area were erased shortly after it had ended. The *New York Journal of Commerce* said that as "a demonstration of the intensity of the economic depression ... the revolt of the farmers is deserving of serious consideration"; but "as a plan for raising farm prices ... it betrays a pathetic ignorance of the causes and the possible remedies for inadequate prices."[32]

When the governors' conference was set for September 9 in Sioux City,

28. W. T. Davis, "The Farmers' Holiday," *New Republic*, LXXII (September 21, 1932), p. 156.
29. "The Farmers' War for Higher Prices," *Literary Digest*, CXIV (September 10, 1932), p. 9.
30. "Rebels Without Ideas," *The Nation*, CXXXV (August 31, 1932), p. 184.
31. *Minnesota Farm Bureau News* (Central Edition, Grand Rapids), September 1, 1932.
32. Quoted in *Literary Digest*, CXIV (September 10, 1932), pp. 9, 11.

Reno ordered a temporary truce, but the farmers persisted in blockading the roads.[33] Before the governors met, there was a meeting of the strikers in Des Moines which drafted a plea asking the executives to endorse the food embargo.[34] About that time, George Shafer, the governor of North Dakota, refused a plea to declare an embargo on wheat with the aid of the state militia, charging that he had no constitutional authority to do so. Governor Floyd B. Olson of Minnesota, however, offered to declare an embargo on farm produce with the aid of state militia, providing that the governors of the neighboring states joined hands with him.[35] On September 9 representatives from nine farm states met in Sioux City to draft a program calling for tariff equality, currency expansion, more agricultural credit at lower interest rates, a moratorium on debts, and surplus-control legislation.[36]

This failed to quiet the holiday association. On September 18 its executive council called upon the grain and livestock farmers of the South and Middle West to declare a holiday; and if prices failed to reach a cost-of-production level within thirty days, then the strike would be extended to perishable products as well. At this time, the League For Independent Political Action, sponsoring a third-party movement, warned that the farmers of the Middle West were determined "to have relief either by ballots or by violence."[37]

Meanwhile, Reno and his associates were planning a parade of farmers in Des Moines for October 4, the date that President Hoover had selected to open his campaign for re-election.[38] Stories circulated to the effect that the Republican national headquarters were worried that hostile demonstrations would break out, and it was felt that the proposed American Legion escort ought to be strengthened by adding companies of regular army soldiers stationed near Des Moines.[39] Democratic leaders also were fearful lest hostile demonstrations against the President hurt the Democratic party; hence Iowa leaders were asked to discourage any such moves.

33. *New York Times,* September 1–3, 1932.
34. *Ibid.,* September 7, 9, 1932.
35. *Fargo Forum,* September 8, 1932.
36. *New York Times,* September 10, 12, 1932.
37. *Ibid.,* September 19, 1932.
38. *Ibid.,* September 25, 1932; *Minneapolis Journal,* September 26, 1932.
39. *New York Times,* October 1, 1932.

On October 4, a few hours before the speech, an estimated crowd of two thousand farmers paraded through the downtown area in protest against Hoover. Among the paraders was Senator Smith W. Brookhart, who had supported Hoover in 1928. Although the demonstration was peaceful, anti-Hoover sentiment in the traditionally Republican state of Iowa was very strong. Some of the placards read: "In Hoover we trusted; now we are busted"; "Cost of production only will save our homes"; "Mr. Curtis: We are not so damned dumb in 1932. Signed Mr. and Mrs. Iowa Farmer"; "Hoover, Hyde, Hell and Hard Times. The Republican 4-H Club." [40]

Angry mobs of farmers must have had some effect on the politicians and others who dared break the strike lines, but there is no evidence that the low prices were cowed by them. In a few regions there were increases in fluid-milk prices; but in other areas the tendency was to flood the market with goods and hence depress prices. For instance, livestock shipments into the Iowa markets were slowed down, but those flowing into the Chicago area were increased and prices lowered. Also, farmers and railroads in the nonstriking areas captured the business of those in striking communities. Truckers who had purchased their trucks on the installment plan stopped their monthly payments because of the strike; some had their trucks taken away and even lost their equities. In Minnesota stories of connivance on the part of holiday leaders were reported. Some were said to have hurried their produce to market before the lid was "clamped down." Market quotations were also lower after than before the strike.[41]

Strike activities slowed down, or else were modified, as 1932 turned into 1933, presumably for the purpose of allowing the new administration to show what it was going to do, and also because of the passing of the marketing season.

One major exception was in the state of North Dakota. There prominent political figures—Congressman Bill Lemke, Usher L. Burdick, later elected to Congress, state legislators, and Farmers' Union leaders—took part. In a convention held in Bismarck early in 1933 strongly worded resolutions urged the farmers to organize councils of defense in each county

40. *Ibid.*, October 5, 1932; *Iowa Union Farmer*, October 5, 1932.
41. *Minnesota Farm Bureau News*, October 1, 1932.

... to prevent foreclosures, and any attempt to dispossess those against whom foreclosures are pending if started; and to retire to our farms, and there barricade ourselves to see the battle through until we either receive cost of production or relief from the unfair and unjust conditions existing at present; and we hereby state our intention to pay no existing debts, except for taxes and the necessities of life, unless satisfactory reductions in accordance with prevailing farm prices are made on such debts.

Other resolutions passed requested farmers to boycott the sale of agricultural repossessions and asked for the enactment of the Frazier bill and the voluntary allotment plan, provided that the prices set were not below the cost of production. President Roosevelt was asked to appoint as Secretary of Agriculture John A. Simpson, whom the North Dakotans regarded as "beyond question agriculture's most fearless and outstanding leader," and a middlewesterner as Secretary of the Treasury. They declared war "on the International bankers and lesser money barons," and said with melodramatic eloquence that the farm home, "the granite foundation of this great republic," must be preserved, for if "that shall crumble, the Government itself must fall."[42]

On March 12 and 13, 1933, less than ten days after Roosevelt took the oath of office, the national convention of the Farm Holiday Association assembled in Des Moines.[43] The motto was "The Farmer Feeds the World and Deserves His Pay." When the convention was called to order, there were delegates present from Montana, North Dakota, Minnesota, Wisconsin, Iowa, Illinois, Ohio, Nebraska, and Kansas; representatives from Colorado, South Dakota, Oklahoma, and Texas were expected to arrive later, and still other states had reported that delegates had been selected but they could not arrive because the bank holiday had made it almost impossible for them to obtain funds to cover their expenses.

Resolutions again were passed calling for prices based on cost of production; moratoria on rural and urban properties; and the exercise of the right of eminent domain by the federal government to take away land from insurance and mortgage companies "on a fair basis of settlement" and to reopen this land for settlement by "actual home-owners" according to the provisions of the Frazier bill, which empowered the government

42. *Farm Holiday News,* February 20, 1933.
43. *Iowa Union Farmer,* March 8, 1933.

to "refund and refinance" land indebtedness, to assume broader control over the money system of the country, and to reach a common understanding with labor, for both were "exploited by the capitalistic owners of the means of production and distribution." These resolutions were accompanied by a warning to the nation's lawmakers that unless legislation was forthcoming in compliance with these demands by May 3, the Farm Holiday Association would prepare for a marketing strike within ten days after the expiration of that date.[44]

Early in 1933 the protestors dropped the farm-strike formula and resorted to the stopping of eviction sales and the waging of agitation to enact moratorium legislation. Forced sales were broken up in Wisconsin, Iowa, and Minnesota, where the holiday movement was the strongest, and also in Nebraska and South Dakota. On January 19, 1933, Governor Clyde Herring of Iowa issued a proclamation asking insurance and mortgage companies to cease making foreclosures until the state was in the position to act. Most of the important life insurance companies holding such mortgages replied that they had been pursuing a policy of leniency with "owner-operators who were willing to cooperate with them," but that they continued "to prosecute foreclosures in cases where the farm was operated by a tenant or where the premises had been deserted."

Violence and ugly tempers, however, continued to flare up. One writer observed that "It became virtually impossible for a life company to prosecute a foreclosure in counties where the Association was strong, no matter how undeserving of consideration the borrower might be. Some few borrowers took advantage of this situation, refused to make any payments, and dared the companies to take action." It is said that the life insurance companies had little trouble with the farm holiday group where "owner-operators" were involved, and that the association "was much less inclined to take up cudgels in defense of nonowner-operators in danger of foreclosure."

Some creditors at times were prone to try to prosecute foreclosures and met with consequent trouble. In one case the agent of foreclosing finance company was "escorted some distance away" and $800 worth of goods were bought for $14. A horse and an automobile were reported sold for ten cents apiece. In North Dakota some sheriffs continued to make forced

44. *Farm Holiday News*, March 22, 1933; *Des Moines Register*, March 13, 1933.

sales despite the warning from the governor to refrain from so doing; when the sheriffs refused to comply, the governor threatened to call out the militia to force them to abide by his proclamation.

The worst case of violence occurred on April 27 in Le Mars, Iowa, when some six hundred persons broke into a courtroom and demanded of the presiding judge that he sign an agreement not to execute any more foreclosure sales. "When he refused, his assailants dragged him out of his courtroom. Upon continued refusal, he was blindfolded, taken to a crossroads, severely beaten, and threatened with death. He did not sign the agreement." This outbreak placed the county under martial law. The assailants were arrested and sentenced, and no further serious outbreaks were reported.[45]

Other action was taken to alleviate the burdens of the farmers. In Iowa, besides the issuance of the proclamation urging mortgagors to refrain from pressing their claims, the millage tax rate was reduced by one-fifth, the period of grace for tax bills was extended and moratoria on property were provided. A study of the financial condition of the State of Iowa, conducted by the Brookings Institution and made public in September, 1933, had recommended a 10 per cent reduction in the direct property tax and increased levies on incomes, business transactions, tobacco, and theaters.[46]

In Minnesota farmers and businessmen informed Governor Olson that the taxpayers would refrain from paying taxes unless state expenditures were cut by one-fourth. During the regular session of the legislature, beginning in January and ending in April, a number of relief measures were passed, perhaps the most drastic of their kind in the nation. In February a proclamation was issued forbidding foreclosures on farms and homes until May 1; this, in turn, was superseded by the act of the legislature which declared a two-year moratorium, extending to May 1, 1935.[47] State direct property taxes were reduced; a tax on individual incomes was enacted ranging up to 5 per cent on incomes over $10,000 to make up

45. Archibald M. Woodruff, Jr., *Farm Mortgage Loans of Life Insurance Companies* (New Haven, Conn., 1937), pp. 101–6.
46. *The New International Year Book, 1933* (New York, 1934), p. 375.
47. *Ibid.*, p. 505; *ibid.*, 1934, p. 433; J. S. McGrath and J. J. Delmont, *Floyd B. Olson* (St. Paul, 1937), pp. 232–33; Woodruff, *Farm Mortgage Loans of Life Insurance Companies*, pp. 108–15.

for what was lost as a result of the reduction in property taxes; some 4,000 miles of roads were to be added to the state highway system to provide more public work; sweeping powers were given the banking commissioner to aid in reorganizing the state banks; the insurance commissioner was granted sweeping powers to regulate insurance company loans; a special levy was placed on chain stores to produce $1,300,000 for state aid to public school districts; a tax of ten cents per pound was imposed on oleomargarine sold in the state; and state appropriations for the next two years were slashed nearly 20 per cent.[48]

Legislation was enacted in other states, too. In South Dakota a tax was enacted on not net but gross income; grace was extended in the payment of taxes; the general levy for 1934 was eliminated; and the assessed valuation of properties was reduced by over $144,000,000. In North Dakota Governor Langer issued a proclamation forbidding the forced sale of farm properties and later that year declared an embargo on all wheat shipments until the cost-of-production level was reached. In Wisconsin legislation which required the governor to levy a state tax when the balance had fallen below the two-million mark was repealed, and the statutory time during which farmers could redeem their property was extended to three years; milk was classed as a public utility and the state department of agriculture and markets was authorized to fix the price paid for it.[49]

In the spring of 1933 Arthur C. Townley, a veteran of other farm campaigns, was asking that Congress adopt a plan which called for the issuance of $1,000,000,000 in scrip to be used in the exchange of products between farmers and organized labor. His plan also provided that workers operate idle factories and plants in which the products needed by the farmers would be produced; the farmers, in turn, were to be pledged to accept the scrip when it was offered them as payment by labor. Townley told his farmer listeners that they could win this strike "if you can provide a plan by which all of these people can pay you cost of production."[50]

As had been predicted earlier, the Farm Holiday Association was to call a national farm strike unless prices had reached the cost-of-production

48. *The New International Year Book*, 1933, p. 504.
49. *Ibid.*, pp. 758, 611, 844.
50. *Farm Holiday News*, April, 1933; *Iowa Union Farmer*, May 3, 1933.

level. This was slated to begin on May 13. But the day before it was to start Governor Olson advised Reno from his hospital bed that the strike was ill advised and that it "would create more unfavorable sentiment toward relief than favorable." After some deliberations, holiday leaders finally agreed to call the strike off with the note that farm prices appeared to be rising, that the farmers were too busy with spring planting to give much attention to it, and further that there was a "sagging of interest" among the farmers. However, the leaders announced that they would closely watch the actions of the Roosevelt administration.[51]

51. *Farm Holiday News,* April, 1933.

A Prophet in Politics: The Public Career of Henry A. Wallace
EDWARD L. AND FREDERICK H. SCHAPSMEIER

FEW IOWANS have reached the pinnacle of national fame achieved by Henry A. Wallace. Born on a farm in Adair County in 1888, Wallace was graduated from Iowa State College (now Iowa State University) in 1910. He edited the family's highly reputable farm journal for several years prior to achieving national recognition as Secretary of Agriculture and ultimately running for the presidency of the United States.

Although active in the political arena for many years, Wallace's greatest lifetime interest was agriculture. As a teen-ager Wallace began experimenting with seed corn and his interest in agricultural genetics continued throughout his lifetime. In 1924 he developed a hybrid seed corn for commercial use and the Wallace family established the Pioneer Hi-Bred Corn Company to market this product. The same year Wallace assumed editorship of the family publication, *Wallaces' Farmer,* a position which he retained until 1933. During his tenure as editor he stressed the superiority of agrarian life and urged improvement of the farmers' economic status.

In 1933 Franklin Roosevelt appointed Wallace Secretary of Agriculture. He later served as Vice-President under Roosevelt and Secretary of Commerce under President Harry Truman. His final public act was to run for President on the Progressive Ticket in 1948, a move that tarnished his image because of association and support from many left wing groups.

In their article on this famous Iowan, Edward and Frederick Schapsmeier emphasize his public career. Their essay provides, however, a many-faceted view of Henry A. Wallace the scholar, the journalist, the geneticist, the humanitarian, the reformer, and, of course, the politician.

A PROPHET IN POLITICS: THE PUBLIC CAREER OF HENRY A. WALLACE

By Edward L. Schapsmeier
Illinois State University
And Frederick H. Schapsmeier
Wisconsin State University (Oshkosh)

As a political figure, Henry A. Wallace was one of the most colorful and controversial personalities to emerge out of the New Deal. With a distinctive agrarian argot, he often sounded like some latter-day prairie prophet summoning a lost generation to the Promised Land.

This unique idealist from Iowa preached reform and predicted the day would come when all Americans would live in affluence. His optimistic outlook brought hope to millions who were poverty stricken during the most dismal period of depression the nation had ever endured. Wallace was an audacious apostle of abundance in a decade when the people were unaccustomed to the pleasures of prosperity. He was labeled by some a dreamer of dreams and a misguided zealot, sincere but impractical. Critics overlooked the fact that he was the architect and successful administrator of massive farm programs. The Triple-A and the Ever Normal Granary were effective measures to raise rural income; they were neither chimerical nor utopian. The confused image of Henry Wallace, compounded by his ill-fated Progressive Party campaign in 1949, arose because of the dual nature of his political activity. As a knowledgeable agricultural economist, Wallace was both realistic and imaginative; but simultaneously he possessed an Edenic vision of a new America. His magnificent rhetoric of reform, punctuated by religious fervor, sought to initiate a transformation of society. The immediate objective was to render assistance to farmers, while the ultimate goal of his endeavor was the attainment of universal social justice.

As the third generation scion of the Wallaces of Iowa, agricultural leadership was part of the family tradition inherited by Henry A. Wallace. His grandfather, a f o r m e r

Presbyterian clergyman, was know affectionately throughout the Midwest as "Uncle Henry." He founded the *Wallaces' Farmer* in 1895 and acquired an outstanding reputation as a farm leader. The first Henry Wallace was appointed to the Country Life Commission in 1908 by President Theodore Roosevelt. This investigative committee discovered and reported a host of deficiencies existing in the rural sector of the economy. It suggested federal legislation to regulate railroads, curtail speculation relative to farm products and proposed means for implementing conservation programs on a vast scale. The report reflected the Progressive philosophy of its members, since it was calling for the use of positive government to aid in the development of a "scientifically and economically sound country life."[1] Some of the findings of the Country Life Commission prompted Congressional action during the Wilson administration, but the floodtide of federal intervention on behalf of the farmer did not come until 1933.

When the venerable Uncle Henry died in 1916, leadership of the family devolved upon Henry C. Wallace. Leaving his post as a professor in the Agriculture Department at Iowa State College (now Iowa State University), Ames, he assumed the editorship of the *Wallaces' Farmer*. The second Henry Wallace, a prominent l a y m a n in the Presbyterian Church, was thrust into public service during World War I. Upon the request of Herbert Hoover, the Food Administrator, Wallace assisted in the formation of a Swine Commission to devise a price formula to increase the production of pork and lard.[2]

In 1920, Henry C. Wallace wrote campaign speeches for Senator Warren G. Harding and, after the Ohioan's victory, became the Secretary of Agriculture. Once in the cabinet, Wallace established the Bureau of Agricultural Economics

---

[1] U. S. Country Life Commission, Report of the Country Life Commission, 60th Cong., 2nd Sess., Senate Document No. 705, pp. 13-20 (Washington, 1909), as quoted in Wayne D. Rasmussen, ed., *Readings in the History of American Agriculture* (Urbana, 1960), 191.

[2] See the Herbert C. Hoover-Henry C. Wallace correspondence and the Report of the Evvard Commission, Food Administration File, Herbert C. Hoover Archives, Hoover Institution On War, Revolution, And Peace (Stanford University).

Henry C. Wallace Taking Oath of Office as Sec. of Agriculture, Succeeding Edwin T. Meredith; R. M. Reece Administering Oath.

and was instrumental in securing administration backing for a considerable amount of remedial legislation.[3] The advent of Coolidge to the presidency brought an end to federal aid for

---

[3] Legislation which was beneficial to agriculture included: extension of the War Finance Corporation, increased capital for the Federal Land Banks, an agricultural representative was placed upon the Federal Reserve Board, Packers and Stockyards Act, Grain Futures Act, cooperatives were exempted from anti-trust prosecution and the Intermediate Credit Act. See the cabinet papers of Henry C. Wallace in the Warren G. Harding Papers (The Ohio Historical Society, Columbus).

the farmer. The unexpected illness and subsequent death of Henry C. Wallace in 1924 deprived the rural populace of an important spokesman within an administration whose interest was focused on fostering private enterprise—and not upon rendering government assistance to agriculture. Even though the Farm Bloc in Congress twice passed the McNary-Haugen Bill to set up a federal agency to dispose of surpluses in overseas markets, the effort was sternly rebuked with vetoes from the White House.[4]

It was during this arid era of Coolidge that the young Henry A. Wallace made the *Wallaces' Farmer* into the most influential farm journal in the nation. The third Wallace was, perhaps, the best qualified of the trio. He was the legatee of the family's heritage and continued the practice of fusing agrarian idealism with agricultural realism. As a student at Iowa State College, he had majored in agronomy—but made a serious study of economics. At that time Wallace came under the influence of Professor Benjamin H. Hibbard, who was to impress upon him a fact he would never forget, namely, that high tariffs were harmful and not helpful to agriculture.[5]

In an effort to broaden his knowledge, Wallace took additional courses at Drake University and read widely in history and economics. His scholarly pursuits led him to the works of Thorstein Veblen. The iconoclast and erratic genius, whom Wallace met only once, became his mentor in economics. Wallace embraced institutional economics as though it were divine revelation. It provided him with a conceptual framework and also confirmed his suspicion that the farmer was the victim of a price system controlled by businessmen whose only interest was private gain. He became aware of the adverse effect of competition, individualism, and laissez faire

---

[4]The position of Henry C. Wallace was a precarious one. Wallace supported passage of the McNary-Haugen Bill, whereas the administration opposed it. Had death not intervened, he may well have been forced to resign his cabinet position. See Case File 1-1A1, Calvin Coolidge Papers, Library of Congress and Department of Commerce, Agricultural Files, Herbert Hoover Archives (West Branch, Iowa).

[5]Henry A. Wallace, "Seminar In Economics," in Russell Lord, ed., *Democracy Reborn, Selected from Public Papers and Edited with an Introduction and Notes* (New York, 1944), 96; Benjamin Horace Hibbard, *Marketing Agricultural Products* (New York, 1921), 281.

economics as it pertained to the farm population. So profound and pervasive was Veblen's impact upon Wallace's thinking, institutional economics became a basic tenet of his political philosophy. When Veblen died in 1929, Wallace penned the following eulogy for his economic tutor: "One hundred years from now people will read Veblen's books and realize that he was one of the few men of the early twentieth century who really knew what was going on."[6] In 1937, as the Secretary of Agriculture, he was still confident that *The Theory of the Leisure Class* and *The Theory of Business Enterprise* were two books which had to be classified "among the most powerful produced in the United States in this century."[7] Wallace believed Veblen's work so valuable, he even recommended to President Roosevelt in 1940 that he read *Imperial Germany And The Industrial Revolution* and *An Inquiry Into The Nature Of Peace And The Terms Of Its Perpetuation.*[8]

While at college, Wallace developed a keen interest in mathematics and the use of statistical studies as a scientific tool. His prowess as a geneticist was proven even as a teenager and, during his college years, he continued to experiment with hybrid corn. His genius in this field assured ultimate success to the Pioneer Hi-Bred Corn Company, a commercial venture he started in 1926. The company prospered, ultimately becoming a multi-million dollar concern.

After his graduation in 1910, Wallace persuaded Iowa State College to establish a statistical laboratory. Wallace's private research covered a wide range of interests. They included price analyses in the cost of production of agricultural commodities, ascertaining the relationship of weather factors on crop yields and studies relating to the effect of extra-terres-

---

[6]HAW, "Odds and Ends," *Wallaces' Farmer,* vol. 54 (August 30, 1929), 1167. The "O & E" was a signed article that appeared in each issue of the paper. Herinafter the *Wallaces' Farmer* will be cited as *WF.*

[7]HAW, "The Power Of Books," Address at the *New York Times* Book Fair, New York City, November 4, 1937, RG 16, National Archives.

[8]Letter, HAW to FDR, April 1, 1940 with enclosure: "Review Of The Book 'Imperial Germany and The Industrial Revolution' Written By Thorstein Veblen In Early 1915" By Henry A. Wallace and "Postscript to Review"; Letter HAW to FDR, March 30, 1940, PSF, Franklin D. Roosevelt Library (Hyde Park, New York).

trial bodies upon the earth's climate.⁹ As early as 1915, the *Wallaces' Farmer* began publishing his corn-hog ratio price charts and in 1925 he co-authored, with mathematician George Snedecor, the work *Correlation and Machine Calculation*. Wallace sought to inform farmers of the importance of economics and in so doing relate to them the significance of tariffs, wage levels, consumer demand, foreign markets and land values. It was in this area, as a publisher, that Wallace performed his greatest service to rural leaders, for he also enlightened them on such matters as war debts, reparations, currency exchange rates, international credit and monetary reform.¹⁰ He, unlike the heads of many farm organizations, viewed agriculture in its totality. His scope was international. He tried to rid farm leaders of their narrow provincialism. Farms were not isolated units, Wallace kept insisting, but were collective parts of world production.

In a scholarly work, *Agricultural Prices*, Henry A. Wallace arrived at some startling conclusions. This study, issued in 1920, was based upon the analyzation of market receipts at Chicago, records of bank clearings, and a tabulation of cost

⁹HAW, "Mathematical Inquiry Into The Effect Of Weather On Corn Yield In The Eight Corn Belt States," *Monthly Weather Review*, vol. 48 (August, 1920), 439-446; Tape Interview-1960, HAW interviewed by Dorothy Kehlenbeck, Iowa State History Collection (Iowa State University, Ames); Letter, Dr. R. E. Buchanan to authors, February 28, 1964; *Annual Report, 1962-1963*, The Statistical Laboratory, Iowa State University, Ames, Iowa, p. 3; Interview with George W. Snedecor, April 18, 1964; HAW, "The Moon And The Weather," *WF & IH*, vol. 53 (May 31, 1930), 1032; "Hot Weather And The Planets," *WF & IH*, vol. 55 (July 26, 1930), 1270; HAW, Review of *The Corn And Hog Surpluses Of The Corn Belt*, by Alonza E. Taylor, *Journal of Farm Economics*, XIV (July, 1934), 510. The *Wallaces' Farmer* merged with the *Iowa Homestead* in 1929, hence the designation WH & IH.

¹⁰"Board Of Trade Speculation," *WF*, vol. 53 (November 30, 1928), 1636; "Tariff And The Farmer," *WF*, vol. 53 (December 28, 1929); 1812; "The New Tariff And Agriculture," *WF*, vol. 54 (June 14, 1929), 873; "Cancelling The War Debts," *WF & IH*, vol. 55 (December 27, 1930), 1976; "Let Us Have More Nation Planning," *WF & IH*, vol. 56 June 6, 1931), 270; "Cutting Down The Surplus," *WF & IH*, vol. 55 (April 5, 1930), 678; "Governor Of The Bank Of England," *WF & IH*, vol. 56 (April 18, 1931), 540; "Time For The Reserve Banks To Act," *WF & IH*, vol. 57 (January 9, 1932), 37; "Ending The Depression Of Plenty," *WF & IH*, vol. 57 (April 16, 1932), 220; "Farm Debts And The Price Level," *WF & IH*, vol. 57 (January 23, 1932), 32.

factors in commodity production. He claimed the so-called free market operated to the disadvantage of the farmer. First, agricultural products were dumped on the market in such a way as to drive prices down and secondly, he discovered the market was actually manipulated in favor of the buyers. Impaled upon the cornucopia of overproduction, the individual farmer could do nothing to help himself. Wallace advised organized effort among farmers. "They will find it necessary," he predicted, "to practice sabotage in the same scientific businesslike way as labor and capital." In addition to deliberate curtailment of production to sustain high prices, he called for an abolition of the "speculative or market price system." The price-fixing authority granted to the government during World War I, Wallace pointed out, was federal intervention for the purpose of managing the economy. Why could it not be done again? No system was sacred and reforms were urgently needed. The farmer received inadequate remuneration for his labor and some change had to be made to assure tillers of the soil at least the cost of their production. Reflecting the influence of Veblen upon his own thought, Wallace cited the need for institutional reform and the necessity for specific economic "machinery." The former meant an alteration of attitudes and habits (e.g. competition and individualism), while the later invited the creation of special agencies to assist the farmer. Such guidance of the economy, Wallace insisted, would stabilize the "violent fluctuations in supply and demand" and would remove personal profit as the "sole motive" for incentive. The primary criteria for controlling the productive capacity of both the farm and factory would be the nation's general welfare. Private exploitation would, in effect, be supplanted by the superior needs of the masses. Needless to say, this type of thinking was equated with Bolshevism in 1920.

The plight of the farmer worsened during the twenties and thirties. The plague of surpluses continued. Technology, such as the tractor and improved farm machinery, increased the output of food and fiber; while domestic consumption diminished and overseas markets disappeared. President Hoover

[11] HAW, *Agricultural Prices* (Des Moines, 1920), 1-17, 27-28, 109-110.

approved the Agricultural Marketing Act of 1929, but the Federal Farm Board it established had no mechanism for preventing excess production. What little assistance was rendered in efficient marketing was negated by other factors. Tightened purse strings due to the severity of the depression, the Hawley-Smoot Tariff and the tangled war debt-reparations problems all served to reduce the demand for agricultural commodities. Wallace used his farm journal to agitate for measures geared to stimulate buying. He urged a lowering of the tariff, cancellation of war debts, drastic reduction of reparations, loans to foreign countries, international monetary agreements, devaluation of the dollar, and an easy credit policy on the domestic scene.[12] As the national economy ground to a halt and showed signs of stagnation, Wallace urged public works, a moratorium on debts and public relief for suffering people.[13] Herbert Hoover, however, remained faithful to his economic dogma. He acted—but with a cautious timidity.

The suffering caused by the depression, and the cruel paradox of poverty amid plenty, served as a catalyst. Henry A. Wallace, while proffering practical solutions, could not refrain from preaching the need for economic reforms leading to a more equitable distribution of the nation's wealth. Compelled by conscience to speak out, he believed the time had

[12]Future Price Trends, Gold And The Farmer," WF, vol. 52 (October 28, 1927), 1396; "For An Honest Dollar," WF & IH, vol. 56 (January 17, 1931), 66; "Tariff Insanity Is World-Wide," WF & IH, vol. 56 (May 9, 1931), 332; "Support Hoover's Program On Moratorium," WF & IH, vol. 56 (November 14, 1931), 1176; "Two Roads Lead Up; One Down," WF & IH, vol. 57 (March 19, 1932), 158; "Foreign Trade And The Depression," WF & IH, vol. 55 (January 31, 1930), 130; Wallace was a long-time vice president of the Stable Money Association and vigorously supported the commodity dollar idea. See Irving Fisher, *Stable Money, A History Of The Movement* (New York, 1934); Letter, HAW to authors, August 4, 1963; Interview with Irving Norton Fisher, Jr., June 27, 1963; Correspondence between HAW and James Harvey Rogers, Papers of James Harvey Rogers (Yale University); Collection of Regional History and Papers of George F. Warren, Olin Research Library (Cornell University).

[13]"Out Of A Job," WF & IH, vol. 55 (June 14, 1930), 1104; "To Bring Back Prosperity," WF & IH, vol. 55 (December 20, 1930), 1954; "Sending Grain To Drouth Sufferers," WF & IH, vol. 56 (February 21, 1931), 250; "Deal Thy Bread To The Hungry," WF & IH, vol. 56 (April 11, 1931), 508; "Depression And The Churches," WF & IH, vol. 57 (September 17, 1932), 485.

come for a total social transformation. The "prophets of both the Old and the New Testament," he affirmed, had a "firm grasp of the fundamental essence of all economics and sociology, namely, justice."[14] To Wallace it was a social sin to tolerate a condition where "whole classes of our people are impoverished at the same time as other classes are made rich."[15] The spectacle of want and privation moved Wallace to editorialize: "So far as the economics of the situation is concerned, Isaiah, 'Uncle Henry' and the modern economists who talk about increasing the consumer's purchasing power are recommending the same cure for hard times. This cure is simply that a greater percentage of the income of the nation be turned back to the mass of the people."[16]

By 1932, Wallace and most of the farm leaders were completely disenchanted with the G.O.P. As the paladin of rugged individualism, Herbert Hoover's impotence in dealing with the calamitous events brought disrepute to his economic philosophy. Franklin D. Roosevelt, well aware of agrarian discontent, took the initiative in making contact with Henry Wallace. The Governor of New York encouraged insurgency and realized he must first win over the farm leaders. A fine reception was accorded to Henry Wallace as he met with the Democratic nominee at Hyde Park. The Iowa editor told his rural readers that Roosevelt revealed a surprising "knowledge and sympathy" for agriculture. "He is better fitted than most," he concluded, "to draw the right kind of men to him."[17] With the favorable image of Roosevelt still in his mind, Wallace informed his friend, William Hirth (editor of the *Missouri Farmer*), that the Democratic nominee was a "most charming gentleman with the right kind of spirit and an open mind."[18]

---

[14]"Biblical Denunciation Of Hoarders," *WF & IH*, vol. 57 (September 3, 1932), 460.
[15]HAW, "O & E," *WF & IH*, vol. 58 (February 4, 1933), 49.
[16]"Deal Thy Bread To The Hungry," *WF & IH*, vol. 56 (April 11, 1931), 508.
[17]HAW, "Sizing Up Eastern Attitudes, Editor Talks With Governor Roosevelt At Luncheon Meeting," *WF & IH*, vol. 57 (September 3, 1932), 460.
[18]Letter, HAW to William Hirth, August 20, 1932, Papers of William Hirth, Western Historical Manuscripts Collection (University of Missouri).

F.D.R. cemented the allegiance of Wallace by asking him to assist in the drafting of a major farm speech. The address, given at Topeka, Kan., on Sept. 14, 1932, committed Roosevelt to the Voluntary Domestic Allotment Plan.[19] This proposal, as codified by M. L. Wilson of Montana State College (now Montana State University), represented the cumulative efforts of many economists.[20] Wallace had been its vigorous champion since 1930. It was a plan to curtail excess production by utilizing acreage allotments with federal supervision. Wallace viewed it as a practical way to cut surpluses and regarded it as a valuable social tool to foster a sense of cooperation among independent farmers.[21] It was the very mechanism he had written about in 1920. The VDAP became the essence of the first Triple-A program in 1933.

The leadership displayed by Roosevelt during the campaign struck a responsive chord within Henry Wallace. The Iowan once wired F.D.R., "It is heart warming to work for appreciation such as yours."[22] In order to win the farm vote for the New York Governor, Wallace wrote an unequivocal endorsement: "Roosevelt is progressive and definitely sympathetic to the farm program. . . . The only thing to vote for in this election is justice for agriculture. With Roosevelt, the farmers have a chance—with Hoover, none."[23]

Following Roosevelt's convincing triumph, he asked Wal-

[19]FDR, "A Restored and Rehabilitated Agriculture," *The Public Papers and Addresses of Franklin D. Roosevelt, with a Special Introduction and Explanatory Notes by President Roosevelt*, Samuel I. Rosenman, collator, (13 vols., New York, 1938-1950), 1932 volume (New York, 1938), 699ff.
[20]The VDAP was the cumulative product of William J. Spillman, John D. Black, Howard R. Tolley, and Milburn L. Wilson. See William J. Spillman, *Balancing The Farm Output, A Statement of the Present Deplorable Conditions of Farming, Its Causes and Suggested Remedies* (New York, 1927); John D. Black, *Agricultural Reform In The United States* (New York, 1929); Letters, HAW to M. L. Wilson, March 24, 1930 and MLW to HAW, April 21, 1930, Papers of M. L. Wilson, Montana State University, Bozeman); Howard R. Tolley, Oral History Collection (Columbia University, New York City).
[21]HAW, "Voluntary Domestic Allotment Plan," *WF & IH*, vol 57 (December 24, 1932), 669, 678.
[22]Telegram, HAW to FDR, August 30, 1932, PPF 41, Franklin D. Roosevelt Library.
[23]HAW, "O & E," *WF & IH*, vol. 57 (October 29, 1932), 565.

lace to join his cabinet. With an intense desire to participate in an administration pledged to action, Wallace accepted the position of Secretary of Agriculture. With zeal and speed, he set about getting a farm bill written so as to take advantage of the emergency session of Congress. His first fight was to repel the onslaught of rural representatives, who were eager to enact every Populist panacea ever enunciated. The final product, the Agricultural Adjustment Act of 1933, was the handiwork of professors, not that of neoPopulists. Wallace and administration supporters thwarted wild schemes that included total price fixing (tantamount to nationalizing the land) and mandatory inflation laws (including the printing of paper money).[24] Economists conceived and carried out the Triple-A program. Its aim was threefold: control of production, elevation of farm income and the inducement of cooperation among the total farm population. The AAA worked with County Committees, set quotas, and enforced compliance.[25]

As acreage allotment payments and government loans began to flow into the farm belt, the rural revolt subsided and threats of violence diminished. The AAA raised income levels of commercial producers while preserving the family sized farm. Little, however, was done to aid the downtrodden sharecropper of the South until Congress passed the Bankhead-Jones Farm Tenancy Act in 1937. A stunning blow came on Jan. 6, 1936, when the Supreme Court declared the AAA unconstitutional. Appalled by the legal logic of the justices,

[24] Rexford G. Tugwell, New Deal Diary, Franklin D. Roosevelt Library; Testimony of HAW, U. S. Senate, Committee on Agriculture and Forestry, *Hearings* on H.R. 3835, *Agricultural Emergency Act to Increase Farm Purchasing Power*, 73rd Cong., 1st Sess., 1933 (Washington, D. C., 1933, 129; Letter, John A. Simpson (President of the Farmers' Union Division of Manuscripts University of Oklahoma, Norman); Elmer Thomas, "40 Years A Legislator," Unpublished Manuscript, 1951, 433 pp., Elmer Thomas Papers (University of Oklahoma); HAW, *New Frontiers* (New York, 1934).

[25] Edward A. O'Neal, "Rebirth Of Agriculture," Radio Address delivered over N.B.C., March 10, 1934, Copy of Manuscript sent to Marvin H. McIntyre, March 13, 1934, PPF 1820, Franklin D. Roosevelt Library; Letter, George N. Peek to FDR, December 15, 1933, Papers of George N. Peek (University of Missouri); Louis H. Bean, Oral History Collection; Interview with Mordecai Ezekiel, December 19, 1963; Interview with Chester C. Davis, August 9, 1963; Letter, M. L. Wilson to authors, August 15, 1963.

Wallace hastened to secure a substitute measure to circumvent the high tribunal's ruling. The Soil Conservation and Domestic Allotment Act of 1936, primarily the work of Howard R. Tolley, was enacted as an interim program.[26] The permanent plan, which would come with the passage of the Agricultural Adjustment Act of 1938, was the product of Wallace's fertile mind.[27] It de-emphasized acreage reduction and stressed storage as a means of handling surpluses. The Commodity Credit Corporation was the instrument used to control the marketing of agricultural commodities. After the Farm Security Administration was established, to aid sharecroppers and tenants, and the Food Stamp program as inaugurated to assure adequate diets for low income families; Henry Wallace felt satisfied. He had helped agriculture while making it serve the general welfare.[28]

When it became obvious the nation was slipping into a recession in 1937, Wallace tried to arouse the President into taking counter-measures to check the decline. "I know you will not let us get into a downward spiralling Hoover tail spin," he wrote to Roosevelt, "even though private capital

---

[26] Letter, Homer Cummings to FDR, November 19, 1935, Franklin D. Roosevelt Library; HAW, "Unconstitutional," Radio Address, January 7, 1936, in Lord, ed., *Democracy Reborn, Selected Public Papers*, 108; HAW, *Whose Constitution, An Inquiry Into The General Welfare* (New York, 1936); Howard R. Tolley; Oral History Collection; Memorandum, HAW to Grace Tully, March 19, 1936, OF AD, Franklin D. Roosevelt Library.

[27] "The Storage of Food," *WF*, vol. 43 (December 6, 1918), 1772; "The Ever Normal Granary," *WF*, vol. 51 (October 8, 1926), 1314; "Joseph, Confucius And The Farm Board," August 19, 1936, in Lord, ed. *Democracy Reborn, Selected Public Papers*, 117-118; HAW, Press Conference, February 10, 1937, RG 16, National Archives; HAW, "The New Agricultural Adjustment Act," *Prairie Farmer*, vol. 110 (February 26, 1938), 1-2.

[28] *Food And Life, Yearbook of Agriculture 1939.* USDA (Washington, D. C., 1939); Interview with Milo Perkins, December 20, 1963; HAW to FDR, February 15, 1938, OF 1, Franklin D. Roosevelt Library; Will Alexander, Oral History Collection; Rexford G. Tugwell, "The Resettlement Idea," *Agricultural History*, vol. 33 (October, 1959), 159-164; Letter, Henry C. Taylor to HAW, March 22, 1937, Papers of Henry C. Taylor (State Historical Society of Wisconsin, Madison); Gladys Baker and others, *Century of Service, the first 100 years of the United States Department of Agriculture* (Washington, D. C., 1963), 211-213.

should become completely demoralized."²⁹ Wallace outlined a comprehensive economic program, which included: public housing, "maintenance of farm purchasing power," labor legislation to sustain consumption, "cheap credit," encouragement of "private capital," and the use of "government capital . . . in case of need."³⁰

Wallace not only played the part of an economic adviser; but with Roosevelt's assent, he assumed the role of ideologist for the New Deal. Using pen and podium, Wallace continued to call for basic reforms. The unholy alliance of social Darwinism, laissez faire economics and the Protestant ethic had created a set of institutions based upon scarcity, he claimed, and the time had come to alter the mores and mental attitude of the American people to fit contemporary conditions. The complexities of an industrial-urban economy had made humans the unwilling victims of unemployment. Faith in frugality, rugged individualism and self reliance did nothing to alleviate the basic malady, namely, an economy that failed to serve the needs of the people. Co-operation, concern for the general welfare and a spirit of altruism, Wallace asserted, would make it possible to have the blessings of an economy of abundance. Technology made universal affluence feasible, he was sure, if only economists would assist in creating the social machinery needed to distribute the wealth equitably among the population. Through regulatory and reform legislation, he argued, the New Deal was fostering social justice. Using the lexicon of the Social Gospel, Wallace enunciated this litany of hope: "The religious keynote, the economic keynote, the scientific keynote of the new age must be the overwhelming realization that mankind now has such control over nature that the doctrine of the struggle for existence is definitely outmoded and replaced by the higher law of co-operation . . . then the vision of Isaiah and the insight of Christ will be on

---

²⁹Letter, HAW to FDR, November 30, 1937, PSF, Franklin D. Roosevelt Library.

³⁰HAW, "Agriculture, Business, Labor And Government," Washington Star Radio Forum, December 6, 1937, PSF, Franklin D. Roosevelt Library.

their way toward realization."[31] Conservative critics heaped scorn upon Wallace. Some labeled him a dangerous radical, while others lampooned his ideas as the apocalyptic daydreams of an impractical visionary. President Roosevelt, however, regarded him as a political asset. Wallace's pronouncements were popular with the electorate. F.D.R. also viewed his Secretary of Agriculture as a knowledgeable, imaginative, and effective administrator. His record and rhetoric, the President reasoned, were merely proof of Wallace's "practical idealism."[32] Thus he personally chose Henry A. Wallace as his running mate in 1940.

On July 30, 1941, President Roosevelt utilized powers granted to him by Congress to establish the Economic Defense Board. By executive order, F.D.R. made Vice President Wallace the Chairman. Soon after, Wallace was also designated Chairman of the newly created Supply Priorities and Allocation Board. In one stroke, Wallace became the most powerful Vice President up to that time.[33] The administrative power delegated to him by the President gave Wallace complete authority over "exports, imports, . . . preclusive buying, transactions in foreign exchange, . . . international investments and extension of credit;"[34] as well as discretionary power relative to the issuance of priorities for the "procurement, production, transmission of materials, articles, power fuel and other commodities."[35] After Pearl Harbor, the Economic Defense

[31] HAW, *America Must Choose, The Advantages and Disadvantages of Nationalism, of World Trade and of a Planned Middle Way* (Boston, 1934), 25.

[32] FDR, Acceptance Speech, 1940, in *Official Report of the Proceedings of the Democratic National Convention Held at Chicago, Illinois, July 15th to July 18th, inclusive 1940*, 255; See also James A. Farley, *Jim Farley's Story, The Roosevelt Years* (New York and Toronto, 1948), 293-294; Frances Perkins, *The Roosevelt I Knew* (New York, Evanston and London, 1964), 133; Letter, Richard Wilson to authors, August 5, 1963; Letter, Samuel I. Rosenman to authors, August 7, 1963; Eleanor Roosevelt, *This I Remember* (New York, 1949), 216.

[33] He utilized his position as a wartime administrator to enhance the war effort and to prepare for the postwar era. Many of his speeches were aimed at preparing public opinion for full international cooperation within the United Nations. See Henry Agard Wallace Papers, Library of Congress.

[34] FDR, *Public Papers*, 1941 volume, 290.

[35] *Ibid.*, 350.

Wallace Campaign Poster

Board was converted into the Board of Economic Warfare and its duties were increased to "advise the State Department on Lend-lease arrangements" and to "conduct negotiations for a post-war economic settlement."[36] Cordell Hull, the Secretary of State, complained that Roosevelt was "virtually creating another State Department"[37] and succeeded in getting the President to reduce some of the powers of the B.E.W. From a pinnacle of power in 1943, Wallace was to plummet to a position of lesser importance. His public controversy with Jesse Jones caused his downfall. Jones, as Secretary of Commerce and Director of the Reconstruction Finance Corporation, regarded Wallace and the B.E.W. as a bunch of "socialist-minded uplifters."[38] The R.F.C. controlled the funds for the B.E.W. and when Wallace and Jones clashed over authorizations for expenditures—Roosevelt summarily removed the Vice President from leadership of the vast wartime agency.[39] In 1944, F.D.R. decided to have Senator Harry S. Truman as his vice presidential candidate. As a consolation prize, Henry Wallace was given a choice of cabinet positions (except that of Secretary of State). He chose Jesse Jones' job. After a stormy hearing, Wallace was confirmed as the new Secretary of Commerce only after the R.F.C. and the office of Federal Loan Administrator were removed from the department's jurisdiction.[40] Jesse Jones, before departing into political exile in Texas, gave vent to his anger by testifying against Wallace's confirmation.

Within a month after Henry Wallace assumed his new

[36]*Ibid.*, 295-296, Letter, FDR to HAW, April 23, 1942, OF 4226, BEW, Franklin D. Roosevelt Library.

[37]Cordell Hull, *The Memoirs of Cordell Hull* (New York, 1949), II, 1154.

[38]Jesse Jones with Edward Angly, *Fifty Billion Dollars, My Thirteen Years With The RFC (1932-1945)* (New York, 1951), 491.

[39]Letter, FDR to HAW, July 15, 1943, FDR, *Public Papers*, 1943 volume, 298; Letter, Leo T. Crowley to authors, March 3, 1964.

[40]Edwin W. Pauley, "Why Truman Is President," as told to Richard English, unpublished memorandum, 37 pp.; Samuel I. Rosenman, *Working With Roosevelt* (New York, 1952), 438-439; Edward J. Flynn, *You're the Boss* (New York, 1947), 180; U. S. Senate, Committee On Commerce, *Hearings on S.375*, 79th Cong., 1st Sess., 1945, 24-84; U. S. *Congressional Record*, 79th Cong., 1st Sess., 1945, vol. 91, Part I, 693.

office, Franklin D. Roosevelt was dead. The mantle of leadership, which for a season seemed destined for Wallace, now passed to the man from Missouri. Wallace's devotion to Roosevelt was never transferred to Truman. As Secretary of Commerce, he proceeded to outline his own program for both domestic and foreign affairs. To insure post-war prosperity, Wallace proposed a plan whereby the government would commit itself to a policy of full employment. It was imperative, he asserted in his book *Sixty Million Jobs* (published in 1945), that Congress immediately "equip government with authority to act in immediate co-operation with private enterprise once incipient unemployment points to the danger of mass unemployment."[41] Wallace envisaged an expanding e c o n o m y, spurred on by federal programs to encourage higher consumption. Fiscal policies should be planned, he urged to promote prosperity. His primary concern was to see the national economy balanced—not the budget. In this same volume, Wallace made many proposals which were anticipatory of things to come. He suggested foreign aid programs, an attack upon domestic poverty, health insurance, guaranteed annual wages, government sponsored research, public works, federal aid to education and civil rights legislation.[42]

Economists and academicians may have winced a bit at Wallace's reference to the "social ideas of the Sermon on the Mount,"[43] but *Sixty Million Jobs* was applauded by those of the Keynesian persuasion. Dr. Alvin H. Hansen, of Harvard University, praised the work as an "education in applied economics" and urged that it be "read and reread by every voter."[44] President Truman requested an autographed copy of the book, informing his Secretary of Commerce: "I have been reading the reviews and they seem to have really gone to town on them."[45] Truman assigned to Wallace the responsibility for overseeing that part of his legislative program dealing with

[41] HAW, *Sixty Million Jobs* (New York, 1945), 33.
[42] *Ibid.*, 49, 111, 116, 126-133, 142, 185.
[43] *Ibid.*, 208.
[44] Alvin H. Hansen, *Economic Policy And Full Employment* (New York and London, 1947), 307.
[45] Letter, HST to HAW, September 10, 1945, OF, Harry S. Truman Library (Independence, Missouri).

federal assistance to small business and government support for the construction of airports.[46] Wallace was zealous in his attempts to help small businessmen. He reorganized the Department of Commerce, which had been neglected by his predecessor (Jesse Jones was more interested in administering the affairs of the Reconstruction Finance Corporation), and sub-divided the Bureau of Foreign and Domestic Commerce into five major offices: International Trade, Small Business, Domestic Commerce, Business Economics, and Field Operations. He asked for a 1946 appropriation of $163 million for his department that he might accomplish the following goals:

1. Promotion . . . of a large . . . foreign trade;
2. Specific services to business . . . in the fields of science, technology, management and marketing;
3. Basic statistical information for business . . . ;
4. To provide more adequate information on the economic situation . . . ;
5. Strengthening . . . the scientific and technical . . . functions of the Department.[47]

Since he was fully aware of the importance of science and technology in the postwar era, Wallace urged the President to inaugurate immediate plans to secure the services of German scientists. In a memorandum to Truman, dated Dec. 4, 1945, Wallace wrote: "The transfer of outstanding German scientists to this country for the advancement of our science and industry seems wise and logical." He even warned the President unless quick action was taken the most talented Germans would be acquired by "our allies, especially the U.S.S.R."[48]

Henry Wallace was privy to the plan of Senator James E. Murray (D-Montana) for the formulation and introduction of a Full Employment Bill. This bill, which became the Employment Act of 1946, received the wholehearted support of the Secretary of Commerce. It was a "mature document," he

---

[46]Letters; HST to HAW, October 4 and 19, 1945, OF, Harry S. Truman Library.

[47]HAW, "Program Of The Department Of Commerce," Statement by the Secretary of Commerce before a Subcommittee of the House Appropriations Committee, January 25, 1946. Papers of Alfred Schindler, Harry S. Truman Library.

[48]Memorandum, HAW to HST, December 4, 1945, OF, Harry S. Truman Library.

asserted, since it sought to "eliminate the deadly threat of instability." This "solemn commitment" on the part of the government to insure full employment was only the first step, he claimed, since action programs would have to follow if needed.[49] Even though Wallace was disappointed over the deletions that had to be made to secure enactment of the bill, he viewed the establishment of the Council of Economic Advisers to the President as an excellent mechanism for fostering intelligent policy making. Democratic planning, rational management of the economy and federal intervention to stimulate buying power were the three pillars upon which Wallace erected his post-war plans for prosperity. During the brief time he held the position as the Secretary of Commerce, Wallace labored inceasingly to assure implementation of policies that would prevent a recurrence of the tragic consequences of World War I.[50]

Wallace's increased involvement in foreign policy affairs ultimately caused his dismissal from the cabinet. His apprehension over the deterioration of Soviet-American relations prompted him to criticize United States foreign policy. When James F. Byrnes, the Secretary of State, complained to Truman, the President asked the Secretary of Commerce for his resignation.[51] Wallace became editor of the *New Republic* in 1946 and from that position launched his ill-fated third party movement. Wallace was sincere in his longings for peace, but his idealism ran rampant. With little comprehension of the aims of the Soviet Union, he more and more placed the onus for the Cold War upon his own country. "Those who put hatred of Russia in their feelings and actions," he wrote in the

[49]Statement by Secretary Henry A. Wallace on the Employment Act of 1946, March 4, 1946, Schindler Papers, Harry S. Truman Library; Letter, Leon H. Keyserling to authors, February 18, 1964; Stephen Kemp Bailey, *Congress Makes A Law* (New York, 1964).

[50]Interview with Mordecai Ezekiel, December 19, 1963; Letters to authors, Alfred Schindler, September 20, 1963; Philip Hauser, August 16, 1963; Bernard L. Gladieux, August 16, 1963; An Address by Henry A. Wallace, Secretary of Commerce, Before Triple-A Regional Meeting, St. Paul, Minnesota, January 10, 1946, Schindler Papers, Harry S. Truman Library.

[51]James F.Byrnes, *Speaking Frankly* (New York and London, 1947), 240, HST, Press Conference, September 20, 1946, Harry S. Truman Library; Harry S. Truman, *Memoirs* (Garden City, 1955), I, 560.

New Republic, "do not believe in peace." Wallace acted from deep convictions. He was motivated by a pacifistic hatred of war and a belief that international amity could be fostered by the application of Christian principles to international relations. "Peace, to endure," he avowed, "Must be built, not on force and deceit, but on understanding."[52] Unfortunately for Wallace, the Progressive Party of 1948 attracted Communists as well as sincere advocates of peace. Thus the taint of disloyalty rubbed off on Wallace and his quixotic crusade for peace ended his political career. A retroactive shadow of doubt, red in hue, was cast over all of his former ideas and activities. Even though he repudiated the Progressive Party in 1950 and supported the United States action in the Korean conflict, he could not undo the damage to his reputation caused by his futile campaign of 1948.[53]

During his long career in public life, Henry A. Wallace had matured from a rural rustic into an astute agricultural economist. Imbued with the Christian idealism of his grandfather and introduced into farm politics by his father, the youngest of the Henry Wallaces evolved his own religio-economic philosophy. Driven by an inner compulsion, he was relentless in his endeavors to bring about the attainment of universal social justice. In the realm of economics, his ideas were sometimes clear and realistic—but at other times were vague and impractical. He was always the conscience of the

---

[52] *New Republic,* vol. 116 (January 20, 1947), 3.

[53] Progressive Party Papers, Special Collections Library (University of Iowa); Papers of Helen Gahagan Douglas, Division of Manuscripts, University of Oklahoma; Papers of Robert Kenny, Bancroft Library, University of California, Berkeley; Curtis D. MacDougall, *Gideon's Army* (New York, 1965), 2 vols.; Jack Redding, *Inside The Democratic Party* (New York, 1958); Karl M. Schmidt, *Henry A. Wallace: Quixotic Crusade 1948* (Syracuse, 1960); Harold Lavine, "Progressives Last Stand," *Newsweek,* vol. 35 (March 6, 1950), 22-25; HAW, "How I'd Stop the March of Stalin," *Coronet,* vol. 29 (November, 1951), 103-108.

New Deal. As an unrelenting crusader, he never let the American people forget that social reforms were both necessary and possible. The moral precepts of the Sermon on the Mount were guides, economics a tool, and politics the means of implementing his ideals. Throughout his tumultuous career he sought to serve humanity. He never waivered from this pursuit, even though forced to endure political pillorying because of his beliefs. With faith in the future, he envisioned a world without war or want. In 1949, Henry Wallace spoke from the pulpit of the Community Church of New York City. In his sermon, he summarized his political philosophy:

> The Kingdom of Heaven here on earth can only be attained when men in their politics, their daily work, their science, their art, their philosophy, and their religion are reaching out continuously for an even higher manifestation and appreciation of that blissful, unmanifested reality which we call God . . . The best way to praise God is right here on earth by helping Him to unfold his joyous plan for all humanity.

Henry A. Wallace spent his last years at Farvue Farm in South Salem, N. Y. The rural atmosphere of his home provided a quiet retreat from the turmoil of politics, but more important to him it was a welcome return to the open countryside. Wallace loved to work with plants and now he had the opportunity to resume his long neglected experiments in genetics. Each passing year was a thrill for him as he observed new and improved varieties of plant life emerge from the soil. A strange muscular affliction, amyotrophic lateral sclerosis, cut short his scientific endeavors. Death came on Nov. 18, 1965, at the age of 77 years. Before succumbing to this incurable malady, however, he allowed his pain wracked body to be used for medical experimentation. Realizing his own case was hopeless, he died knowing he had tried to help future sufferers of this dreadful disease. It was his last gesture of good will to mankind.

The Post World War II Legislative Reapportionment Battle in Iowa Politics
CHARLES W. WIGGINS

IN THIS SELECTION an Iowa State University political scientist, Charles Wiggins, presents documentation and analysis of Iowa's legislative reapportionment struggle as it has developed throughout the past twenty years. Clearly one of the major, if not *the* major political issue in Iowa's recent past, the reapportionment controversy reflects the makeup and orientation of the major political interest groups as well as the thinking and behavior of Iowa's political parties.

Beginning with Iowa's early statehood days, Wiggins presents a brief history of reapportionment. He then describes the positions and motivations of the various participants in the struggle, such as the Iowa Farm Bureau (conservative) and the Iowa League of Women Voters (liberal). Carefully detailing the attempts, both successful and unsuccessful, to implement change in the makeup of the legislature, he follows the episodes from the first attempt for reform in 1955 through the last court action in 1972.

What lies ahead for the Hawkeye State in the area of legislative redistricting and behavior? In other related research Professor Wiggins has predicted that as liberal urban forces gain strength and become better organized, we will see political parties play more active roles and political interest groups wield less influence.

A HISTORICAL ANALYSIS of the legislative reapportionment controversy in Iowa after World War II can be regarded as a useful exercise for several reasons. First, it tends to dramatize the fact that the Iowa governmental system, like that of any other state, cannot function as a completely autonomous, or independent, political decision-making unit if a significant federal interest lies in the issue area under consideration. Under our federal system of government in the United States and the national supremacy clause in the U.S. Constitution, the national government is always in a position, potentially at least, to impose a constraint upon the decision making of state governmental institutions. The study which follows emphasizes the role of the federal government, especially the role of the federal courts, in imposing constraints upon reapportionment decision making by two state governmental institutions—the Iowa general assembly and the Iowa supreme court.

An examination of the reapportionment controversy is useful also because it tends to bring into sharper focus the role of interest groups and political parties in Iowa politics. Reapportionment was viewed by the participant groups as being an especially salient question since it dealt with the basic allocation of political power and influence within the state political system. The manner in which seats in the general assembly were to be allocated was perceived by many interest groups as having a significant impact upon their ability to marshal support from future legislatures for their policies and programs. The political parties, on the other hand, viewed apportionment as being directly related to their ability to win elections and to capture control of one of the three major branches of Iowa government—the state legislature. Given its primacy, reapportionment was an issue in which the activities of interest groups and political parties became highly visible, with their spokesmen not only intensely lobbying legislators on the issue, but also frequently making distinct appeals to the electorate and becoming litigants in major court cases dealing with the question.

The reapportionment controversy is also interesting in that it tends to underscore the important role played by the Iowa supreme court within the state governmental system. The supreme court is the final interpreter of all questions surrounding what the various provisions in the state constitution really mean. Where federal laws or court decisions conflict with the Iowa constitution, the state court applies the federal standards when relevant to given cases, fully recognizing the supremacy clause in the national constitution. Unlike the other branches of state government, however, the state supreme court assumes a more passive posture in its decision making. Whereas legislators and governors may actively solicit support for a new program or policy, the supreme court must wait for someone to bring before it a case involving a critical policy question, such as reapportionment, before it becomes involved.

Early History of Apportionment

Throughout most of the nineteenth century, seats in the Iowa legislature were apportioned on the basis of population. Seats in the senate were apportioned among the counties according to population, while those in the house of representatives were apportioned among districts of up to four counties on the basis of population.[1] As long as Iowa was a state whose settled areas consisted mainly of sparsely scattered farms, no concern was directed at apportioning both chambers of the legislature on this basis. With the closing of the Iowa frontier toward the latter part of the 1800s, population growths and movements began to become rather uneven. Some areas, especially those with urban communities, grew at a much faster pace than other areas. The constitutional population requirements for apportioning seats in both houses of the legislature were followed until 1886, when regular redistricting was replaced by legislative inaction.

During the first half of the twentieth century, the legisla-

---

1. A review of early apportionment practices in Iowa is found in Robert B. McKay, *Reapportionment: The Law and Politics of Equal Representation* (New York: The Twentieth Century Fund, 1965), pp. 323–24.

ture became more rural-dominated and reluctant to apportion itself on a population basis. Two amendments to the Iowa constitution were approved, both of which subsequently were to make the apportionment of either chamber on a population basis virtually impossible. In 1904, an amendment was passed providing for a 108-member house of representatives with one representative from each county, except for the nine most populous counties which were granted two representatives. In 1928, another amendment was passed which provided that no county could have more than one senator in the 50-member senate, even though seats in the upper chamber were supposed to be allocated according to population. Presumably, urban residents were not numerous enough or enough aware of the implications of these amendments to obtain their defeat at the polls. Anyway, both amendments prevented any future apportioning of either chamber on a population basis.

Early Post World War II Developments

Reapportionment gradually developed into a major political issue during the decade following the end of World War II. The heightened interest in reapportionment at this particular point in time was probably partly a function of the fact that Iowans had more time to devote to state public policy considerations, given the absence of the demands generated by the war effort. Another factor related to this heightened interest was the recognition on the part of many citizens that significant urbanization had occurred in the state over the past several decades and was continuing to occur at a fairly steady pace. Whereas in 1900 only one-fourth of the state's residents lived in urban areas, by 1950 this figure had jumped to almost one-half. Given constitutional restrictions and legislative inaction, neither chamber of the legislature had been reapportioned to compensate for this redistribution in the state's population since 1886.

Conflict over reapportionment during the decade following World War II generally centered on the question of whether or not reapportionment was necessary at all. Conservative and, in most cases, rural interest groups argued that there was no need for reapportionment. These groups, most of whom wielded much influence in the legislature, argued that the malapportioned legislature had done an adequate job of serving the state's public policy needs over the years. The more liberal and, in most cases, urban proponents of reapportionment argued that steps should be taken to bring about reapportionment that would provide for greater urban representation in at least one chamber of the general assembly.

WHICH CHAMBER ON POPULATION?

Around 1955, the conservative interests changed their position on reapportionment, probably out of recognition for the increased public interest in and demand for some type of reapportionment. Their new position was one favoring reapportionment with the condition that adequate safeguards be provided to assure area representation in one chamber of the legislature. Their new position was translated into a proposed constitutional amendment—originally drafted in the headquarters of the Iowa Farm Bureau Federation—which eventually became known popularly as the Shaff Plan.[2] (David Shaff was a state senator from Clinton and the proposal's chief legislative sponsor.) The plan called for the apportioning of the senate on a population basis and the house on an area basis, with one representative from each county. In effect, the conservative, rural interests were proposing a plan which would have assured them a future veto power in one chamber.

The original proponents of reapportionment reacted to the new rural proposal from a mixed, yet still on the whole negative, perspective. While gratified that their opponents no longer completely opposed reapportionment, proponents of the more liberal, urban viewpoint argued that this "little federal" plan should not be the exact opposite of the national scheme. Instead, the state house of representatives should be apportioned along the same lines as its federal counterpart—meaning population—while the area factor should be given greater weight in the apportionment of the state senate as is the case with the upper chamber's federal counterpart. Besides, the members of the house were elected to shorter terms (two years) than members of the senate (four years) and would be more subject to changing public opinions about political issues.

2. For a brief period, Senator Stevens of Greene County was the plan's major legislative sponsor.

From 1955 to 1960, neither urban nor rural forces were able to muster enough strength in the legislature to pass a reapportionment plan. In order for an amendment to the Iowa constitution to be properly initiated by the legislature, it must pass both chambers in identical form by constitutional majority votes during two consecutive assemblies before being submitted to the electorate in a ratification referendum. But each side in the reapportionment controversy was not able to muster enough support for its proposal even for one assembly; better yet, each side was able to muster enough support to block passage of the other side's proposal during the 1955, 1957, and 1959 sessions. Undoubtedly, each side played upon the concerns of the members of the chamber most detrimentally affected by the other side's proposal. In other words, the urban forces tended to rely upon much senate opposition to the rural forces plan, while the rural forces were bolstered by opposition on the part of many representatives to the proposals advanced by the urban interests. Thus, both sides of the reapportionment conflict were effectively playing the game of "legislative checkmate."

Who Were The Liberal and Conservative Forces?

What interest groups tended to associate with the liberal forces on the reapportionment question? What groups tended to coalesce around the conservative position? In addition, what were the positions of the political parties in this emerging controversy?

LIBERAL FORCES

The groups supporting the urban position on reapportionment constituted what might be referred to as the "liberal coalition." Two factors tended to characterize this coalition. First, all its members felt with varying degrees that the state legislature had ignored many of its public policy proposals over at least the past few decades. Second, for reasons both external and internal to several of the groups belonging to this informal coalition, the coalition as a whole tended to be more loosely joined, or less cohesive, than its conservative opponents.

A foremost member of the liberal coalition was organized labor, represented by the Iowa Federation of Labor (AFL-

CIO). The IFL, which had approximately 80,000 members in 1960, felt that the only way in which organized labor was to become more effective in state governmental affairs was by urban areas being granted a larger proportion of seats in the general assembly. After all, the leaders of organized labor emphasized, the bulk of union members was concentrated in the approximately fifteen underrepresented urban counties in Iowa. Foremost among the legislative objectives of the IFL at the time was repeal of the state right-to-work law, a law forbidding union shop contracts which had been passed by the legislature in 1947.

The Iowa League of Women Voters was also a member of the liberal coalition. In 1960, the league had approximately 1,800 members, most of whom resided in the larger urban communities of the state. The ILWV's position on reapportionment was consistent with its traditional interest in governmental reform; after all, the ILWV was an organization that had grown out of the woman suffrage movement which occurred around the turn of the century. In the late 1950s, and early 1960s, in addition to its liberal position on reapportionment, the league was proposing such reforms as a shorter ballot for selecting the state's top executive officials, annual sessions of the legislature, and a civil service system for state employees.

Although less active and somewhat ambivalent on the reapportionment question in the late 1950s, the Iowa League of Municipalities was also regarded as a member of the liberal coalition. Composed of municipal officials from all sizes of urban communities in the state, the league's less than enthusiastic endorsement of the liberal position on reapportionment stemmed in part from the inclination of its permanent staff not to become involved in such a heated political issue for fear of antagonizing many members of the rural-dominated legislature. Following the 1960 general elections, however, the League of Municipalities underwent a major reorganization. A new and enlarged permanent staff was added and a greater degree of unity among members was achieved. As a result, it almost immediately began to undertake a more active and influential part in reapportionment politics.

Chambers of commerce of a number of Iowa's larger cities were also members of the liberal coalition. (Unlike many other states in the U.S., there never had been a state organization of chambers of commerce in Iowa.) For example, the Des Moines and Cedar Rapids chambers were especially active on the reapportionment issue. The concern expressed by these chambers about reapportionment probably resulted from experiences quite similar to those of municipal officials. For example, prior to 1963 when basic changes were made in the law, these chambers voiced their opposition to the state's anti-liquor-by-the-drink law. In addition, they voiced support for more municipal home rule and a larger share of state road money.

With only a few exceptions, larger city newspapers were also strong proponents of the liberal position on reapportionment. The most influential of them were undoubtedly the *Des Moines Register* and *Tribune,* newspapers with large and extensive statewide circulations. These big city newspapers, via their editorial pages, had expressed for many years what they perceived to be desirable progressive changes in state public policies. Among them were the need for county consolidation, school district reorganization, longer terms and a shorter ballot for the state's major executive officials, annual sessions of the legislature, municipal home rule, and greater state financial support for primary and secondary schools, institutions of higher learning, and mental health programs. In many cases, the big city press related slow progress in these areas to rural domination of the legislature.

A curious and relatively weak member of the liberal coalition was the Iowa Farmers' Union. Since the 1930s, the union had not played a major, active role in Iowa politics. Because of its small membership of approximately 7,600 in 1960 and limited financial resources, it had not found it possible or desirable to become involved in most public policy matters. Yet, the union aligned itself quite solidly with other liberal interests on the reapportionment question in the late 50s and early 60s. Although the more concrete reasons for the group's position on reapportionment were not clear, it was probably in part a reflection of the friendly, mutually beneficial alliance that it had enjoyed with organized labor for many years. Undoubtedly another factor was the traditional hostility between the union and a major force in the conservative coalition—the Farm Bureau—stemming from disagreements about many national (especially agricultural) policy questions. In other words, it was only "natural" for the Iowa Farmers' Union to be on a side of reapportionment opposite to that taken by the Iowa Farm Bureau Federation.

An important group which indirectly joined the liberal coalition later on in the reapportionment controversy was the Iowa Civil Liberties Union. Since its initial formation in the mid-1930s, this group had played a relatively active, though by no means exceedingly influential, role in attempting to protect what it viewed as important fundamental civil rights and liberties of individual Iowans. Over the years, the group attracted a fairly small but strongly dedicated group of civil libertarians to its ranks. Liberal academicians at institutions of higher learning as well as liberal attorneys had played significant roles in this organization's activities. As will be demonstrated later, the president and chief counsel of the ICLU were major litigants in a reapportionment battle before the Iowa supreme court in the early 1970s.

CONSERVATIVE FORCES

Aligned in opposition to the liberal coalition on reapportionment were the members of the conservative coalition. Members of this coalition had wielded the most influence in Iowa politics for at least the previous three or four decades. Thus, these groups were concerned primarily with protecting their interests in both short and long runs by taking the conservative position on reapportionment.

The most powerful member of the conservative coalition was the Iowa Farm Bureau Federation. The influence which this group had wielded in Iowa politics for the previous three or four decades was a function of several factors. Among them were its large, well-distributed membership (around 120,000 in all 99 counties), its excellent organization and leadership, and its ample financial resources. For some time the IFBF had effectively opposed many of the public policy proposals advanced by member groups of the liberal coalition. For example, it opposed (1) measures to increase the municipal streets share of state road money at the expense of the secondary road system, (2) a shorter ballot for the state's executive officers, and (3) organized labor's attempt to repeal the right-to-work law.

Aligned with the Farm Bureau on the reapportionment issue was the Iowa Manufacturers Association, an organization made up of the owners and managers of over 500 manufacturing establishments in the state. The IMA's position on reapportionment probably stemmed from its fear that organized labor would become quite powerful in Iowa politics if urban areas were given increased representation in the state legislature. More liberal worker benefit programs and rigid working condition policies would result from such increased political influence on the part of organized labor. Above all else, something exceedingly dear to the hearts of most IMA members—the right-to-work law—would probably be repealed. It is interesting to note that the IMA's role in the conservative coalition was similar to that of the Iowa Farmers' Union in the liberal grouping. In other words, IMA members were for the most part residents of cities and towns who thought that their political interests would be advanced or protected more by the conservative, primarily rural position on reapportionment. The Farmers' Union, on the other hand, was a rural group that felt its political interests would be advanced more through the liberal, primarily urban reapportionment perspective.

Many county government officials also took the conservative position on reapportionment. Their position on this question was consistent with their stands on two other issues. First, they were opposed to the efforts of municipal officials to obtain a larger share of state road money at the expense of the secondary, or rural, road system, since county boards of supervisors had the responsibility of administering the secondary road fund. Second, many county officials adamantly opposed those proposals advanced by liberal interests that called for county consolidation, partly because they feared elimination of their jobs.

Finally, one other informed group, the rural press, was also regarded as a member of the conservative coalition. This group, with a few individual exceptions, looked with disfavor upon many of the proposals advocated by members of the liberal coalition. For example, members of this group looked with disfavor upon proposals giving urban municipalities home rule authority.

What positions did the two major political parties take on the reapportionment question? Given its traditional minority position in Iowa politics since the Civil War, the Democratic Party in Iowa was an adamant proponent of legislative reapportionment. Most state Democratic leaders perceived malapportionment as working against their chances of capturing a greater share of legislative seats, since Democratic voting overall tended to be stronger in urban areas than in rural areas. In the late 50s and early 60s, the official Democratic position was that one house of the legislature should be apportioned on the basis of population and the other on area; more specifically, it argued that the house of representatives should be the population chamber with the senate the area chamber.[3] Most Democratic leaders undoubtedly believed that putting the house of representatives on an area basis, with one representative from each county, would virtually guarantee the Republican Party control of the lower chamber, even in election years when strong voting tides occurred in favor of the Democrats. After all, there were many more safe Republican counties—many also sparsely populated—than there were safe Democratic counties in the state. Thus, the Democratic Party aligned itself quite strongly with the liberal coalition.

The Republican Party, on the other hand, took a more ambivalent, or middle-of-the-road, position on reapportionment. Reapportionment, as mainly an urban versus rural controversy, tended to produce a higher level of disunity within the Republican leadership ranks than was the case with the Democrats. Since the Civil War years, the Republicans had been the majority party in Iowa politics, capturing most major elective offices and controlling the legislature. In maintaining this dominant position, a key part of the Republican strategy had been to accommodate within its structure as many political interests as possible, even those involving potential conflict.[4] But as Iowa became more socially and economically diversified, especially during the post World War II period with more rapid urbanization and industrialization, the Republicans experienced more and more difficulty in accommodating these emerging interests. Reapportionment was an issue associated with these changes and the Republicans had a more difficult time handling it than the traditionally weak Democrats. For the Republicans to have taken the liberal position on this question would probably have meant alienating many

---

3. For example, see *The 1960 State Platform and Candidates of the Democratic Party of Iowa* (Des Moines: The Democratic State Central Committee of Iowa, 1960), p. 12.
4. Harlan Hahn, *Urban-Rural Conflict: The Politics of Change* (Beverly Hills: Sage Publications, 1971), especially pp. 101–31.

traditional loyalists in the rural areas; if they had taken the "pure" conservative position (house on area and senate on population), they would have disturbed many present and potential future voters in the growing urban communities. Thus, the Republican state platforms in 1958 and 1960 urged passage of reapportionment with one chamber on population and the other on area, without specifying which chambers should be apportioned on which basis.[5] As we will see later, most Republican leaders eventually worked for the passage of the Shaff Plan after realizing that it was the only one having a chance of legislative passage. Overall, therefore, the Republicans aligned themselves more closely with the conservative coalition, even though they were not as solidly linked with this coalition as the Democrats were with the liberal coalition.

THE 1960 CONSTITUTIONAL CONVENTION QUESTION

From 1955 to 1960, neither the conservative nor liberal coalition was able to muster enough strength in the legislature to pass a reapportionment plan that either side favored. By 1960, two things were quite evident to the liberal interests. First, both chambers of the legislature were heavily weighted in favor of residents of rural areas in that 35 percent of the state's population theoretically could elect a majority of senators and only 27 percent could elect a majority of representatives. Secondly, the liberal urban forces considered it quite unlikely that the legislature would pass a reapportionment plan acceptable to them. As a result of these two factors, they concluded that the best route to reapportionment was via a constitutional convention.

At the November election of each year ending in "0" the state constitution requires that the voters be given the opportunity to vote on the question of whether a constitutional convention should be held for the purpose of revising the constitution. Although there was historical precedent for other action, the next legislature would presumably have to establish a convention if a majority of voters voting on the question

---

5. *1958 Republican State Platform* (Des Moines: Republican State Headquarters, 1958), p. 9; *1960 Republican State Platform* (Des Moines: Republican State Headquarters, 1960), p. 7.

favored the convention call.⁶ During the 1960 election campaign, members of the liberal coalition worked hard to bring about a favorable convention vote, feeling that this was the only way reapportionment could truly be achieved.⁷ In addition to campaigning for a convention on an individual group basis, the members of the liberal coalition formed a special *ad hoc* group—the Citizens Committee for a Constitutional Convention—to coordinate and provide greater publicity for their "pro" convention efforts. Leaders of the groups belonging to the coalition served as directors of the Citizens Committee. As expected, the 1960 Democratic state platform urged Iowans to vote "yes" on the convention question.⁸

Members of the conservative coalition, for the most part, actively opposed the calling of a constitutional convention, arguing that reapportionment was an issue which could be better handled by a more expert governmental body, meaning the legislature. The conservatives further argued that such a convention could propose changes to the constitution other than just reapportionment, and many of these frequently mentioned changes (liquor-by-the-drink, new or higher taxes, and legalization of union shops) were highly questionable, if not downright undesirable. Besides, they argued, the constitution did not explicitly state that all convention-proposed changes to the state's basic document had to be submitted to the electorate in a referendum for ratification. Generally, then, the conservatives pictured the convention as a dangerous, even possibly dictatorial, mechanism for bringing about reapportionment. They, too, organized a special statewide *ad hoc* interest group—Iowans for Reapportionment by Legislative Action—to convey their message to voters.

Neutrality on the convention question was the theme of the constitutional convention plank in the 1960 Republican

---

6. A majority of those who voted on the question in 1920 had favored the convention call, but the 1921 legislature refused to provide the mechanisms for the establishment of a convention—another unusual event in Iowa political history.
7. A more thorough treatment of the 1960 convention controversy is found in: John R. Schmidhauser, *Iowa's Campaign for a Constitutional Convention in 1960* (New York: McGraw-Hill Book Co., Inc., 1963); and Charles W. Wiggins, "Constitutional Convention Issue in Iowa (1960)," *Annals of Iowa* (Winter, 1970), pp. 171–90.
8. *The 1960 State Platform and Candidates of the Democratic Party of Iowa* (Des Moines: The Democratic State Central Committee of Iowa, 1960), p. 6.

state platform.[9] The plank suggested that both sides on the convention controversy had some good points to make and urged Iowa citizens to study these points carefully before deciding which way to vote. The Republican candidate for governor in 1960, unlike his Democratic opponent, reiterated this official Republican middle-of-the-road convention position as he campaigned throughout the state.[10]

The November, 1960, vote on the convention question resulted in a victory for the conservative interests, with 470,034 persons voting in favor and 532,762 against. Voting occurred primarily along urban-rural lines, with a significantly higher proportion of urban voters than rural voters supporting the calling of the convention. An analysis of the convention voting also concluded that the proportion of general election voters voting on the convention question was significantly less in urban areas where electric voting machines were employed than in rural areas where separate paper ballots were still used.[11] Thus, given the urban-rural voting pattern on the question, most analysts concluded that the mechanics of balloting cost the proponents a significant—perhaps decisive—number of "yes" votes at the election.

THE SHAFF PLAN AND THE BEGINNING OF LITIGATION

Having won at the polls, the conservative coalition focused its efforts on the 1961 legislature in an attempt to get its reapportionment proposal, the Shaff Plan, passed. After experiencing a few initial setbacks, it was eventually successful. The critical votes on this plan occurred in the senate, where opposition to it was much stronger. On final passage, the plan carried the upper chamber by a single vote, with a single Democrat "bolting" his party's caucus position to put it over the top. Otherwise, all Democrats and most urban Republicans voted against the plan, but together they constituted a slim senate minority.

---

9. *1960 Republican State Platform* (Des Moines: Republican State Headquarters, 1960), pp. 5-6.
10. The Republican candidate was Norman Erbe, while the Democratic candidate was Edward McManus.
11. George B. Mather, *Effects of the Use of Voting Machines on Total Votes Cast: Iowa—1920–1960* (Iowa City: Institute of Public Affairs, The University of Iowa, 1964), pp. 53-57.

The proposed constitutional amendment was considered again and approved by the 1963 legislature. Although voting on the plan this time generally occurred along the same lines as it had in 1961, it received somewhat greater support from urban Republicans who acquiesced under the realization that it was the only viable reapportionment plan that could be passed and submitted to the electorate at the time.

A special election was called December 3, 1963, to provide the voters with an earlier than normal opportunity to approve or reject the plan. At the election, voters rejected the proposed amendment, with 191,421 voting in favor and 271,214 against. Although the proposal carried in 64 of the 99 counties, voters in urban counties voted heavily against it, assuring its defeat. Liberal interests, especially the Iowa Federation of Labor, had conducted a very aggressive campaign against the Shaff Plan (referred to frequently as the "Shaft" Plan by its opponents). Defeat of this plan was also attributed to the opposition of a popular first term Democratic governor, Harold Hughes, who had spoken against it throughout the state.

Some months prior to the December, 1963, vote on the Shaff Plan, the head of the Iowa Federation of Labor had filed suit in federal district court in Des Moines claiming that the apportionment scheme currently in effect was unconstitutional. In addition, he asked the court to rule on the constitutionality of the Shaff Plan. The filing of the suit in federal court resulted from a decision of the United States Supreme Court the previous year. In the 1962 *Baker v. Carr* decision, the U.S. court had overturned a previous ruling by declaring that the federal courts did have jurisdiction in matters involving legislative apportionment.[12] Thus, individuals experiencing what they viewed as discrimination under an apportionment scheme could have their cases adjudicated in the federal court system. The federal district court in Des Moines, in rendering its decision, declared the current apportionment scheme unconstitutional, but refused to grant immediate relief to the plaintiff in his challenge of the Shaff Plan, since a referendum was to be held shortly on it.[13] However, the court indicated that it was retaining jurisdiction in the latter challenge.

12. *Baker v. Carr*, 369 U.S. 186 (1962). The court overturned its previous ruling in *Colegrove v. Green*, 328 U.S. 549 (1946).
13. *Davis v. Synhorst*, 217 F. Supp. 492 (S.D. Iowa 1963).

With the defeat of the Shaff Plan at the polls, the federal district court in January, 1964, reiterated its previous findings that the present apportionment scheme was unconstitutional according to the national constitution and suggested that a special legislative session should be called to enact a new apportionment plan.[14] A special session convened upon the call of Governor Hughes the following month. The legislature proceeded to pass two reapportionment plans, a temporary plan according to which legislators were to be elected at the November, 1964, elections and a permanent one which would follow the constitutionally prescribed procedures of passage by two successive assemblies and approval in a state-wide referendum. The temporary plan provided for substantially increased representation for urban areas in the house of representatives (for example, the number of representatives from Polk County was increased from 2 to 11), with slighter increases in the senate. Under the plan, 47 percent of the electorate theoretically could elect a majority of representatives, while 39 percent could elect a majority of senators. In order to affect the smallest number of incumbents, the number of representatives was increased from 50 to 59.[15] The proposed permanent reapportionment amendment called for a house on population and a senate on area, with the number of seats in the two chambers being reduced to not more than 100 and 50 respectively when ratified by the voters and implemented.

THE IMPACT OF REYNOLDS V. SIMS

Shortly after the 1964 general elections, the head of the Iowa Federation of Labor requested the federal district court in Des Moines to review both the temporary and permanent plans passed by the 1964 special session. He claimed that neither plan was in accord with the U.S. Supreme Court's historic *Reynolds v. Sims* decision in June of that year.[16] In the

---

14. *Davis v. Synhorst*, 225 F. Supp. 689 (S.D. Iowa 1964). This federal district court decision was subsequently appealed to the U.S. Supreme Court. The major plaintiff in the appeal case, E. Howard Hill, was the head of the Iowa Farm Bureau Federation. On June 22, 1964, the nation's highest court upheld the lower court's ruling; see *Hill v. Davis*, 378 U.S. 565 (1964).
15. The temporary plan was subsequently approved by the federal district court in Des Moines on March 27, 1964; see *Davis v. Synhorst*, 231 F. Supp. 540 (S.D. Iowa 1964).
16. *Reynolds v. Sims*, 377 U.S. 533 (1964).

Reynolds case, the court had ruled that both chambers of state legislatures must be apportioned on a population—or "one man-one vote"—basis, for otherwise it would constitute a state depriving residents of the equal protection of the laws granted to them by the fourteenth amendment of the U.S. Constitution. In the prevailing opinion in the case, Chief Justice Earl Warren argued that the legal relationship between a state government and its local subdivision (such as counties) was essentially a unitary one in that all local subdivisions were considered as creatures of the state. Thus, the federal analogy, or the argument that representation in the two chambers of a state legislature could, or should, be similar to that in the national congress, was recognized by the U.S. Supreme Court as being inapplicable to the question of state legislative apportionment.

The federal district court rendered its decision on the second major IFL reapportionment challenge in February of 1965.[17] It concluded that the temporary reapportionment plan passed by the 1964 special session was unconstitutional since the "one man-one vote" principle enunciated by the nation's highest tribunal in the *Reynolds* case had been violated in the apportioning of state senate seats. The district court declared that this deficiency had to be corrected by the time of the 1966 elections. Although it did not rule specifically on the permanent reapportionment amendment passed for the first time by the 1964 special session, most political leaders concluded that the amendment would eventually be declared unconstitutional if action was pursued further on it, so it was not considered by the subsequent legislative session.

DEMOCRATS AND SINGLE-MEMBER DISTRICTS

The 1965 legislature proceeded to make the necessary changes in the apportionment of senate districts required by the court's decision. In drawing new districts, the legislature also increased the number of senate seats from 59 to 61. However, a new controversy erupted when the assembly considered a new permanent apportionment amendment to the Iowa constitution. Legislators from counties with more than one legislator had been elected on an at-large basis in 1964. The Dem-

---

17. *Davis v. Cameron*, 238 F. Supp. 462 (S.D. Iowa 1965).

ocratic landslide victory of that year (Democrats had won all major state offices and had captured control of both chambers of the legislature—101–23 in the house and 34–25 in the senate) resulted in most urban county delegations being composed totally of Democratic legislators. Republicans, reacting to this rather novel and, to them, certainly undesirable situation, urged that a mandatory subdistricting provision be written into the new amendment, with all legislators elected from single-member districts. The Democratic majority, enjoying the fruits of legislative control for the first time since the Great Depression years, easily defeated Republican efforts to write such a provision into the new amendment.

Following the 1965 legislative session, three prominent Republicans and a rural, conservative Democrat filed suit in state district court in Polk County charging that the temporary apportionment plan in effect at the time was unconstitutional on both federal and state grounds in that voters in multilegislator counties were permitted to vote for more than one representative or senator. The plaintiffs charged that this constituted a breach of (1) the equal protection of the laws clause of the fourteenth amendment of the national constitution, and (2) a provision in the bill of rights section (article I, section 6) of the Iowa constitution requiring that all laws passed by the legislature shall be of such nature that they apply to all individuals in a uniform manner. The plaintiffs further argued that multiple-member districts discriminated against minority political groups in urban counties; for example, a great deal of emphasis was given to the argument that the election of all eleven Polk County legislators at large (where the Democrats were the dominant party) made it exceedingly difficult for the Republicans to elect any legislators from it, even though the Republicans enjoyed certain pocket areas of strength within the county (especially the western region of Des Moines). Thus, people in these pocket areas of Republican strength were being discriminated against by the multiple-member district system. The plaintiffs further argued that residents of rural, single-member districts were discriminated against because they could vote for only one legislator. In addition, they argued that a typical voter in a multiple-member district, especially Polk County, was confronted with an unjustifiably long ballot at the polls and this made rational voting on his part quite difficult.

The state district court found the arguments on the part of the plaintiffs to be unconvincing and ruled against them. The plaintiffs immediately appealed the case to the state supreme court which, in April of 1966, reversed the lower court ruling and by a 5 to 4 vote declared that all state legislators in the future would have to be elected from single-member districts.[18]

Republicans and members of the conservative coalition were generally pleased with the court's decision. Most Republicans had favored the single-member district concept since it had first been inserted in their 1960 state party platform.[19] The 1964 election outcome obviously had reinforced their belief in the virtue of single-member districts. Members of the liberal coalition, on the other hand, did not form anything approaching a united front against the single-member district concept. Especially noteworthy was the position taken by the urban press—the *Des Moines Register and Tribune,* for example—in support of the election of all legislators from single-member districts. Since the Democratic Party had no formal position on the question, many of its leaders, especially in rural areas, were not particularly disturbed by the court's decision in *Kruidenier v. McCulloch.*

Bipartisan Reapportionment

The 1967 legislature was faced with two tasks. First, under the direction of the state's highest court, it was required to subdistrict those counties from which more than one legislator had been elected under the 1965 temporary reapportionment plan. Second, it was confronted with the problem of what action to take on the 1965 permanent reapportionment constitutional amendment. As noted before, the 1965 Democratic controlled legislature had refused to include a mandatory subdistricting provision in the proposed amendment before its initial legislative passage. Yet, the state's highest tribunal subsequently had declared that subdistricting was required under

---

18. *Kruidenier v. McCulloch,* 258 Iowa 1121 (1966). Mrs. Kruidenier, the major plaintiff and a Republican, was a resident of Polk County and the wife of a high executive of the *Des Moines Register and Tribune.* One of her co-plaintiffs was Robert Rigler, Republican floor leader in the state senate.
19. *1960 Republican State Platform* (Des Moines: Republican State Headquarters, 1960), p. 7.

the "uniform application of the laws" clause in the state constitution. Thus, the solons were faced with two alternatives on the permanent apportionment amendment: (1) scrap it and initiate a completely new amendment with a subdistricting requirement, even though this would delay passage of *any* amendment for an additional two years, or (2) pass the 1965 amendment for the second time and initiate for the first time a separate amendment dealing specifically with subdistricting.

The 1966 elections had resulted in a very unusual situation in terms of partisan control of the general assembly. For the first time since the Depression years, the legislature was under divided party control, with the Republicans controlling the house (89–35) and the Democrats maintaining a slight edge in the senate (32–29). This unusual situation probably had much to do with leaders of both parties agreeing to a proposal for the establishment of a special bipartisan commission outside the legislature to draft a new temporary apportionment plan for the 1968 elections which would include subdistricting. The legislative resolution establishing the commission provided that the state chairman of each major party was entitled to appoint seven members to the commission. Each chairman proceeded to select one commission member from each congressional district. The commission met and hammered out a new temporary apportionment plan, a process which required much bargaining or give and take, between the commission members representing the two parties. The commission then submitted its proposal to the legislature, where it easily passed both chambers. The passage of any amendments by a partisan majority in one chamber would have certainly been resisted by the partisan majority in the other chamber and produced a stalemate. Thus, 1967 marks the year when a substantially bipartisan reapportionment plan was passed by the assembly.

The second problem confronting the 1967 legislature—what to do about the permanent reapportionment amendment—was resolved by the passage of the 1965 amendment for the second time and the initial passage of a new amendment making subdistricting mandatory.

THE ARRIVAL OF PERMANENT REAPPORTIONMENT

During the 1968 general elections, the electorate overwhelmingly approved the permanent reapportionment amendment first initiated by the 1965 legislature, with 469,449 in favor and 263,886 against. This amendment, which had a substantial impact upon subsequent reapportionment developments, contained five major provisions. First, it provided for a legislature made up of a house of no more than 100 members and a senate of no more than 50 members. Second, it provided for the apportionment of both legislative chambers on a population basis, with the territory of districts being as compact and contiguous as possible. Third, for the first time in Iowa history, the amendment permitted the crossing of county lines in the establishment of legislative districts. Fourth, an automatic reapportionment provision for future years was involved whereby the state supreme court would be required to redistrict the assembly if a legislature meeting in the year following a federal decennial census failed to reapportion itself. Finally, and certainly not least important, was a provision granting to any qualified voter the right to file suit directly with the state supreme court if he believed that the legislature had not complied with the previously mentioned constitutional requirements in apportioning itself. In granting the court original jurisdiction in reapportionment cases (the only area of original jurisdiction granted the court by the state constitution), the amendment provided that the court itself should draw up a new apportionment plan within ninety days after finding any plan passed by the legislature to be unconstitutional.

The 1969 legislature took on the task of implementing the 1968 permanent reapportionment amendment. One of its biggest hurdles was to reduce the size of both chambers, which meant eliminating at least 24 seats in the lower chamber and 11 in the upper chamber. For assistance in this dilemma, the legislative leaders opted for the 1967 format: a special bipartisan 14-member commission from outside the legislature should be appointed to draft a reapportionment scheme. The legislative resolution establishing the commission specified that it should come up with a plan providing for a 100-member house and 50-member senate.

The bipartisan commission reported back to the assembly during the latter part of the 1969 session, after interparty compromises similar to those in the 1967 commission were struck. This time, however, the legislature approved several substantial amendments to the commission plan, changes which were mostly designed to protect the seats of incumbent Republican lawmakers. The major difference between the 1967 and 1969 legislatures related to these developments was that the Republicans firmly controlled both chambers in 1969 (86–38 in the house and 45–16 in the senate), whereas they had controlled only the lower chamber in 1967. In other words, the Republicans in 1969 had the votes needed in both chambers to alter a reapportionment plan that was the product of bargains struck by an "outside" bipartisan reapportionment commission.

In addition to implementing the permanent reapportionment amendment, the 1969 assembly passed for the second required time the mandatory subdistricting amendment approved originally in 1967. Little controversy surrounded the second passage of this proposed amendment.

Rasmussen v. Ray—THE COURT WARNS

Shortly after the 1969 legislature adjourned, Democratic state chairman Clark Rasmussen brought suit in state supreme court charging that the new reapportionment plan was unconstitutional in that it provided for too much population deviation among districts and for districts that were not as compact in territory as they could be. Governor Ray and other high state officials were listed as defendants in the case. Rasmussen also emphasized that the legislature had not made a good faith effort to provide for substantial equality of population among districts, and that Republican supported and approved alterations to the bipartisan commission proposal represented a movement away from greater population equality. Therefore, so Rasmussen argued, the 1969 plan violated the 1968 permanent reapportionment amendment to the state constitution and the fourteenth amendment to the federal constitution as interpreted by the nation's highest tribunal.

In late spring of 1970, the state supreme court unanimously upheld Rasmussen's contentions and declared the 1969 plan to be unconstitutional on both federal and state grounds.[20] However, a majority of the members of the court agreed that no relief could be granted the plaintiff, since the filing date for the 1970 June primary elections was so near. In other

20. *Rasmussen v. Ray*, 175 N. W. 2d 20 (Iowa 1970).

words, the court refused to order the calling of a special legislative session to draft a new apportionment plan to be used in electing legislators during the 1970 June primary and November general elections. Even more interesting was the court's refusal to draft a new districting plan itself, even though it appeared to have been given this responsibility under the 1968 permanent reapportionment amendment! But the court majority argued that there just wasn't enough time before the primary elections to do this. The end result was that those who were elected to the legislature during the 1970 elections were chosen according to an apportionment plan already declared unconstitutional by the state supreme court. Although there was no court test of the situation, some observers questioned whether all laws passed by the "unconstitutional" 1971–72 assembly might also be regarded as unconstitutional!

Noun v. Turner—THE COURT ACTS

As a result of the 1970 general elections, Republicans retained their tight grip on the 1971–72 assembly, controlling the upper chamber by a 37 to 13 margin and the lower chamber by a 62 to 37 margin. At the same elections, the somewhat redundant constitutional amendment requiring single-member legislative districts was also approved by voters by more than a 2 to 1 margin (289,200 for, 132,590 against).

The 1971 legislature set about to rectify the constitutional wrongs ascertained by the court in the *Rasmussen* decision. Unlike in 1967 and 1969, however, no outside bipartisan commission was established to prepare a reapportionment plan. Instead, working closely with Republican leaders, the regular constitutional amendment and reapportionment standing committees were assigned the laborious task of formulating a reapportionment proposal. In turn, these committees relied quite extensively upon the technical expertise and assistance of the Legislative Service Bureau—the research arm of the legislature—in preparing the plan. Using 1970 census data and the aid of a computer, the bureau was directed to devise several alternative plans which contained small, but varying, population deviations among districts. The reapportionment committees, with the house committee taking the lead, agreed to commence work on one of the service bureau-devised alternative plans, although it was not the one with the lowest population deviation among districts. Changes were subsequently made to this working plan in committee and via amendments on the floor of the legislature once it was reported out of committee. These changes were mainly designed to eliminate as many situations as feasible where incumbent legislators, especially Republican incumbents, were placed together in the same districts and would have to run against each other in the next election. The Republican leadership strategy was to attempt to obtain as broad a base of support for the plan as possible; thus, a few concessions were even granted Democratic legislators, when possible. Following a few interparty—many Democrats charged partisan gerrymandering—and interchamber skirmishes, a new reapportionment plan cleared both chambers.

Upon adjournment of the 1971 assembly, leaders of five groups belonging to the liberal coalition—Iowa Civil Liberties Union, League of Women Voters, United Auto Workers, Iowa Federation of Labor, and the Democratic Party—filed three separate suits in the state supreme court challenging the constitutionality of the 1971 apportionment plan.[21] Richard Turner, the state's attorney general, was named as defendant in these cases. Since the three suits were quite similar in nature, the court decided to consolidate them for hearing and disposition purposes. In essence, the plaintiffs' arguments were similar to those lodged by the Democratic state chairman two years previously. The legislature, they argued, had not made a good faith effort to reapportion itself into districts containing the lowest possible population deviations and ones which were as compact as possible. The decision of the reapportionment committees, with the consent of Republican legislative leaders, to work from a plan which did not contain the lowest population deviation of the several alternative plans made available by the service bureau meant in fact that the legislature had established an unconstitutional minimum population deviation standard (*de minimis* standard in legal parlance) at some point in the legislative process.

21. *Noun v. Turner* (Iowa supreme court decision of January 14, 1972). Mrs. Noun, head of the Iowa Civil Liberties Union, maintained throughout the proceedings that she was involved in the case as a private citizen, and not the head of the ICLU. Her activity in this case, along with that of her attorney (ICLU attorney), however, established at least the indirect involvement of the ICLU in Iowa reapportionment politics.

In presenting its case, the League of Women Voters presented to the court a reapportionment plan which it had prepared after legislative adjournment and which contained smaller population deviations and more compact districts than provided for in the reapportionment law being tested. Furthermore, the league suggested that the court should consider adopting its plan to replace the one passed by the legislature. The plaintiffs also urged the court to draw up a new apportionment plan, a responsibility it apparently had refused to assume in the 1970 *Rasmussen* decision. Finally, as if to add insult to injury, the plaintiffs requested the court to order the state government to reimburse them for the expenses they incurred in preparing to bring their cases before the state's highest tribunal.[22]

On January 14, 1972, to many a memorable day in Iowa constitutional and political history, the state supreme court unanimously declared that the 1971 apportionment plan was unconstitutional and announced that it was assuming responsibility for drafting a reapportionment plan. The court agreed that the legislature had erred in establishing a minimum population standard initially in drawing districts; the acknowledged availability of alternative plans (prepared by the Legislative Service Bureau) containing lower deviations was adequate proof of this. Furthermore, the legislature acted illegally in permitting changes to the alternative, or working, plan accepted because these changes brought about even larger deviations. In other words, the court argued that protecting incumbent legislators and other motivations (gerrymandering for partisan advantage or to keep urban and rural areas separate, etc.) were "impermissible considerations" employed by the legislature in attempting to justify population deviations in the plan. Thus, the plan involved "invidious discrimination" against voters in more populous districts, and this arrangement constituted violation of "equal protection" under the federal constitution and the "apportionment according to population" provision in the state constitution.

---

22. The plaintiffs in the first suit (leaders of the Iowa Civil Liberties Union, League of Women Voters, and United Auto Workers) reported expenses of $2,300; the two IFL leaders in the second suit reported expenses of $300, while the Democratic state chairman indicated expenses of $5,400. Altogether, then, expenses totaling $8,000 were reported by all of the plaintiffs in this consolidated case. Attorneys' fees were not included in these figures.

Legislative Reapportionment Battle

The court also declared the 1971 apportionment act unconstitutional on the grounds that districts violated the compactness requirement of the state constitution. The assembly had erred in establishing districts which were not as compact as they could have been. The court noted that the legislature had established less compact districts when it amended the computer-drawn working plan in order to protect incumbent legislators. The justices emphasized that the only justifiable reason for violations of compactness would be if the legislature were attempting to achieve greater population equality among districts, but the defendant had failed to prove that this was the case.

After courteously declining the offer of the League of Women Voters to adopt its plan, the court announced that it would proceed to draw up new legislative districts itself. The court further ordered that the terms of all senators, including those who were serving in the middle of their four year terms, would be terminated, a point which drew the ire of many of the senators falling into that category. Finally, the court concluded that it could find no authority for ordering the state to compensate the plaintiffs for the expenses they incurred in bringing their cases before the court.

A careful examination of the *Noun* decision lead most students of reapportionment politics to the following conclusions. First, throughout the decision, the court appeared to be strongly irritated by what it viewed as the legislature's unwillingness to heed its warning in the *Rasmussen* decision two years before and make a good faith effort to reapportion itself on a strict "one man-one vote" basis with districts as compact as possible. Second, the decision emphasized that the burden of proof was on the state to demonstrate clearly that considerations other than population equality and compactness did not enter into the legislative reapportionment decision. In other words, the state was charged with the burden of justifying why its plan was not unconstitutional, as opposed to the burden being placed on the plaintiffs to demonstrate why a plan was unconstitutional.

The Aftermath

The court proceeded to draw up a new apportionment plan, using technical assistance borrowed from the legislative service bureau. Before adjourning, the 1972 legislature expressed its somewhat reluctant willingness to comply with the court's ruling by passing a law postponing the primary elections until August 1.

The court completed its task on March 31 and decreed that its new plan be put into effect. The 1971 reapportionment plan struck down by the court had contained maximum population deviations of 3.8 percent between the largest and smallest house districts and 3.2 percent between the largest and smallest senate districts. The court-drawn reapportionment plan, on the other hand, contained population deviations substantially below those in the 1971 law, to the point that the deviations in both chambers were only a small fraction (less than .1) of 1 percent. Iowa had become the state with the most equitably apportioned legislature in the Union![23]

Political observers wondered whether the court's rather stringent standards for fair apportionment meant that future legislatures would find it exceedingly difficult, if not impossible, to pass a plan that could survive a test of constitutionality. Some conjectured that the legislature in effect had now permanently abdicated its traditional constitutional responsibility for reapportionment. Events following the 1980 federal census would certainly shed some light on these penetrating questions.

---

23. "42 States Reapportion; Plans are 'Final' in 21," *The American Legislator* (May, 1972), p. 2.

Agrarian Stability in Utopian Societies: A Comparison of Economic Practices of Old Order Amish and Hutterites
DOROTHY SCHWIEDER

TODAY the Old Order Amish Mennonites are perhaps Iowa's most distinctive ethnic group. Emigrating from Europe in the early 1700s, Amish initially settled in Pennsylvania but soon were spreading out and making settlements in many eastern and midwestern states. The Amish were among Iowa's first settlers when several families moved into the Kalona area in the late 1830s. In 1917 a second Amish community was started when several Kalona families moved to Hazelton to establish a more conservative settlement. Largely because of their need for additional land, the Amish began a third community near Milton in 1969.

The Iowa Amish live much the same as the eastern Amish, believing in a simple, agrarian way of life. Their activities are dictated by their religious beliefs; they reject worldly conveniences, electricity, telephones, and automobiles, and rely on horses and buggies for transportation. Often called the "plain people," they dress in an Old World manner; the men wear wide-brimmed hats and long, full beards while the women appear in bonnets and long, dark skirts. Church services are held in the home. One room schoolhouses cover the countryside in Amish communities as the plain people believe that an eighth grade education is adequate for their children and strongly resist sending their children to non-Amish schools. Among the Iowa Amish are slight variations in beliefs and practices; for example, many Kalona Amish use tractors for field work while the Hazelton farmers use only horses.

In order to present a contrast and comparison the following essay examines the economic practices of the Iowa Amish in relation to the South Dakota Hutterites. Sharing similar backgrounds, religious beliefs, and present-day lifestyles, the Amish and Hutterites present views of two midwestern utopian societies. Moreover, in terms of longevity, these societies are the most successful utopian populations in the United States.

During the mid-1800s two separate religious utopian societies moved into America's Middle West in search of land and freedom. Amish Mennonites from Pennsylvania and Ohio numbered among the first settlers moving into southeastern Iowa in the 1840s, while Russian Hutterites migrated to the Dakota Plains in the 1870s. At the time of their respective settlements, Iowa and Dakota were in the early frontier stage and offered both groups the necessary land for initial settlements with opportunity for further growth. Both Amish and Hutterites succeeded in their venture and today represent two of the most successful utopian societies in existence. Even though they appear in some ways to be strikingly different— Hutterites live communally and utilize the most modern farm machinery while Amish believe in private property and generally farm with outdated equipment—both groups share vitally important agricultural convictions and practices. Their common beliefs in superiority of agrarian life, isolation from outside influences, self-sufficiency in economic needs, large families, mutual assistance, minimum education, and restriction of expenditures have enabled both groups to achieve a high degree of economic and social stability. The primary purpose here is to identify past experiences and characteristics which have produced agrarian stability for Old Order Amish and Hutterites and secondly to focus on current similarities which allow both to maintain that condition successfully.

The Hutterites

Hutterites and Amish Mennonites share a common origin and early-day adversities. Born of the religious upheavals stemming from the Protestant Reformation, both groups grew out of Anabaptism and today represent two of the three surviving

Anabaptist groups in North America.[1] Because of deviant religious convictions they suffered severe persecution throughout their European history and both established patterns of migration to new lands whenever persecution and demands for change became overwhelming.

The Hutterites became established in 1528, several years prior to the formation of Mennonite congregations. Before migrating to the new world, Hutterites lived for 350 years in Europe where they founded major settlements in Moravia, Slovakia, Transylvania, and Russia. Early in their history they adopted the principle of communal property believing that if they held "all things common" they practiced the one true religion and hence experienced a superior life.[2] Alternating between prosperity and persecution and at times finding their membership reduced to a mere handful, the Hutterites nevertheless managed to survive and continued their religious communal practices throughout their European existence.

Originating in Moravia, the earliest Hutterites were soon forced to leave the country because of religious persecution. After the Peace of Augsburg in 1555 they returned to their Moravian homes and remained there throughout the sixteenth century. Surrounding manorial lords soon recognized the Hutterites' craft skills and invited them to settle on their manorial estates. Once on the estates, Hutterites established settlements called Bruderhofs which enabled them to better follow their religious-communal convictions. Living conditions were arranged to facilitate the Hutterites' desire for isolation and communism. Each Bruderhof was a community in itself and usually consisted of several large, three-story buildings and several smaller houses arranged around a village square. The ground floor contained rooms for community living, such as dining hall, kitchen, and nursery, while the upper floors contained private living quarters for each family. The Hutterites in each Bruderhof strove for self-sufficiency and, with their own fields, woods, ponds, and workshops, they often achieved their goal. Each settlement had a manager, a member appointed to handle the business matters of the Bruderhof which consisted

---

1. William Albert Allard, "The Hutterites, Plain People of the West," *National Geographic Magazine*, July 1970, p. 98.
2. "Anabaptism," *Encyclopedia of Religion and Ethics*, 1913, I, 410; Victor Peters, *All Things Common: The Hutterian Way of Life* (Minneapolis: The University of Minnesota Press, 1965), p. 11.

of buying and selling goods, and making work assignments. Within their community most occupations were represented: masons, blacksmiths, sicklesmiths, dyers, shoemakers, furriers, wheelwrights, saddlers, cutlers, watchmakers, tailors, weavers, glass and rope makers, brewers, and other occupations.[3] Under these conditions the Hutterites prospered and attracted many new members; they often refer to this period as the Golden Age.[4]

With the coming of the eighteenth century, prosperity faded as dominant religious groups began once more to persecute the small sect. Moravian officials eventually expelled all Hutterites and for the next 150 years they suffered extreme persecution as they wandered eastward, settling for a time in Transylvania and later Slovakia. Continuous pressure from the Catholic Church resulted in confiscation of their manuscript books, placement of many members in monasteries, and removal of many Hutterite children from their homes. Caught up in a Turkish-Russian War and with their numbers drastically reduced, they decided to leave Slovakia and move further eastward in search of yet another new home.[5]

While still in Slovakia, the Hutterites consulted with an official of the Russian crown who desired settlers in the Ukraine. They agreed to emigrate to Russia when they were guaranteed exemption from military service, retention of their German language, and control of their own schools. Movement into this area required some adjustments, however, in the Hutterites' economic activities. The region lacked resources and markets for their craft products, but contained a great abundance of available land. The result was heavier emphasis on agricultural production, a practice which has continued to the present. Even with de-emphasis on craft work the Brethren remained highly self-sufficient through home production.[6]

In 1870, after 100 years of considerable prosperity in

---

3. C. Henry Smith, *The Story of the Mennonites,* 4th ed. (Newton: Mennonite Publication Office, 1957), pp. 353–54; "Bruderhof," *The Mennonite Encyclopedia,* 1955, I, 445–46.
4. V. F. Calverton, *Where Angels Dared to Tread* (Indianapolis: The Bobbs-Merrill Company, 1941), p. 171.
5. "Hutterian Brethren," *The Mennonite Encyclopedia,* 1956, II, 856.
6. John W. Bennett, *Hutterian Brethren* (Stanford: Stanford University Press, 1967), p. 165.

Russia, the Czar decreed that Hutterites must give up their special status. Once more, forced to choose between changing their traditional behavior or movement to a new region where they might continue their old ways, the Hutterites chose to migrate. This time they looked to the New World; the plains of southeastern Dakota were selected because they believed them to closely resemble the Russian steppes.

Throughout their European existence the Hutterites' religious and social beliefs changed very little; following their migration, life in America continued much the same as they had experienced it in Russia. Believing that God sanctioned their way of life and desired them to live communally, they also believed that they must practice nonresistance, isolate themselves from the world, live in a simple manner, and refuse to take any oaths except to God. These beliefs—called Central Beliefs—were set down in the sixteenth century and still guide the Hutterites today.[7]

Hutterites' religious beliefs controlled all aspects of their lives; they defined each new situation in reference to their Central Beliefs. No break existed between the past and the present; the past was not a separate, bygone age, but continued to govern their daily actions, their education, their beliefs, and even constituted their reason for existence. Hence, their total being continued all that had gone before. Religious convictions governed even the placement of buildings. Because all authority came from God who created the universe and arranged all things in order and harmony, they ordered their social life and physical world to conform to this ideal. Within a settlement all buildings had to be placed properly in terms of direction and distance from the others. The buildings faced toward the center of the community, symbolic of the group's rejection of worldly things. Individuals had their proper place in society also since God had so ordered their lives: husband over wife, older members over younger people, and parents over children.[8] Through their 400 year history there have been subtle and slight modifications to changing social and cultural

---

7. Lee Emerson Deets, *The Hutterites: A Study in Social Cohesion* (Gettysburg: Times and News Publishing Company, 1939), p. 22; Peters, *All Things Common*, pp. 76–77.
8. John A. Hostetler and Gertrude E. Huntington, *The Hutterites in North America* (New York: Holt, Rinehart and Winston, 1967), pp. 6–19.

situations as Hutterites moved from one land to another, but basic beliefs and living patterns remain unchanged.

In 1874, the sparsely settled Dakota Territory offered the Hutterites land as well as an unstructured social environment where they might isolate themselves from worldly influences and continue their Old World ways. This was a period of extreme hardship, however, as Dakota had proven a hostile environment to the earliest settlers throughout the 1860s and early 1870s. Moving into an area traditionally characterized by marginal rainfall, lack of timber, blizzards, hail, and prairie fires, the settlers also experienced a period of extended drought. Because of geographical and climatical conditions in Dakota, settlers discovered that farming required more capital than in prairie states. Farmers faced initial costs of purchasing food, farm equipment, fencing materials, livestock, housing materials, and well digging. To compound farmers' problems, it was often difficult to secure credit and farm prices remained low.[9] The drought and natural adversities of the region greatly reduced crop yields and many of the earliest farmers admitted defeat and headed back east.

While other early Dakotans were giving up in despair, the Hutterites quickly adjusted their economic institutions to the plains environment. The Hutterites were not typical pioneers because unlike the average pioneer setting up an individual household, the Brethren came as a "large scale diversified enterprise."[10] In the areas of land, labor, and capital, the Hutterites had a decided advantage over their neighbors. The exact amount of money brought by them from Russia is not known, but it was obviously substantial since they purchased land rather than utilizing the Homestead Act. With large amounts of capital the Hutterites purchased large acreages and quickly diversified their farming operations. Within the first year of their operations they were experiencing economies of large scale farming and hence greater economic stability.[11] Moreover, Hutterites continued their European practice of "selective adoption" whereby they adopted technological changes in farm machinery and methods without any corre-

---

9. Gilbert C. Fite, *The Farmers' Frontier 1865–1900* (New York: Holt, Rinehart and Winston, 1966), pp. 103–4.
10. Bennett, *Hutterian Brethren*, p. 165.
11. Ibid., pp. 179–80.

sponding change in their religious attitudes or behavior patterns.[12] In this way the Hutterites transplanted their European society—a fully developed social, economic, and religious system—to the hostile Dakota plains with minimal adjustment problems.

Thus, beginning originally as Anabaptists and quickly adopting the "community of goods" principle, the Brethren have successfully retained their traditional society for 350 years in Europe and almost 100 years in the United States. Throughout their European experience—in Moravia, Transylvania, Slovakia, and Russia—when confronted with demands for change, they chose instead to forego land and possessions and sought new frontiers where they might continue their old ways. In spite of 300 years of persecution and continued relocation, the Hutterites established set religious beliefs and community behavior that resulted in strong cohesive ties and clear-cut goals for their future. Immigrating to the United States their religious-communitarian society not only survived the hostile Dakota environment in the 1870s but the Hutterites initiated a policy of expansion that they have continued to the present.

THE AMISH

The Mennonites—parent group of the Amish—originated in the early 1500s in Switzerland and were first called Swiss Brethren. Following an early Anabaptist reformer, Menno Simmons, the Mennonites took his name and adopted his teaching as the fundamentals of their faith.[13] The Mennonites failed to maintain the unity of the Hutterites, and after considerable internal dissension, they divided into several distinct branches, one of which is the Amish.[14]

A major controversy arose among Mennonites in 1693 over the practice of shunning, a method of punishing members for the violation of church rules by totally avoiding them until they repented. Believing that his fellow churchmen had become too lax regarding shunning, Jakob Ammons, a Swiss Mennonite minister, advocated a most extreme position that

---

12. Deets, *The Hutterites*, pp. 49–50.
13. Smith, *The Story of the Mennonites*, p. 122.
14. "United States of America," *The Mennonite Encyclopedia*, 1959, IV, 776.

shunning should be upheld as rigidly as possible, even to the extent of wives and husbands refusing to live with their banned spouses. The controversy split most European Mennonites into two factions and the group that remained with Ammons came to be known as Amish.[15]

The Amish, always an agrarian people, frequently suffered intolerance and persecution because they were not members of the established churches. At times persecution took the form of banishment from land ownership or tenancy in certain districts. Often Amish were able to secure only marginal or mountainous land, and sometimes paid special taxes and higher rents simply to be accepted as tenants. Under the pressure of these adverse conditions, they quickly discarded old, traditional farming methods and devised new ways to build up the fertility of the poor soil. Their very existence depended on their willingness and ability to experiment. Because of these economic and social pressures they became the first in central Europe to experiment with new methods of fertilizing, cattle feeding, and fodder cultivation.[16]

Crop rotation was another innovation the Amish devised in their attempts to offset low crop yields resulting from poor land. Importing clover from Holland, they first adapted it to the Palatine area and after several decades were recognized as excellent clover farmers. Clover improved the soil producing more feed for stock which produced more manure for fertilizer. This marked the initiation of the four-year crop rotation system which the Amish continue to use today. In the Palatinate this practice checked the problem of soil destruction and improved the economy of the entire section. Very early then, the European Amish established the practice of agricultural experimentation and often the adoption of new and improved farming techniques and crops.[17]

A second characteristic was their sharing of new agricul-

---

15. John A. Hostetler, *Amish Society*, rev. ed. (Baltimore: The Johns Hopkins Press, 1970), pp. 28–34.
16. J. C. Getz, "Economic Organization and Practices of the Old Order Amish of Lancaster County, Pennsylvania," *Mennonite Quarterly Review*, XX (1946), 63; Hostetler, *Amish Society*, p. 42; Walter Kollmorgen, *Culture of a Contemporary Rural Community: The Old Order Amish of Lancaster County, Pennsylvania, No. 4: Rural Life Studies No. 106* (Washington, D.C.: Government Printing Office, 1942), pp. 19–20; Fred Knopp, "The Amish Know How," *The Farm Quarterly*, I (1946), 88.
17. Hostetler, *Amish Society*, p. 42; Getz, "Economic Organization," p. 64.

tural information. The different Amish congregations kept in close contact and members passed along new farming methods that could be tried and evaluated by other church people. In this way they developed a broader understanding of different agricultural practices being used as well as new methods. It gave them a decided advantage over peasant farmers who knew little or nothing about practices other than their own.[18]

Even with superior farming methods and rapid agricultural adaptability it is doubtful if the Amish could have continued in Europe. They lived in compact, tightly structured communities and to maintain their living pattern they needed either additional adjacent land or large areas of new land. During the late 1600s and early 1700s land became increasingly difficult to obtain in Europe. This, along with sporadic religious persecution, convinced the Amish to look to a totally new area for future settlement.

The first Amish came to America in the early 1700s in response to William Penn's invitation to settle his colony; within a few years they had moved to Lancaster County.[19] Settlement in the region proved a wise decision because of excellent farming conditions; fertile soil, gentle rolling terrain, adequate rainfall, moderate temperatures, and a long growing season all aided the Amish. In later years the area also proved advantageous as excellent market facilities developed for Amish products.[20] Applying to fertile Pennsylvania soil their time proven agricultural techniques, the Amish quickly became known as superior family sized farmers.[21]

From the beginning of their settlement in Pennsylvania, the Amish exhibited a high degree of geographical mobility. Spreading out from southeastern Pennsylvania, Amish soon moved into Maryland, Delaware, Ohio, Indiana, Illinois, and by 1839 were among the first settlers moving into the territory of Iowa. The earliest Iowa Amish were from Ohio and settled for a brief time in Lee County. Within a few years they moved

---

18. Kollmorgen, *Culture of a Contemporary Community*, p. 19; Knopp, "The Amish," p. 91.
19. Calvin George Bachman, "The Older Amish of Lancaster County," *Pennsylvania German Society: Proceedings and Addresses*, ed. by the Society (Norristown: Norristown Herald, Inc., 1942), p. 51.
20. Kollmorgen, *Culture of a Contemporary Community*, p. 3.
21. Knopp, "The Amish," p. 94.

to Johnson County and settled in Washington Township.²² Like their Pennsylvania forefathers, Iowa Amish selected an excellent location. Southeast Iowa offered adequate rainfall, fertile soil, sufficient timber, and a growing season of approximately 170 days.²³ The agricultural practices which had served them so well both in Europe and in the eastern United States were applied to southeastern Iowa, bringing them the same economic prosperity they had previously experienced.

Around 1850 a significant division took place in Amish society when a segment of the group began to resist further innovations and change in their way of life. The resulting split produced two groups—the Old Order and the New Order. The Old Order were distinguished by their resistance to social change, nonconforming manner, religious worship in their homes, and use of the horse and buggy. Their wearing apparel also set them apart since women wore long dark dresses and white prayer bonnets and men grew beards and wore large-brimmed hats, collarless shirts, and front-drop trousers. At the time of the division approximately one-third of the group remained with the Old Order.²⁴ The Amish split affected Iowa communities as it did all other Amish settlements in America.²⁵

To understand Amish society and its commitment to the soil, one must consider its religious convictions as well as its history. The Amish central values are religious beliefs and practices which totally permeate their daily lives; Amish occupations, hours of work, means and destination of travel, choice of friends and mates, and economic habits are all structured by religious beliefs and considerations. The Amish view themselves as divine in the sense that they are "a chosen people of God."²⁶ To the Amish the only acceptable occupation is farming. One reason, of course, is that they have never known any other environment but, more importantly, their religious belief is that as farmers they live closer to God and can better serve Him in their rural way of life. They consider themselves

22. Melvin Gingerich, "The Mennonites in Iowa," *Palimpsest*, LX (1959), 225–26.
23. Iowa State Department of Agriculture, *Iowa Book of Agriculture* (Des Moines: published by the State of Iowa, 1968), pp. 327–37.
24. "Old Order Amish," *The Mennonite Encyclopedia*, 1959. IV, 43.
25. Subsequent references in this paper to Amish or Amishmen refer to the Old Order unless otherwise specified.
26. Hostetler, *Amish Society*, pp. 9–10.

excellent farmers and feel there is a "special kind of divine blessing" responsible for their success.²⁷

Their rural setting enables them to better maintain other religious convictions as well. They believe that God desires them to be "not conformed to this world" (Romans 12:2), "not unequally yoked with unbelievers" (II Corinthians 6:14), and to be a "peculiar people" (Titus 2:12); they must therefore live apart from non-Amish people as much as possible. As true Christians they must shut out evil conditions by turning away from worldly things. This leads specifically to the view that cities are centers of evil and must be avoided. In addition, marriages with outsiders are forbidden.²⁸

Their religious convictions also affect their farming methods. If an Amishman farms in a way that causes the soil to lose its fertility, it is considered as sinful as adultery or theft. The matter is brought before the church membership for they believe that "he who robs the soil of its fertility sins against both God and man."²⁹

These convictions combined with a rural way of life have enabled Amish people to successfully resist change in their social and religious behavior. From this background "a mentality has developed that prefers the old rather than the new." While most applicable to religious convictions this attitude has become a generalized one. Living in compact settlements where customs are socially reinforced and a strong sense of community and mutual aid exists, they have very successfully maintained a "slow-changing society, still reminiscent of peasant life several centuries ago."³⁰

Amish and Hutterites Today

The history of the Amish and Hutterites in the New World is a successful one. As it did for so many others, America offered these two utopian societies available land and freedom.

---

27. Knopp, "The Amish," p. 91; Getz, "Economic Organization," p. 58; Kollmorgen, *Culture of a Contemporary Community*, p. 23.
28. Hostetler, *Amish Society*, pp. 47–49; Kollmorgen, *Culture of a Contemporary Community*, p. 21; Fredric Klees, *The Pennsylvania Dutch* (New York: The Macmillan Company, 1950), p. 46.
29. Klees, *The Pennsylvania Dutch*, p. 48.
30. Hostetler, *Amish Society*, p. 11.

Bringing with them from Europe tightly structured, well-developed economic and religious systems that produced high degrees of social and economic stability, both groups have succeeded in maintaining that stability in the United States. In comparing their societies at the present time, similar economic patterns appear that were first evident in their Old World existence; they share agrarian based, agrarian dominated lives which are tradition-oriented, and very slow to change.

The great, all encompassing feature of Amish and Hutterite societies is their belief in the superiority of agrarian living. Their religion demands that they work as farmers and it is this foundation that makes possible most of their other common economic practices. A rural environment allows them separation from the outside world and makes possible a high degree of economic self-sufficiency. In a rural setting with a minimum of economic expenditures and limited formal education, large families produce an abundant labor supply and are assets rather than liabilities. Their simple manner of living allows them to tightly restrict all expenditures. The Hutterites' communal pattern and the Amish policy of mutual assistance provide a pooling of community resources that results in greater strength and solidarity. Without the agricultural setting it is highly doubtful that either group could survive.

Hutterite and Amish families strive to be as self-sufficient as possible and both groups exhibit near self-sufficiency in food and clothing needs. Large gardens and orchards (wherever climate permits) are considered essential; during the summer months wives and children spend many hours planting, hoeing, and harvesting the produce. Food is then canned and provides the family with a year's supply of vegetables and some fruit. In many Amish homes, canning is a family affair and all members help out. One Amish family canned almost 2,000 quarts of food in one summer. The families' meat supply is also filled at home with the seasonal slaughtering of livestock; chickens are a part of all farmsteads. The Hutterites' food production methods are much the same only carried out on a larger scale. Self-sufficiency is equally evident with clothing needs as Amish and Hutterite wives and daughters make most, if not all, of their families' garments. With their unchanging styles, an article of clothing is never discarded but handed down from one family member to the next and used until it is totally worn out.³¹ These activities have several important results: first, they significantly reduce expenditures, particularly in view of the large number of children. Second, these activities maintain families as productive units. The family not only functions as a unit with a sense of togetherness, but the family unit takes on increased importance; Amish and Hutterite families have not suffered disintegration from loss of functions as have so many other American families.³²

Their self-sufficiency is in part made possible by their large families which produce an ample labor supply. Both Hutterites and Amish have birthrates among the highest in the world and everyone except the smallest children have work assignments.³³ About the time Hutterite children reach age twelve, they enter a period of apprenticeship where they work in all different areas of colony life. Young men rotate from one department to another, learning procedures in different work areas. Girls follow the same pattern working in the laundry, kitchen, garden, and doing babysitting.³⁴ At fifteen they begin eating with adults. By the time young people reach eighteen, they have been thoroughly indoctrinated in Hutterite beliefs and religion, and schooled in all aspects of Hutterian work; they are then ready for baptism which ushers them completely into the adult Hutterite world. In this manner, the Hutterites' living arrangement utilizes the abilities of all members, from the smallest through the eldest.³⁵ Life is styled somewhat along the same lines as the plantation system in the antebellum South where division of labor efficiently utilized all age groups.

In Amish society the pattern is similar although less structured. Children begin to assist their parents when they are four years old and are given limited responsibility by the time they are six. The Amish believe deeply that they must teach their children to work hard and accept responsibility. Boys

---

31. Old Order Amish Community, Kalona, Iowa, interviews with a selected group of Old Order Amishmen and women, April, 1970. Because of the desire of the interviewed persons to remain anonymous, specific names have been omitted. This information has been recorded, however, and is on file.
32. Floyd Martinson, *Family in Society* (New York: Dodd, Mead Company, 1970), p. 6; John Bennett, "Communes, the Oldest 'New' Movement in Western Civilization," *Washington University Magazine*, Winter, 1971, pp. 21–25.
33. Hostetler, *Amish Society*, pp. 81–82, 155; Bennett, *Hutterian Brethren*, p. 199.
34. Peters, *All Things Common*, p. 135.
35. Bennett, *Hutterian Brethren*, pp. 174–79.

help their fathers with farm chores, care for the livestock, and, during the proper season, assist with field work. Girls care for younger children, hoe gardens, and perform household chores. Their many children allow the Amish to reject labor-saving devices, relying instead on hand labor. Before they are twenty-one Amish young people are not paid by their parents and if they work for outsiders, the wage is turned over to their parents. When they reach twenty-one, however, their parents begin paying them or they hire out to nonfamily members and are allowed to retain their earnings.[36]

The children's role as well as other features of Amish and Hutterite life makes possible the two groups' policy of restricted expenditures. In Hutterite life the "ideal of austerity" governs acquisitions. They believe that ownership of personal possessions is sinful and they buy only absolute necessities such as farm implements or items they cannot produce. Television sets and radios are regarded as worldly and therefore forbidden. This results in increased savings for the entire colony which can be used later to finance additional colonies.[37] Hutterites make a distinction, however, between personal possessions and adoption of economic and technical devices which they believe have a useful function in colony life. Believing that their very existence depends on their use of large, modern farm machinery, most Hutterite colonies have more up-to-date equipment and processing methods than their non-Hutterite neighbors. The Hutterites thus believe that their adoption of such new technology as larger combines and tractors, conserves rather than destroys their way of life. An exception, however, concerns Hutterite women. A strong effort is made to prevent their work habits from changing so adoption of new equipment for gardening, painting, and domestic work is restricted.[38]

The Amish also practice consumption austerity; expenditures are sharply limited as money is spent only for necessities. Their religious beliefs prohibit spending on jewelry, nonbiblical storybooks, commercial entertainment, cosmetics, and haircuts. They are more selective in their spending habits than the Hutterites as they reject not only worldly devices like tele-

---

36. Hostetler, *Amish Society*, pp. 154–55; Old Order Amish Community, Kalona, Iowa, private interviews, April, 1970.
37. Bennett, *Hutterian Brethren*, pp. 167, 173–74.
38. Ibid., pp. 269–71.

vision sets and radios, but also electricity, telephones, and automobiles.[39]

The Amish are particularly frugal about the purchase of farm machinery and weigh expenditures very carefully; unless there is an absolute need for a new or different implement, it is not purchased. In the Kalona area, the average amount invested in machinery per farm has been estimated at approximately $1,500. Most machinery is about forty or fifty years old, but will continue to be used as long as it can be repaired. Amishmen are highly adept at fashioning replacement parts since in many instances new parts are no longer available. Many Amish farmers use horses for field work so equipment needs are simplified and the life of equipment definitely prolonged.[40]

In observing similarities between Amish and Hutterites, it appears that one area of incompatibility is the basic economic organization of the communities—Hutterites' communism and Amish private property holdings. Upon closer observation, however, differences are minimized. While Hutterites hold everything common, Amish people practice a high degree of mutual assistance that results in what could be termed a semicommunal society. It is one of the most significant advantages the Amish enjoy in maintaining their economic stability.

The Amish practice of mutual aid extends to all areas of their lives, but perhaps is most significant in regard to their financial needs. Young Amishmen desiring to purchase their own farms can depend on assistance from their families as well as other Amishmen. Sometimes the son or son-in-law receives the farm as an outright gift; in other cases they purchase it but at a much lower price than if sold to a non-Amishman. When money is loaned to a family member the interest rate is about half the rate charged by a commercial firm; money loaned to nonfamily members is slightly higher. Outside investment is discouraged with money retained in the community for loans to young Amishmen. This system gives them an atypical but highly advantageous financial system with the following features: (1) no money is borrowed unless necessary, (2) when money is borrowed, interest rates are low, (3) fore-

---

39. Kollmorgen, *Culture of a Contemporary Community*, p. 46; Old Order Amish Community, Kalona, Iowa, private interviews, April, 1970.
40. Old Order Amish Community, Kalona, Iowa, private interviews, April, 1970.

closures are nonexistent, (4) bank failures and business failures only remotely affect them, and (5) interest earnings remain within the community.[41]

Mutual aid is highly beneficial to Amish people in other financial areas as well. Amishmen do not believe in commercial insurance, but have an agreement among church members that covers loss of farm buildings due to fire or windstorm. The farmer suffering the loss will pay one-fourth the cost himself and the remaining three-fourths is divided among other church members. Settlement is usually reached within sixty days. When an Amishman borrows from an outside source, church members draw up an agreement in which they guarantee the repayment of the loan. This is then signed by the farmer requesting the loan and the bishop of the church district. If Amish families are unable to pay medical bills or other expenses these are paid by the entire church district. The matter is handled by the bishop who collects the bills, assesses each family in the district according to its ability to pay, and then reimburses the creditor.[42]

Two other significant areas of mutual assistance are building construction and agricultural cooperation. Amish frugality is reflected in the practice of buying old buildings that they then either move to their own farms, or tear down to retrieve the lumber. These tasks are shared among many Amish neighbors. When new construction is necessary—particularly barns but also houses—many Amishmen assist with the project. Agricultural cooperation is evident in threshing rings where several farmers—usually five—band together to purchase a thresher and then at harvest time, rotate from one member's farm to another, pooling their labor as well as their capital. This results in considerable savings both in machinery investment and labor costs.[43]

The result of the Amishmen's mutual aid policy is a tightly knit, unified community where each family, although operating as a separate unit, has the backing of all community members and potential use of all community resources. It is a practice which approximates to a significant degree the communal organization of the Hutterites.

41. Ibid., Kollmorgen, *Culture of a Contemporary Community*, pp. 22, 50–52.
42. Old Order Amish Community, Kalona, Iowa, private interviews, March, 1971.
43. Ibid.

Although not economic activities, two other shared practices are closely allied to their economic life and therefore deserve attention; these are attitudes and activities regarding community size and education. Community size is a major concern of both Amish and Hutterites and their agrarianism makes it possible to carefully control the number of members in individual settlements. The Hutterites believe that optimal colony size is approximately 150 people so when population reaches between 130 and 150 people, they begin preparations for "branching." This is their method of establishing a new colony—referred to as a daughter colony—under the close supervision of the older or mother colony. Members draw lots to determine who will move. They then elect a second minister, purchase land, send out work crews to construct necessary buildings, and train managers for the various enterprises in the new colony. When the time arrives for the actual move, the mother colony's assets are equally divided between the two groups. The mother colony maintains a supervisory role until the daughter colony achieves self-sufficiency (usually five years) when the tie is ended and each group becomes autonomous.[44]

The total number of Amish within a locality is relatively unimportant, but the size of individual church districts is closely supervised. Every Amish community is divided into districts containing approximately twenty-five families whose members then elect a bishop and two ministers. When their congregation grows beyond that number they can no longer accommodate everyone in one household for church services. Since Amish travel by horse and buggy they must also control church membership in terms of area to be traveled in a short period of time. When church membership exceeds the limit, a new district is created, bishops and ministers elected, and the new district soon becomes autonomous.[45]

In the area of education Amish and Hutterites share methods and goals through which they seek to maintain their unchanging ways. Since education of the young is a major way of maintaining their way of life, it must be controlled and limited. Both groups believe that education beyond the eighth grade

---

44. Paul K. Conkin, *Two Paths to Utopia* (Lincoln: University of Nebraska Press, 1964), pp. 51–52; Norman Thomas, "The Hutterian Brethren," *South Dakota Historical Collections*, XXV (1950), 297.
45. Old Order Amish Community, Kalona, Iowa, private interviews, March, 1971.

is unnecessary and possibly dangerous. Hutterites maintain that further education will discourage or weaken the fear of God in their children. They place heavy stress upon the education of their children as a means of instilling in them obedience to God and indoctrinating them in their communal-religious ways. The Hutterites maintain their own colony schools but in compliance with state law, hire a certified individual to teach what they refer to as "English school." They view the state required educational system as contrary to their goals and counteract the influence wherever possible. Before the regular school session children attend one-half hour of "German School" where they learn the German language, catechism, history, and beliefs of their people. At the end of the day, following "English School," the children remain for an additional half-hour of "German School." This system has been described as a "blanket of counter-indoctrination" which surrounds the English school session.[46]

The Amish maintain that their children do not need any education beyond eighth grade to be competent farmers; nor do their children need subjects like the new mathematics. They contend that they teach the four Rs—reading, writing, arithmetic, and respect—and that is sufficient. They maintain rural parochial schools but in many instances their teachers are not certified. Some Amish children attend public rural schools, but only where the other children are New Order Amish or Conservative Mennonites. They have strenuously resisted attempts to send their children to public schools. Like the Hutterites, Amish believe that limited formal education is a tool to further their own social-religious behavior as well as to achieve the rudiments of basic education, and where they maintain their own schools, religious training is incorporated into the curriculum.[47]

Summary

In a rapidly changing world, the Amish and Hutterites exercise time-proven traditions and beliefs which enable them to retain a great many of their Old World ways. With the exception of Hutterites' constant adoption of new farm tech-

---

46. Deets, *The Hutterites*, p. 46.
47. Old Order Amish Community, Kalona, Iowa, private interviews, March, 1971.

nology, the two societies live much the same as they did centuries ago. Both are part of the American utopian movement because of their shared convictions that they are a chosen people and are living a superior life, but while most utopian groups have hoped to change society, Amish and Hutterites have desired only to maintain the status quo. Their great need has been land and isolation and at the time of their respective migrations, both were plentiful in America.

The location of their settlements had far reaching effects on their North American agrarian practices; the Hutterites, settling on the Great Plains, found it necessary to continue their innovative agricultural ways while the Amish, because of their locations, were allowed to retreat from their European patterns. The Hutterites' settlement in Dakota placed them on the eastern border of the Great Plains. This locality with its characteristics of limited rainfall and special weather phenomena demanded that Hutterites farm extensively rather than intensively as most agriculturists had done in the prairie and woodland regions. Large acreages, increased capital, and an abundant labor supply meant the Hutterites could succeed in the Plains even in times of great stress. Equally important, their advantages led to quicker diversification to offset frequent intervals of drought and locust. As larger and more efficient machines were marketed, the Hutterites in keeping with their European experience, quickly adopted them. Their special advantages derived from communal living plus modernized, efficient farming aided them in effectively competing with non-Hutterite neighbors. Thus the agricultural practices that Hutterites brought from Europe were perpetuated by the American locality in which they settled; moreover, because of their particular environment, the Brethren had and continue to have no other option but to continue these policies.

The Amish fared differently. They brought from Europe careful farming methods and a predisposition for rapid adoption of new methods, but their settlements in the New World allowed them to partially discard these characteristics. Land in southeastern Pennsylvania was very different from Amish land in Europe and no special techniques or new crops were necessary to make it produce abundantly. Their four year crop rotation program, heavy use of manure for fertilizing, and meticulous farming habits all produced successful farming; with this experience the Amish gradually ceased to be experimenters or quick adaptors, relying instead on their time-proven, traditional methods. With their movements into Ohio, Delaware, Maryland, and other eastern states—all somewhat standard in agricultural features—the same methods continued to bring success. Settlement in Iowa proved no exception; fertile soil, adequate rainfall, and available land allowed the Amish to continue their agrarian patterns. Today in Iowa, Amish continue the same methods used 200 years ago in Pennsylvania. Some use tractors for field work, but most prefer horses, and new methods, such as contour farming, are regarded suspiciously. Only in these predictable agricultural regions could Amish ignore change, retain small acreages, and rely almost exclusively on the same procedures for more than 200 years.

Perhaps if early settlements had been reversed their lifestyles and agrarian practices would have developed significantly differently. There is little reason to doubt the Hutterites' success almost anywhere, particularly in the eastern half of the United States, if land was available. Initially, perhaps, the Amish could have adapted to the Plains environment but if they should immigrate today with their great resistance to all change, their success in that area is highly doubtful. At present, both groups appear well situated in their respective localities. If, however, old patterns are repeated and further migrations necessary, the Hutterites would appear to have a decided advantage because of their American experience which demanded retention of adaptability and hence flexibility.

In assessing the comparative qualities of Amish and Hutterites which might account for their successes, both their self-sufficiency and interdependency should receive special emphasis. Their locations allowed them to retain a high degree of independence from outsiders; the available land plus their living patterns so firmly ingrained during their European experience has perpetuated this quality. Today these groups operate in what might be called satellite worlds which revolve around our general society, but operate almost exclusively outside that society. Their needs are fulfilled, with very few exceptions, by their own group and they continue to make few demands upon society at large other than to ask to be left alone. The second quality—interdependency—is aided by the first and is vital to the continuance of Amish and Hutterite life. Agrarianism is the foundation of their interdependent nature; all other characteristics flow from and are nurtured by this condition and all combine to make continuation of the agrarian base possible. An example of these interrelationships is evident if one begins with the characteristic of family size. In both groups large families are assets rather than liabilities because of the children's labor value. Near economic self-sufficiency, particularly in food and clothing but also in educational needs, is then imperative to support their many offspring. That same economic self-sufficiency, however, is only possible because each family contains many members and hence many workers. Features like isolation are also supportive. Their agrarian setting makes possible the rejection of worldly influences and hence isolationism. Isolation is in turn reinforced by their rural, eight-grade schools, their self-sufficiency, restricted expenditures, and mutual assistance or communal living. The interrelationship of all aspects of their societies suggests a weblike structure: each major facet supports and yet is sustained by each of the other major facets. The results are highly integrated, cohesive, stable communities characterized primarily by an exceptionally high degree of interdependency. Moreover, the different practices are interlocked to such a degree that the destruction of any one could alter their lifestyle sufficiently to result in their demise, or at least a significant change in lifestyle.

Today, both groups are expanding in members and developing new communities. Between 1960 and 1969, Hutterites established nine new colonies in South Dakota alone, while also establishing additional colonies in Montana and Canada. Today they have over 200 colonies which contain approximately 200,000 people with a South Dakota population of nearly 3,000.[48] The Amish are also increasing, both in members and settlements. Three communities now live in Iowa, the most recent established near Milton in 1969. The same year a new settlement was begun in Jamesport, Missouri, located forty miles south of the Iowa border. Within each locality even though a few families leave the Old Order each year (usually to join a Conservative Mennonite congregation) the high birth-

---

48. Marvin P. Riley, *South Dakota's Hutterite Colonies: 1874–1969* (Brookings: Agricultural Experiment Station, Bulletin 565, 1970), p. 14.

rate produces a continual increase of members.[49] South Dakota Hutterites and Iowa Amish, reflective of their total groups, today represent two of the most unchanging but rapidly expanding utopian societies in North America and will undoubtedly receive more attention in the future.

---

49. Old Order Amish Community, Kalona, Iowa, private interviews, March, 1971.

What Happened to Main Street?
PETER SCHRAG

LIKE MANY midwestern states, Iowa abounds in small towns. With their particular social institutions, their small businesses, and their main streets, they offer an insightful look at the way in which many Iowans live. This article by Peter Schrag describes his visit to an Iowa community—Mason City—which he projects as a somewhat typical small town. There Schrag interviewed a cross section of the population—teen-agers, politicians, social and economic elites— all to help him develop a sense and a feel for the town where, as he observes, it is the "fashion to worry slow." Like countless other writers before him, Schrag has looked to the heartland of the country for reassurances that Americans' lifestyles, social and political attitudes, and perhaps most importantly work motivations (particularly the Protestant Ethic) have not changed greatly over the past half century.

Many eminent figures have attempted to capture the essence of the land and the people that reside here in rural mid-America. Authors like Hamlin Garland have written despairingly but accurately of life in the Middle West; musicians like Meredith Willson have captured the sometimes puritanical moral attitudes of Iowans; poets like Paul Engle and artists like Grant Wood, each with his own artistic form, have delightfully portrayed Iowans' pride, humor, smugness, as well as countless other forms of human emotion.

Like Peter Schrag, however, they are all essentially dealing with small, rural communities. Perhaps this is, as he observes early in his essay, because we are all in some way "just small town boys come home."

From Peter Schrag,
Out of Place in America: Essays for the End of An Age
(New York: Random House;
© 1970 by Peter Schrag),
pp. 52–73.

WHAT HAPPENED TO MAIN STREET?

MASON CITY, IOWA. Pop. 32,642. Meat packing, Portland cement, brick and tile, beet sugar, dairy products, commercial feeds, soybean oil and meal, thermopane windows and mobile homes. At the intersection of Highways 18 and 65, 135 miles south of Minneapolis, 125 miles north of Des Moines. Three major railroads. Ozark Airlines. Daily newspaper, one local television station. Library, art museum.

Among the most difficult things in any small American town is to stay more than a few days and remain an outsider. There seems to be a common feeling that anyone—even a writer from New York—is, somewhere in his heart, a small-town boy come home. The light but unceasing stream of traffic which moves through Main Street—Federal Avenue in Mason City—north to Minneapolis and beyond, south to Des Moines, reinforces the belief that this flat, open place is part of a great American continuity extending through other Main Streets, across the fields of corn and beets, past tractor depots and filling stations, past grain elevators and loading pens to the very limits of the national imagination. It must make it difficult to conceive of anyone as a total stranger, for being here—local pride notwithstanding—cannot seem very different from being anywhere else.

They take you in, absorb you, soak you up; they know whom you've seen, where you've been, what you've done. In Mississippi hamlets the sheriff follows you around; here it is The Word. *Small towns co-opt (you tell yourself) and nice small towns co-opt absolutely.* But it is not just them, it's you. The things that you bring with you—your sense of yourself as a friendly sort, the wish to believe that the claims of small-town virtue are valid, and your particular kind of chauvinism—all these make you a willing collaborator. So maybe they're right. *Maybe we're all just small-town boys come home.* Yes, you're willing to come to dinner, to visit the Club, to suspend the suspicion that all this is some sort of do-it-yourself Chamber of Commerce trick. Later perhaps (says the Inner Voice of Reason) you will be able to sort things out, to distinguish Main Street from the fantasies that you and a lot of other people from New York have invented for it. Later.

You have come here to see what is happening to the heart of this country, to ask how the great flat democracy responds to Vietnam and Black Power, to marijuana and Mark Rudd, to see how it is taking technology and the

Bomb—all the things that overwhelm the visible spectrum of public concern. Is there something here that can survive in New York and Chicago, is there an Americanism that will endure, or will it perish with the farm and the small town? What, you ask, is happening to Main Street? Later. For the moment you are simply in it, listening to them worry about a proposed civic center, about the construction of a mall, about taxes and industrial development, and about something called "the traffic problem" which, by even the more placid standards of New York, seems more imagined than real.

There are ghosts in this country—local ghosts, and ghosts that you bring with you, that refuse to stay behind: shades of brawling railroad workers and dispossessed farmers; frontiersmen and Babbitts; the old remembered tales of reaction and America First, of capital R Republicanism and the Ku Klux Klan; the romance of Jefferson and Frederick Jackson Turner, the yeoman farmer and the self-made man. As a place of literary irony, Middle America is celebrating its golden anniversary. "Main Street," wrote Sinclair Lewis in 1920, "is the climax of civilization. That this Ford car might stand in front of the Bon Ton Store, Hannibal invaded Rome and Erasmus wrote in Oxford cloisters. What Ole Jensen the grocer says to Ezra Stowbody the banker is the new law for London, Prague and the unprofitable isles of the sea; whatsoever Ezra does not know and sanction, that thing is heresy, worthless for knowing and wicked to consider." But that irony, too, may be a ghost—now as much myth, perhaps, as the self-flattering cultural propositions invented to answer it. ("Right here in Mason City," someone tells you, "we sell three hundred tickets each year for the Metropolitan Opera tour performances in Minneapolis.") The life of Babbittry, you tell yourself, follows the life (and art) of others.

But the models are no longer clear. Main Street once insisted on rising from Perfection (rural) to Progress (urban): Sauk Centre and Zenith were trying to do Chicago's Thing, but what does Chicago have to offer now? The Main Street boosters are still there, hanging signs across the road proclaiming "A Community on the March," but their days are numbered. How would Lewis have portrayed the three hundred marchers of the Vietnam moratorium in Mason City? How would he deal with the growing number of long-haired pot-smoking kids? Here, too, Mason City follows New York and Chicago (The Mafia, you are told, controls the floating dice games that occasionally rumble through the back rooms of a local saloon.) The certainty of Lewis's kind of irony was directed to the provincial insularity that war, technology, and television are rendering obsolete. Main Street lives modern not in its dishwashers and combines—not even in Huntley-Brinkley and Walter Cronkite—but in its growing ambivalence about the America that creates them, the America that crosses the seas of beets and corn—and therefore about itself.

It is not a simple place, and perhaps never was. You see what you expect, and then begin to see (or imagine) what you did not. Standard America, yes: the Civil War monument in the Square; the First National Bank; Osco's Self-Service Drugs; the shoe store and movie theaters; Damon's and Younkers' ("Satisfaction Always"); Maizes's and Penney's; Sears and Monkey Ward. Middle America the way it was supposed to be; the farmers come to shop on Saturday afternoon; the hunting and fishing; the high school football game Friday night; the swimming and sailing at Clear Lake, a small resort nine miles to the west. You cannot pass through town without being told that Mason City is a good place to raise a family, without hearing praise for the schools, and without incessant reminders that Meredith Willson's musical play *The Music Man* was *about* Mason City, that Willson was born here, and that the town was almost renamed River City because of it. (There *is* a river, the Winnebago, which makes itself known only at times of flood.) Mr. Toot, the figure of a trombone-blowing bandsman (says a man at the Chamber of Commerce), is now the town symbol. "We hope," says the man, "that we can make our band festival into a major event." Someday, you imagine, this could be the band capital of the nation, and maybe the whole wicked universe.

Mason City, they tell you, is a stable community: steady population, little unemployment, no race problem (there are, at most, 300 Negroes in town), clean water and, with some huffy qualifications (dust from one of the cement plants, odor from the packing house) clean air. A cliché. In the *Globe Gazette*, the editor, Bob Spiegel, suggests that the problems and resources of the large cities be dispersed to all the Mason Cities in America. A Jeffersonian, Mr. Spiegel, and a nice guy: "The smaller communities need the plants and the people that are polluting the urban centers—not in large doses, but steadily, surely . . . The small communities are geared up. They have comprehensive plans. They know they can't stand still or they will be passed by." Stable, perhaps, but what is stable in a relativistic universe? The very thing that Spiegel proposes seems to be happening in reverse. The community is becoming less pluralistic: it has fewer Negroes, fewer Jews, and fewer members of other minorities than it had twenty years ago. "After the war," said Nate Levinson, an attorney, who is president of the synagogue, "we had eighty Jewish families. Now we have forty. We can't afford a rabbi any more." On the few occasions that

Mason City has tried to attract Negro professionals, they refused to come or to stay. There is nobody to keep them company, and the subtle forms of discrimination—in housing and employment—are pervasive enough to discourage pioneers. ("My maid says if she hears any more about Black Power she'll scream . . . I wouldn't mind one living next door, if he mowed the grass and kept the place neat.") The brighter kids—black and white—move away, off to college, off to the cities, and beneath that migration one can sense the fear that the city's declining agricultural base will not be replaced by enough industrial jobs to maintain even the stability which now exists.

Mason City is not a depressed town, although in its stagnating downtown shopping area it often looks like one. (Shopping centers are thriving on the periphery: the farmers come in to shop, but not all the way.) The city shares many of the attributes of other small Middle Western communities, competing with them for industry, counting, each week, another farm family which is selling out or giving up, counting the abandoned houses around the county, counting the number of acres (now exceeding two hundred) required for efficient agricultural operation. An acre of land costs $500, a four-row combine $24,000. If you stop in places like Plymouth, a town of 400, nine miles from Mason City, you hear the cadences of compromise and decline: men who have become part-time farmers who make ends meet, at $2.25 an hour, by working in the sugar mill in Mason City. Independence becomes, ever more, a hopeful illusion belied by abandoned shops and boarded windows, and by tales of success set in other places: an engineer in California, a chemist in Detroit, a teacher in Oregon.

Iowa, you realize, not just from statistics, but from faces, is a state of old people: "What do the kids here want to do? What do the kids in Mason City want to do? What do the kids in Iowa want to do? They want to get out. I'd get out, go to California if I could." There is a double migration, from farms into towns, from the towns into the cities, and out of state. More than 10 percent of Mason City's work force is employed at the Decker Packing Plant on the north side of town. (The plant is a division of Armour and Co.) At the moment the plant is prosperous; it pays good wages. (A hamboner—who does piece work—can make $6 to $7 an hour.) But what would happen, said one of the city's corporate managers, if the place should succumb to the increasing efficiency of smaller plants? "What'll we do the day—and don't quote me—when the place has to shut down?"

It is the fashion to worry slow, worry with a drawl. Urgency and crisis are not the style. Through most of its history, Mason City was dominated by a few families, and to some extent it still is, not because they are so powerful, but because Federal Avenue once thought they were. Small towns create their own patriarchs, tall men who look even taller against the flatness of history, producing, inevitably, a belief that civic motion and inertia are the subtle work of Big Men—bankers, real estate operators and corporate managers. Mason City still talks about the General, Hanford MacNider (banking, cement, real estate) who was an assistant secretary of war under Coolidge, ambassador to Canada, an aspirant for the 1940 Republican nomination for president, and, for a time, a supporter of America First. (In Mason City, MacNider was *Secretary* of War and barely missed becoming president). The MacNiders gave the city land for parks, for the public library and for a museum. (The General was also a founder of the Euchre and Cycle Club, a lunch-and-dinner club—all the best people—which still has no Jewish members, and he is remembered, among other things, as the man who did not lower his flag for thirty days after John F. Kennedy was killed.) "My father," said Jack MacNider, now president of the Northwestern States Portland Cement Co., "was quite a guy. Some people thought he was tough. To some he was a patron saint. You should have known him."

The General's shadow survived him, and there are still people who are persuaded that nothing of major consequence can be accomplished in Mason City against the opposition of the family. Is that true, you ask Jack, sitting in his second-story office overlooking Federal Avenue. (There is a picture of the General, in full uniform, behind Jack's desk). "I'm flattered," he answers, not defensively, but with some amusement, saying more between the lines than on the record, telling you—you imagine—that the MacNiders take the rap for a lot of small-town inertia they can't control, and that they suffer (or enjoy) a visibility for which they haven't asked. At this very moment a young lawyer named Tom Jolas, a second-generation Greek, is challenging the Establishment (such as it is) in his campaign for mayor; you both know that Jolas is likely to win (on November 4 he did win, handily) and that the city's style and mood is now determined as much by younger businessmen and professionals—and by hundreds of packing-house workers and cement workers—as it is by the old families. "This must be a fishbowl for the Mac-Niders," you say, and Jack offers no argument. And when you speak about prejudice in Mason City, Jack agrees—yes, there is—but you can't be sure whether he means against Catholics, Jews and Negroes (or Greeks and Chicanos) or also against the MacNiders. The shadow is still there, but the General is dead.

Mason City's traditional style of politics and political

behavior was nicely represented by sixty-five-year-old George Mendon, who was mayor for sixteen years until Jolas beat him. Small towns always create the illusion of responsiveness—you can call any public official, any corporate manager, with little interference from secretaries who ask your business, your name, and your pedigree—and you thus can walk into Mendon's office unannounced and receive an audience. But you are never sure that, once in, you have really arrived anywhere. The action must be someplace else. The room is almost bare, the desk virtually clean, the man without visible passion. Yes, jobs and industrial development are a problem, and Mason City has done pretty well, but there are twenty thousand other towns trying to attract industry and, you know, these things take time. Yes, they would like to hire some Negoes for the police force, but none have been qualified. Yes, the MacNiders had been good to the city—all that land they'd given (and all those tax deductions?) but . . . When Mendon was challenged during the campaign about operating an underpaid and undertrained police force, he answered that the city had the most modern equipment, including riot guns, mace, and bulletproof vests. What are they for, you ask, and Mendon, rattling the change in his pocket, identifies himself. "Our colored population is peaceful," he said. "They wouldn't riot. But you never know when people from the outside might come in and try to start something." Mason City is prepared for Watts and Newark, and somewhere in its open heart there lurks an edge of apprehension that the fire next time might burn even here. But when Mendon spoke about his riot guns at an open meeting, the general response was tempered by considerable facetious amusement, and the people who were amused went out to vote against him, and beat him.

There is no single current running against the old style

of politics, or against the Mendons and the Establishment they are supposed to represent. In 1968 Mason City voted for Nixon, for the conservative Congressman H. R. Gross, and for Harold Hughes, a liberal Democrat. ("We helped elect Gross the first time he ran," said a union official, "and we've been sorry ever since.") Sociology and political calculations don't help much. "The issue here," said Bud Stewart, who runs a music store and worked for Jolas, "is generational," implying that whatever was young and progressive supported the challenger against the older Establishment. Jolas campaigned under the slogan "Time for a Change," including, among other things, concern for public housing (which the city does not have but desperately needs), more attention to the problems of youth, and the creation of a modern police force that could meet what he called the rising rate of crime. (And which meant, I was told, getting rid of the reactionary police chief who had bought all the riot junk.) But what Jolas said was clearly not as important as what he is: young, energetic and, beneath it all, ambiguously liberal and unambiguously decent. "I had my hair long and wore sideburns," he tells you (two years ago, he managed a teen-age rock band), "but my friends said I couldn't win with it, so I cut it short. But maybe after the election I might get a notion and let it grow again."

Jolas's great political achievement before he ran for mayor was to force the State to re-route a projected interstate highway so that it would pass within a few miles of Mason City, but it was undoubtedly personality rather than politics that elected him. ("You know what they're saying about me," he mused one day toward the end of the campaign. "They're saying that if I'm elected the Greeks and the niggers are going to take over Mason City. I even had someone charge that I belong to the

Mafia, the Greek Mafia.") More than anything else, Jolas seems to have a sense of concern about youth—not a program but an awakening awareness of how kids are shortchanged by schools, politicians, by adults. ("He knows," I write in my notes, "that the world screws kids.")

What Jolas can achieve is doubtful. He will not have a sympathetic city council, or perhaps even a sympathetic community, and his commitment to a downtown Civic Center and mall as a means of restoring the vitality of the central business area may be more the tokens of modernism than the substance of progress, yet it is clear that Jolas received the support, and represented the aspirations of whatever liberalism (black, labor, professional) that the city could muster. If you sit in his storefront headquarters long enough you learn how far Main Street has come from Babbittry. You meet Mary Dresser, the recently widowed wife of a lawyer who, as president of the Iowa League of Women Voters, carried a reapportionment fight through the legislature and who speaks of how, when their son decided to grow a mustache, she and her husband decided to back him up against the school authorities and how, eventually, they won; Jean Beatty, the wife of a psychologist, answering phone calls and stuffing Jolas envelopes, and shuttling between meetings of the League and the local branch of the NAACP, knowing that the organization should be run by black people but knowing also that its precariously weak membership cannot sustain it without help; or Jim Shannon, the County Democratic chairman, who has worked for the Milwaukee Railroad all his life and who has gone back to the local community college (working nights, studying economics during the day), speaking in his soft, laconic, infinitely American cadences about the campaign for Bobby Kennedy in 1968, about a decade of legislative fights, reminding you, without meaning to or even mentioning it, that liberalism wasn't invented in New York, that the Phil Harts, the Frank Churches, the Fred Harrises and the George McGoverns weren't elected by professors.

If that were all—if one could merely say that Mason City and Middle America are going modern—it would all be easy, but they are not. (What, after all, is modern, uniquely modern, after you've dispensed with the technology?) The national culture is there, mass cult, high, middle and low, mod and trad: Bud Stewart in the Edwardian double-breasted suits which he orders from advertisements through the local stores; the elite trooping off to Minneapolis to hear the Met when it comes on tour, or to Ames to catch the New York Philharmonic (mostly, say the cynics, to be conspicuous, not for love of music); the rock on the radio and in the jukes (The Fifth Dimension, Blood, Sweat and Tears, new Dylan and old Baez, plus some leavening from the likes of Johnny Cash); the long hair and the short skirts, the drugs and the booze. (At the same time, beer, rather than pot, seems still to be the preponderant, though not the exclusive, form of adolescent sin.) But somehow what Mason City receives through the box and the tube, and from its trips to Minneapolis and Des Moines, where some of the ladies do almost weekly shopping, it seems to shape and reshape into its own forms. There is a tendency to mute the decibels of public controversy and social friction, perhaps because people are more tolerant and relaxed, perhaps because they are simply less crowded. There is talk about crime and violence, but the most common local examples seem usually to involve the theft of bicycles and the destruction of Halloween pumpkins. (Another way of staking a claim on the modern?) If you ask long enough, you can get some of the blue-collar workers to speak about their resentment against welfare, taxes, and student demonstrators (not at Harvard, mind you, but at the State University of Iowa), but it is commonly only television and the newspapers that produce the talk—and so it tends to be dispassionate, distant, and somewhat abstract. Bumper stickers and decals are scarce; you rarely see American flags on the rear windows of automobiles because, one might assume, there aren't many people at whom to wave them, not many devils to exorcise. The silent majority here is an abstraction, a collage of minorities, except when it comes to the normalcy of the ladies' study clubs and bridge clubs, the football, the hunting and fishing, and the trip to the lake. And every two years they go back, most of them, and vote for H. R. Gross.

And yet, here are the kids, high school students and students at the Community College, organizing a moratorium march, running a little newspaper, semi-underground within the high school, and with the blessing of the school authorities; here are the clergymen, not all, but a few, giving their support for the march from the pulpit (when she heard her minister that Sunday, one prominent parishioner promptly resigned from the church); and here are ordinary people responding to the critics of dissent with their own protest. In a letter to the *Globe Gazette:*

> We supported the Moratorium Day demonstration. We have a son in Vietnam. We love our country. We fly the American flag.
>
> But we do not believe in blindly following our leader as the Germans did when their leader decided to exterminate the Jews or as some Americans would do if our leader should decide to exterminate the Indians.
>
> We feel our country was wrong to send 40,000 of our boys to their death, not defending their own shores.

> Supporting the Moratorium was our way of saying we love our country right or wrong, and this time it was wrong.

Given the reputation of the average small town in America, the greatest surprise is the school system which, under Rod Bickert, the superintendent, and John Pattswald, the high school principal, has managed to move well beyond the expected, even in the conventional modern suburb. Mason City has abandoned dress codes in its high school, has instituted flexible-modular scheduling (meaning that students have only a limited number of formal lecture classes, and can do their own thing—in "skill" and study centers, in the library or the cafeteria—as they will) and has begun to experiment, in the high school, with an "open mike" where any student can talk to the entire school on anything he pleases. There are no bells, no monitors. As you walk through the halls (modern, sprawling, corporate style), Pattswald, a Minnesotan, explains that he first came to the school as a disciplinarian. "It was a conservative school and I ran a tight ship." When he became principal he turned things around. "We're something of an island, and when some of the parents first heard about it they thought it was chaos. We had an open meeting—parents and students—to explain the flex-mod schedule, but most of the parents wanted to know about dress. (You know, we have everything here, including girls in miniskirts and pants suits.) The students helped us carry it. They know that some sort of uproar could blow this thing right out of the water, but I think they can do the job."

Every day Pattswald spends a couple of hours visiting classes, asking students irreverent questions that are, at least tangentially, directed to the teachers. "I ask them why they're doing what they're doing; what's the significance of this, why study it at all? Sure, we have some weak teachers, but now when I hire people I role-play with them a little, I want to see how they take pressure. In the classroom it's too easy for the teachers always to be the last resort and to put the screws down. That's no way to improve the climate of learning." The conversation is frequently interrupted while Pattswald stops to talk with students (he knows many by name), and later to tell you about them. "Kids are my life," he says, rounding a corner after a brief encounter with two boys. "The whole point is to get them to appreciate the worth of an individual. We have to reach the ones who are overlooked, like one boy they were taunting and who talked about himself as 'a ball that they always kick around.' Those are the ones we have to reach. But I think we're coming."

The militant students seek you out. Mason City is still a confining place, and they find the visitor from New York, the outsider, walking through the hall alone: the organizers of the moratorium, the editors of the mimeographed paper, the *Bitter End* (not quite underground, not quite official), the activists, sons and daughters of the affluent lawyers and doctors, all local people, not carpetbaggers from the East. The school, they say, is divided between "pointy heads like us" and "the animals." (A group passes through the hall after school and the pointy heads, through a glass door, follow the herd with "Moo-moo," "Oink-oink.") The radicals still see the school as a fraud. "There is no way to get a decent education in a public school. Everybody's too uptight." Like what? "Like being allowed to leave school during your unstructured time to make a movie. You can get a release to dish hamburgers at McDonald's, so why not to make movies?" One of them gets threatening letters for his part in the peace movement, another loses his allowance because he won't cut his hair. Their lives are no different, nor are their parents', from those of similar people in Scarsdale or Shaker Heights or Winnetka. (Some of them, said Pattswald, "have told their parents to go to hell.") What is surprising is that, although they are a lonely minority, they are in Mason City (bands, football, cheerleaders, Toot)—that they are in this community at all.

For the majority of the young, the concerns are universal: cars, dances, sports. You hear them in Vic's ("Real Dago Pizza"): "It's a '65 Chevvy. I traded it for that car that was sitting in the grass by the Hub . . . paid three hundred and fifty dollars and put a new engine in it and it runs great." They want to go to college, to get jobs—more than half the high school students work—so they can maintain those automobiles, get married. The modest dream is to become an airline stewardess; "if I'm not too clumsy," to enlist in the Army; to learn a trade. On Friday nights they cruise up and down Federal, shuttling from a root-beer stand at the south end to a drive-in at the other. There is some talk about establishing a teen center, a place Where Kids Can Go, but the proposal draws little enthusiasm from adults and less from the kids. And yet, even among the majority—the animals, the apathetic—something may be happening. The war perhaps, or television, or the music. There was a time, said a school administrator, "when the war seemed very distant." Mason City's enlistment rate was always high, the college students were exempt anyway, and the draft wasn't much of an issue. But in the past year eight recent graduates of Mason City High were killed in Vietnam, making death and change more personal. Nearly a hundred turned out to hear discussions about the war inside the school, and while the patriotic speakers still come to address the assembly, other messages are being heard as well. The hair gets longer, the music a little harder, and the news is on everybody's set.

The young are slowly becoming mediators of the culture, they receive the signals from the outside and interpret the messages for adults. And that's new for all America, not just for Mason City. "The kids are having an effect on their parents," said a mental-health worker, one of the few clinicians in town, apparently, that the adolescents are willing to trust. "People here are friendly and uptight at the same time. Many of them take the attitude that the children should have their fun, that eventually they'll come around to their parents' view. But people have been jarred—by TV and by their own children, and they know, some of them at least, that they've got to listen. They're trying to become looser."

But becoming looser is still a struggle and, given the conditions of life, an imperative that can be deferred. ("I'm *not* going to send my son to Harvard," says a Harvard graduate. "An eighteen-year-old is not mature enough to handle SDS and all that other garbage.") The space, the land, the weather, the incessant reminders of physical normalcy make it possible to defer almost anything. Church on Sunday, football on Friday and the cycle of parties, dinners, and cookouts remain more visible (not to say comprehensible) than the subtleties of cultural change or social injustice. If the churches and their ministers are losing some of their influence among the young (and if the call for psychiatrists is increasing), they are still holding their members, and if the Catholic Monsignor, Arthur Breen, has to schedule a folk mass at Holy Family every Sunday (in addition to four other masses) he nonetheless continues to pack them in.

What you see most of all (see is not a good word—feel, maybe) is a faith in the capacity of people and institutions to be responsive, the belief that, finally, things are pretty much what they seem, that Things Work. "This is just a big farm town," said a Mason City businessman. "You don't check people's credit here; you just assume they'll pay their bills. In Waterloo, which is really an industrial city, even though it isn't very big, you check everybody out." The answer to an economic problem is to work harder, to take a second job, or to send your wife to work, usually as a clerk or a waitress. (Wages for women are extremely low.) On the radio, Junior Achievement makes its peace with modernism by setting its jingle to "Get With It" to a rock beat, but the message of adolescent enterprise (Babbittry?) is the same, and around the lunch tables at the Green Mill Restaurant or the bar at Tom MacNider's Chart House it is difficult to convince anyone that sometimes even people with the normal quota of ambition can't make it.

The advantages of that faith are obvious, but their price is high. "This is a nice town as long as you don't rock the boat," said Willis Haddix, a meat packer who is president of the struggling Mason City chapter of NAACP. "What's wrong here is in the secret places": in subtle discrimination in housing and jobs; in the out-of-sight dilapidated frame houses at the north and south ends of town, buildings surrounded with little piles of old lumber, rusting metal chairs, decaying junk cars once slated for repair; in the lingering aroma of personal defeat; and in the cross between arrogance and apathy that declares "there are no poor people in this area." On Sundays, while most people are packing their campers for the trip home, or making the transition between Church and television football, the old, who have little to do, wander into the Park Inn for lunch (hot roast-beef sandwiches for $1.25), and talk about medicare. And against theirs you hear other voices: Murray Lawson, for example, a civilized, compassionate man who represents Mason City in the legislature, saying, "We've been generous with education, but not so generous with the old; we've had a rough time with nursing homes"; Jim Shannon who supports his wife and seven children on the salary of a railroad clerk and janitor, describing the effects of a regressive sales tax that victimizes the small man but makes little impact on the rich; the official of the local OEO poverty agency talking about the county's third welfare generation and reflecting that "an admission of poverty is an admission of failure, and people here don't do that"; Tom Jolas describing Mason City's enthusiasm for the New York Mets when they won the World Series after a ninth-place finish in 1968 because "people believe in coming off the bottom."

And then you learn something else—about yourself, and about the phenomenon you choose to call Main Street. You hear them complain about Eastern urban provincialism, people who cannot believe that Mason City has television ("You must get it from the West Coast"), let alone an art museum, a decent library, or a couple of go-go joints (or that you can buy Philip Roth, Malcolm X and Henry Miller in the bookstore), and you begin to understand, almost by suggestion, what the barriers of comprehension are all about. Is it really surprising that Main Street cannot fully comprehend talk about police brutality, police rigidity, or social disillusionment? If the system works here, why doesn't it work everywhere else?

Main Street's uniquely provincial vice lies in its excessive, unquestioning belief in the Protestant ethic—hard work, honesty—and conventional politics; New York's in the conviction that most of the time nothing may make much difference, that institutions and public life are by their very nature unresponsive. And if New York has come to doubt the values and the beliefs of tradition, it still hasn't invented anything to replace them. The anger of the blue-collar worker—at welfare, students, Negroes—is rooted in the frustrated ethic of Main Street, frustrated not only in its encounters with urban problems and technology but also in the growing doubt of the Best People —Wallace's pointy heads, Agnew's effete impudent snobs— that it still has merit. Among the characteristic excesses of rural populism (whether expressed by William Jennings Bryan, Joe McCarthy or Spiro Agnew) was a paranoia about Them: the Bankers, the railroads, the Eastern Establishment, the Communists in government. But paranoia is surely also one of the characteristic defenses of almost every other inhabitant of New York. (If you try to explain the vicissitudes of dealing with Con Edison or the New York Telephone Company, most people in Mason City stare at you in disbelief; if you speak about rents and housing they're certain you've gone mad.) Every rural or small-town vote against some proposal for the alleviation of a problem in New York or Chicago or Cleveland is not merely an act of self-interest (keeping taxes low, protecting the farmers) but also a gesture of disbelief that Main Street's ethic and tactics—if they were really applied—would be ineffective in the Big City.

At the end, sitting in the waiting room at the municipal airport (all flights from Chicago are late, naturally), you detach yourself. You hear, still, one of the Federal Avenue lawyers saying, "This town is solid; it's solid as a commercial center and as a medical and cultural center for a large region." You see his nearly bare office—the brown wood furniture, the linoleum floors, and the fluorescent lights—see his partner, in a sleeveless gray pullover, walking through the outer office (Clarence Darrow?), and hear the trucks stopping for the red light at the intersection below. You hear Jack MacNider speaking about the gradual movement of the "iron triangle," the Midwestern industrial region, into north central Iowa, speaking about the ultimate industrialization of the area around the city. You see the high school homecoming queen, fragile and uncomfortable in the back of an open convertible in the wind-chilled stadium; see the wide residential streets with their maples and time-threatened elms, the section of magnificent houses by Prairie School architects, one of them by Frank Lloyd Wright, and the crumbling streets at the south end, near the Brick and Tile, and you hear, in that same neighborhood, two NAACP ladies, one white, one Negro, discussing the phrasing of a letter to the school board politely protesting the use of *Little Black Sambo* in the elementary grades. And then, finally, you hear again all those people speaking about how good Mason City is for raising a family, and you wonder what kind of society it is that must separate growing up and the rearing of children from the places where most of its business is transacted, its ideas discussed and its policies determined. And then you wonder, too, what would happen if something ever came seriously to disturb Main Street's normalcy, if direct demands were ever made, if the letters ceased being polite, if the dark places—the discrimination and disregard—were probed and, for the first time, tested. Small towns do co-opt, you think, not by what they do, not by their hospitality, but by what we wish they were— because all of us, big city boys and small, *want* to believe. And yet, when Ozark 974 rises from the runway, off to

Dubuque, over the corn and beets, over the Mississippi, off to Chicago, you know that you can't go home again, that the world is elsewhere, and that every moment the distances grow not smaller but greater. Main Street is far away.

[1970]